SYBASE SQL SERVER 11

An Administrator's Guide

JOHN KIRKWOOD

JOIN US ON THE INTERNET VIA WWW, GOPHER, FTP OR EMAIL:

WWW: http://www.thomson.com
GOPHER: gopher.thomson.com
FTP: ftp.thomson.com
EMAIL: findit@kiosk.thomson.com

WebExtra℠

WebExtra gives added value by providing updated and additional information about topics discussed in this book. Items included in the WebExtra for *SYBASE SQL SERVER 11 An Administrator's Guide* are:

- Material describing disk space allocation and the creation of databases
- A description of the requirements for rebuilding the master database and for carrying out a complete system rebuild
- Corrections to the book contents

The WebExtra features outlined above are available free of charge (except for the charges associated with accessing the Internet and the World Wide Web). Just go to the Web site for International Thomson Computer Press. The URL is:

http://www.thomson.com/itcp.html

A service of I(T)P™

SYBASE SQL SERVER 11

An Administrator's Guide

JOHN KIRKWOOD

INTERNATIONAL THOMSON COMPUTER PRESS

I(T)P™ An International Thomson Publishing Company

London • Bonn • Boston • Johannesburg • Madrid • Melbourne • Mexico City • New York • Paris
Singapore • Tokyo • Toronto • Albany, NY • Belmont, CA • Cincinnati, OH • Detroit, MI

I(T)P™ A division of International Thomson Publishing Inc.
The ITP logo is a trademark under license.

For more information, contact:

International Thomson Publishing Europe
Berkshire House 168-173
High Holborn
London WCIV 7AA
England

International Thomson Computer Press
20 Park Plaza, 13th Floor
Boston, MA 02116
USA

International Thomson Publishing Gmbh
Königswinterer Strasse 418
53227 Bonn
Germany

International Thomson Publishing Asia
221 Henderson Road #05-10
Henderson Building
Singapore 0315

Thomas Nelson Australia
102 Dodds Street
South Melbourne, 3205
Victoria, Australia

International Thomson Publishing Japan
Hirakawacho Kyowa Building, 3F
2-2-1 Hirakawacho
Chiyoda-ku, 102 Tokyo
Japan

Nelson Canada
1120 Birchmount Road
Scarborough, Ontario
Canada M1K 5G4

International Thomson Editores
Campos Eliseos 385, Piso 7
Col. Polanco
11560 Mexico D.F. Mexico

International Thomson Publishing Southern Africa
Bldg. 19, Constantia Park
239 Old Pretoria Road, P.O. Box 2459
Halfway House, 1685 South Africa

International Thomson Publishing France
1, rue st. Georges
75 009 Paris France

British Library Cataloging-in-Publication Data
A catalogue record for this book is available from the British Library

Library of Congress Cataloging-in-Publication Data
A catalogue record for this book is available from the Library of Congress

First Printed 1996

ISBN: 1-85032-287-2

Commissioning Editor: Liz Israel Oppedijk
Publisher/Vice President: Jim DeWolf, ITCP/Boston
Project Director: Chris Grisonich, ITCP/Boston
Marketing Manager: Kathleen Raftery, ITCP/Boston
Production: Jo-Ann Campbell • mle design • 562 Milford Point Rd. • Milford, CT 06460

Printed in the U.S.

Contents

APPENDIX C—STORAGE STRUCTURES AND INDEXING 477

APPENDIX D—MULTIUSER CONSIDERATIONS: CONCURRENCY AND MEMORY 515

Foreword

I am pleased to have this opportunity to present John Kirkwood's *Sybase SQL Server 11: An Administrator's Guide* as the first book in Sybase Press. This book provides timely coverage of the newest release of our relational database management system, Sybase SQL Server 11. SQL Server 11, which has demonstrably achieved our design goals of performance, scalability, and quality, is a powerful, many-faceted software product that deserves book-length coverage on topics ranging from managing the data in a distributed enterprise, to performance and tuning for mission-critical applications.

With this book, aimed at developers and database administrators, John Kirkwood once again demonstrates his ability to explain Sybase SQL Server software with clarity, grace, and precision. John has been a hands-on user, eloquent proponent and dedicated teacher of Sybase SQL Server since 1987. With the welcome addition of humor and candor, John presents SQL Server features in the order that a user would logically encounter them, based on his practical experience in his consulting practice. John never lets his long-term familiarity with our products cloud his ability to pick out the salient aspects of new features, telling users what to do first, and what to avoid. With the sureness of years of experience, John selects those topics and examples that most usefully complement the standard Sybase documentation and training.

Indeed, this book is another instance of John's ongoing contributions to the Sybase user community, as represented by his active participation in the International Sybase User Group and its Enhancements Committee. We are fortunate to have the flagship offering from our new line of books come from one of our best customer advocates, John Kirkwood.

Mark Hoffman
President and CEO
Sybase, Inc.

Introduction

This book is a complete description of SQL Server System 11.0 from Sybase. It is structured in two parts to make it easier to find what you want, depending on your existing experience of SQL Server. Part One describes all of the new features introduced since version 4.9.2 and Part Two completes the full picture by describing the features which are mainly unchanged from version 4.9.2. So, if you already know how SQL Server works read Part One first and then review Part Two. If you are new to SQL Server, please start with Part Two, which explains the basics, before you attempt Part One. It will not make that much difference but you might find it a little more logical.

Organization

Chapters 1–13 constitute Part One, which covers the new features; Appendices A–D constitute Part Two, which covers the unchanged features. Chapters 1–11 cover the features introduced in System 10, and Chapters 12 and 13 describe the new features introduced in System 11. Appendices A and B are a complete list of the system tables and the command/system procedure syntax.

Chapter Coverage

Chapter 1 Declarative Integrity

This chapter discusses the new declarative integrity feature introduced in System 10 that allows domain and referential integrity to be defined in the create table command. The syntax and use of each new clause are discussed in detail, followed by a general treatment of integrity, relating it to the System 10 implementation and highlighting the aspects which are not yet covered in the declarative integrity clauses. The full create table syntax is then given with some examples. The chapter concludes with a comparison of the new declarative clauses and the existing nondeclarative integrity of default, rule and trigger.

Chapter 2 Cursors

This chapter describes the System 10 support for cursors that allows access to a set of rows returned by an SQL statement on a one by one basis from the first row to the last. The difference between using a loop and using a cursor to step through a set of rows is explained, followed by a description of the types of cursor that System 10 recognizes. The cursor commands are then described in detail with examples, both for T-SQL server-based cursors and for ct-library client-based cursors. The chapter concludes with a discussion of cursor locking.

Chapter 3 Datatypes

This chapter covers the datatypes available in System 10 and System 11.

Chapter 4 Threshold Manager

This chapter describes the threshold manager introduced in System 10. This provides the ability to fire a stored procedure when the free space in a segment falls below a specified amount. As thresholds are defined on segments, I have included a discussion on segments in this chapter.

Chapter 5 Auditing

This chapter describes the System 10 auditing feature. A description of the components and the installation is followed by a detailed discussion of the setting and use of the various audit options.

Chapter 6 Security

This chapter describes the System 10 security system including the setting of the appropriate names, IDs and passwords to enable login to the server and the use of databases once login is achieved. The new administration roles and the granting and revoking of command and access privileges to the users in the databases are then described. The chapter concludes with a description of configuring remote access between servers.

Chapter 7 Miscellaneous New Sybase Features

This chapter describes a collection of new features added in System 10 by Sybase. These include transaction status, rollback trigger, trigger self-recursion, sort timing parameters, join density and customized error messages. I have also included the SET command options here.

Chapter 8 Miscellaneous New ANSI Features

This chapter describes a collection of new features added in System 10 to comply with ANSI 89. In general, these are switchable between the version 4.9.2 settings, which are usually the default settings to make life easier. The principal features are chained transaction mode, locking isolation levels, view with check option, null testing, a schema definition and subquery changes.

Chapter 9 Backup and Recovery

This chapter discusses the System 10 backup server which controls the dump and restore of databases and transaction logs to ensure full recovery from failure. The transaction management is discussed first to describe the transaction log entries and the actions taken to recover from media and system failures, followed by a detailed description of the commands and procedures necessary to enable this.

Chapter 10 The Optimizer

This chapter describes the System 10 optimizer. Because of the number of changes, and the importance of this topic, I have not just listed the System 10 features but have given a full treatment of the subject. The chapter first gives a definition of the various terms with explanations of how they effect the optimization. This is followed by two detailed optimization sections: one on the simpler optimization plans of single tables and joins and the other on the more complicated plans of nested statements.

Chapter 11 What If? Problem Anticipation and Solving

This chapter is a collection of configuration, monitoring and problem-solving techniques and tools related to System 10.

Chapter 12 New System 11 Features

This chapter describes the new features introduced in System 11. These include data cache and buffer pool management, partitioning heap tables, optimizer improvements, update in place rules, the housekeeper task, the maximum rows per page feature and lock promotion thresholds.

Chapter 13 System 11 Configuration Parameters

This chapter is a description of the new sp_configure configuration parameters in System 11.

Appendix A—Allocating Space and Creating Databases

This appendix describes the initialization of disk space and its allocation to databases and logs including disk mirroring and use of the default device. Creation and expansion of databases and logs is covered with a treatment of how to estimate the necessary sizes.

Appendix B—Master Database and Logical System Rebuild

This appendix describes the requirements for rebuilding the master database and for carrying out a complete system rebuild.

Appendix C—Storage Structures and Indexing

This appendix takes a detailed look at the SQL Server B-tree index structures: clustered and nonclustered. The appendix covers the data storage structures, the index structure and the processing involved in insert/update/delete against each combination of index. The other types of page structure—allocation, distribution and text/image—are also discussed.

Appendix D—Multiuser Considerations: Concurrency and Memory

This appendix describes the SQL Server approach to the important aspects of a multiuser environment such as concurrency and locking and the allocation of memory.

The Purpose of this Book

As with my previous book on version 4.9.2, the material is not a rehash of the existing literature but is based on my practical use of System 10 and some initial work with System 11. I have tried to show how to use the new features, along with discussions of the problems I encountered and any solutions that I found. This is not a list of bugs associated with the software—and there have been a few—but is advice on how to use the new features and my personal opinion on what is good and bad about them. As I always say: you may or may not agree with me but I hope that it makes you aware of potential problems and prompts you to check even the simplest-looking statement.

As always, I hope that you enjoy this book and find it useful. If you have any comments—especially bits that you think are incorrect—please contact me as I will be delighted to hear from you.

Finally, my thanks to Jim Panttaja for his review of the early material, and to several people at Sybase—Karen Paulsell, Scott McCargor, Marc Sugiyama, Brijesh Agarwal, Judy Bowman, Robert Garvey, dan Scanlan—for their detailed technical comments and corrections.

John Kirkwood

1

Declarative Integrity

This chapter discusses the new declarative integrity feature of System 10 which allows domain and referential integrity to be defined in the create table command. The syntax and use of each new clause are discussed in detail, followed by a general treatment of integrity, relating to the System 10 implementation and highlighting the aspects which are not yet covered in the declarative integrity clauses. The full create table syntax is then given with some examples. The chapter concludes with a comparison of the new declarative clauses and the existing non-declarative integrity of default, rule and trigger.

System 11 has added to the identity property features and a maximum rows per page to the definition of a table.

COMMAND SYNTAX

```
alter table
create table
```

SYSTEM PROCEDURE SYNTAX

```
sp_addtype
sp_addmessage
sp_bindmsg
sp_configure
sp_dboption
sp_helpconstraint
```

1.1 Schema-based Declarative Integrity

1.1.1 New Clauses in Create Table

System 10 has introduced integrity constraints in the definition of a table. Such constraints are called declarative as they do not involve any programming effort; in other words, you simply declare them. They are included in the **create table** command as **default**, **constraint**, **unique**, **primary key**, **references** and **check** clauses. These declarative integrity constraints can completely replace the rules and defaults. However, the foreign key references clause is rather limited in scope and less comprehensive than the referential integrity that you can specify in a trigger. Because of this, it will have to be used in a complementary fashion to triggers. In my opinion, the primary key constraints should be defined in **create table** but the rules and defaults should be left as they are; that is, as separate objects defined using **create rule** and **create default**. The declarative references clause should be used for the referential integrity which it defines (existence and restrict) and triggers used to provide any cascade and nullify requirements. (Reasons for this will be discussed in more detail in section 1.4.) Whether you agree with me or not, please be consistent and ensure that you have company standards defined for the implementation of integrity using System 10.

In summary, the declarative integrity involves the following clauses.

default specifies a column default value to be used when a record is created without a value assigned to the column.

identity specifies that the column contains a sequential number generated by the server to uniquely identify each row. This is not really an integrity feature but including it here completes the new `create table` syntax.

constraint specifies an integrity constraint at the column or table level and may contain the following clauses.

unique specifies unique non-null values for a column.

primary key specifies the column(s) which make up the unique identifier (`primary key`) of the rows of the table.

references specifies foreign key referential integrity for a single column.

foreign key ... references ...
specifies foreign key referential integrity for one or more columns at the table level.

check specifies a validation rule at the column or table level.

Although it's a bit boring, the best place to start is with the syntax of the new clauses. I'll fit these into **create table** later in section 1.3.

1.1.2 Default

```
DEFAULT {constant_expr|user|null}
```

where:

constant_expr	may not reference any database object but may include functions;
user	inserts the user name;
null	inserts null.

This specifies a default value for a column to be used if no value is supplied on insert. For example:

```
DEFAULT 'ZZZZ'
DEFAULT getdate()
DEFAULT user
```

The column datatype must be compatible with the default value. For **user**, the datatype must be char(30) or varchar(30).

Declaring a default on an **identity** column has no effect. The identity column is always assigned the next sequential number by the server. In my opinion, it would be better to get an error message, or at least a warning, since the likelihood is that you have made an error somewhere. Be careful of this and check the identity columns carefully.

1.1.3 Identity Property

```
IDENTITY | null | not null
```

This indicates that the column has the identity property which means that it contains a sequential number generated by the server to uniquely identify each row. (Note that it replaces the null|not null specification for the column, which is not unreasonable as it cannot be null.)

Only one column in the table may have the identity property. The column automatically does not allow nulls and may not be updated. The column datatype must be **numeric** of scale 0 (see section 3.1.1 for an explanation of this new datatype). There is no wrap around of the identity value for a column; you simply get an error message and no more rows may be inserted into the table. So be careful; since the maximum range of the numeric datatype is $10^{38} - 1$, this should not present much of a problem, but if you are trying to save space with a smaller precision, you can block the application when you run out of values.

The column value starts at 1 and increases in increments of 1. The server does not make one number at a time available but instead divides the set of possible values into blocks of consecutive numbers and makes one block at a time available for allocation. This block is memory resident and is an attempt to improve server performance when allocating the number. However, it can leave gaps in the number allocation if there is a failure and the current block of numbers is lost. On recovery from a failure, the unused numbers in the current block are no longer available and the identity value for the table starts at the beginning of the next block of numbers. SQL Server calls this the "pre-burned algorithm."

If a column is declared as:

```
a numeric(3, 0) identity
```

and the server allocates identity values in blocks of 10, then if the server fails after value 16 has been allocated, the values 17–20 will never be used. The new block will start from 21 when the server has recovered.

Similarly, rollback of a transaction which is setting an identity column value will result in gaps in the sequence. On a rollback, the identity value rolled back is discarded and the next insert uses the next available identity value. So, if an identity value of 104 is rolled back, 104 is discarded and the next insert—even a repeat of the same command—uses 105.

The size of the block of numbers made available by the server can be configured using:

```
sp_configure 'identity burning set factor', value
```

This is explained in detail in section 11.2.

The system administrator can insert explicit values into an identity column by having the identity_insert option set as follows.

```
SET identity_insert table_name on
GO
INSERT INTO table_name (column_name)
VALUES (20)
GO
SET identity_insert table_name off
GO
```

When you insert an identity field value you must specify the column names in the insert command. You cannot issue an insert command while the **set identity_insert** is on without including the identity column.

```
SET identity_insert orders on
GO
INSERT INTO orders
(order_key, cust_no, order_date)
VALUES (8000, 1234, getdate())
GO
INSERT INTO orders (cust_no, order_date)
VALUES (1235, getdate())
```

```
Msg 585, level 16, state 1:Explicit value must be specified for identity field in
the table 'orders' when IDENTITY_INSERT IS ON.
```

```
SET identity_insert orders off
GO
```

If order_key is an identity column, then gaps can occur when an identity value is manually inserted. When the identity_insert property is set to off, the server restarts from the max(value) + 1. If the current values are 1–243 and a manual insert of 329 is made, the next identity value used is 330. If the current values are 1–243 and a manual insert of 189 is made to replace a deleted record, the next identity value used is 244.

Only one table at a time may have the identity_insert option on. You can display the last inserted value via the global variable **@@identity**. When using **select into** to create a table, an identity column is created as:

```
SELECT id_key = identity(precision), col_a, col_b
INTO new_tab FROM old_tab
```

where precision determines the maximum range of the identity value as $10^{precision} - 1$.

When using **select into** from a table with an existing identity column, the new table column inherits all of the identity properties of the source table as long as you select on a row by row basis and do not alter the identity values or include them more than once. Therefore, the new column will not have the identity property if you:

- included a UNION, join, GROUP BY or aggregate in the select;
- select the identity column more than once (Be careful of this one; it does not generate a failure based on two identity columns but treats the two result columns as no longer having the identity property.);
- include the identity column in an expression.

If you try to include the old identity column as well as creating a new one, the select into fails as you can have only the one identity column in a table.

The **syb_identity** keyword may be used in place of the identity column name at any time to reference the identity column. This eliminates the need to disclose the name of the identity column when using it as an internal surrogate key.

```
SELECT max(syb_identity) FROM tab_name
-----------
 3457
```

A new database option **auto identity** allows a ten-digit identity column to be included automatically on new tables which are created without a primary key, a unique constraint or an identity column.

sp_dboption

```
sp_dboption db_name, 'auto identity', true
```

This automatically generated identity column is not available with a **select** * and may be viewed only by using the SYB_IDENTITY_COL column name in the select statement (the uppercase is mandatory).

System 11 Additions

There are some System 11.0 additions to the control of the identity property.

A new System 11 database option may be used to enforce uniqueness for use with cursors and isolation level 0 (dirty read) processing.

```
sp_dboption db_name, 'identity in non unique index', true
```

This automatically includes an existing identity column in the indexes of a table, so that all the indexes are now unique. Note that the table MUST have an existing identity column for this to be applicable. The unique index is required for cursor update processing and for isolation level 0 reads.

A new System 11 configuration option **identity grab size** specifies a number of sequential identity values which are reserved for a specific session of insert processing against a table.

sp_configure

```
sp_configure 'identity grab size', number
```

This reserves the number of identity values for each insert process against the table. If there are two processes inserting against a table and the identity grab size is set at 20:

```
sp_configure 'identity grab size', 20
```

then process one will have identity values 1–19 reserved and process two will have identity values 20–39 reserved. If process one inserts 15 rows and process two inserts eight rows, the table will contain identity columns 1–15 and 20–28. If process one logs off after inserting the 15 rows then the identity values 16–19 are lost and not available for use by other processes.

Be careful with this one as gaps will be common.

1.1.4 Constraint

```
CONSTRAINT constraint_name
{{UNIQUE | PRIMARY KEY}
       [CLUSTERED | NONCLUSTERED]
       [WITH {FILLFACTOR | MAX_ROWS_PER_PAGE} = x]
       [on segment_name]
| REFERENCES table_name [(col_name)]
| CHECK (check_condition)}
```

This specifies an integrity constraint on a column as a choice of:

UNIQUE

No two rows may have the same non-null value. Null is allowed but only one row may have a null value. This is consistent since null signifies an unknown value. If the value is unknown, it is not possible to determine if it is the same as any other value. This automatically creates a unique index which is dropped only by dropping the constraint using **alter table**. By default, the index is nonclustered.

PRIMARY KEY

No two rows may have the same value and null is not allowed. Again a unique index is automatically created. By default this is clustered. It is a pity that SQL Server does not insist on primary key declaration on every table as this conform with the referential integrity rules. However, it is easy to understand as the legacy of pre-System 10 tables would have to be catered for, which could incur duplication of indexes and triggers and make the change to System 10 rather wearisome.

It is also annoying that SQL Server defaults this index to clustered. If it is the only index on the table, this is OK. But in general the clustered index is wasted as a primary key which is most often used for single record access. Always be aware that it is usually necessary to override this default index choice and make this index nonclustered.

Apart from the default index choice, this declaration is the same as unique. However it is useful, even just from a documentation aspect, to declare the primary key of a table. I would recommend the use of this clause for the primary key and unique for other candidate keys. Use of the primary key clause is advantageous as the references clause links to the primary key by default.

REFERENCES

This indicates a referential integrity constraint between this column and a single column in the named table. If the column in the other table is specified, it must have been defined as unique, primary key or in a create unique index. If no column is specified, the link is made automatically to a primary key column. The table in the references clause must exist. SQL Server uses this references clause to check that the data values being input exist on the referenced table column. Therefore, when a row is added to a table, any references columns are checked to see if the primary key occurrence exists. If not, the input fails. Similarly, if a references column is updated, SQL Server checks to see if the new column value exists as a primary key occurrence.

CHECK

This is a rule which the column must conform to. The check_condition has the same format as a rule condition; that is, as if it were in a where clause except that it may not contain a subquery or reference table objects (except the column it is defined on).

```
CHECK (loc_code IN ('01', '02')
OR loc_code LIKE '[A-Z][0-9]')
```

Note the mandatory parentheses around the check_condition.

The **constraint_name** is optional. However, specifying a constraint name is useful when the constraint condition creates an index (unique/primary key) since the index name is set to the constraint name. If you do not specify a constraint_name, the constraint is named as:

references/check constraint	
tabname_colname_object_id	for a column constraint;
tabname_object_id	for a table constraint;

unique/primary key constraint	
tabname_colname_tabindid	where tabindid is the table_id:index_id.

To limit the size of these default names, the first ten characters of the table name and the first five characters of the column name are used.

The indexes created for unique and primary key may be dropped only by using alter table to drop the constraint.

alter table

```
ALTER TABLE tab_name
DROP CONSTRAINT constraint_name
```

This makes it good practice to explicitly name constraints. Also, this automatic creation of an index on the single column primary key is rather annoying as it does not allow the index to be redefined to include other columns. SQL retrievals on the primary key plus additional columns will benefit from a composite index which covers the query. This will have to be created in addition to the primary key index created for the constraint. Performance will suffer, either as a reduction in performance of the retrieval because the single column index is used or as a reduction in performance of maintenance commands because more indexes have been created than is necessary for the SQL. (See the query optimizer for a full description of index covering.)

The constraint clauses may be declared as table level constraints.

```
CONSTRAINT constraint_name
{UNIQUE | PRIMARY KEY}
       [CLUSTERED | NONCLUSTERED]
              (col_name[, col_name]...)
       [WITH {FILLFACTOR|MAX_ROWS_PER_PAGE} = x]
       [on segment_name]
| FOREIGN KEY (col_name[, col_name]...)
       REFERENCES tab_name [(col_name[, col_name]...)]
| CHECK (check_condition)
```

Again the **constraint_name** is optional although I prefer to use it at the table level as opposed to the column level. It is not that important—index names are about the best argument—as it is not a reusable dictionary object. If you cannot reuse it, why bother to name it? However, the default index name at the table level (tabname_number) may either interfere with or contradict your naming convention. Naming the constraint makes life easier.

The table level constraints perform the same function as the column level constraints. The obvious difference is that the table level constraints may operate on more than one column. This is a particularly useful aspect of the table level check constraint which can reference any column in the table and therefore permits cross-checking of data in several columns.

```
CHECK (price < 50 and qty > 100)
```

The foreign key references check needs a new keyword at the table level—**FOREIGN KEY**—to allow you to specify the column names which make up the foreign key.

Note that defining the **primary key** at the table level allows you to nominate more than one column. This can get around the composite index problem above. If the primary key is a single column but SQL would benefit from having other columns in the primary key index, simply define all of the columns in the primary key at the table level. The columns will still be unique and the index will include all of the columns. Of course, this does mess up your schema documentation.

Be careful about placing the clustered index on a different segment from the data. As always, SQL Server will move the data to the index segment.

1.1.5 Error Handling

The default error messages are not a lot of fun.

```
Foreign key constraint violation occurred, dbname = 'prod_db', table_name =
'orders', constraint_name = 'orders_cust_1040006736'""Check constraint violation
occurred, dbname = 'prod_db', table_name = 'orders', constraint_name =
'orders_order_160003601'
```

Therefore it is advisable to override them with user-defined error messages. For integrity constraints, you add the message using **sp_addmessage** and then bind it to the constraint using **sp_bindmsg**. The definition and use of user-defined error messages is covered in detail in Chapter 7, section 7.10.

sp_addmessage, sp_bindmessage

```
sp_addmessage 50100, 'orders still exist'
sp_addmessage 50200, 'date out of range'
go
sp_bindmsg 'orders_cust_1040006736', 50100
sp_bindmsg 'orders_order_160003601', 50200
go
```

The error messages are held on the system table **sysusermessages**.

Any error message is displayed on the first constraint violation and the command aborted. Subsequent integrity checks are not made until the current error has been corrected and the command resubmitted.

1.1.6 User-defined Datatypes

User-defined datatypes in SQL Server are a very useful means of creating a domain based on the system datatypes, rules and defaults. However, none of the constraint clauses are available to attach to user-defined datatypes. Although the **check** constraint may be named, it cannot be bound to a user-defined datatype. The **sp_addtype** gives an error message of `"You cannot bind a declared constraint."`

sp_addtype

You can specify the **identity** property when creating a user-defined datatype (as this is not a constraint).

```
        sp_addtype type_name, datatype [, "identity|null|not null"]
sp_addtype pkey_type, "numeric(8)", "identity"
```

(The quotes are necessary for the datatype numeric(8) as it contains special characters—the open and close brackets—and for identity as it is a reserved word.)

The mixing of defaults, rules, user-defined datatypes, check and default clauses is worth mentioning. In general, the user-defined datatype rule/default is overridden by the check and default clauses. More specifically, the following apply.

- A rule bound to a column and a check clause are accumulative; they both apply.
- A check clause overrides a user datatype rule.
- A default clause overrides a user datatype default.
- A default object bound to a column defined with a default clause gives an error message `"The column already has a default. Bind disallowed."`

1.2 Integrity Theory

Let's look at the integrity theory and see how the SQL Server implementation relates to it. There are three distinctions normally applied to data integrity:

1. domain integrity	the validation of the column independent of other data in the database;
2. entity integrity	the specification of what columns make up a unique non-null primary key;
3. referential integrity	the validation of the data—row or column—against the other data in the database.

1.2.1 Domain Integrity

This is covered by a combination of several parts of the column definition:

- datatype
- unique | null | not null

- default
- check.

Simply defining a column with these does not automatically imply a domain as the default and check clauses have to be defined against every column that they apply to. Therefore, in my opinion, true domain integrity is not possible with declarative integrity and requires the separate objects of user datatype, default and rule.

1.2.2 Entity Integrity

This is covered by the primary key definition, although it needs to be mandatory to be fully ANSI compliant.

1.2.3 Referential Integrity

This is the most interesting one as it relates to other data and has several parts to it. Referential integrity exists between two tables in the database and defines the actions which occur in the relationship. Let me define a few terms.

primary key — one or more columns of a table that have non-null unique values to uniquely identify each row in the table.

foreign key — one or more columns of a table that exist as a primary key on another table.

Referential integrity states that if a foreign key has a non-null value then the value must exist on the table where the foreign key is a primary key. Note that this definition allows the foreign key column(s) to contain null. This means that there are several referential integrity conditions which define the primary key to foreign key relationship: existence, restrict, cascade and nullify.

The **existence** check deals with the foreign key end of the relationship being processed. The foreign key value must exist as a primary key. An insert or update of a non-null foreign key must check that the value exists as a primary key on the related table. This is the situation which SQL Server checks automatically with the references clause.

```
FOREIGN KEY (prod_no)
 REFERENCES product(prod_no)
```

This will ensure that any insert or update of prod_no is allowed only if the value exists as a prod_no on the product table.

The more interesting referential integrity is when the primary key end is processed as we now have to cope with deletions and updates. Consider an orders:item:product relationship as in Figure 1.1. (I use ** to denote a primary key.)

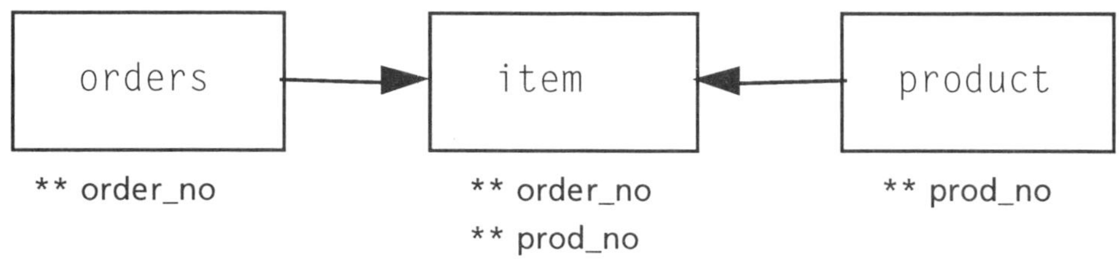

Figure 1.1 *1:M:1 relationship.*

Both item.order_no and item.prod_no are foreign keys as they are primary keys of orders and product, respectively. When we add an item record, we need to have both the orders and product records existing, which we would do with a references clause on the order_no and the prod_no as:

```
CREATE TABLE item
        ( order_no char(6) not null
                REFERENCES orders(order_no),
          prod_no char(12)     not null
                REFERENCES product(prod_no))
```

This handles the detail:master relationship existence checks; that is, the many:one relationship as described above. What we need to cater for now is the opposite direction of master:detail, i.e. the one:many relationship. In our example, we need to consider the integrity constraints when we process the orders and/or the product table.

Using orders as the example, we need to consider what to do for the actions insert, update and delete.

Inserting an order is no problem as it is independent of the item records and therefore no integrity constraints are required. (In fact, the referential integrity existence check on the detail record, item, means that item records cannot exist until the order is created.)

Updating the primary key or deleting the order record does require some integrity constraints. I shall discuss deleting as it is easier to visualize. The same discussion applies to updating the primary key to a new value. You do not allow primary key updating in your systems as it is not a normal thing to do. Why change the identifier of an object? Maybe you have chosen the wrong candidate as primary key? But maybe you assigned the wrong primary key by mistake, in which case you will need to provide some functionality to change the primary key value.

To preserve referential integrity when I delete the order record, I cannot leave any item records with that order_no on them. If I do, I conflict with the referential integrity rule that says that non-null foreign key values must exist as the appropriate primary key values. So I have three options:

1. restrict do not allow the delete/update while foreign key values exist;
2. cascade delete (or update) all foreign key records for the primary key value;
3. nullify set all values of all foreign key occurrences of the primary key to null. This applies to deletes only (as a primary key on the orders table is not allowed to be null by definition of a primary key) and is not possible in our example as the foreign key order_no is part of the primary key of item and therefore may not contain null.

There is another option in the ANSI standard—set default—which is equivalent to nullify except that the foreign key value is set to the default value for the field, assuming the field has a default. I personally do not like this option as it requires the default value to have business meaning in the system. If this is the case there will, no doubt, be some deletes which should not be allocated to the default value and special code will need to be constructed for these special cases. I think that it is much better to restrict delete and have a business function to transfer item records to the default key when required. I'm not going to lose sleep if you disagree with me, it's only my personal design opinion after many years of building specials in nonrelational systems to cater for such situations.

Nullify is unusual and almost all practical situations are a choice between cascade and restrict. System 10 does not support nullify or cascade (or set default) so the only option supported by System 10 is restrict. Although the restrict constraint will be the most common, this means that triggers are still necessary for specific referential integrity which cascades or nullifies.

So the table based referential integrity of the references/primary key combination will automatically check that:

- a record will not be inserted if references column value input does not exist as a primary key in the referenced table;

- a referenced table value will not be deleted/updated if foreign key values exist on the referencing table.

1.3 Create Table Syntax

The full syntax is rather complicated as it contains the new integrity clauses at both the column and the table levels.

create table

```
CREATE TABLE table_name
(column_name   datatype
        [DEFAULT {constant_expr|user|null}]
        {[{IDENTITY|null|not null}]
        |  [[CONSTRAINT constraint_name]
                {{UNIQUE|PRIMARY KEY}
                        [clustered|nonclustered]
                        [with {fillfactor|max_rows_per_page} = x]
                        [on segment_name]
                 | REFERENCES table_name[(column_name)]
                 | CHECK (check_condition)}]}...
        | [CONSTRAINT constraint_name]
                {{UNIQUE|PRIMARY KEY}
                        [clustered|nonclustered
                                (col_name[,col_name]...)
                        [with {fillfactor|max_rows_per_page}  = x]
                        [on segment_name]
                | FOREIGN KEY (col_name[,col_name]...)
                        REFERENCES table_name
                                [(col_name[, col_name]...)]
                | CHECK (check_condition)}

        [{,{next_column|next_constraint}}...]
        [with max_rows_per_page = x]
        [on segment_name]
```

Note the interesting position of the default clause directly after the datatype definition. This is awkward initially because the phrasing that you are used to is col_name datatype null|not null. However, the null|not null is now part of the identity clause which comes after the default clause. So the sequence is col_name datatype default identity|null|not null. You will get it wrong several times at first and the error message is not too informative, so be careful.

The fillfactor and max_rows_per_page (System 11 only) are page packing densities which give you control over the amount of data stored on each page. The fillfactor is the percentage to which a page is filled on initial load and the max_rows_per_page is the maximum number of rows that will be contained on a page for the life of the data.

The fillfactor is important for providing space for growth after the initial load of the data to minimize page splitting. The maximum rows per page is important for limiting the rows stored in a page to minimize the number of rows locked by a data maintenance command, which helps to reduce locking contention. These ideas are dealt with in more detail in Appendix F.

Let's look at some examples by defining the tables and constraints of a customer:orders:item:product schema as in Figure 1.2.

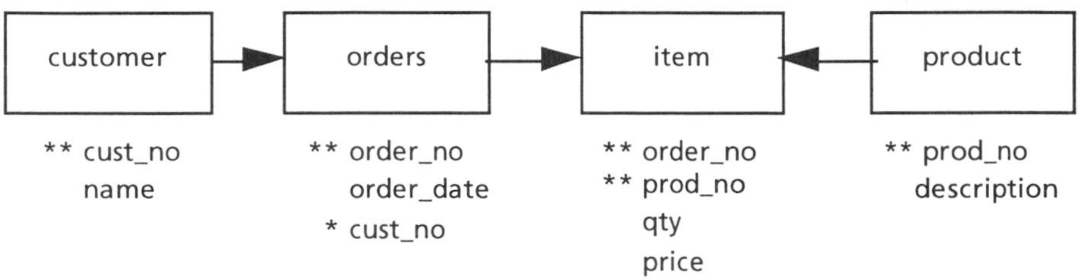

***Figure 1.2** Integrity example schema.*

where:

---

key fields are char(6);
character fields are varchar(30);
numeric fields are numeric(8, 2);

with the standard referential integrity and specific domain integrity of:

order_date must not be prior to today and default to today;
qty between 1 and 1,000;
price > 0;
price * qty must not be > 50,000.

```
CREATE TABLE customer
        (cust_no char(6) not null
                CONSTRAINT customer_pkey
```

```
                    PRIMARY KEY nonclustered,
         name    varchar(30) not null)

CREATE TABLE product
        (prod_no char(6) not null
                CONSTRAINT product_pkey
                        PRIMARY KEY nonclustered,
         description varchar(30) not null)

CREATE TABLE orders
        (order_no char(6) not null
                CONSTRAINT orders_pkey
                        PRIMARY KEY nonclustered,
         order_date datetime
                DEFAULT getdate()
                not null
                CHECK
                (convert(char(9),order_date,6)
                               >= convert(char(9),getdate(),6)),
         cust_no char(6) not null
                REFERENCES customer(cust_no))

CREATE TABLE item
        (order_no char(6) not null
                REFERENCES orders(order_no),
         prod_no char(6) not null
                REFERENCES product(prod_no),
         qty numeric(8, 2) not null
                CHECK (qty between 1 and 1000),
         price numeric(8, 2) not null
                CHECK (price > 0),
        CONSTRAINT item_pkey PRIMARY KEY
                CLUSTERED (order_no, prod_no),
        CONSTRAINT item_valuechk
                CHECK (qty * price <= 50000))
```

(The not null clauses are optional, of course, as SQL Server defaults columns to not null. However, I like to include them as it is nicely self-documenting.) You may decide from a standards viewpoint to declare all constraints at the table level and to name them explicitly. This has merit for legibility, ease of maintenance and ease of comprehension. It makes no difference to the execution. However, when you use sp_help to see the table definition, it shows the column level defaults and checks under the default and rule heading but the table level checks do not show.

```
sp_help orders
```

```
column_name     type                 length    prec          scale   nulls
                default_name                   rule_name                      identity
order_no        char                 6         null          null    0
                null                           null                           0
order_date      datetime             8         null          null    0
                orders_order_14400354 orders_order_160003601        0
cust_no char                         6         null          null    0
                null                           null                           0

index_name      index_description
       index_keys
orders_pkey     non-clustered, unique located on default
       order_no

No defined keys for this object.
```

```
sp_help item
```

```
column_name     type          length      prec           scale     nulls
                default_name              rule_name                         identity
order_no        char          6           null           null      0
                null                      null                              0
prod_no         char          6                          null      null     0
                null                      null                              0
qty             numeric 5     8           2              0
                null                      item_qty_224003829       0
price           numeric 5     8           2              0
                null                      item_price_240003886     0

index_name      index_description
                index_keys
item_pkey       clustered, unique located on default
                order_no, prod_no

No defined keys for this object.
```

The constraints are held on sysobjects as normal objects with the default and check constraints sharing the same object types as the default and rule objects. References constraints use the new object type of "RI". (Although the manuals say that there is a new type of "RI," I could not create it.)

```
SELECT name, id, type FROM sysobjects
       WHERE type in ("D", "R", "RI")
```

```
name                        id              type
orders_order_14400354       14400354        D
orders_order_160003601      160003601       R
item_qty_224003829          224003829       R
item_price_224003886        224003886       R
item_value_chk              112000721       R
```

(or a simple sp_help)

The constraints (not the defaults) are also held on sysconstraints.

```
select * from sysconstraints

colid   sparel   constrid     tableid      error   status   spare2
3       0        1721017858   1689017714   0       128      0
2       0        1817018200   1801018143   0       64       0
```

This is not really a lot of help and it is better to use **sp_helpconstraint**.

sp_helpconstraint

```
sp_helpconstraint table_name [, detail]
```

where

detail	returns information about the constraint's user and error messages

```
sp_helpconstraint item

name                        defn
item_pkey                   PRIMARY KEY INDEX (order_no, prod_no):
                                    CLUSTERED
item_valuechk               CONSTRAINT item_valuechk
                                    CHECK (qty * price <= 50000)
item_order_no_              1817018200  item FOREIGN KEY (order_no)
                                    REFERENCES orders(order_no)
item_prod_no_1721017858     item FOREIGN KEY (prod_no)
                                    REFERENCES product(prod_no)
item_qty_224003829          CHECK (qty between 1 and 1000)
item_price_240003886        CHECK (price > 0)
```

Note that the referential integrity applies to the schema as well as the data, so you must drop the tables in the correct sequence. In the above examples, we cannot drop the orders table before we drop the item table because there is a referential integrity constraint between them.

1.4 Comparison with Nondeclarative Integrity

The declarative integrity constraints all have an equivalent method in SQL Server which existed prior to System 10 and these are still available. They are listed in Table 1.1.

***Table 1.1** Integrity methods comparison*

declarative	existing method
unique	create unique index
primary key	create unique index
default	create default
	sp_bindefault
references	create trigger
check	create rule
	sp_bindrule
	or
	create trigger

The rule equivalent for check applies at a column level only so I have included create trigger as an equivalent to check at the table level when it provides multiple column checking.

There is no real difference as far as indexing overhead. Therefore, there should be no performance degradation when using declarative integrity although you may have to define the primary key at the table level to include columns for a composite index, as explained in section 1.1.4. So for the referential integrity of the references constraint compared with a trigger, I would go for the declarative approach as it cannot lose and has considerable merit in being completely defined in the table command. Sybase should expand this as quickly as possible to include cascade and nullify integrity on the primary key record processing. At present, the references constraint covers only restrict from the primary key occurrence and existence from the foreign key occurrence. However, this covers the majority of referential integrity processing and the occasions when a trigger will be necessary will be few.

The unique and primary key constraints are also worth consideration, but be careful. SQL Server has the annoying habit of automatically making the primary key a clustered index, when clustered indexes are usually more useful for the foreign key or sequential retrieval. Most primary key access is single record on the primary key, which is just as efficient by nonclustered index. The clustered index should be reserved for other access which retrieves ranges of records. This is not a major drawback; just be aware of it and maybe make it standard to always specify the index type.

Where I have more of a problem with the declarative integrity is with default and check constraints. One of the major benefits of defaults and rules is that they are independent objects and therefore are reusable. The default and check constraints are declared per table and must be repeated for each table to which they apply. This makes testing and maintenance more difficult and moves away from the concept of columns belonging to domains. However, the declarative check clause does allow you to validate against more than one column of the table, which you cannot achieve with a rule.

The availability of defaults and rules as separate objects to permit the creation of domains when bound to a user-defined datatype sways me to continue using them instead of the declarative default and check clauses, except when the useful new feature of cross-column checking is required.

The same comment applies in a limited extent to the references clause when it is used to validate a column against a look-up table. This is the type of referential integrity you would also like to execute when the field is input. However, this is a more wide-ranging discussion which includes distribution of data and the population of pop-up lists. It does not deter you from placing such referential integrity in a declarative references clause rather than a trigger.

Triggers are still required for the cascade and nullify referential integrity processing and to include any additional integrity checking which is not an inherent part of the data relationships, such as maintaining denormalized data.

1.5 Summary

The System 10.0 declarative integrity goes a long way to providing the necessary schema-based integrity. The use of the integrity clauses—default, check, unique, primary key, references—provide all but the cascade and nullify options of referential integrity. Inclusion of these options in the references syntax will allow all referential integrity to be carried out as declarative and reserve the use of triggers for other integrity checks and business processing.

The principal problem with the domain integrity of default and check is that it does not create server-wide objects which may be used for other column validation. This is not a unique SQL Server problem, but it does defeat the purpose of domain integrity and makes it more laborious and error-prone to define column validation. In my opinion, the combination of user-defined datatype, rule and default creates a powerful object for enforcing domain integrity and you may need to seriously consider retaining this approach if you currently use it.

2

Cursors

This chapter describes the System 10 support for cursors. The support allows access to a set of rows returned by an SQL statement on a one by one basis from the first row to the last. The difference between using a loop and using a cursor to step through a set of rows is explained, followed by a description of the types of cursor that System 10 recognizes. The cursor commands are then described in detail with examples, for both T-SQL server-based cursors and for ct-library client-based cursors. The chapter concludes with a discussion of cursor locking.

System 11 has added to the available cursor locking levels by allowing isolation level 0 (dirty reads) locking.

COMMAND SYNTAX

```
declare cursor
open
fetch
close
deallocate cursor
update
delete

ct_cursor
ct_param
```

SYSTEM PROCEDURE SYNTAX

```
sp_cursorinfo
```

2.1 What is a Cursor?

A cursor provides access to the set of rows returned by an SQL query by stepping through them one by one from the first row to the last row. Without a cursor, this has to be contrived in T-SQL by using set rowcount 1 or a min/max primary key variable within a loop construct and repetitive iteration of the select command.

For example:

```
DECLARE         @min int,
                @cnt int,
                @name varchar(20),
                @credit_limit numeric(8, 2),
                @msg varchar(70)

SELECT @cnt = count(*) FROM customer
       WHERE county = 'Berkshire'

SELECT @min = min(cust_no) FROM customer
       WHERE county = 'Berkshire'

WHILE (@cnt > 0)
BEGIN
       SELECT @name = name,
                @credit_limit = credit_limit
              FROM customer
              WHERE cust_no = @min

       IF (@credit_limit = 0)
       BEGIN
              SELECT @msg = 'customer' + @name +
                                      ' has no credit limit'
       PRINT @msg
       END

       IF (@credit_limit > 10000)
       BEGIN
              SELECT @msg = 'customer' + @name +
                              ' has corporate credit limit'
              PRINT @msg
              END
              SELECT @min = min(cust_no)
                     FROM customer
                     WHERE cust_no > @min
                     AND county = 'Berkshire'
              SELECT @cnt = @cnt - 1
       END
```

With a cursor, we can avoid the repetitive execution of the select command by executing it once to return the set of rows, and then fetching each row in turn from that result set with a loop construct. For example:

```
DECLARE read_csr CURSOR FOR
        SELECT name, credit_limit
                FROM customer
                WHERE county = 'Berkshire'
                FOR READ ONLY
GO

/* the declare cursor must be in its own batch  */

DECLARE @name varchar(20),
                @credit_limit numeric(8,2),
                @msg varchar(70)

OPEN read_csr

FETCH read_csr INTO @name, @credit_limit

IF @@sqlstatus = 2
BEGIN
        PRINT 'no records'
        CLOSE read_csr
END

ELSE
BEGIN
        WHILE (@@sqlstatus = 0)
        BEGIN
                IF (@credit_limit = 0)
        BEGIN
                SELECT @msg = 'customer' + @name + ' has no credit limit'
                PRINT @msg
        END

        IF (@credit_limit > 10000)
        BEGIN
                SELECT @msg = 'customer' + '@name + ' has corporate credit limit'
                PRINT @msg
        END

        FETCH read_csr
                INTO @name, @credit_limit

        END

IF (@@sqlstatus = 1)
```

```
BEGIN
        PRINT 'error occurred'
END

CLOSE read_csr

END

DEALLOCATE CURSOR read_csr
GO
```

The cursor allows us to access each row in turn from the set of rows returned by the SQL command. A cursor is associated with the select statement in the declare cursor command and controls the current position within the cursor result set.

The cursor result set is the set of rows returned by the select command. The cursor position is a pointer to a single row in this result set. The fetch command then activates the row currently pointed to and makes it available for display and/or deletion/update.

2.2 Types of SQL Server Cursors

Cursors may be defined in the client application or in server-based T-SQL. The previous example is a server-based cursor where the cursor is fully declared, opened and closed at the server and the row by row processing takes place at the server. In this case, the client application processes the returned rows as normal as if they had been returned from a standard T-SQL command. For a server-based cursor, the cursor may be fully contained in a stored procedure. Again, the client application will have no knowledge at all of the cursor, simply making the db-library/ct-library calls to execute the procedure and process the results.

Using the same approach as a server cursor but with a different set of function calls, the client application may take complete control of the cursor by issuing the SQL statement in a series of cursor function calls to declare, open, close and process the results rows. In this case, the server does not know of the cursor control and all row buffering and cursor position control is based at the client. Again, the result set may be generated from a T-SQL select command or a procedure execution of the select command.

The literature rather confusingly names these as:

client cursor	a cursor controlled by the client issuing a T-SQL select;
execute cursor	a cursor controlled by the client executing a stored procedure;
language cursor	a cursor controlled by the server issuing a T-SQL select;
server cursor	a cursor controlled by the server executing a stored procedure.

So, quite simply, there are two types of cursor. **Client cursors**, which are completely under the control of the client routine via Open Client calls and **server cursors**, which are completely server-based using the declare cursor, open, fetch, close and deallocate commands. The client cursor statements are described in section 2.5 and the server cursor commands in section 2.3.

2.3 Server Cursor Commands

There are five commands to use with server cursors:

declare cursor

The declare cursor command defines the cursor, specifying the select statement which defines the rows and columns comprising the cursor result set. Declare cursor also indicates whether the result set is updatable or read only.

open

The open command opens a cursor for processing, evaluating and executing the select command and making the cursor result set available for processing.

fetch

The fetch command returns one or more rows from the cursor result set. The default of one row per fetch may be changed using the **set cursor rows**.

```
SET cursor rows 10 for cursor_name
```

The fetch may specify a list of variables to read the column values into. In this case, only one row at a time is fetched regardless of the cursor rows value, because SQL Server variables are scalar and can accept only one value at a time. Contrary to the standard variable assignment which puts the last value read into the local variable if the select command returns more than one row, the cursor fetch reads only one row from the result set and places the value in the local variable regardless of the set cursor rows setting.

close

The close command closes a cursor, disabling access to the cursor result set. You may reopen a closed cursor to reposition to the beginning of the result set.

deallocate cursor

The deallocate cursor command deletes the cursor, making it inaccessible and deleting the result set and any other memory resources allocated to the cursor.

2.3.1 Declare Cursor

declare cursor

```
DECLARE cursor_name CURSOR
FOR select_statement
[FOR {READ ONLY | UPDATE [OF column_list]}]
```

where

select_statement	a standard select that defines the cursor result set. The only additional restrictions on this select are that it must contain a FROM clause and cannot contain: COMPUTE FOR BROWSE INTO HOLDLOCK
read only/update	specifies if the cursor result set may be updated or is read only. The default depends on the syntax of the select statement. If the select statement does not create the result set directly from the base table but requires an intermediate worktable, then the default is read only. Otherwise the default is update. It is always worth specifying this to avoid confusion. This means that the default is read only if the select statement contains: DISTINCT GROUP BY

ORDER BY
UNION
an aggregate function

A cursor that is a join statement cannot have records deleted even if the cursor is updatable.

update of column_list specifies the columns of the cursor result set which may be updated. If **of column_list** is omitted, all columns of the result set may be updated. If you explicitly declare the cursor as **for update** you must have a unique index on the table which is on a column not in the update of column_list.

tab_1 indexed on (a, b)

```
DECLARE csr_2 CURSOR FOR
  SELECT a, b, c FROM tab_1
       FOR UPDATE OF c
```

is valid, but:

```
DECLARE csr_3 CURSOR FOR
  SELECT a, b, c FROM tab 1
       FOR UPDATE OF b, c
```

gives an error message of:

```
"The optimizer could not find a unique index which it could use to table scan
'tab_1' for the cursor."
```

If you specify **for update**, you must have a unique index on the table. If uniqueness is not a natural property of the data, then you can force uniqueness by defining an identity column and including it in the index. In System 11 the new database options **auto identity** and **identity in non unique index** will establish index uniqueness automatically for you (see section 1.1.3).

Examples

```
DECLARE csr_1 CURSOR
 FOR SELECT cust_no, name, address
       FROM customer
       WHERE county = 'Berkshire'
```

An updatable cursor of all customer records in Berkshire.

```
DECLARE csr_2 CURSOR
 FOR SELECT prod_no, description
        FROM product
        ORDER BY description
```

A read only cursor (because of the order by) of all product records in description sequence.

```
DECLARE csr_3 CURSOR
 FOR SELECT order_no, prod_no, qty, price*qty gross_price
        FROM item
        WHERE prod_no like 'ABC%'
 FOR READ ONLY
```

A read only cursor of order items for a product range.

```
DECLARE csr_4 CURSOR
 FOR SELECT order_no, prod_no, qty, price
        FROM item
        WHERE qty > 100 AND price > 100
 FOR UPDATE OF qty, price
```

An updatable cursor of items, for update of qty and price (with a unique index containing neither qty nor price).

The declare cursor must be in a batch by itself.The scope of the cursor (the range over which the cursor is accessible) is not limited to the batch but depends on where it was declared.

T-SQL

A cursor is available for the length of the user session, i.e. from server login to logout. Therefore a cursor need be declared only once in a session. Even if the cursor is in its own batch, it spans all batches until the end of the session. To redefine the cursor it must be deallocated before a new declare cursor is issued. To refresh and go back to the beginning of the cursor result set, you simply close and reopen the cursor.

procedure/trigger

A cursor declared in a procedure/trigger is available for the length of time the procedure/trigger executes. Cursors may not span the procedure/trigger boundary, i.e., cursors declared inside a procedure/trigger are not known outside of the procedure/trigger and vice versa. This means that although cursor names must be unique in the same scope, the same cursor name may be used inside and outside the procedure/trigger and the cursor result sets are not available across the procedure/trigger boundary. In practice, the detection of duplicate cursor names is done at run time, so the same name may be used in the syntax as long as the cursors do not coexist at run time. The following is valid since the duplication of the cursor name will not be visible at run time, as only one of the cursors is declared for each execution.

```
CREATE PROC proc_1 (@flag char(1) = 'Y')
AS
BEGIN
IF @flag = 'Y'
        DECLARE update_csr_1 CURSOR
        FOR SELECT cust_no, name
                FROM customer
        FOR UPDATE
ELSE
        DECLARE update_csr_1 CURSOR
        FOR SELECT prod_no, description
                FROM product
        FOR UPDATE
RETURN
END
```

Cursors that are not direct mappings from the base table (e.g., GROUP BY, ORDER BY) cannot be guaranteed to reflect the current values of the base table rows. These cursors are read only by nature of their indirect row mapping and will have created an internal work table to produce the cursor result set. As SQL Server does not retain read locks at the server, other transactions may update rows at the server. These updates will not be reflected in the cursor result set, which is working from the internal work table created by the open cursor.

The corollary of this is that the cursor result set of an updatable cursor must be the actual base table rows. When a SQL Server row is updated, there are several conditions which will cause it to be deleted from its current page and reinserted in another page. SQL Server does update in place but the rules for this are very stringent. In System 10, you should assume that an update will move the row. In summary, SQL Server will move the row if one of the following is satisfied:

- update of a variable length column;
- update of a column which allows nulls;
- update of a column which is part of an index;
- update of more than one row;
- update of a table which has an update trigger;

- update of more than half of the row;
- update of three nonconsecutive columns separated by more than 8 bytes;
- the table is replicated.

The rules are less strict in System 11 (see Appendix E) when only replication and update including a join are guaranteed to move a row. In all other cases, if the updated row fits into the page, it is placed back in its current page.

Of course, if the primary key of the row is clustered, the row must be reinserted in sequence of the key which will place it back into the same page. Even in this situation, data page splitting could cause the row—and several others—to be moved to a new page.

If this does happen, there is the possibility that the row will be accessed again during the cursor processing. This problem is not unique to SQL Server cursor processing, so you may be well prepared for it. If not, you may wish to include some application checking to ensure that a row is not updated more than once.

If you make a mistake in a T-SQL server cursor in the declare cursor statement, it is in a batch of its own and, although that batch fails, execution continues at the next batch which tries to use the cursor. However, the cursor has not been declared and the cursor commands in this batch fail. But the failure is not trapped by an @@sqlstatus setting and you can get a never-ending loop as @@sqlstatus is not being set. So the previous example code for cursor processing is not really correct and you should test for @@error=102 after the declare cursor.

```
DECLARE csr_1 CURSOR FOR
 SELECT * FROM tab_1
 FOR READ ONLY
GO
IF @@error=102
BEGIN
        PRINT "error in cursor declare"
        RETURN
END
ELSE
        /*  cursor processing as before  */
```

2.3.2 Open

open

```
OPEN cursor_name
```

This opens the cursor ready for processing.

```
OPEN upd_csr_1
```

The open cursor statement checks the syntax of the SQL command defined in the declare statement, sets up the appropriate memory structures for the cursor result set and positions the cursor before the first record, ready to fetch it. Be a little careful here as the open statement does not always create the cursor result set. System 10 optimizes the open statement processing so that, in most cases which do not need a work table, the select command is only partially processed and the rows are retrieved by the fetch command. As mentioned above, if the update moves the row out of the current page, subsequent fetch commands can cause the updated row to be read again and reappear in the result set.

2.3.3 Fetch

fetch

```
FETCH cursor_name [INTO fetch_list]
```

The fetch command returns one or more rows from an open cursor. The columns may be returned into an optional set of variables specified in the fetch_list.

```
FETCH upd_csr_1
FETCH read_csr_1 INTO @id, @name, @address
```

Fetching data from a cursor result set is done row by row in a forward direction; that is, always fetch the next row. There is no way to go backwards through the cursor result set to fetch a row which has already been retrieved. To fetch a row which has already been retrieved, you need to close and reopen the cursor to start at the beginning again. You can cause more than one row to be fetched at a time by specifying the number of rows in the **cursor rows** option of the set command.

```
SET cursor rows value for cursor_name
SET cursor rows 100 for read_csr_1
```

The latter set command will return 100 rows for each fetch. If you use the INTO clause of the fetch command, then any set cursor rows value is ignored and one row at a time is returned. This is perfectly reasonable as fetch INTO assigns the returned values into variables which are scalar and can hold only one value at a time.

Each fetch returns a row from the cursor result set and makes the returned row the current row so that it is now available for update or delete processing. If you issue a fetch with the cursor currently positioned on the last row of the result set, the cursor position moves beyond the end of the set and a warning is returned by setting the global variable **@@sqlstatus** to 2. As there is no valid cursor position, an update or delete cannot be issued against the cursor when this happens.

The fetch statement sets the global variable **@@sqlstatus** as:

0 successful fetch statement;

1 error occurred in the fetch statement;

2 fetch past the last row in the cursor result set.

The fetch statement also sets the **@@rowcount** global variable to the number of rows that have been returned by the fetch commands (in other words, a running total of the number of rows currently in the cursor result set). The @@rowcount value is available until the cursor is closed or deallocated.

Be careful where you place the fetch and the @@rowcount test as seemingly innocuous commands which do not retrieve data—such as while and if—will reset @@rowcount to zero.

```
FETCH read_csr
...
WHILE (@@sqlstatus = 0)
BEGIN
        FETCH read_csr
        IF (@@rowcount > 20)
        BREAK
.
.
.
END
```

This works fine but:

```
FETCH read_csr
...
WHILE (@@sqlstatus = 0)
BEGIN
        IF (@@rowcount > 20)
        BEGIN
                BREAK
        END
        FETCH read_csr
END
```

does not work. Even though there are no select statements between the fetch and the @@rowcount test, the while statement changes the @@rowcount to zero so the break command is not executed.

The processing structure to fetch and process each row is therefore:

- fetch the first row;
- check if there are no records;
- fetch and process subsequent rows in a loop until end of set;
- check for an error.

```
FETCH cursor_1

IF @@sqlstatus = 2
BEGIN
        PRINT 'no records'
        CLOSE cursor_1
END
ELSE
BEGIN
        WHILE (@@sqlstatus = 0)
        BEGIN
        .
        .
        FETCH cursor_1
        .
        .
        END
IF (@@sqlstatus = 1)
BEGIN
        PRINT 'error occurred'
END
```

```
CLOSE cursor_1
END

DEALLOCATE CURSOR cursor_1
```

When using server cursors, the output is multiple single row results. The @@sqlstatus value is not set to 2 until the fetch has been processed to read past the end of the result set, which produces an empty output row at the end of the processing. This does not cause any problems when you execute the procedure from a client application using db-library or ct-library, but it always displays when you execute the procedure from ISQL. The only way that I could find to eliminate it was to fetch into variables and control the output display in the code.

```
CREATE PROC csr1 AS
        BEGIN
        DECLARE @var1 int, @var2 int, @var3 int
        DECLARE csr_1 CURSOR FOR
                SELECT col_1, col_2, col_3 FROM tab_1
                FOR READ ONLY
        OPEN csr_1
        FETCH csr_1 INTO @var1, @var2, @var3
        IF (@@sqlstatus = 2)
        BEGIN
                print "no records"
                CLOSE csr_1
                DEALLOCATE CURSOR csr_1
                RETURN 1
        END
        PRINT "col_1 is: %1!  col_2 is: %2!  col_3 is %3!",
                @var1, @var2, @var3
        WHILE (@@sqlstatus = 0)
        BEGIN
                FETCH csr_1 INTO @var1, @var2, @var3
        PRINT "col_1 is: %1!  col_2 is: %2!  col_3 is %3!",
                @var1, @var2, @var3
        END
        IF (@@sqlstatus=1)
        BEGIN
                PRINT "error occurred"
        END
        CLOSE csr_1
        DEALLOCATE CURSOR csr_1
        END
        RETURN
        GO
```

2.3.4 Close

close

```
CLOSE cursor_name
```

This deactivates a cursor, removing access to the cursor result set.

```
CLOSE read_csr_1
```

Closing a cursor does not deactivate the cursor, it simply does not allow any further access to the results set and leaves the cursor position undefined. The closed cursor may be reopened to permit refetching of rows from the beginning of the cursor result set. This requires a reissue of the open statement which will reexecute the SQL command. If there has been any maintenance of the data since the first open, this open will pick up the new data.

2.3.5 Deallocate Cursor

deallocate cursor

```
DEALLOCATE CURSOR cursor_name
```

This command deallocates a cursor, making it inaccessible and releasing all memory resources linked to the cursor.

```
DEALLOCATE CURSOR upd_csr_1
```

A deallocated cursor must be declared again before it can be reused. An open or closed cursor may be deallocated but it is good practice to close before deallocating.

2.3.6 Cursor Information

The system procedure **sp_cursorinfo** provides information about the cursor status and result columns.

sp_cursorinfo

```
sp_cursorinfo [cursor_level] [, cursor_name]
```

where

cursor_level	0	a cursor declared outside a stored procedure;
	n	a cursor declared inside a stored procedure at nesting level n;
	-1	either of the above;
	null	all cursors irrespective of level.

```
sp_cursorinfo 0, orders_csr
```

```
Cursor name 'orders_csr' is declared at nesting level 0.
The cursor id is 367142.
The cursor has been successfully opened 18 times.
The cursor was compiled at isolation level 1.
The cursor is not open.
The cursor will remain open when a transaction is committed or rolled back.
The number of cursor rows returned for each FETCH is 1.
The cursor is updatable.
The result columns are:
Name='order_price', Table='orders_tab', Type=numeric(6, 2).
Length=6 (updatable).
Name='order_qty', Table= 'orders_tab', Type=numeric(8, 3).
Length=8 (updatable).
```

2.4 Update and Delete Extensions

The **update** and **delete** command syntax has been extended to allow for cursor-based processing.

update

```
UPDATE table_name
       SET column_name = value
             [, column_name = value]...
       WHERE CURRENT OF cursor_name
```

Note that there is no FROM clause in this version of the update.

delete

```
DELETE [FROM] table_name
       WHERE CURRENT OF cursor_name
```

These update or delete the current row of the table (or view) for the named cursor. Current row is the row just fetched. Note that the commands do not include a separate where clause on the record to be updated, as we already know which record is to be updated because of the cursor pointer.

A simple example of the syntax is:

```
DECLARE csr_1 CURSOR FOR
       SELECT pkey, col_a FROM tab_1
              WHERE pkey = 1
              FOR UPDATE OF col_a
GO

OPEN csr_1
FETCH csr_1
UPDATE tab_1 SET col_a = col_a + 20
       WHERE CURRENT OF csr_1
GO
```

2.5 Client-based Cursor Commands

This is by no means a detailed description of ct-library processing structures and describes only the command syntax for cursor processing. (If you are not a programmer or have not written a line of "C" in your life, most of this section will be incomprehensible and I would recommend that you ignore it.)

There are two commands to process client-based cursors.

The **ct_cursor** command is a generic command which initiates one of the cursor commands. The cursor actions initiated by ct_cursor are:

- declare cursor
- define read only/update
- open
- define number of rows returned by each ct_fetch
- update/delete current record

- close
- deallocate cursor.

The **ct_param** command defines any variables required by the cursor statement such as:

- select statement host variables
- stored procedure parameters
- columns in update of list.

The sequence of events is still the same: declare, open, fetch and process in a loop, close, deallocate. However, all of the cursor-related commands are issued with ct_cursor. Do not forget that you need a unique index on the table if you intend to update it.

2.5.1 ct_cursor

ct_cursor

The syntax of the **ct_cursor** command is:

```
ct_cursor(cmd, type, name, namelen, text, textlen, option)
```

where

cmd	a pointer to the CS_COMMAND structure which holds the commands sent to the server and the results of these commands;
type	the type of cursor action to initiate. These types are explained in detail below;
name	the name of the cursor or the name of the table being updated/deleted;
namelen	the length of the name field in bytes;
text	the select command being declared or the update statement if the action is update;
textlen	the length of the text field in bytes;
option	an action dependent on the type, as explained below for each type.

Declare Cursor

```
ct_cursor(cmd, CS_CURSOR_DECLARE, "read_csr",
        CS_NULLTERM, "SELECT ord_no, prod_no, qty, price from ord_item",
        CS_NULLTERM, option)
```

where

option	CS_READ_ONLY	a read only cursor;
	CS_FOR_UPDATE	an updatable cursor;
	CS_UNUSED	not defined;

Number of Cursor Rows

```
ct_cursor(cmd, CS_CURSOR_ROWS, NULL, CS_UNUSED,
               NULL, CS_UNUSED, (CS_INT)2)
```

Open

```
ct_cursor(cmd, CS_CURSOR_OPEN, NULL, CS_UNUSED,
               NULL, CS_UNUSED, CS_UNUSED)
```

Close

```
ct_cursor(cmd, CS_CURSOR_CLOSE, NULL, CS_UNUSED,
               NULL, CS_UNUSED, option)
```

where

option	CS_DEALLOC	closes and deallocates;
	CS_UNUSED	closes but does not deallocate.

Deallocate

```
ct_cursor(cmd, CS_CURSOR_DEALLOCATE, NULL,
               CS_UNUSED, NULL, CS_UNUSED, CS_UNUSED)
```

Update

```
ct_cursor(cmd, CS_CURSOR_UPDATE, "ord_item",
        CS_NULLTERM, "update ord_item
        set price = price * 1.05 where current of upd_csr",
        CS_NULLTERM, CS_UNUSED)
```

Delete

```
ct_cursor(cmd, CS_CURSOR_DELETE, "ord_item",
        CS_NULLTERM, NULL, CS_UNUSED, CS_UNUSED)
```

Example of a Processing Sequence

```
strcpy(select, "select * from sal_pur");
ct_cursor(cmd, CS_CURSOR_DECLARE, "curs_1", CS_NULLTERM,
select, CS_NULLTERM, CS_READ_ONLY);

ct_cursor(cmd, CS_CURSOR_ROWS, NULL, CS_UNUSED, NULL,
          CS_UNUSED, (CS_INT)1);

ct_cursor(cmd, CS_CURSOR_OPEN, NULL, CS_UNUSED, NULL,
          CS_UNUSED, CS_UNUSED);

ct_send(cmd); /* sends the declare, rows and open to the server  */

/*  ct_results, ct_bind, ct_fetch as always for results  */

ct_cursor(cmd, CS_CURSOR_CLOSE, NULL, CS_UNUSED, NULL,
          CS_UNUSED, CS_DEALLOC);

ct_send(cmd); /*  send the close (and deallocate) to the server  */

/*  ct_results to check results of ct_close  */
/*  clearly the close does not produce any regular rows  */
```

2.5.2 ct_param

ct_param

The syntax of the ct_param command is:

```
ct_param(cmd, datafmt, data, datalen, indicator)
```

where

cmd	a pointer to the CS_COMMAND structure which holds the commands sent to the server and the results of these commands;
datafmt	a pointer to a CS_DATAFMT structure which describes the parameter. This array describes: • name • length • datatype • scale and precision • status: CS_UPDATECOL update column; CS_INPUTVALUE input parameter.

```
format.status = CS_UPDATECOL;
ct_param(cmd, &format, "price", CS_NULLTERM, CS_UNUSED);
```

2.6 Cursor Locking

SQL Server uses update locks by default for updatable cursors. Therefore, the statement:

```
DECLARE upd_csr_1 CURSOR
       FOR SELECT a, b, c FROM tab_1
              WHERE c > 50
       FOR UPDATE
```

places update locks on the records read from tab_1. However, these are not permanent locks which last until the end of the transaction. They are temporary on the basis that SQL Server is expecting you to escalate them to an exclusive lock with an update statement. If you do not update immediately, there is a chance that SQL Server will lose the update lock on that record as the update lock is released when the cursor position moves off the current data page. In other words, the record has an update lock only for as long as the page is read; there is the possibility that a row will be read and the update lock will be lost before it is updated. In this case, there is a finite time when another transaction may update a row which has been displayed at the client.

This is saying that SQL Server follows an optimistic locking strategy and you MUST employ some check on the data you are updating to ensure that it has not changed since you last read it. This is no different from normal SQL Server updating, but in this case there is no system-provided functionality as the **for browse** clause is not permitted in the **declare cursor** statement.

If it bothers you to have update locks on records that you are only reading (it bothers me as there is no guarantee that the record is locked anyway), you can specify a standard shared lock in the from clause of the select statement.

```
DECLARE upd_csr_2 CURSOR
FOR SELECT a, b, c FROM tab_2 SHARED
       WHERE c > 50
FOR UPDATE
```

This will place a shared lock on the data page as standard as if a normal select had been issued. You really are only swapping an update lock for a shared lock but it will improve concurrency and, as there is no guarantee that you still have the record lock, it seems to be a straightforward gain.

In general, cursors should access the data on a unique index, although this is necessary only for update cursors. Be aware that if you declare an update cursor without using a unique index on the table, then any update of the table will automatically close all cursors on the table. So use unique indexes for updatable cursors.

The locks have the following effects.

- A read only cursor takes standard shared locks, which means that other users may read the pages but not update them until the shared lock is off. The shared lock lasts only for the duration of the page fetch.
- An update only cursor takes update locks on the pages being scanned so that other users may read the data until an exclusive lock is placed on the page by an **update** or **delete** command. Again, the update lock lasts for the duration of the page read. The exclusive lock lasts until the end of the transaction.
- If you specify the **shared** option, the update only cursor takes shared locks instead of update locks when scanning the pages
- If you also specify **holdlock**, then the locks are retained on all pages fetched. Other users may read the data but may not update it. The holdlock forces the locks to be retained until the end of the transaction. Be wary of holdlock as it can significantly increase contention.

SQL Server locking is described fully in Appendix F.

System 11 Additions

System 11 has introduced a "dirty read" facility called **isolation level 0** which uses no locks on the pages and allows data to be read even if it is exclusively locked. This is defined in the **select** command of the **declare** statement.

```
DECLARE read_csr CURSOR FOR
        SELECT * FROM orders
        AT ISOLATION READ UNCOMMITTED
```

Isolation level 0 cursors are automatically read only and require a unique index on the table. Isolation levels are discussed in detail in section 8.2.

2.7 Summary

At last, we have the ability to use server-based cursors in SQL Server and a very nice implementation of client cursors in ct-library. The System 10.0 implementation lacks nothing which will prevent you using this feature.

I have tested the server-based cursor performance (in late 1994 using 10.0.1) compared to multiple set based commands and, unfortunately, there is rather a large performance overhead in using the server-based cursors. The "official" figures admit to a "slight" overhead but I found a minimum of 100% overhead.

As with all performance benchmarks, please check the results in your own environment. The benchmark I ran was on VAX VMS with version 10.0.1 of the server and a db-library client on a separate machine. You may get different results but, based on my experience, I can only say that SQL Server-based cursors should be used sparingly. You must be prepared for a significant performance hit.

I have not checked the client-based cursors for performance but there is little to suggest a large overhead as they are fully client-controlled. However, be careful of the network overhead of making multiple fetches.

3

Datatypes

This chapter covers the datatypes available in System 10. The new and changed datatypes in System 10 are detailed, followed by a summary of all of the datatypes. The chapter concludes with a discussion of the resultant precision and scale in arithmetic.

System 11 has made no addition to the System 10 features.

COMMAND SYNTAX

None

SYSTEM PROCEDURE SYNTAX

None

NEW DATATYPES

```
numeric (precision, scale)
decimal (precision, scale)
double precision
float(precision)
```

3.1 New Datatypes

System 10 has introduced two new datatypes:

numeric (or decimal) an exact numeric value with precision and scale to indicate number of digits and number of decimal places, e.g., numeric(6), numeric(8, 2). The default scale is 0.

double precision a float datatype that may use 8 bytes of storage.

There are two changes to existing datatypes.

float(precision) float may now accept an optional precision.

character datatypes the default length for all character datatypes—char, varchar, nchar, nvarchar—is now one. The exception to this is in the **convert** function, where the default length for character is 30.

```
CONVERT(CHAR, @var_1)
```

and

```
CONVERT(CHAR(30), @var_1)
```

are equivalent.

However, there have been several additions and changes during the later version 4 releases. The System 10 datatypes are summarized in Table 3.1.

Table 3.1 *System 10 datatypes*

datatype	range	bytes	comments
tinyint	0 to 255	1	
smallint	2^{15}-1 to 2^{-15}	2	
int	2^{31}-1 to 2^{-31}	4	
numeric(p, s)	10^{38}-1 to 10^{-38}	2 to 17	Max precision = 38 default precision = 18 default scale = 0
decimal(p, s)	10^{38}-1 to 10^{-38}	2 to 17	Synonym for numeric
float(p)	h/w dependent	4 or 8	p<16: 4 bytes p>=16: 8 bytes

Table 3.1 (Continued)

datatype	range	bytes	comments
real	h/w dependent	4	
double precision	h/w dependent	8	
small money	$2^{31}/10^{4}$-1 to $2^{-31}/10^{4}$	4	Fixed scale of 4
money	$2^{63}/10^{4}$-1 to $2^{-63}/10^{4}$	8	Fixed scale of 4
char(n)	0 - 255	n	
varchar(n)	0 - 255	entry length	
nchar(n)	0 - 255	n*@@charsize	allows for national character set where 1 character uses > 1 byte
nvarchar(n)	0 - 255	n*@@charsize	allows for national character sets where 1 character uses > 1 byte
text(n)	2^{31} - 1	multiples of a page	
binary(n)	0 - 255	n	
varbinary(n)	0 - 255	entry length	
image	2^{31} - 1	multiples of a page	
bit	0 or 1	1	
smalldatetime	1 Jan 1900 to 6 June 2079	4	
datetime	1 Jan 1753 to 31 Dec 9999	8	

The system datatype names are now case insensitive, so the following are all equivalent.

```
DECLARE @var_1 CHAR(10)
DECLARE @var_2 char(10)
DECLARE @var_3 ChAr(10)
```

There are now several synonyms for system datatype names. The following are equivalent.

integer	and	int
double precision	and	float
character	and	char
character varying	and	varchar
national character varying	and	nvarchar
national char varying	and	nvarchar
nchar varying	and	nvarchar

The float, double precision and real datatypes cannot be guaranteed to hold exact values. This is not specific to SQL Server but is a common feature of such datatypes.

Therefore, a column defined as qty float displaying a value of 20.12345 cannot be guaranteed to be retrieved by the command:

```
SELECT * FROM tab_1
       WHERE qty = 20.12345
```

as the actual internal stored value may be something like 20.1234499999.

Use numeric when you are confident of the maximum scale of a number. Even if you are a little unsure, it is often advisable to define such columns as numeric to ensure no problem with exact matching.

Float is physically held as real or double precision, depending on the precision. If the precision is < 16, then the column is held as real in 4 bytes. If the precision is >= 16, then the column is held as double precision in 8 bytes. However, unless the column is defined with the datatype **real**, it always displays as float on sp_help, with a length of four or eight.

Although the minimum storage size for a bit datatype is 1 byte, multiple bit columns are collected into bytes. Therefore 1–8 bit columns use 1 byte; 9–16 bit columns use 2 bytes, etc.

An important aspect of System 10 support for exact numeric datatypes with a scale (such as non-integer) is that numeric literals which include a decimal point are treated as numeric. Only literals entered with the "e" notation (e.g. 1.6e-10) are treated as float.

This is obviously different from version 4.x when numeric did not exist. It means that there may be a difference in precision or scale as a result of arithmetic operations. So be careful to check the calculations involving numeric literals when you move to System 10.

There is one other change to the System 10 result datatype that involves money. In version 4.x, if a money datatype and a literal were in a calculation, the result was money. In System 10, the result will conform to the datatype hierarchy and is liable not to be money. The only way around this is to use money variables or the convert function.

```
SELECT price * 2.5 FROM tab_1
```

will result in a numeric result datatype because the literal is numeric, which is higher in the datatype hierarchy than money. Float, real and numeric are higher than money and result in a non-money result datatype.

```
SELECT price * $2.5 FROM tab_1
```

or

```
SELECT convert(money, price * 2.5)
 FROM tab_1
```

will result in a money result datatype.

The datatype hierarchy is held in systypes.

```
SELECT name, hierarchy FROM systypes
ORDER BY hierarchy
```

name	hierarchy
floatn	1
float	2
datetimen	3
datetime	4
real	5
numericn	6
numeric	7
decimaln	8
decimal	9
moneyn	10
money	11
smallmoney	12
smalldatetime	13
intn	14
int	15
smallint	16
tinyint	17
bit	18
varchar	19
sysname	19
nvarcharn	19
char	20
nchar	20

```
varbinary            21
timestamp            21
binary               22
text                 23
image                24
```

The names with a suffix of "n" are SQL Server reserved datatypes which are allocated to the fixed length datatypes which allow nulls, as SQL Server always holds a column which allows null as variable length.

However, be very careful of the aggregate functions which still return float datatypes if the result is non-integer. I used an integer column and a numeric(2, 1) literal and obtained the results:

int_col * 1.0 gave numeric result;

avg(int_col) * 1.0 gave numeric result;

avg(int_col * 1.0) gave float result.

So be careful. You need to check the result datatype of your important arithmetic. Some functions now return numeric datatypes instead of float (see section 3.5).

3.2 Precision and Scale in Arithmetic

The precision and scale of numeric datatype arithmetic is shown in Table 3.2.

Table 3.2 *Arithmetic precision*

operation	precision	scale
addition	max(s1,s2) + max(p1-s1,p2-s2)+1	max(s1,s2)
subtraction	max(s1,s2) + max(p1-s1,p2-s2)+1	max(s1,s2)
multiplication	s1 + s2 + (p1-s1) + (p2-s2) + 1	s1 + s2
division	max(s1+p2-s2+1,6)+p1-s1+p2	max(s1+p2-s2+1,6)

Wow! Let's look at these more closely.

3.2.1 Addition

result = n1 + n2 e.g., 12.43 + 9.127 = 21.557

The formula for addition is:

scale(result) = max(scale(n1), scale(n2))
precision(result) = scale(result) + integer_part(result)

where

---

integer_part(result) = max(integer_part(n1), integer_part(n2)) + 1

The new scale is easy; it is the maximum of the scale of the datatypes.

The new precision is: the new scale
+
the maximum integer portion of the input datatypes
i.e., max(p-s) of the input datatypes
+
1 (because the most we can go is 1 up in precision)

3.2.2 Subtraction

result=n1– n2 e.g., 12.43 – 9.127 = 3.303

The argument is the same as addition although the +1 is not really necessary.

3.2.3 Multiplication

result = n1 * n2 e.g., 12.43 * 9.127 = 113.44861

The formula for multiplication is:

scale(result) = scale(n1) + scale(n2)
precision(result) = integer_part(n1) + integer_part(n2) + 1

where integer_part is as before:

integer_part(result) = max(integer_part(n1), integer_part(n2)) + 1

The new scale is the sum of the input scales. Check if you like; it's basic arithmetic.

The new precision is: the new scale
+
the sum of the input precisions
+
1 (as with addition)

3.2.4 Division

This one is not so simple as the scale can be as big as you want if it is a repeating decimal (for example, 7÷3) and the true formula depends on which type of number the divisor is (e.g., even, odd, multiple of 5, prime, etc.). So the easiest approach here is to accept the formula and check individual cases if you wish. Of course, there will always be a problem with scale and precision on division, so maybe a standard rounding policy is best.

The formula for division is:

scale(result) = max(scale(n1) + integer_part(n1) + 1, 6)
precision(result) = scale(result) + integer_part(result)

where the 6 is included to ensure some information about the decimal portion.

Watch your version 4.x arithmetic calculations when you move to 10.x, as the abort and overflow default actions have changed. In 4.x, the default settings of arithabort and arithignore returned an error message and continued processing. In 10.x, the default settings return an error and abort the command.

3.3 Conversions

When assigning one numeric datatype to another, you will get an error message if there is loss of precision or scale on conversion.

```
DECLARE @num6_2 NUMERIC(6, 2)
DECLARE @num6_1 NUMERIC(6, 1)

SELECT @num6_2 = 1234.56
SELECT @num6_1 = @num6_2
```

This will produce an error message:

```
Scale error during implicit conversion of NUMERIC value '1234.56' to a NUMERIC
field."
```

Such assignments require an explicit conversion using the convert function:

```
SELECT @num6_1 = CONVERT(NUMERIC(6,1), @num6_2)
```

The above message was what the manual said was produced. What I actually got was:

```
Truncation error occurred."
Command has been aborted."
```

which is a little terse and uninformative if a transaction with lots of arithmetic fails.

3.4 Changes to System Tables

3.4.1 systypes

There are three new columns in the systypes table:

1. prec the precision;
2. scale the scale;
3. hierarchy The position within the datatype hierarchy (see section 3.1). User datatypes are assigned the hierarchy of the base datatype.

3.4.2 syscolumns

There are two new columns in the syscolumns table:

1. prec the precision;
2. scale the scale.

Those system procedures (for example, sp_help) that display information from these tables, have been altered to include the new columns.

```
sp_help orders
```

```
column_name  type               length          prec   scale  nulls
             default_name                       rule_name            identity
order_no     char               6               null   null   0
             null                               null                 0
order_date   datetime           8               null   null   0
             orders_order_14400354  orders_order_160003601 0
cust_no char           6                 null   null   0
             null                               null                 0
price        numeric 8                 6        2      0
             null                               null   null          0
```

```
index_name      index_description
        index_keys
orders_pkey     non-clustered, unique located on default
        order_no

No defined keys for this object.
```

3.5 Changes to functions

Because of the new exact numeric datatypes, some of the numeric functions can now return a numeric datatype instead of a float datatype. These are: abs, ceiling, degrees, floor, power, radians, round and sign.

3.6 Summary

System 10 has introduced new exact numeric datatypes—numeric and decimal—and altered the nonexact numeric datatype—float—to accept a precision that allows 4 byte and 8 byte float values. This is long-awaited but means you will have to check your existing code that involves numeric literals to ensure that there is no loss of precision or scale. Another important change is in the datatype hierarchy that effects money calculations. These no longer automatically produce money datatype results and you will need to check how the result datatype of these calculations effect the precision and scale of the calculation.

4

Threshold Manager

This chapter describes the threshold manager, which provides the ability to fire a stored procedure when the free space in a segment reaches a specified amount. As the threshold manager maintains free space in a segment, I have included a discussion on segments in this chapter. The other space allocation topics of devices and databases are dealt with in Appendix C.

System 11 has made no addition to the System 10 features.

COMMAND SYNTAX

None

SYSTEM PROCEDURE SYNTAX

```
sp_addsegment
sp_dropsegment
sp_extendsegment
sp_placeobject
sp_addthreshold
sp_dropthreshold
sp_modifythreshold
sp_dboption
sp_helpthreshold
sp_helpsegment
```

NEW FUNCTION SYNFTAX

```
curunreservedpgs
lct_admin
```

4.1 Introduction

The threshold manager keeps track of free space in a database, firing a procedure when the number of free pages in a segment falls below a specified value, known as the threshold value. The principal purpose of this is to monitor free space in syslogs so that log full may be avoided, but it is available in any named segment of the database. The log segment has a mandatory threshold called the **last chance threshold**. All other threshold values, including additional thresholds on the log segment, must be defined explicitly. In all cases, even the last chance threshold on the log segment, you must define what is to happen in the called procedure.

Before describing the use of thresholds, let's cover the concept and use of segments. Segments in SQL Server are logical space allocations which permit the placement of specific objects on disk. The physical allocation of space using **disk init** and **create database** is described in Appendix C.

4.2 Segments

4.2.1 Using Segments

Segments are defined on the devices so that we can specify the placement of the objects (tables and indexes) that we create in each database. Initial creation of the database causes three segments to be created automatically:

system segment	for the system tables;
default segment	for the data and indexes;
log segment	for the database log.

By default, these are used by the server when allocating space unless there is a specific segment allocation. Allocating the log to its own log segment allows it to be monitored by the threshold manager.

```
CREATE DATABASE fred
  ON dev1 = 5,
  ON dev2 = 1
  LOG ON dev3 = 8
```

will give an initial segment allocation as shown in Figure 4.1.

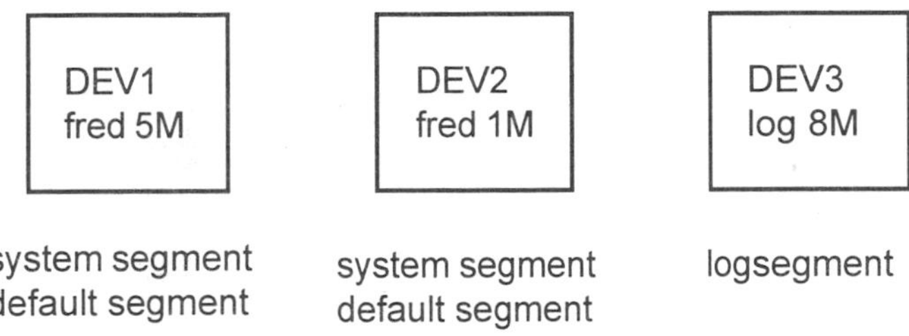

Figure 4.1 *Initial segment allocation.*

As we create tables and indexes on this database, they will be allocated to one default segment on one device (say devl) until it fills up and then to the next default segment on the other device (dev2). Choice of device is based on the device number in sysdevices with the lowest device number used first.

We are aiming for the smoothing of the disk activity on each device (in reality on each physical disk but I shall assume a device per disk just to make the discussion easier). To do this we need to place objects on specific devices. We do not place objects directly on the device, but create named segments on the devices and place the objects in the segments. The limit is 31 segments per database so do not get too carried away with this logical space allocation.

Creating segments is done with the system procedure **sp_addsegment**.

sp_addsegment

```
sp_addsegment  segment_name,
               db_name,
               device_name
```

To create segments for our database fred in Figure 4.1, the following is used.

```
sp_addsegment seg_a, fred, devl
sp_addsegment seg_b, fred, dev2
```

Note that the database name is mandatory in System 10 although some of the SQL Server documentation omits it.

This gives a segment allocation as shown in Figure 4.2.

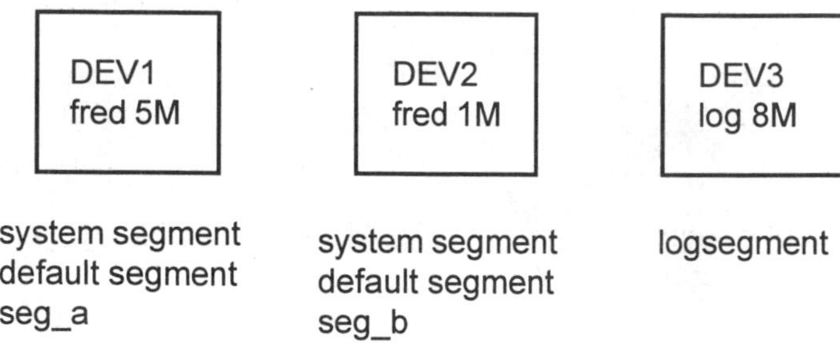

Figure 4.2 *Named segment allocation.*

We can now create tables and indexes on these named segments by adding the segment name to the create statement. This ensures that they are allocated to a specific device.

```
CREATE INDEX ind_1 ON tab_1(col_1) ON seg_b
```

Unfortunately we have not reserved dev2 exclusively for seg_b as it still has the initial allocations of the system segment and the default segment. Any objects allocated to the default segment will use dev2 when the space on dev1 is full.

To ensure that a device is reserved only for those objects that we specifically allocate to it, we also need to drop the initial system and default segment allocations. Dropping segments is done using the system procedure **sp_dropsegment**.

sp_dropsegment

```
sp_dropsegment segment_name,
               db_name
               [, device_name]
```

So to reserve dev2 for seg_b we need to drop:

```
sp_dropsegment "system", fred, dev2
sp_dropsegment "default", fred, dev2
```

We now have a segment allocation as shown in Figure 4.3 and complete control over the use of dev2.

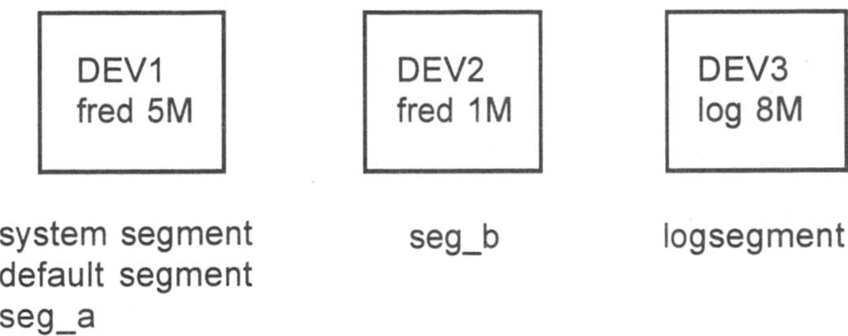

Figure 4.3 *Exclusive segment allocation.*

Note that in System 10 you cannot drop all instances of the default segment from the database. Be careful because you can now accidentally place an object on the wrong device.

The optional use of the device name is important. If you do not quote the device name, the segment is dropped from the database. If you do use the device name, the segment is unmapped from the device but not actually dropped from the database. This unmapping can be useful when you have a segment spanning more than one device and wish to remove the segment from one of the devices but leave it mapped to the other. A segment is extended to more than one device using **sp_extendsegment**.

sp_extendsegment

```
sp_extendsegment        segment_name,
                        db_name,
                        device_name

sp_extendsegment seg_a, fred, dev2
```

Dropping a segment automatically drops any thresholds associated with it. Unmapping a segment from a device automatically drops any thresholds which now exceed the total segment space. Unmapping a log segment from a device, or extending it, automatically recalculates the last chance threshold.

Let's summarize the steps and do another example.

1. Create the database on specific devices.

```
CREATE DATABASE fred
 ON devl = 10,
 ON dev2 = 8
 LOG ON dev3 = 5
```

2. Create segments on the data devices to allow controlled placement of objects.

```
sp_addsegment seg_a, fred, dev1
sp_addsegment seg_b, fred, dev2
```

3. Remove the default and system segments from all but one device. The removal of the system segment is not mandatory.

```
sp_dropsegment "default", fred, dev2
sp_dropsegment "system", fred, dev2
```

Be careful that this device does not fill up, as the system tables are allowed on only one device.

Now let's create a database on two devices, log on a third; extend the database to a third device; create two segments on one device and one segment on the others; reserve the two segment device for our exclusive allocation.

1. Create the database.

```
CREATE DATABASE fred
 ON dev_a = 10,
 ON dev_b = 8
 LOG ON log_dev = 4
```

2. Extend the database.

```
ALTER DATABASE fred ON dev_c = 6
```

3. Create the named segments.

```
sp_addsegment myseg_1, fred, dev_a
sp_addsegment myseg_2, fred, dev_a
sp_addsegment myseg_3, fred, dev_b
sp_addsegment myseg_4, fred, dev_c
```

4. Reserve dev_a.

```
sp_dropsegment "default", fred, dev_a
sp_dropsegment "system", fred, dev_a
```

We now have exclusive control of dev_a for allocation of objects and controlled placement on dev_b and dev_c. However, dev_b and dev_c will also contain the system tables and any objects that we do not specifically place on a segment.

The commands:

```
CREATE TABLE tab_1 (col_1 int) ON myseg_1

CREATE INDEX ind_1 ON tab_1(col_1) ON myseg_3
```

```
CREATE TABLE tab_2 (col_1 int) ON myseg_1

CREATE TABLE tab_3 (col_1 int)

CREATE INDEX ind_2 ON tab_2(col_1) ON myseg_4

CREATE INDEX ind_3 ON tab_3(col_1)

CREATE TABLE tab_4 (col_1 int) ON myseg_2
```

will give an allocation as shown in Figure 4.4.

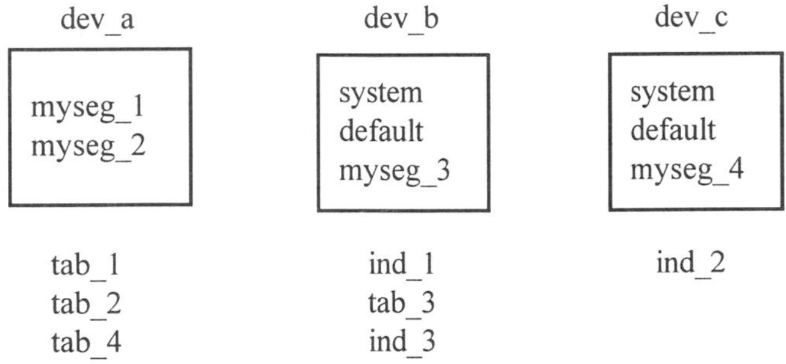

Figure 4.4 *Object allocation.*

Remember that the clustered index and the data of the table are the same object although they are created in separate commands. Therefore, the clustered index and the table may not reside on different devices. SQL Server will allow you to create the clustered index on a segment that is on a different device than the table but will migrate the data records to the index device on index creation. You might think this is crazy but if the devices are on different physical disks, it may speed up the clustered index creation by introducing parallel disk activity into the process. This is minimal as the new device will be used only for the write at the end of the process, but it cannot be slower. (Famous last words!)

The above example used an alter database to get the database onto dev_c. When alter database is used to expand a database onto a new device, the system and default segments are created normally. When the device is already in use by the database, the existing segments are used.

4.2.2 Object on More Than One Device

So far we have looked at how to place objects on specific disks to even out the disk activity. The logical extension of this is to spread an individual object over two or more disks so that disk access is shared across the disks.

This uses the system procedure **sp_placeobject**.

sp_placeobject

```
sp_placeobject seg_name, object_name
```

The approach is to define a segment that covers the devices:

```
sp_addsegment dual, fred, diska
sp_extendsegment dual, fred, diskb
```

and inform the server that the object has to use this segment:

```
sp_placeobject dual, tab_1
```

in which case the server will allocate free space from diska first and then from diskb when diska has been filled up. What you really want, however, is control over record placement. As this is not possible, I personally have very little time for this approach. Splitting the allocation of records in a table across more than one disk is normally required to increase parallel disk activity, which requires control over which records go on which disk. This is not possible with the SQL Server approach. I would suggest splitting the table into several tables and placing each object on a different segment on a different disk. This allows you program control of record placement by table_name, which gives the required parallelism. (However, this requires a union to get the data back together, so consider your options, especially as union is not supported in views.)

When you use sp_placeobject to provide a new segment for an object to use, this new segment is used for all future space allocation. The existing segment space allocation is not affected.

4.3 Thresholds

4.3.1 Creating a Threshold

Thresholds are defined on segments to provide a free space value at which a procedure is executed to provide a warning or to take remedial action. The principal use of thresholds is on the log segment to provide free space warnings about the proximity of the log filling up and to clear space by dumping the log. A last resort threshold is called the **last chance threshold** and is created automatically by SQL Server on all logs that are defined on a separate segment from the database.

You can, of course, define your own thresholds or have several free space warning thresholds on the log. These are defined using **sp_addthreshold**.

sp_addthreshold

```
sp_addthreshold        db_name,
                       segment_name,
                       free_space,
                       proc_name
```

where

free_space	the number of free pages at which the threshold procedure executes;
proc_name	the stored procedure which the threshold manager executes when the number of free pages falls below the free_space value. This procedure must be on the current SQL server, but may be in a different database, such as sybsystemprocs, or on a remote open server.

Even though you must quote the database name, you need to be in the database of the segment before you can execute this procedure. In other words, you must specify the current database.

```
sp_addthreshold        jk_db,
                       logsegment,
                       200,
                       jk1_proc

Adding threshold for segment 'logsegment' at '200' pages."
DBCC execution completed. If errors occurred contact your System Administrator.
```

Do not panic about the DBCC message; it's a part of the sp_addthreshold execution.

This updates a new system table, **systhresholds**, which stores the above information about the threshold: segment number, free space, proc_name and a status to indicate "last chance threshold." When a threshold fires, the server looks in systhresholds to get the procedure name for the segment and calls it with four parameters as:

```
EXEC seg1_thresh_proc
     @dbname = prod_db,
     @segmentname = prod_seg1,
     @space_left = 50,
     @status = 0
```

where

@dbname	varchar(30)	
@segmentname	varchar(30)	
@space_left	int	
@status	int	(1 = last chance)

What you put in the procedure is entirely up to you. You may even change the parameter names if you wish, as SQL Server uses positional parameters in the exec statement. However, the use of positional parameters in the procedure call means that you must keep the same sequence and the same datatypes. Useful things to do would be to archive some data or to dump the transaction log. You must not maintain any records in the current database if you are executing the last chance threshold procedure, as processes which write to the log are not allowed to execute. Once the last chance threshold has fired, any process which writes to the log is automatically suspended or aborted. (The choice is a database option—see 4.5.1.)

Any error and other messages from the threshold procedure go to the error log. Any other output, such as a select statement, is thrown away by the server. The threshold procedure is run as a "background" task with no associated terminal or user session, and with the permissions of the user who created the threshold. (Note that this is the permission at the time the threshold was added, less any permissions that have since been revoked but not including any new permissions granted.) As this process does not have a network connection, there is nowhere to send regular output. Because of this, you will not automatically see any evidence in the error log that the threshold procedure has fired. It is useful to include a print statement in the threshold procedure to indicate what has happened.

Be careful when you enter the threshold procedure name, as SQL Server does not check that it exists at this time. The only check is when the threshold procedure executes, at which point it might be a little late. When the procedure executes, SQL Server simply returns an error message if the procedure name does not exist.

4.3.2 Last Chance Threshold

As the name suggests, this is the threshold which is the final warning at which point you must do something or the segment will be full. This is set automatically on a log segment when the log is on a separate segment from the database. You should have a last chance threshold on every syslogs that is on a separate segment. If you do not, then something has gone wrong with the upgrade and you need to use lct_admin to set it (see 4.4.2). This special threshold is there to prevent the log becoming full and a "dump tran...with no_log" having to be run.

The server maintains this log segment threshold at the value which allows enough free space to allow dump tran to write a record to the log (plus a little for safety). The server maintains this value as you alter the size of the log segment with sp_dropsegment, sp_extendsegment and sp_logdevice. When the last chance threshold executes, it means that you cannot do anything else in the database that attempts to write to the log, as you will then be unable to run dump tran. So the server automatically suspends or aborts all processes that try to write to the transaction log. The choice of suspend or abort is set using sp_dboption (see 4.5.1) with a default of suspend.

This means that the last chance threshold procedure can only perform:

- select
- print
- raiserror
- dump tran.

As the output from the select does not display, I would suggest that you simply print an error message to the error log and dump the transaction log. Once the dump tran has cleared enough space from the log, the suspended transactions are awakened. Aborted transactions must be resubmitted by the users.

A special procedure, **sp_thresholdaction,** is executed for the log segment last chance threshold procedure. It's not really a system procedure as you have to write it yourself (with the previous four parameters) but it directs your mind towards one procedure for all last chance thresholds on all log segments. Since you are simply going to dump the transaction log, it might as well be a system procedure and be in sybsystemprocs. The dump command can now accept variables for all of its parameters, so one sp_thresholdaction is sufficient. If you have not created this procedure, SQL Server will simply suspend processing of the transaction with the following error message in the error log.

```
Space available in the log has fallen critically low in database 'fred'. All
future modifications to this database will be suspended until the log is success-
fully dumped and space becomes available.
The transaction log in database 'fred' is almost full. Your transaction is being
suspended until space is made available in the log."
```

Note that the inability to write to the log when the last chance threshold procedure has fired prohibits a checkpoint and a dump database. Dump database is under your control, so do not run it. Any checkpoint which is attempted by the server once the last chance threshold has fired on the log segment does not try to checkpoint the database, but instead writes messages to the error log. These messages state the database name and how many tasks are currently suspended. This also means that the recovery routine will not attempt to recover a database that has reached the last chance threshold on the log segment.

So issue a dump tran as fast as possible to allow the database to get back to normal.

```
CREATE PROCEDURE sp_thresholdaction
(@dbname varchar(30), @segmentname varchar(30),
 @space_left int, @status int)
AS
DUMP TRANSACTION @dbname TO disk1_dump
PRINT "dumped log:  '%1!' for database '%2!'",
        @segmentname, @dbname
```

This is also an area where long-running transactions can give you problems. If a long-running transaction which is writing many records to the log causes the last chance threshold to fire, you will initiate a dump tran. However, this dump tran can only clear completed transactions prior to the oldest open transaction. The long-running transaction will remain on the log and be restarted when the threshold procedure completes. It is quite possible that insufficient space will have been removed from the log to allow the long-running transaction to complete and the threshold will fire again, almost immediately. Drastic action will be required to get out of this one, such as abandoning the transaction or using lct_admin to unsuspend the transaction (with the old problems of a log full). So try to avoid such long-running transactions. If you cannot avoid them, it may be advisable to abort transactions when the last chance threshold fires.

4.3.3 Remove an Existing Threshold

A threshold is removed using the system procedure **sp_dropthreshold**.

sp_dropthreshold

```
sp_dropthreshold        db_name,
                        segment_name,
                        free_space
```

```
sp_dropthreshold production, data_seg_1, 1024
```

Note that free space is mandatory as you can have several thresholds (max 256) on the same segment giving you progressive warnings until you reach the last chance threshold. Make sure that you have a note of where the thresholds are defined.

Although you must specify the database name, you need to be in the current database. You cannot drop the last chance threshold on the log segment.

4.3.4 Changing a Threshold

You may alter the segment name, free space and threshold procedure associated with a threshold using **sp_modifythreshold**.

sp_modifythreshold

```
sp_modifythreshold      db_name,
                        segment_name,
                        free_space
                        [, new_procedure]
                        [, new_free_space]
                        [, new_segment_name]
```

As always, you must quote the current database name.

To alter the free space of an existing threshold:

```
sp_modifythreshold prod_db, prod_seg_1, 300, NULL, 200
```

The owner and permission of the threshold procedure are changed to the user who modified the threshold. If the threshold is a last chance threshold, you may change only the threshold procedure name.

4.4 New Functions

4.4.1 Number of Free Pages in the Disk Allocation

curunreservedpgs

```
curunreservedpgs(dbid, lstart, free_pages)
```

where

dbid, lstart	the database ID which contains the page number defining the piece of the disk to be reported on;
free_pages	the number of free pages in the disk piece containing lstart. Include this value to specify a default to be returned. If the database is open, the function succeeds and the actual number of free pages stored in memory is returned.

```
SELECT curunreservedpgs(u.dbid, u.lstart, u.unreservedpgs)
       FROM master.dbo.sysusages u
       WHERE u.dbid = db_id()

       ------
       2968
       224
```

A free space figure for the segment is recorded in the column **unreservedpgs** in **sysusages**. This is not maintained dynamically while the database is open but is updated in cache when extents are allocated and deallocated. The cache value is flushed to unreservedpgs when the database is closed at shutdown of the server. Do not rely on the sysusages figure as it is wrong while the database is open. If you really want to know the current value, use the curunreservedpgs() function.

The sequence for the maintenance of the unreservedpgs column is:

- count free space when the database is recovered;
- update in cache from extent allocation/deallocation;
- update unreservedpgs when the database is closed at shutdown.

On every update to unreservedpgs—allocation and deallocation of extents—the new value is checked against the free space for the segment. If the threshold has been reached, the specified stored procedure is executed.

4.4.2 Log Segment Last Chance Threshold Management

lct_admin

```
lct_admin(item, dbid)
```

where item:

reserve	the number of pages in syslogs which would be required to do a dump tran. In this case, the second argument is not dbid but the total number of pages in the log segment. The server uses this option internally when creating the last chance threshold for the log segment. `lct_admin("reserve", 20480)`
lastchance	creates the last chance threshold for the log segment, updating systhresholds and the memory resident value. This is only necessary when upgrading existing databases to System 10 as the last chance threshold is not automatically acquired.
logfull	indicates if the last chance threshold has been reached. A return of 1=yes, 0=no.

unsuspend	wakes up any suspended tasks in the database and marks the last chance threshold of the log segment as "inactive" so that no future transactions will be suspended. This gets you out of a hole if necessary but it will probably cause the log to fill up which will need a dump tran...with no_log and then a dump database. So do not use it.

The values of item are strings and require quotes:

```
select lct_admin("logfull", 8)

        ----
         0

select lct_admin("reserve", 10240)

        ----
         456
```

4.5 Changes to Existing Procedures

4.5.1 sp_dboption

sp_dboption

This has two new options.

abort tran on log full

This option aborts transactions that try to write to the log segment after the last chance threshold procedure has fired. The default is to suspend transactions.

```
sp_dboption fred_db, "abort tran on log full", true
```

no free space acctg

This option turns off free space management on all segments except the log segment. Free space management cannot be turned off on the log segment.

```
sp_dboption fred_db, "no free space acctg", true
```

4.6 Hysteresis Value

Specifically in the log, but also in other segments, it is useful to create more than one threshold to give progressive warnings on the available free space. The log is especially important as the last chance threshold suspends all tasks except for the dump tran.

However, in a normally active system, the amount of free space will fluctuate as space is allocated and deallocated. If this happens around the threshold value, the threshold procedure will fire frequently and become an unnecessary overhead. To prevent this, SQL Server use a **hysteresis** value to control the execution of the threshold procedure. After a threshold procedure is executed, the amount of space used in the database must increase by at least the hysteresis value before the threshold procedure is executed again.

The hysteresis value determines the midpoint between two thresholds. Therefore, two thresholds must be at least two times the hysteresis value apart, as shown in Figure 4.5.

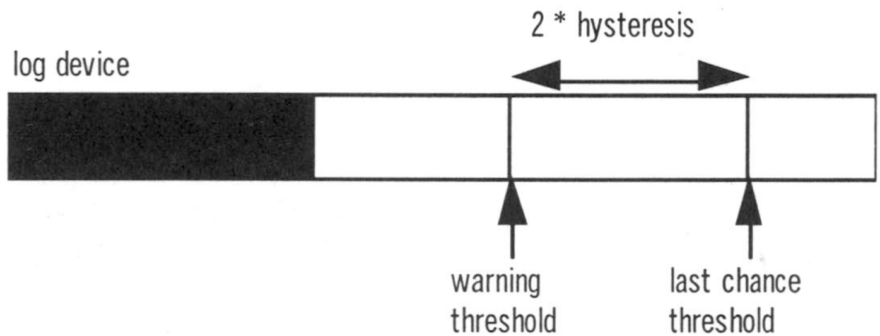

***Figure 4.5** Multiple thresholds on the log device.*

The hysteresis value is controlled by the server and is stored in the global variable **@@thresh_hysteresis**.

```
SELECT @@thresh_hysteresis

    ----
     64
```

With the above hysteresis value, a segment with a threshold of 64 pages must place the next threshold at 64 + 2 * 64 = 192 pages.

A threshold procedure is executed the first time the threshold is crossed, i.e. when free space has fallen below the threshold value. (Thresholds are not executed when the threshold is crossed in the other direction; that is, when free space is increasing.) However, this check is too simple as it would cause the threshold to execute if free space increased past the threshold and then decreased across it again. Therefore, the system checks that it is the first time the threshold has been crossed since the amount of free space came within the hysteresis value of the threshold. This is illustrated in Figure 4.6.

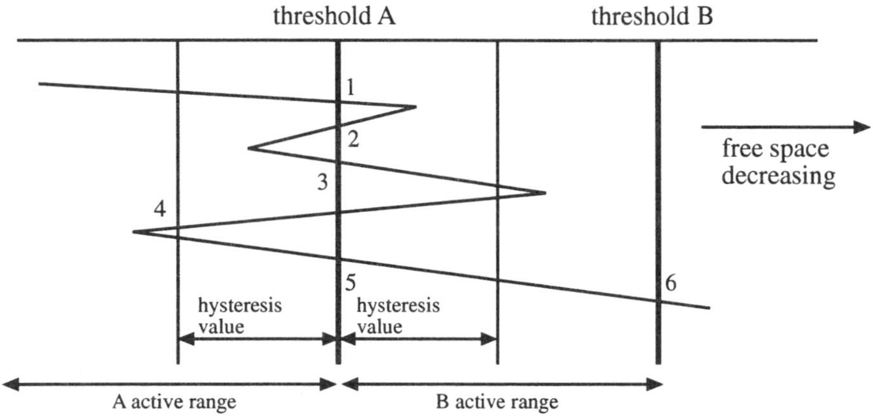

***Figure 4.6** Hysteresis control.*

1. This is the first time that the threshold has been crossed, so A fires. After it fires, it is deactivated so that is does not fire again and B is activated.
2. As we cross A with free space increasing, no threshold fires. But we have now gone out of the range of B and B is deactivated.
3. We now recross A but the free space is not increased beyond the hysteresis value so A is not reactivated and does not fire. However, we are now back into the range of B, which is activated.
4. We now cross the point where the free space has increased beyond the hysteresis value about A, so A is activated.

5. This is the first time across the A threshold since the free space came within the hysteresis value of the threshold, so A fires. A is deactivated and B is activated.

6. This is the first time across the B threshold since the free space came within the value of the threshold so B fires. B is deactivated.

4.7 System Tables

4.7.1 systhresholds

There is one row for each threshold on a segment.

```
select * from systhresholds
```

segment	free_space	status	proc_name	suid	currauth
logsegment	40	1	sp_thresholdaction	1	0x27

This is displayed using the system procedure **sp_helpthreshold**.

sp_helpthreshold

```
sp_helpthreshold [seg_name]
```

```
sp_helpthreshold
```

segment_name	free_pages	last_chance?	threshold_procedure
2	40	1	sp_thresholdaction
1	200	0	jkl_proc

where 1 indicates the last chance threshold.

4.8 Threshold Placement on the Log Segment

Because the last chance threshold on the log segment suspends transactions, it can be a considerable overhead on the system. It is useful to have an earlier threshold which dumps the log but, as it is not a last chance threshold, does not suspend transactions and has minimum overhead on the system. Careful placement of this is important, as you are doing it for performance reasons and do not want to issue a dump tran too often.

The ideal situation is to have the early warning threshold so that transactions that are still writing to the log do not cause the last chance threshold to fire while you are dumping the log, but also do not leave too much unused space in the log before the last chance threshold. In other words, while the dump tran is occurring, the log should fill up as close to the last chance threshold as possible without causing it to fire. This is illustrated in Figure 4.7.

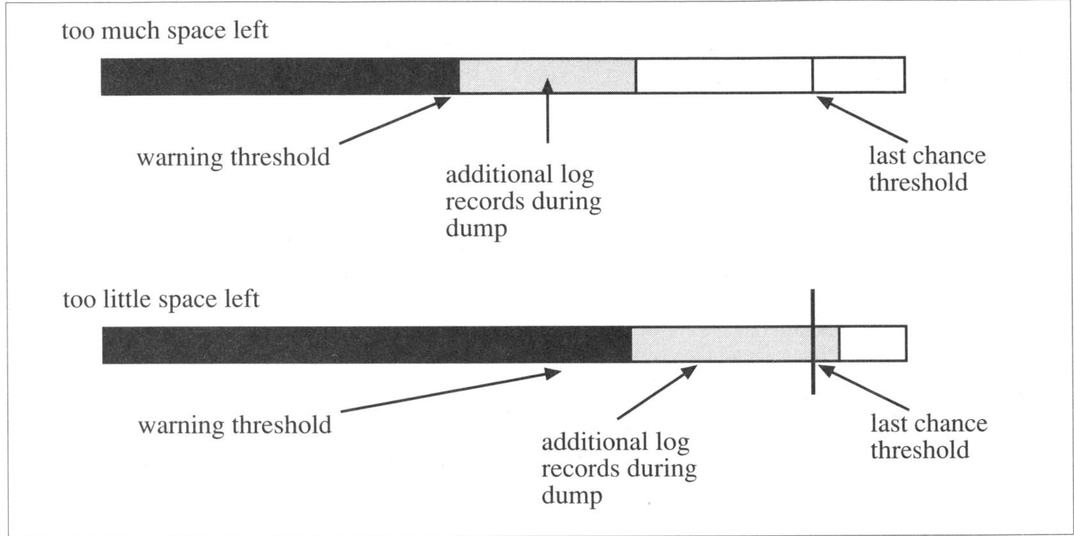

Figure 4.7 *Placement of warning threshold on log segment.*

In the first diagram, the dump tran has been fired too early, as there is considerable unused space after the dump tran has finished. This means that the early warning threshold is placed too soon and the dump tran will fire more often then necessary.

In the second diagram, the placement is wrong as the log has filled to the last chance threshold before the early warning threshold dump tran has completed.

Placement of the early warning threshold is easily checked by monitoring the log usage during the dump tran fired by the early warning threshold and seeing how close it comes to the last chance threshold. Log usage monitoring is best done in this case using **sp_helpsegment** to show the space available in the log segment.

sp_helpsegment

```
sp_helpsegment logsegment
```

```
segment name            status
2           logsegment      0

device      size        free_pages
jklogdev    2.0MB       224

table_name  index_name  indid
syslogs syslogs 0
```

The number of pages is given by:

```
SELECT sum(size) FROM sysusages
       WHERE dbid = db_id("prod_db")
       AND (segmap & 4) = 4
```

4.9 Summary

System 10 has the excellent feature of thresholds on segments to provide warnings when free space falls to a specified level. It is interesting that the threshold is defined on a segment which is a logical object with no independent physical allocation of space. This means that,if you place a threshold on every segment of a device, you can get several warnings when free space falls below the threshold. The reverse also holds true; if you miss one the device can still fill up. Clearly, controlled use of thresholds on the production databases will give you ample warning of space problems before the devices fill up. The important use of thresholds is for the automatic last chance threshold on the log segment. Suitable action to this proactive warning of little free space on the log can eliminate the log full problem on production databases.

5

Auditing

This chapter describes the System 10 auditing feature. A description of the components and the installation is followed by a detailed discussion of the setting and use of the various audit options.

System 11 has made no addition to the System 10 features.

COMMAND SYNTAX

None

SYSTEM PROCEDURE SYNTAX

```
sp_auditinstall
sp_auditoption
sp_auditdatabase
sp_auditobject
sp_auditsproc
sp_auditlogin
sp_addauditrecord
```

5.1 Introduction

System 10 provides an audit trail feature to write events to an audit table. This table is called sysaudits and is in a separate database called sybsecurity. You may specify the events for which auditing takes place. A record is written to sysaudits each time a specified event occurs.

The audit system consists of three principal components:

1. The sybsecurity database which contains the audit tables;
2. the system procedures which set up the auditing options;
3. the audit queue, which is used to hold the audit records before they are written to the audit table.

5.1.1 Sybsecurity Database

The audit database sybsecurity consists of the normal system tables plus the two audit-specific tables:

sysaudits	the audit records;
sysauditoptions	one row for each global audit option.

In practice, sybsecurity is no different from any other database and will contain all of the tables which are defined in model at the time of the installation of auditing, in addition to the above two audit-specific user tables. Note that these two are user tables in sybsecurity and not system tables, although they start with "sys."

5.1.2 System Procedures

There are six new system procedures available to define and use the auditing facility:

sp_auditoption	sets server mode audit option;
sp_auditdatabase	sets database level audit requirements;
sp_auditobject	sets table and view level audit requirements;
sp_auditsproc	sets procedure and trigger level audit requirements;
sp_auditlogin	sets specific user login audit requirements;
sp_addauditrecord	writes ad hoc audit records to sysaudits.

These are described in detail in section 5.4.

The events you may audit are at four levels.

1. server level — auditing of server events such as login, logout, remote connections and commands that require specific authorization;
2. database level — auditing of database events such as the use command and the use of grant, revoke, truncate and drop;
3. user level — auditing of the text of commands submitted by a specific user and of attempts to access tables and views;
4. object level — auditing of access to specific tables, views, procedures and triggers.

5.1.3 Audit Queue

The audit queue is a shared memory stack that stores the audit record until it is processed by the audit process and written to the audit trail in sybsecurity. This separates the writing of the audit records from the application tasks to impose a minimum overhead on the applications.

The sequence of events for auditing user events is shown in Figure 5.1.

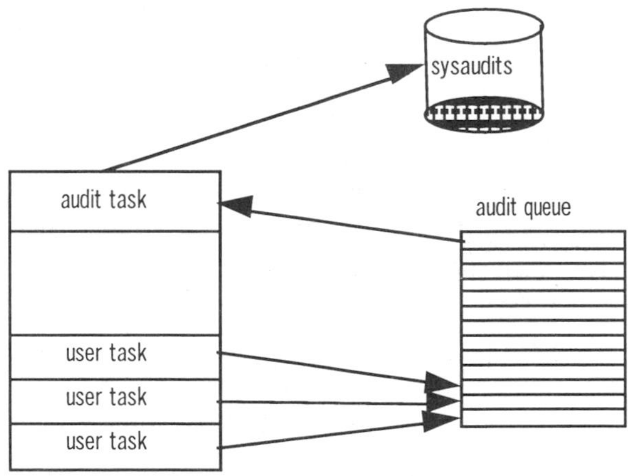

Figure 5.1 *Audit sequence.*

User tasks write to the audit queue in shared memory. The server audit process removes the audit records from this queue and writes them to sysaudits.

5.2 Installation

5.2.1 Automatic Installation

Auditing is installed using sybinit. The installation creates the sybsecurity database, the two auditing system tables and the auditing stored procedures. Sybsecurity is installed on its own device and sysaudits on its own segment. This allows the space to be monitored by the threshold manager. As sysaudits may be used heavily, you should place sybsecurity on a disk, which avoids other heavily-used data such as master, tempdb and syslogs.

Calculating the size of the audit device is similar to the transaction log; that is, it depends on activity, what you are auditing and how often you clear it out. Default size after initialization is 5 MB. Sybsecurity is installed with the option trunc log on chkpt to keep it as small as possible. This option means that the transaction log is cleared of all completed transactions at each checkpoint. (The use of the transaction log and a checkpoint in SQL Server is explained in Chapter 9.) This keeps the transaction log as small as possible by continually clearing it out. It also means that the log records written to the transaction log are not being dumped. Therefore, transaction log-based recovery is not set for the audit trail and you could lose all records since the last sybsecurity database dump. Clearly, this default option is used to keep the audit transaction log as empty as possible to avoid log full or threshold events.

It is up to you but, if you feel that you cannot afford to lose this amount of audit data, keep in mind that the audit records are never fully recoverable. There may be several audit records in the audit queue when a failure occurs and these will be lost, as they have not been written to a table at this point.

When the server is booted, the audit process starts automatically if the sybsecurity database exists. An audit queue exists in shared memory to buffer audit records generated by user audit activity. The size of the audit queue may be configured using sp_configure, with a default of 100.

```
sp_configure "audit queue size" [, number_of_records]
```

```
sp_configure "audit queue size", 200
go
```

This does not take effect until after reboot.

The size of the audit queue is important to the overall system performance. When the audit queue is full, any application task which tries to write to the audit queue is forced to "sleep" until space becomes available in the queue. This is an obvious overhead to the application and, therefore, a properly-sized audit queue is important.

If the queue is too small, it will fill up frequently and application processes will sleep until space is available. If the queue is too large, it will take longer for an individual audit record to be written to sysaudits, with a corresponding higher number of audit records that may be lost if the system crashes. The maximum number of audit records that can be lost in a system crash is the size of the audit queue plus 20 records. Writes to sysaudits are not forced and are buffered after leaving the audit queue before being written to sysaudits on disk. Flushing to disk depends on system activity, but is no worse than every 20 records.

The actual sysaudits records have a maximum size of 424 bytes but may be as small as 22 bytes. It depends on what you are auditing. It is worth checking in sysaudits after you have been running auditing for a while.

Administering the audit system requires a user with sso_role. This system security officer role can execute all of the audit procedures and access the audit trail. Make sure that you grant the appropriate user access to sybsecurity. The security roles sa_role, sso_role, oper_role are explained in Chapter 6.

5.2.2 Sysaudits Restoration

If recovery is not an issue with you, but you do lose the sysaudits table, it may be recreated using the undocumented system procedure sp_auditinstall, which simply creates an empty sysaudits table.

sp_auditinstall

```
sp_auditinstall        @segname = segment_name,
                       @devname = device_name
```

You need to be in the audit database sybsecurity and you must supply both the segment and device names.

Remember that the use of a segment does not guarantee space and sysaudits gets no special treatment. If some other table uses the segment or device, it can use up the space you think that you have for sysaudits. So keep it on its own device and segment. Treat it like the transaction log and you will avoid any complications. The definition and use of segments is explained in Chapter 4.

5.3 Removing Auditing

To completely remove auditing from the server you need to disable it first before dropping the audit database.

sp_auditoption

```
sp_auditoption "enable auditing", "off"
go
drop database sybsecurity
go
```

You cannot drop sybsecurity with auditing enabled.

5.4 Auditing Levels

Having installed auditing, you (or a user with sso_role) need to establish which events you need audited and then execute the appropriate procedures. No auditing actually takes place until you have enabled auditing using sp_auditoption. This means that you can create all of the necessary audit events and then turn auditing on. Conversely, turning auditing off does not remove any of the specified audit events; it simply stops them being written to the audit queue and the audit trail.

Event auditing occurs at the levels:

- server
- database
- table and view
- procedure and trigger
- user login

with the current settings being held in **sysauditoptions**.

5.4.1 Server Level

This level allows the auditing of events which are not tied to a specific database, object or user, such as:

- login and logout;
- incoming remote procedure connection;
- server reboot;
- setting of a role during a session;
- executing commands that require a specific role;
- errors;
- writing ad hoc audit records;
- enabling/disabling auditing.

This is set up with sp_auditoption.

```
sp_auditoption [option [, action]]
```

where option/action

enable auditing	sets server-wide auditing on/off. Server-wide auditing must be on before any other auditing takes place; `sp_auditoption "enable auditing", {"on|off"}`
all	sets all options on/off (except "enable auditing"). Using "all" is equivalent to using "on" or "both" for a specific option; `sp_auditoption "all", {"on|off"}`
logins	enables auditing of login attempts: successful, failed or all attempts; `sp_auditoption "logins", {"ok|fail|both|off"}`
logouts	enables auditing of logout attempts, including unintentional logouts such as dropped connections; `sp_auditoption "logouts", {"on|off"}`
server boots	enables auditing of server boots; `sp_auditoption "server boots", {"on|off"}`

rpc connections — enables auditing of remote connections to run a procedure via a remote procedure call: successful, failed or all connection attempts;

```
sp_auditoption "rpc connections", {"ok|fail|both|off"}
```

roles — enables auditing of the set role command: successful, failed or all attempts;

```
sp_auditoption "roles", {"ok|fail|both|off"}
```

sa|sso|oper|navigator|replication commands — enables auditing of the use of privileged commands which require sa_role, sso_role, oper_role privilege to execute: successful, failed (because the user lacks the proper role) or all attempts;

```
sp_auditoption "{sa|sso|oper|navigator|replication}command",
               {"ok|fail|both|off"}
```

errors — enables auditing of errors: fatal, nonfatal or both;

```
sp_auditoption "errors", {"nonfatal|fatal|both|off"}
```

adhoc records — allows ad hoc user records to be written to the audit trail using sp_addauditrecord.

```
sp_auditoption "adhoc records", {"on|off"}
```

The initial, default action for all options is "off." With no parameters, sp_auditoption displays the current audit settings.

```
sp_auditoption

name                  sval
enable auditing       off
logins                off
logouts               off
server boots          off
rpc connections       off
roles                 off
sa commands           off
sso commands          off
oper commands         off
navigator commands    off
errors                off
ad hoc commands       off
replication command   off
```

5.4.2 Database Level

This level allows the auditing of security-related events at the database level, including:

- use command;
- "outside access" i.e. access to an object in the audited database from another database;
- grant command;
- revoke command;
- drop command;
- truncate command.

sp_auditdatabase

```
sp_auditdatabase [db_name [, action [, {"d u g r t o"}]]]
```

where

action	"ok|fail|both|off" Failure occurs because the user lacks the permission to access the database;
dugrto	the types of database events that can be audited. If omitted, all event types are audited; d drop commands: database, table, view, procedure, trigger u use command g grant command r revoke command t truncate table command o outside access, i.e. execution of commands from another database that reference objects in this database.

```
sp_auditdatabase prod_db, "ok", "d"
sp_auditdatabase prod_db, "fail", "gr"
sp_auditdatabase prod_db, "both", "o"
```

The settings are displayed as:

```
sp_auditdatabase

"prod_db" has the following audit options available

name
-----------
successful drop
failed grant
failed revoke
successful outside access
failed outside access
```

Individual database settings are displayed as:

```
sp_auditdatabase  db_name
```

5.4.3 Table and View Level

This level allows the auditing of the regular data manipulation language (DML) commands.

- delete
- update
- insert
- select.

This auditing takes place only when a permission check is carried out on the user of the command. The permission check to see if a user is allowed to carry out the issued command is not fired at every execution of the command, but depends on how the command is executed. If the command is a raw T-SQL command, then the permissions are always checked and the commands are always audited. However, if the command is in a stored procedure or view, then the permissions are checked and auditing occurs only if the ownership changes. If the owner (creator) of a procedure and/or view also owns the objects referenced within the procedure/view, then the only permission checked is the execute/select permission on the procedure/view. Therefore, the DML commands on tables and views will not be audited. If an object within a procedure/view is owned by a user other than the owner of the procedure/view, the permission of the user executing the procedure/view will be rechecked when the object is accessed and auditing will occur.

sp_auditobject

```
sp_auditobject object_name, db_name [, action [,"d u s i"]]
```

where

db_name	must be the current database when specifying object_name auditing;
action	"ok|fail|both|off" Failure is caused by lack of privilege;
dusi	the kind of access to audit. If omitted, all access is audited; d delete i insert s select u update

```
sp_auditobject salary_tab, prod_db, "both", "disu"

sp_auditobject totals_tab, prod_db, "fail", "diu"
```

Newly created tables/views are not audited automatically and the options "default table/default view" have to be set to define the auditing requirements for new tables/views. In this case, the database does not need to be the current database.

```
sp_auditobject {"default table"|"default view"},
db_name [, action [, "dusi]]
```

```
sp_auditobject "default table", prod_db, "both", "du"
```

Note that this is the auditing of object access in a specific database. Auditing of object access by specific users on a server-wide basis is done using sp_auditlogin, which is explained later in this section.

The object level settings are displayed as:

```
sp_auditobject

dbo.salary_tab" has the following audit options set
```

```
name

successful deletes
failed deletes
successful updates
failed updates
successful selects
failed selects
successful inserts
failed inserts

dbo.totals_tab" has the following audit options set

name

failed deletes
failed updates
failed inserts
```

Individual object settings are displayed as:

```
sp_auditobject tab_name
```

The "default" settings are not displayed unless explicitly requested.

```
sp_auditobject  "default table"

name

successful deletes
failed deletes
successful updates
failed updates
```

5.4.4 Procedure and Trigger Level

This level allows the auditing of stored procedure and trigger execution.

Again, auditing occurs only when user permission is checked and not all procedure accesses cause permissions to be checked. If a procedure is called within a procedure and the owner of both is the same, the embedded call does not cause any permission checks and the embedded procedure execution will not be audited.

Although the execution of a trigger never causes permissions to be checked (the objects in the trigger may cause permission checks but not the execution of the trigger), trigger access is always audited if this level is enabled.

(This type of permission checked access is sometimes called "mediated" access in the SQL Server literature. See, you learn something every day when you least expect it.)

sp_auditsproc

```
sp_auditsproc [obj_name|"all", db_name [, action]]
```

where

obj_name	the name of the procedure or trigger;
db_name	must be the current database if specifying the "proc_name" or "all" option;
action	"ok|fail|both|off" Failure is caused by lack of permission to execute the procedure;

```
sp_auditsproc "all", prod_db, "fail"
sp_auditsproc "salary_trig", prod_db, "both"
```

Newly-created stored procedures or triggers are not audited automatically and the "default" option has to be defined for all new procedures and triggers. As before, the default option may be set for any database in the server.

```
sp_auditproc "default", db_name [, action]
```

```
sp_auditsproc "default", prod_db, "fail"
```

The procedure/trigger auditing settings may be displayed using sp_auditsproc.

```
sp_auditsproc

"salary_trig" has the following audit options enabled

name

successful sproc/trigger
failed sproc/trigger
```

Individual procedure/trigger settings are displayed as:

```
sp_auditsproc proc_name
```

The "default" settings are not displayed unless explicitly requested.

```
sp_auditsproc "default"
```

5.4.5 User Login Level

This level audits the table and view access of a specific login name with the option of recording the text of all commands sent to the server by the login name. The latter option obviously may use a lot of disk space but can be very useful when trying to debug what a user is doing. Be careful here as it does not record all text/actions that the user carries out, only those sent to the server (which is usually enough). Again, auditing takes place at a permission check, so not all access is audited, as described before.

sp_auditlogin

```
sp_auditlogin  [login_name [, "table"|"view"|"cmdtext"
               [, "ok|fail|both|on|off"]]]
```

where

table|view	audits attempts to access tables or views. Associated options are: ok audits successful access; fail audits permission failures; both audits both successful access and failures; off disables table/view auditing.
cmdtext	audits the text of command batches submitted to the server. Associated options are: on enables cmdtext auditing. off disables cmdtext auditing.

```
sp_auditlogin john, "table", "fail"
sp_auditlogin jill, "cmdtext", "on"
```

Watch this one; the error messages are in a world of their own. I input a login name that was not on syslogins and got the error message:

```
"Invalid second argument. Valid choices are 'ok', 'fail', 'both' or 'both'"
```

User login audit settings may be displayed as:

```
sp_auditlogin

"john" has the following audit options set.

name

failed table ref

"jill" has the following audit options set

name

command batch text
```

Individual user login settings are displayed as:

```
sp_auditlogin login_name
```

The setting of a specific option is displayed as:

```
sp_auditlogin login_name, option
```

5.4.6 User-defined Audit Records

sp_addauditrecord

```
sp_addauditrecord      [text]
                       [, db_name] [, obj_name]
                       [, owner_name] [, dbid]
                       [, objid]
```

where

text	message text inserted to sysaudits.extrainfo;
db_name	database name inserted into sysaudits.dbname;
obj_name	object name inserted into sysaudits.objname;
owner_name	owner of the object inserted into sysaudits.objowner;
dbid	database ID inserted into sysaudits.dbid;
objid	object ID inserted into sysaudits.objid.

For example:

```
sp_addauditrecord
        @text="allowed access to fred in salary_tab",
        @db_name="personnel", @obj_name="salary_tab"
```

System 10 specifies the use of the parameter names but System 11 specifies the positional parameter format, which is why I have shown both. Note that sp_addauditrecord does not check any of the information you enter, so make sure that you get the names and ids correct.

5.5 System Tables

The general information recorded in each audit record is:

- type of event;
- date and time of event;
- login ID and name of user who caused the event;
- IDs and names of objects invoked in the event;
- success or failure, i.e. permission check result;
- additional information, depending on event.

The full layouts of the auditing tables are:

sysaudits

```
select * from sysaudits

event          eventmod       spid   eventtime       sequence      suid    dbid
objid          xactid         loginname       dbname          objname
objowner       extrainfo
8              1              1      Sep 8 1994 2:05PM       1       1       6
null           null           sa              ftest_db        null
null           USE
8              1              1      Sep 8 1994 2:02PM       1       1       6
2124534602     null           sa              ftest_db        tab_1
dbo            TRUNCATE TABLE
```

Clearly your own routine will give more readable information.

```
SELECT spid, eventtime, suid, dbname, objname, extrainfo
       FROM sysaudits
```

sysauditoptions

```
select * from sysauditoptions
```

```
num     val            minval  maxval  name
sval    comments
1       0              0       1               enable auditing
off     Indicates whether or not system wide auditing is enabled
7       0              0       3               roles
off     Role change auditing
```

sp_auditoption (as shown in section 5.4.1) is good enough here.

5.6 Archiving Audit Data

Clearly, auditing can use a lot of space, depending on the level of auditing that you have set. Regardless of the growth rate, it is not a good idea to let sysaudits grow continuously until it fills up the device you have placed it on. When this happens, the audit process fails and each user process that tries to write an audit record fails. In addition, if you have global login accounting enabled (sp_auditoption "logins," "on") the SSO would not be able to login. If you have sso_role auditing on (sp_auditoption "sso_role," "on") the sso_role would not be able to execute any commands, such as turning auditing off. To get you out of this potential disaster, the sso_role is temporarily taken out of the audit system when the audit device is full. Any audit record generated by the sso_role is written to the error log to enable the SSO to archive and truncate sysaudits. In addition, the sso_role is able to issue a shutdown to stop the server.

So keep a close watch on sysaudits size. The simplest way is with a threshold. As sysaudits is installed in its own segment, you can set a threshold on this segment to monitor sysaudits, which is the only table on this segment. The least you should do in the threshold procedure is to copy the sysaudits data to an archive table (in a separate archive database) and truncate sysaudits.

```
INSERT INTO archive_db.dbo.audit_archive_tab
       SELECT * FROM sysaudits
TRUNCATE TABLE sysaudits
```

You could use:

```
SELECT * INTO archive_db.dbo.audit_archive_tab
       FROM sysaudits
```

to copy the data, but this requires select into/bulk copy to be set on in the archive database. As select into does not log the record inserts to the transaction log, it renders the transaction log useless for a database recovery. Therefore, you need to take an immediate dump database to ensure that the archive database can be recovered from the transaction log. The choice is yours. Select into is faster and dumping the archive database is not really a problem.

5.7 Summary

System 10 has introduced a new database sybsecurity with a new table sysaudits which allows the auditing of defined events. This auditing is at four levels: server, database, user and object, to provide a comprehensive audit capability. Be careful of the performance overhead when auditing is installed and make sure that the sybsecurity database is on its own device away from the other active data. In addition, do not let the sysaudits table fill the device as this will cause all audited commands to fail.

6

Security

This chapter describes the System 10 security system, covering setting of the appropriate names, ids and passwords to enable login to the server and use of databases once login is achieved. The new administration roles and the granting and revoking of command and access privileges to the users in the databases are then addressed. The chapter concludes with a description of configuring remote access between servers.

System 11 has made no additions to the System 10 features. But watch the new sp_configure option names (system-wide password expiration and allow remote access) which are detailed in Chapter 12.

COMMAND SYNTAX

```
grant
revoke
setuser
```

SYSTEM PROCEDURE SYNTAX

```
sp_changedbowner
sp_addlogin
sp_password
sp_locklogin
sp_modifylogin
sp_droplogin
sp_role
sp_displaylogin
sp_adduser
```

```
sp_addalias
sp_dropuser
sp_dropalias
sp_addgroup
sp_changegroup
sp_dropgroup
sp_helpuser
sp_helpgroup
sp_helprotect
sp_addserver
sp_addremotelogin
sp_remoteoption
sp_serveroption
sp_helpserver
sp_helpremotelogin
sp_clearstats
sp_reportstats
```

6.1 Introduction

We need to create logins (accounts) for people to get to the server and then create user names in each database for them to use the databases. You can make this as simple or as complicated as you wish but you need to define two stages: a login to the server and a user name in each database that the login requires access to. Once allowed access to the server, a separate user name must be defined in each database that you wish the login to have access to. The simple approach is to retain the same name but there are various grouping and aliasing facilities to make life a little easier for the system administrator when defining users in databases.

Each person who needs access to the server has to be defined as a login in master and then as a user in each database to which access is allowed, as shown in Figure 6.1.

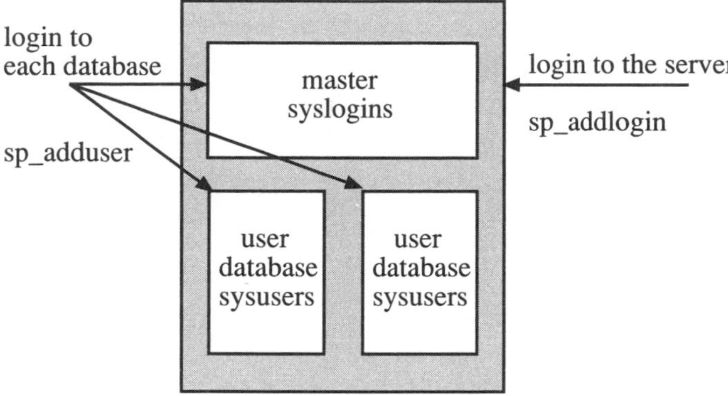

Figure 6.1 *Server and database access.*

The login to the server is defined in master and creates entries in **syslogins**. Each login is identified with a unique server-wide identifier, called server_id or SUID.

To use a database (including master), each user is defined in the database, which creates an entry in **sysusers** in the respective database. Each user is identified in each database with a database unique identifier, called user_id or UID.

The characteristics of login are:

- permission to attach to the server;
- entry in syslogins;
- no default access to any user database;
- identified by SUID;
- also called "account" in SQL Server literature.

The characteristics of user are:

- permission to use a database;
- entry in sysusers;
- access to single database only;
- identified by UID;
- two special cases: groups and aliases.

6.2 Classes of User

There are three classes of user in SQL Server: system administrator, database owner, and user. The system administrator (SA) has absolute rights everywhere. (S)he can go everywhere and do anything. The database owner (DBO) is as powerful as the SA but only in the database which (s)he owns. The regular user is controlled completely by the SA or the DBO and can do only what (s)he is allowed to do by the more-privileged SA and DBO. In System 10, the SA capabilities have been subdivided into roles to allow users other than the superuser "SA" to function as SA/DBO. This improves the accountability of the administrator, as we are now able to identify individual SUIDs against the SA function.

Database ownership is automatically given to the person who creates the database. I recommend that this is the SA. If you adhere to that, you may want to pass ownership of some of the databases to other users. This is done with the system procedure **sp_changedbowner**.

sp_changedbowner

```
sp_changedbowner login_name [,true]
```

```
use fred
go
sp_changedbowner prog_1
go
```

The option "true" causes all aliases and permissions to be transferred to the new database owner.

I believe that the SA has more control by doing all database creation and conferring database ownership to a few users. I prefer to retain ownership by the SA and, if necessary, alias specific users as DBO (see 6.5.1). This gives fewer problems during recovery as SA/DBO is always SUID of 1.

System 10 has introduced roles to the security system to allow many administrative users to be assigned to a role that has specific commands it may execute. From the security point of view, the roles function as groups. What they really achieve is the removal of the superuser SA and introduce individual accountability by SUID against users who have system administration capabilities.

There are three roles.

1.sa_role The role equivalent to the SA login with the exception of security functions. The sa_role responsibilities include:

- install the server;
- allocate and manage disk space (devices, segments, databases);
- modify, drop and lock login accounts;
- create users, groups and grant/revoke permissions.

The sa_role user behaves as the old SA login by becoming the DBO when in a database and assumes user_id 1.

2. sso_role The SQL Server security role to perform tasks related to login, password and auditing. The sso_role responsibilities include:

- create login accounts;
- change login passwords and expiration intervals;
- manage the audit system.

The sso_role does not have any special permissions on objects and commands, only on system procedures.

3. oper_role An operations role to perform dumps and loads in every database. The oper_role responsibilities include: dump and load databases and transaction logs.

In addition to these explicit roles—which effectively split the old SA login into three roles—the implicit database owner (DBO) and object owner roles still apply.

The DBO responsibilities include:

- create users in the database;
- grant/revoke permissions in the database.

The object owner responsibilities include:

- create objects in a database;
- grant/revoke permissions on these objects.

6.3 Logins

Prior to System 10, the server had a rather loose login and password mechanism which has now been addressed by SQL Server. All that was required to access the server was a login name and a password. This suffered from several deficiencies that are addressed in System 10.

Minimum Length Password

This problem was not all that serious as any characters may be used in the password. There is now a minimum password length of six characters.

Password Expiration

A number of days for expiration can now be set on a server-wide basis. This is more important from a security aspect but forced change of password is really going to hurt those of us who have hard-coded (or no) passwords in command files. (Avoidance is at the server level—see section 6.3.2. I know that passwords in command files are very bad practice, but I bet there are always a few lying around.) You need to turn this on as it is disabled by default.

Password Encryption

Passwords are now encrypted in syslogins. One wonders why they never were in the first place. Encryption may also be requested by the client.

Reuse of Server IDs

Login names may now be locked to prevent reuse of server IDs. Again, this never seemed like a good idea the first time round.

6.3.1 Creating Logins

Logins are created in master using the system procedure **sp_addlogin**.

sp_addlogin

```
sp_addlogin login_name, password [, default_db
                                  [, deflanguage [, fullname]]]
```

If you do not specify the default database, the default is master, which is not a good idea since you do not want users to have access to master. If you do not specify the default language to be used when the user logs in, the default used is the default for the server as defined at installation.

You must be in the master database and have sso_role to add logins.

```
isql -Usa -Pwhatever

use master
go
sp_addlogin fred, spiderman
go
```

System 10 has introduced a minimum password length of 6 bytes. This applies to sp_addlogin and sp_password. You will not be forced to change existing passwords which are fewer than 6 bytes. But the password expiration will get you. In **sp_addlogin**, the password is now a mandatory field of at least six digits.

6.3.2 Password Expiration

System 10 has introduced a server-wide password expiration level, which may be set as a number of days using **sp_configure**.

```
sp_configure   'password expiration interval', [, no_of_days]
```

This option does not need a server reboot but takes effect after the reconfigure command.

```
sp_configure 'password expiration interval', 30
go
reconfigure
go
```

The number of days is counted from the last time the password was changed (or since the login was created if the password has not been changed). The default number of days is zero which means that password expiration is disabled as in versions 4.x.

When a user's password expires, (s)he is allowed to login but gets a message to change the password. The only command that may be run is sp_password. As with most expiration systems, a warning is issued upon login that the password is about to expire in a number of days. This warning is issued seven days before expiration or when 25% of the interval is left, whichever is the greater.

To change their own password, users employ the system procedure **sp_password**.

sp_password

```
sp_password old_pw, new_pw  [, login_name]
sp_password spiderman, punisher
```

Only a user with sso_role can use the login_name to change another user's password. If you have to change another user's password you must input your password for the old password.

If all of the SSOs forget their passwords (it does happen if there is only one) there is a new parameter (-p) in dataserver that generates a random password for the specified login_name. This allows one login. Once one SSO has logged in, (s)he can alter all of the other passwords using sp_password.

```
dataserver... -plogin_name
```

After the usual boot messages, the message:

```
new SSO password for login_name:  xxxxxx
```

appears to allow the SSO to login, change their own password and those of any other SSOs.

6.3.3 Password Encryption

The passwords stored in syslogins are now encrypted and always displayed in encrypted form even with **select * from syslogins** run by the SA. The algorithm is based on a combination of Data Encryption Standard and Fast Encryption Algorithm.

As advantageous as this is from a security aspect, it presents problems when someone forgets their password. This is why the operation of sp_password was changed to allow the SSO to change another user's password without knowing the old one.

Password encryption may also be requested by the client at login to allow passwords to be sent over the network in encrypted form when making remote procedure calls. The initial login is made without a password and the server returns an 8-byte encryption key that the client uses to encrypt the password. The server knows the key and can decipher the password when the user logs in. The db-library call to use password encryption is:

```
dbsetlencrypt( loginrec, enable)
```

where

enable	true or false.

The client password encryption may be installed between remote servers using sp_serveroption.

sp_serveroption

```
sp_serveroption server_name, 'net password encryption', {true|false}
```

Network password encryption may be set in isql and bcp using the -X (/encrypt) option.

6.3.4 Login Locking

SUID/UIDs are unique throughout the server and each database, respectively, and are allocated sequentially in syslogins and sysusers. If a login/user is dropped, the SUID/UID is not reused unless it is the last used number. Therefore, there is no guarantee that the same login/user on different servers/databases will have the same SUID/UID. This is important in privilege checking, which is done by ID and not name. Checking is done on UID in each database with the SUID being mapped in each database to the UID. Do not assume that servers with identical login_names and user_names will be the same internal ID numbers. The only exception to this is the SA, who is always SUID number 1.

Login names may now be locked to prevent future use and thus disable reuse of server IDs. More importantly, it means that a login name may be disabled for a period of time and then retains its original SUID when reenabled. Previously dropping and readding the login could cause the login to have a new SUID, which would effect all the privilege checking for that login. Login locking is done using **sp_locklogin**.

sp_locklogin

```
sp_locklogin [login_name , "{lock|unlock}"]
```

Once a login_name is locked, no access to the server is possible using that login_name. Unlocking a locked login reenables access to the server. (The server user

ID has not changed so nothing is different.) The procedure may be executed when you get a warning message that the login is active, while the user is logged in. Once the user logs out no, further access is allowed to the server. When you try to login to a locked account, you simply get the standard "login incorrect" message. Server user ID is a smallint (32,767) so you have plenty of available numbers if you adopt a policy of locking logins instead of dropping them.

Use of **sp_locklogin** with no arguments displays the current login lock status.

```
sp_locklogin john, "lock"
go

Warning: the specified account is currently active
Account locked

sp_locklogin
go

Locked account(s)

name
----------
john
```

Fortunately, the system will not allow you to lock the last unlocked sa_role or sso_role login.

6.3.5 Modifying Login Accounts

Some of the login information may be changed using **sp_modifylogin**. This changes the default database, default language and/or the full name of the login account. Note that this replaces sp_defaultdb which no longer exists. When a login is initially created, the default database is master, which is not a good idea as access to the master database should be as restricted as possible. A user default database should be specified when the login is created or modified using **sp_modifylogin**.

sp_modifylogin

```
sp_modifylogin login_name, option, value
```

where option

defdb	modifies the default database;
deflanguage	modifies the default language;
fullname	modifies the full name of the login.

```
sp_modifylogin john, defdb, fred
sp_modifylogin john, fullname, 'john kirkwood'
```

There is no check to confirm that the user is allowed to use the database which has been set as their default (which is the same when the login is created). You need this unchecked database access situation because the logical steps are to create the login and default database attachment before you define the user in the database. Why not just drop the login and add it again to redefine the default database? Because the SUID will change and all the privilege checking will be wrong.

6.3.6 Dropping a Login

When a login is no longer required (such as if the person has left the company) it should be dropped using the system procedure **sp_droplogin**.

sp_droplogin

```
sp_droplogin login_name
```

```
use master
go
sp_droplogin user_1
go
```

Dropping a login is no longer allowed if the login name is a user, is aliased in any database, or is defined as the DBO of a database. You must remove all users/aliases and database ownership before you can drop the login.

There are two important points to this.

- Only the SA or the DBO should create objects.

- When a person leaves the company, it may be advisable to lock the login to bar them from any external access to the server. Then, create a new login for any staff replacement and alias the new login to the old user in the database. (This is covered later when we discuss database users.) This prevents unauthorized access but minimizes the changes that have to be made at the privilege level.

As with sp_locklogin, the system gives you a level of protection from stupidity and will not allow you to drop the last unlocked sso_role login.

6.3.7 Displaying Login Information

Information on a login name may be displayed using the system procedure **sp_displaylogin**.

sp_displaylogin

```
sp_displaylogin [login_name]
```

```
sp_displaylogin fred

Suid:  11811
Loginame:  fred
Fullname:
Configured authorized:
Locked:  No
Date of last password change:  Feb 20 1996 11:04 AM
```

The configured authorization is a list of administration roles available to the login name. This is described in more detail in section 6.4.2. Not supplying a login name displays information for the current login; i.e. yourself.

Accounting information of the CPU and I/O usage of logins may be displayed using the system procedure **sp_reportstats**.

sp_reportstats

```
sp_reportstats [login_name]
```

```
sp_reportstats fred
```

```
Name          Since         CPU    Percent CPU    I/O    Percent I/O
Total CPU     Total I/O
fred          Feb20 1996    1      0.0010%        0      0.0000%
91581         2100692
```

You can reset the statistics for the login using the system procedure **sp_clearstats**. This calls sp_reportstats before it initializes the values but does not clear the total figure.

sp_clearstats

```
sp_clearstats [login_name]
```

```
sp_clearstats fred
```

You need to have sa_role to execute these procedures.

6.4 Roles

The administration function has now been split into three distinct roles. This split allows specific functional roles to be taken by different people: sa_role for administration duties, sso_role for security duties and oper_role for operations duties. In addition, the roles allow many users to function as one of the roles but to retain their individual login name and server user ID.

The roles function as groups and may be assigned whatever regular privilege you wish using grant and revoke.

```
grant execute on jkl_proc to sso_role
```

On initial installation, there are no user logins defined on the system. You still need to login initially as SA which has all three SA, SSO, and oper role capabilities. You can continue to use SA if you wish, but the recommendation is to create the administration, security and operation user logins and assign them to the relevant roles. Having done this, you can then lock the SA login so that it cannot be used. As the use of roles gives you full accountability in the audit system, it is strongly advised that you use them. You can, if you want, assign the administration logins to all three roles so that the user logins function as SA.

6.4.1 Assigning Roles

Roles are assigned to a login_name using **sp_role**.

sp_role

```
sp_role        {'grant'|'revoke'}, {'sa_role'|'sso_role'|'oper_role'},
               login_name
```

```
sp_role 'grant', 'sa_role', john
go
sp_role 'grant', 'sso_role', john
go
```

An annoying little "feature" of some of the role commands is that you must use the quotes around "sa_role", "sso_role" and "oper_role". The initial releases of System 10 insisted on quotes all of the time. This is gradually being removed but there are a few occasions still lying around. You may find it easier to use quotes all of the time when using roles to avoid intermittent syntax errors.

Role assignment does not take place until the next login, so if a user is currently logged in when a role is assigned, it does not take effect until (s)he logs out and in again. All roles for a user are automatically activated on login.

During a login session, a user may switch a role on and off using the **set role** command.

```
set role      {'sa_role'|'sso_role'|'oper_role'} {on|off}
```

sp_role is issued in master where the login name is defined but the role for the login is automatically available in all databases in which the login is a valid user. Again, the system prevents you revoking the last sa_role/sso_role from a login account.

6.4.2 System Tables

There are three new system tables: two in master—**syssrvroles** and **sysloginroles**—and one in each database—**sysroles**.

syssrvroles

This allows a row for each system defined role.

```
select * from syssrvroles
```

```
srid    name
0       sa_role
1       sso_role
2       oper_role
3       sybase_ts_role
4       navigator_role
5       replication_role
```

where

navigator_role	used by the Navigator server for internal purposes;
replication_role	used by the Replication server for internal purposes;
sybase_ts_role	the Technical Services role to allow certain nondocumented DBCC commands to be executed. It is not recommended that you grant this to anyone.

sysloginroles

This contains a row for every system defined role possessed by a server user. Note that the old SA user has five roles on installation.

```
select * from sysloginroles

suid  srid  status
1     0     0
1     1     0
1     2     0
1     5     0
1     3     0
3     0     0
```

where

status	not currently used.

This table is updated by sp_role and is simply a mapping of the server user ID to the server role ID in syssrvroles.

sysroles

sysroles is a mapping from the server role ID to the local database role ID.

```
select * from sysroles
```

```
id    lrid     type  status
0     16384    0     0
1     16385    0     0
2     16386    0     0
3     16387    0     0
4     16388    0     0
5     18389    0     0
```

where

id	server role id;
lrid	local database role id;
type/status	not currently used.

The local role ID (lrid) is treated like a group ID and therefore starts at 16,384 and shares this number range with groups.

Role information is displayed using **sp_displaylogin**.

sp_displaylogin

```
sp_displaylogin [login_name]
```

```
sp_displaylogin john
```

```
Suid:  3
Loginame:  john
Fullname: Configured authorized:  sa_role  sso_role
Locked:  No
Date of last password change:  Sep 22 1993 11:29 AM
```

Only the sso_role can display login information about another user.

6.4.3 Built-in Functions

There are two built-in functions associated with roles which return role information:

show_role()	returns a string of all active roles;
proc_role(role_name)	returns 1 if role is active, 0 if not.

```
select show_role()
go
```

```
sa_role  sso_role
```

```
select proc_role('sa_role')

  ------
     1
```

Again, remember the quotes when using roles.

6.5 Users

Login gives the user the right to use the server and to be attached to a database, but gives no rights to do anything in the database. To work in a database, the login_name is mapped to a user_name in the database. The server unique SUID is mapped to a database unique UID. This mapping must be done in every database in which the user wishes to work.

The login to user mapping is done using the system procedure **sp_adduser** and creates an entry in sysusers.

sp_adduser

```
sp_adduser login_name [, user_name [, group_name]]
```

Make sure that you are in the correct database before you add the user.

```
use production
go
sp_adduser fred
go
```

This maps the login fred to the user_name fred in the production database.

```
use test
go
sp_adduser fred, controller
go
```

This maps the login fred to the user_name controller in the test database. This is useful if one person carries out a specific function, since the login may be changed as the person changes, but the user_name may remain the same in the database so all privilege checking is unchanged. This is a one-to-one mapping; if several logins carry out the same function, the alias feature is needed.

A special user_name of "guest" is used as a default to allow anyone to access a database. This is not created automatically in the database but must be added like any other user.

```
sp_adduser "guest"
```

This means that anyone who can login to the server will have access to a database which has a guest user defined. The server first checks to see if there is an entry in sysusers. If there is no entry for the SUID but there is a guest entry, the user will be treated as a guest in the database with all the privileges attached to the guest UID. (This is not recommended in production systems but I find it useful in a training database used to train new staff when I do not know the logins which will require access to the database.) A guest user is always present in master and tempdb to allow access to these databases by all users. This is used in master to allow the initial check against syslogins to determine if the login is valid. The guest user in master and tempdb can no longer be dropped.

Guest users have a UID of 2 and SUID of -1 as there is no one-to-one mapping of SUID to UID for guest users. The DBO or SA is always UID of 1. So create all objects in a database as SA or DBO. Then the UID does not change and the privilege checks are easier. In production databases, create objects as the SA—you want complete control over the production systems anyway. In test and development databases where designers and programmers want freedom over what objects they create and when they are created, alias everyone to the DBO. This is important as all objects are identified by a composite primary key of object_name and UID on sysobjects. So if the programmers are all different UIDs, the procedures, tables, indexes that they create are owned by them and not automatically available to other designers/programmers in the database. If everyone appears to be the DBO there is no problem as everyone has access to everything in the database. On the other hand, if everyone is a different user in development databases, then the objects which they create belong exclusively to them. This means that their program development is totally under their own control. Some installations which I have worked with prefer this situation but it is not my personal favorite.

6.5.1 Aliases

We do not need to call the user in the database the same name as the login to the server. However, the user_name parameter in sp_adduser is a one-to-one mapping of login to user. If we wish several logins to be known as the same user in the database—as above for the DBO—then we need to use aliases. These are defined by the system procedure **sp_addalias**.

sp_addalias

```
sp_addalias login_name, user_name
```

```
sp_addalias user_1, dbo
```

If login_name is already defined as a user in the database, it cannot be aliased to another user_name. Any one login may have only one user_name in the database, so being both a user and aliased to another user is not allowed. You cannot alias anyone to SA.

As mentioned before, this is most useful in a development database when all developers may be aliased to the DBO, which is easiest to maintain and causes the fewest problems.

Why not just give all developers the same login?

It has the same effect but is a little different from a control viewpoint. An alias allows you to login to the server uniquely and gives the SA better control over who has access to the server. The same login has the same SUID, which has the same UID. So, the SA is not only unable to keep people out of the server but cannot tell which individual is causing any trouble. If different logins are aliased to the one user_name in the database, then you are yourself on the server. The SA controls who gets to the server on an individual basis as well as having the SUID available in the database to write to the audit trail if someone misbehaves.

Aliases are recorded in the system table **sysalternates**. Yes, I know that the name is different. In general, the system procedure is singular and it updates the plural table name. So sp_addlogin updates syslogins, except for sp_addalias which updates sysalternates.

6.5.2 Uses of Aliases

Aliases are useful to the administrator in two ways.

The first is that they make life easier in a test/development database by having everyone look like the DBO and therefore ownership of all objects is the same, no matter who creates them.

If the SA is the DBO in test_db and fred is aliased to be the DBO in test_db, the system table entries are:

```
use test_db
go
sp_addalias fred, dbo
go
```

syslogins

name	SUID
sa	1
fred	20

sysusers

name	SUID	UID
dbo	1	1

sysalternates

SUID	ASUID
20	1

Note that the checking sequence to see if a login is a valid user in a database is sysusers for SUID, sysalternates for SUID, sysusers for guest. So use of aliases is a small overhead.

The second use of aliases for the administrator is in moving databases from one server to another. Because we can never guarantee that the same login names have the same SUID on different servers, we cannot move a database to another server and expect people to be able to login and use the databases. Because the SUIDs will have changed, all of the object ownership and privilege checking will be different and many routines will fail to execute. By aliasing everyone to the DBO, all objects are owned by the DBO (who is always UID 1) and therefore there is no change to the ownership when the database is moved. I would not recommend this for production databases as you will not wish regular users to have DBO rights in a production database, but it is extremely useful for non-production databases.

I would like to stress that it is only my personal preference that the easiest object ownership scenario is to have the SA create all of the production databases and objects in them and alias everyone who uses development and test databases to DBO. This does give the SA a lot of work in the production databases but you really do want this level of control anyway, so do it.

6.5.3 Dropping Users

Depending on how they have been set up, user names are dropped using the system procedure **sp_dropuser** or **sp_dropalias**.

sp_dropuser

```
sp_dropuser user_name
```

sp_dropalias

```
sp_dropalias login_name
```

Note the use of the login_name when dropping an alias. An aliased user is not known by a unique user_name as there may be several logins aliased to the one user_name. But the SUID which is mapped to the common UID is unique, so dropping of an alias is by login_name.

You cannot drop a user who owns objects in the database or who has granted permissions to other users in the database.

6.6 Groups

Groups have nothing to do with allowing access to the server or a database but are simply a means to facilitate assigning privileges to users. Each user may have privileges granted and revoked to the user_name or users may be grouped together and the privileges granted and revoked to the group_name. Privilege setting to groups is easier for the administrator and the checking is slightly less of an overhead as the system tables are smaller.

Groups are added to sysusers using the system procedure **sp_addgroup**.

sp_addgroup

```
sp_addgroup group_name
```

The group_name is unique in the database and is added to sysusers with a UID greater than 16,383. There is a default group of "public" which is UID of 0. Groups look like users as far as the system tables and privilege mechanisms are concerned.

Having added a group, users in the database are attached to it either when the user is added with sp_adduser or by moving them out of the default public group into the named group using the system procedure **sp_changegroup**.

sp_changegroup

```
sp_changegroup group_name, user_name
```

```
sp_changegroup programmer, fred
```

or

```
sp_adduser  fred, fred, programmer
```

Notice that there is no default setting of the second parameter of sp_adduser. If you set the group_name when you add the user, you must repeat the user_name in the second parameter of sp_adduser or use null.

A user may be attached to only one named group and the group_name must exist before users are attached to it. In fact, everyone is always in public no matter how you attach them to a group so each user may be in public and one named group.

```
sp_adduser fred, fred, analyst
go
sp_adduser john
go
sp_changegroup programmer, john
go
```

Fred is in the group analyst, john is in the group programmer and both of them are in the group public.

6.6.1 Dropping Groups

A group_name is dropped from the database using the system procedure **sp_dropgroup**.

sp_dropgroup

```
sp_dropgroup  group_name
```

A group may not be dropped if there are users currently attached. To drop a group while the users are still active in the database you need to change the users back to public. (They are already in public; it is only to remove them from the named group, and then drop the empty group.)

```
sp_changegroup "public", fred
go
sp_dropgroup programmer
go
```

Note that public is a reserved word and must be enclosed in quotes.

6.7 System Tables

There are three system tables—**syslogins**, **sysusers**, **sysalternates**—associated with logins and users.

6.7.1 syslogins

syslogins contains one row for each login to the server containing the information.

```
select * from syslogins

suid    status accdate                    totcpu totio   spacel timeli result
dbname  name   language          pwdate                  audflags      fullname
password
1       1      Mar 30 1992 11:00 am  0       0       0      0      0
master  sa     NULL              Sep 22 1993 1:52AM      0             NULL
0x3103 ... etc
2       0      Mar 30 1992 11:00 am  0       0       0      0      0
master  probe  NULL              Sep 22 1993 1:52AM      0             NULL
0x3103 ... etc
3       0      Mar 30 1992 11:00 am  0       0       0      0      0
sales   clerk  NULL              Sep 22 1993 1:52AM      0      NULL
0x3103 ... etc
4       0      Mar 30 1992 11:00 am  0       0       0      0      0
test    prog   NULL              Sep 22 1993 1:52AM      0             NULL
0x3103 ... etc
5       0      Mar 30 1992 11:00 am  0       0       0      0      0
manufac store  NULL              Sep 22 1993 1:52AM      0             NULL
0x3103 ... etc
```

There are no system procedures to display this table and "select *" is available only to the SA as the password field is protected from access by any other user. The password is always displayed in its encrypted form. Spacelimit, timelimit and resultlimit are all columns reserved by SQL Server and I have no information on them, although they are reasonably obvious.

6.7.2 sysusers

sysusers contains one row for each user, group and administration role in the database containing the information.

```
select * from sysusers
```

suid	uid	gid	name	environ
-2	0	0	public	null
-1	2	0	guest	null
1	1	0	dbo	null
2	3	0	probe	null
18	4	16390	fred	null
-16390	16390	16390	programmer	null
-16389	16389	16389	replication_role	null
-16388	16388	16388	navigator_role	null
-16387	16387	16387	sybase_ts_role	null
-16386	16386	16386	oper_role	null
-16385	16385	16385	sso_role	null
-16384	16384	16384	sa_role	null

where

suid	the unique server_id: • SA is always 1; • probe is always 2; • public is always -2; • guest is always -1. Guest and public may have many logins attached to them so a special SUID is allocated. Probe is a system login/user which is used by the two-phase commit process. Do NOT drop it. If using two-phase commit if you are not using two-phase commit, you might as well drop it.

uid	the user_id unique in this database: • SA/DBO is always 1; • guest is always 2; • public is always 0; • groups/roles are always greater than 16,383.
gid	the group_id unique in this database. Groups are treated like users with UID/gid > 16,383 and have a row in sysusers. There is no separate system table for groups.
environ	again reserved by SQL Server and I have no information on this column.

The data in sysusers is displayed with the system procedure **sp_helpuser**.

sp_helpuser

```
sp_helpuser

users_name    Id_in_db    group_name    login_name    default_db
dbo               1       public        sa            master
guest             2       public        null          null
probe             3       public        probe         master
fred              4       programmer    fred          sales_test
```

The group information on sysusers is displayed using the system procedure **sp_helpgroup**.

sp_helpgroup

```
sp_helpgroup

group_name           group_id
programmer           16390
public               0
navigator_role       16388
oper_role            16386
replication_role     16389
sa_role              16384
sso_role             16385
sybase_ts_role       16387
```

Information on the users in a group is displayed with sp_helpgroup and a specific group_name.

```
sp_helpgroup  programmer
```

group_name	group_id	users_in_group	user_id
programmer	16390	fred	11
programmer	16390	john	14

6.7.3 sysalternates

sysalternates contains one row for SUID and one for alternate SUID combination.

```
select * from sysalternates
```

suid	altsuid
1	12
6	8
6	10
6	9

This is really only a link table and is meaningless by itself. **sp_helpuser** on a specific user_name displays the aliased users.

```
sp_helpuser  dbo
```

user_name	ID_in_db	group_name	login_name	default_db
dbo	1	public	sa	master

```
Users aliased to user
login_name
fred
john
jill
```

If the name supplied to sp_helpuser is aliased, the sp_helpuser shows the alias user name information.

```
sp_helpuser fred

The name supplied is aliased to another user.
```

alias_name	id_in_db	group_name	login_name	default_db
dbo	1	public	sa	master

6.7.4 System Table Summary

table	procedures	commands
syslogins	sp_addlogin	none
	sp_droplogin	
	sp_password	
	sp_modifylogin	
	sp_displaylogin	
	sp_reportstats	
	sp_clearstats	
sysusers	sp_helpuser	none
	sp_helpgroup	
	sp_adduser	
	sp_dropuser	
	sp_addgroup	
	sp_dropgroup	
	sp_changegroup	
sysalternates	sp_helpuser	none
	sp_addalias	
	sp_dropalias	

There is a set of built-in functions which displays login, user and database identification:

suser_id(user_name)	returns SUID;
suser_name(SUID)	returns login_name;
user_id(user_name)	returns UID;
user_name(UID)	returns user_name;
user	returns user_name;
db_name(db_id)	returns database_name;
db_id(db_name)	returns database_id.

```
select suser_id("fred")

----
 11

select suser_name()

----
 sa
```

The null argument returns the current login, user or database identification.

6.8 Privileges

Assigning privileges is a simple matter using two commands, **grant** and **revoke**, with privileges being assigned to the execution of commands (create, drop, etc.) and to the access of objects (select, update, etc.). These privileges may be assigned to users, administration roles, groups and public.

In addition, SQL Server has an object hierarchy which limits the amount of privilege checking and can provide significant access limitations; for example, all access via stored procedures with no direct execution of the select command.

The users/groups to which privileges may be assigned also have a hierarchy in which the privileges are checked, as shown in Figure 6.2.

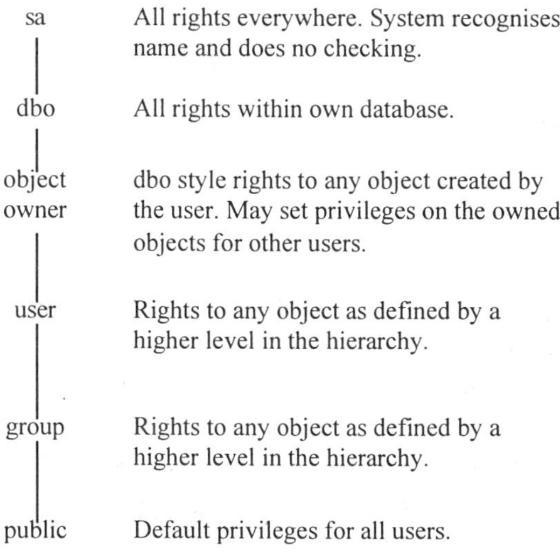

***Figure 6.2** User privilege hierarchy.*

The privileges are checked in this sequence, so users are checked before groups before public. This means that if a user has access to an object and you add the user to a group which has no access to the object, the user still retains access to the object. This is a standard means of having a group setting with individual user exceptions. Permissions granted to roles override those granted to users or groups.

6.8.1 Command Privileges

The administrator may grant command privileges within a database. This is unusual within a production system where you simply want the user to be able to operate the production system from the client applications, but will be required in a test/development database. The simplest settings are as stated before: alias everyone in the test/development databases to the DBO and they will have all rights in those databases.

Some commands may not be transferred to other users, as follows.

SA only	disk init
	disk reinit
	disk refit
	disk mirror
	disk unmirror
	disk remirror
	kill
	reconfigure
	shutdown
SA/DBO only	checkpoint
	dbcc
	drop database
	revoke (commands)

Of the remaining transferable commands, **create database** may be transferred by the SA only. Note that if you grant create database privilege to another user, the command updates sysdatabases in master so the user will need to be defined in master with update capability on the system tables. Not a good idea!

The default command and object privileges are summarized as follows, with an indication whether or not they may be transferred.

sa_role		**oper_role**		**dbo**		**object owner**	
alter database	Y	dump database	N	checkpoint	N	alter table	N
create database	Y	load database	N	create default	Y	create index	N
disk init	N	dump tran	N	create proc	Y	create trigger	N
disk mirror	N	load tran	N	create rule	Y	delete	Y
disk reinit	N			create table	Y	drop (obj)	N
disk refit	N			create view	Y	execute	Y
disk remirror	N			dbcc	N	grant (obj)	Y
disk unmirror	N			drop database	N	insert	Y
kill	N			grant (cmnds)	Y	readtext	Y
reconfigure	N			revoke (cmnds)	N	references	Y
shutdown	N			setuser	Y	revoke (obj)	N
				select	Y	truncate table	N
						update	Y
						update stats	N
						writetext	Y

(Remember: the sso_role has no privileges on commands, only on system procedures.) The remaining T-SQL commands are available to all users under the general permission grouping of public.

The default system procedures privileges are:

sa_role	**dbo**	**sso_role**	**object owner**
sp_addlanguage	sp_addalias	sp_addauditrecord	sp_bindefault
sp_addremotelogin	sp_addgroup	sp_addlogin	sp_bindmsg
sp_addumpdevice	sp_addsegment	sp_addserver	sp_bindrule
sp_changedbowner	sp_addthreshold	sp_auditdatabase	sp_commonkey
sp_changegroup	sp_adduser	sp_auditlogin	sp_dropkey
sp_clearstats	sp_dropsegment	sp_auditobject	sp_dropmessage
sp_configure	sp_dropthreshold	sp_auditoption	sp_droptype
sp_dboption	sp_dropuser	sp_auditsproc	sp_foreignkey
sp_dbremap	sp_extendsegment	sp_configure	sp_placeobject
sp_diskdefault	sp_logdevice	sp_displaylogin	sp_primarykey
sp_displaylogin	sp_modifythreshold	sp_dropserver	sp_procxmode

sa_role	dbo	sso_role	object owner
sp_dropalias		sp_locklogin	sp_rename
sp_dropdevice		sp_password	sp_unbindefault
sp_dropgroup		sp_remoteoption	sp_unbindmsg
sp_droplanguage		sp_role	sp_unbindrule
sp_droplogin		sp_serveroption	
sp_dropremotelogin			
sp_locklogin			
sp_modifylogin			
sp_monitor			
sp_renamedb			
sp_role (sa_role)			
sp_serveroption			
sp_setlangalias			

The remaining system procedures are available to all users under the general permission grouping of public.

Command privileges are set using the **grant** and **revoke** commands.

grant/revoke

```
GRANT {all | command_list} TO name_list

REVOKE {all | command_list} FROM name_list
```

where

name_list	user name; group name; role name; public.

```
GRANT create proc TO public
go
GRANT all TO fred, programmers
go
REVOKE create table, create view FROM john
go
```

Clearly, the use of groups makes this an easier task for the SA and makes maintenance easier.

6.8.2 Object Privileges

The owner of an object has the ability to modify the schema of an object (commands such as alter, create and drop). These schema modification privileges may not be transferred to other users by the object owner, only by the SA or DBO. Other users in the database are granted or revoked privileges on the data in the object by the SA, DBO or object owner, which allows them to select, delete, and insert on the object.

System 10 has a new feature, **with grant option**, which confers the authority to issue the grant and revoke commands on objects to a regular user. Prior to System 10, the right to grant/revoke privileges on objects was restricted to the SA or the object owner. The **with grant option** extension now allows this to be extended to other users.

I'll treat the commands separately. Grant is reasonably straightforward but there are some interesting effects of revoke when a hierarchy of privileged users has been established.

grant

```
GRANT action_list
ON object_name [(column_list)]
TO grantee_list
[WITH GRANT OPTION]
```

where

action_list	the actions which are allowed: ALL SELECT INSERT UPDATE DELETE EXECUTE REFERENCES

grantee_list	the users being granted the privilege: user_name group_name role_name public

The **with grant option** may be made only to a user_name. A grant with grant option is not allowed to a group or public.

References permission is required before you can create a table that includes a referential integrity references constraint.

Note that the column_list may be specified with the object _name, which is the current Sybase syntax, or with the action_list, which is the ANSI syntax. It is not valid to specify a column list in both places.

ANSI:

```
GRANT UPDATE (col_1, col_3) ON tab_1
       TO jill WITH GRANT OPTION
```

Sybase:

```
GRANT UPDATE ON tab_1 (col_1, col_3)
       TO jill WITH GRANT OPTION
```

Using the **with grant option** when conferring a privilege on an object to a user allows that user, as well as the DBA and object owner, to grant that privilege to other users. So:

```
GRANT EXECUTE ON jk_proc_1
       TO jill WITH GRANT OPTION
```

gives jill the ability to execute jk_proc_1 and to grant the execute privilege to other users. This now allows a user to have the same privilege granted from multiple sources.

john:

```
grant select on tab_1 to jill with grant option
```

john:

```
grant select on tab_1 to margaret
```

jill:

```
grant select on tab_1 to margaret with grant option
```

jill:

```
grant select on tab_1 to hugh
```

margaret:

```
grant select on tab_1 to colin
```

which gives the relationship shown in Figure 6.3.

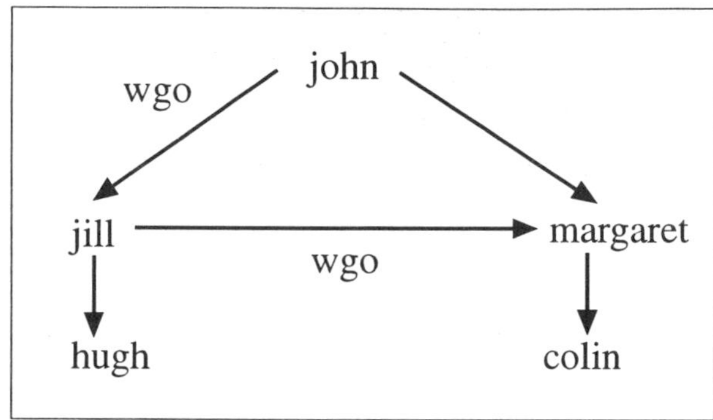

Figure 6.3 *Grant privilege hierarchy.*

The two grants to margaret are treated as independent grants because they come from different sources and create two rows in sysprotects. As always, the entries in sysprotects are kept to a minimum. If the source is the same, several grants on the same object to the same user are merged by updating the existing sysprotects row instead of creating a new one.

```
GRANT DELETE ON tab_1 TO fred
GRANT DELETE ON tab_1 TO fred
        WITH GRANT OPTION
```

If both grants are issued by the same user, then the first creates a row in sysprotects and the second updates it to **with grant option**.

```
select * from sysprotects where uid = 10
```

id	uid	action	protecttype	columns	grantor
1465056255	10	197	1	0xf0	1

Similarly:

```
GRANT UPDATE ON tab_2(col_1, col_3) TO fred
GRANT UPDATE ON tab_2(col_2, col_4) TO fred
```

results in one row in sysprotects with update granted on col_1, col_2, col_3 and col_4 although sp_helprotect shows it as separate output lines.

```
sp_helprotect fred
```

grantor	grantee	type	action	object	column	grantable
dbo	fred	Grant	Select	tab_1		
dbo	fred	Grant	Upd	tab_2	col_1	FALSE
dbo	fred	Grant	Upd	tab_2	col_3	FALSE
dbo	fred	Grant	Upd	tab_2	col_2	FALSE
dbo	fred	Grant	Upd	tab_2	col_4	FALSE

revoke

```
REVOKE [GRANT OPTION FOR] action_list
       ON object_name[(column_list)]
       FROM grantee_list
       [CASCADE]
```

where

grant option for	removes the grant privilege only. Normal command privileges are not effected. Omitting this clause revokes both command and grant privilege.
cascade	cascades the revoke of the grant privilege down the chain if the person from whom the grant privilege is being revoked has granted it to any other users.

The revoke is best explained with a few examples. Using the previous privilege hierarchy of Figure 6.3, then:

```
REVOKE SELECT ON tab_1 FROM jill
```

- jill loses the select privilege and the grant privilege for the select;
- hugh loses the select privilege since he received it from jill;
- margaret retains the select privilege because it also came from john, but loses the grant privilege as it came from jill.

```
REVOKE GRANT OPTION FOR SELECT ON tab_1
       FROM jill CASCADE
```

- jill loses the grant privilege for the select on tab_1;

- margaret loses the grant privilege for the select on tab_1;
- they still both retain the select privilege as the 'grant option for' removes only the grant privilege.

```
REVOKE GRANT OPTION FOR SELECT ON tab_1
       FROM margaret
```

- margaret loses the grant privilege for select on tab_1.

```
REVOKE GRANT OPTION FOR SELECT ON tab_1
       FROM jill
```

- This command fails as jill has conferred grant privilege on another user but the cascade keyword has not been used.

The rules for revoking are summarized in Table 6.1.

Table 6.1 *Rules for revoking grant option*

command	command privilege	grant option	cascade
revoke ...	Y	Y	Y
revoke grant option for ... with cascade	N	Y	Y
revoke grant option for ... (no grant priv. conferred on other user)	N	Y	N
revoke grant option for ... (grant priv. conferred on other user)	command fails	command fails	command fails

If revoking the command privilege (not the grant option for):

- the named user loses the command privilege and the grant privilege if granted;
- any users that have had privilege conferred by the named user lose the command privilege and any grant privilege, i.e. automatic cascade.

If revoking the grant privilege only with cascade:

- the named user loses the grant privilege;

- any users which have had the privilege conferred on them by the named user lose the privilege.

If revoking the grant privilege only without cascade:

- the named user loses the grant privilege unless the named user has conferred the grant privilege to any other user, in which case the command fails.

In other words, the basic revoke removes the named command privilege plus any grant privilege and cascades the revoke. However, revoking just the grant privilege cascades only if explicitly requested in the revoke.

If you allow named users to create objects in a database, then the DBO of the database (who did not create the object and is just another user) does not get automatic privileges on the object. However, the DBO cannot be barred from any object in the database as the DBO may issue the setuser command to look like any user in the database.

setuser

```
setuser  ["user_name"]
```

Use a null user_name to get back to yourself.

Care is required in the sequence of grant and revoke both to avoid mistakes and to save you input effort.

To revoke privilege from one user in a group:

```
GRANT create proc TO programmer
go
REVOKE create proc FROM fred
go
```

Even though fred is in the group programmer, he has no create proc capability because of the checking hierarchy which checks the user first. Also, if you issue more than one privilege (grant and/or revoke) against a user/group, the last one issued is the one which is active.

Similarly, to exclude one column from a group or user:

```
GRANT select on tab_1 TO programmer
go
REVOKE select on tab_1(col_1) FROM programmer
go
```

This is a standard approach—bar one, grant to all and revoke from the one.

In general, SQL Server keeps sysprotects as small as possible. A revoke will simply delete the grant from the table. However, when the revoke does not match the grant exactly, a separate revoke entry is made in sysprotects. This occurs in the following situations.

when the grant and revoke levels are different
grant at public, revoke at user or group; grant at group, revoke at user.

when the grant privilege is at table level but revoked at column level

```
grant select on tab_1 to john with grant option
revoke grant option for select on tab_1(col_1) from john
```

In this case, john still retains select on all columns of tab_1, so the current row is modified to reflect the grant option at column level and a new row is created to reflect the select privilege on tab_1(col_1) equivalent to:

```
grant select on tab_1(col_1) to john
```

Note that the sequence of issuing the grant and revoke commands is very important. The above sequence of granting to the large group and revoking from the few users is the recommended one as it allows exceptions to be created for individual users. This is possible as the privileges are checked in the hierarchy of user:group:public. However, a definition sequence of revoke from the user and grant to the group or public will cause the grant to override the revoke.

```
revoke select on tab_1 from john
grant select on tab_1 to public
```

will cause the sysprotects entry for john:tab_1 to be deleted and replaced with an entry for tab_1:public. Make sure that you define in the sequence of large to small (that is, public:group:user) so that the privileges are checked in the sequence user:group:public.

The sequence:

1. grant to public
2. evoke from group
3. revoke from user

will cause separate entries to be set up in sysprotects for public, group and user. However, the sequence:

1. revoke from user
2. revoke from group
3. grant to public

will delete the user and group entries and replace them with the public entry.

6.8.3 Privilege Hierarchy of Objects

Procedures/triggers use views and tables, and views use tables, all of which may have different privileges set on them. However, the privileges of the contained objects are not checked when the procedure/trigger/view is created, only when they are executed. The amount of checking when the object is executed depends on the ownership of each object in the hierarchy. If the ownership of objects in a hierarchy is the same, then the access privileges are checked only once on the initial entry. If the ownership of objects in a hierarchy changes, then the access privileges are checked on initial entry and at each level at which the ownership changes.

The hierarchy of object privileges in SQL Server allows you to restrict users to a particular level of access, such as view access to tables. This is very useful. If I want to ensure that all users access data via stored procedures I can:

```
GRANT execute on proc_1 TO public
go
REVOKE select on tab_1 FROM public
go
```

This ensures that everyone can execute the procedure proc_1 which selects from the table tab_1 but cannot directly use the select command on tab_1.

The hierarchy is shown in Figure 6.4.

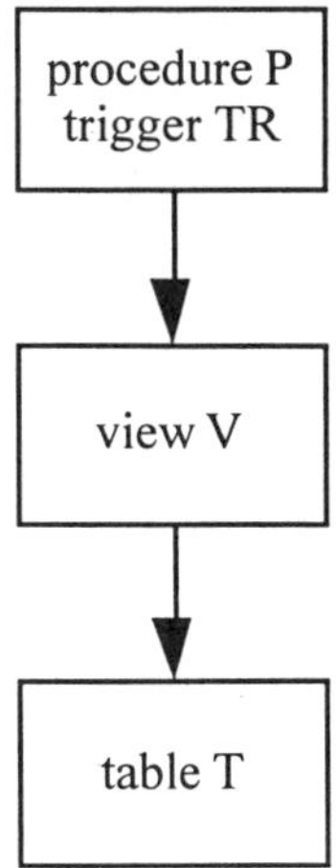

Figure 6.4 *Object privilege hierarchy.*

If the ownership of the objects in a hierarchy is the same, SQL Server does not recheck the privileges but uses the privileges at the entry point. Executing a procedure which uses a view which uses a table will not cause the privileges on the view or the table to be checked if the ownership of the view and the table is the same as the procedure. So, keep all production database objects owned by the SA and all test/development database objects owned by the DBO.

Consider the ownership hierarchies in Figure 6.5.

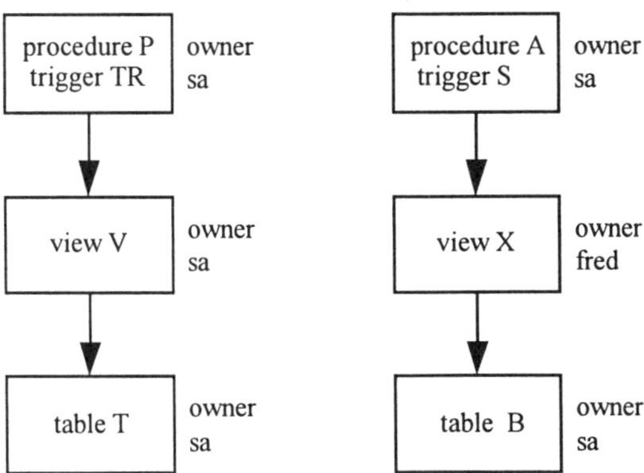

Figure 6.5 *Example privilege hierarchies.*

We have no problem with procedure P, view V, table T.

```
GRANT execute on P TO public
go
GRANT select on V TO public
go
REVOKE select on T FROM public
go
```

This means that access to table T is available via procedure P or view V, but not directly on table T.

However:

```
GRANT execute on A TO public
go
GRANT select on X TO public
go
REVOKE select on B FROM public
go
```

means that nobody can access table B (except SA who has access everywhere). Entry at the view is allowed but the change in ownership at the table rechecks the privileges which bars access. Entry at the procedure level is allowed, change of ownership at the view causes the privileges to be rechecked but still allowed. However, the next change of ownership at the table causes privileges to be checked again and access is not allowed.

The privileges are checked at the entry level and not rechecked for any dependent or referenced objects unless the object ownership changes from the level above. Keep the ownership chains simple: SA in production and DBO everywhere else. This is particularly relevant in views and must not be forgotten when triggers are defined on tables.

Consider the following table and view.

```
CREATE TABLE emp_tab
        (emp_id int, name varchar(30))
go
REVOKE select on emp_tab FROM public
go
CREATE VIEW employee AS
        SELECT emp_id, name FROM emp_tab
                WHERE emp_id = user_id()
go
GRANT select on employee TO public
go
```

If the owner of the view and the table is the same, then everyone can use the view. If the owner of the view and the table is different, then no one can use the view.

Triggers act as any other object in the hierarchy. However, you need to be careful as not everyone can create triggers. Only the owner of the table may create a trigger on the table. This helps in the privilege hierarchy but you need to be careful that the trigger does not access a table owned by someone else, as the privileges will be rechecked and the trigger will fail which causes the invoking command to fail.

user_2

```
CREATE TABLE tab_2 (ctrl int)
go
```

user_1

```
CREATE TABLE tab_1 (a int, b int)
go
GRANT insert on tab_1 TO public
go
CREATE TRIGGER trig_1 ON tab_1
        FOR INSERT AS
BEGIN
        UPDATE user2.tab_2 SET ctrl = ctrl + 1
RETURN
END
go
```

An insert on tab_1 will fail unless update access is allowed on tab_2 to the users inserting on tab_1. So keep ownership simple.

6.9 Access to System Procedures

System procedures are globally available and reside in their own database called **sybsystemprocs**. Users have global access privileges to system procedures, which means that any user has privilege to execute a system procedure in all databases or in no databases.

You cannot deny access to a system procedure in the user database. You have to attach to sybsystemprocs and deny the access there. This means that you must define the user in sybsystemprocs and revoke execute from that user.

```
USE sybsystemprocs
go
sp_adduser fred
go
REVOKE execute on sp_configure FROM fred
go
```

6.10 System Tables

6.10.1 sysprotects

Grant and revoke update **sysprotects**, which has changed to cater for the new grant privilege.

```
select * from sysprotects
```

id	uid	action	protecttype	columns	grantor
1	0	193	1	0xfeff0b	1
1	16390	193	1	0x01	1
1	0	193	1	0x01	1

where

id	object ID to which privilege applies;	
uid	user, group or role ID to which privilege applies;	
action	the privilege type:	
	references	151
	insert	195
	delete	196
	update	197
	create table	198
	create database	203
	create view	207
	create procedure	222
	execute	224
	dump database	228
	create default	233
	dump transaction	235
	create rule	236
protecttype	0	grant with grant
	1	grant
	2	revoke

columns	a column list bit map for select, update, references;
grantor	user ID of the grantor.

This is not very helpful and is better displayed by the system procedure **sp_helprotect**.

sp_helprotect

`sp_helprotect` (all permissions for all objects)

```
grantor grantee type   action  object        column grantable
dbo     public  grant  update  tab_1         all    false
dbo     public  grant  select  sysalternates all    false
dbo     public  grant  select  syscolumns    all    false
```

`sp_helprotect john` (all permissions for the named user)

```
grantor grantee type   action  object        column grantable
dbo     public  grant  update  tab_1         all    true
```

```
sp_helprotect @name = 'john', @option = 'grant'
```

(all grant permissions for the named user)

The naming of parameters in the last example is necessary because there is a second parameter to sp_helprotect: the name of the user in the database. The full syntax of sp_helprotect is:

```
sp_helprotect [name [,name_in_db [, option]]]
```

The only valid option at present is "grant" and you must enter the quotes.

6.11 Managing Remote Access

The preceding logins and users allow use of databases on the local server. In a networked configuration, SQL Server allows access to procedures on remote servers; that is, servers on other network nodes.

The sequence of events to establish remote access between servers is:

sp_configure	to enable remote access;
sp_addserver	to add the server;
sp_addremotelogin	to add the logins.

```
sp_configure "remote access", on
go
```

Having set remote access to on with sp_configure, we need to define the servers which are involved in remote access using the system procedure **sp_addserver**.

sp_addserver

```
sp_addserver   server_name [, {local|null} [, network_name]]
```

where

network_name	the interfaces name for server_name when this is different from the interfaces entry. This allows you to establish local aliases for the remote servers. When the alias is used, the null option is used in place of local.

```
sp_addserver glenlivet, local
go
sp_addserver tomintoul
go
```

Every server taking part in the remote access must have every other server defined as remote and itself as local. Consider three servers: glenlivet, aberlour and tomintoul:

glenlivet:

```
sp_addserver glenlivet, local
go
sp_addserver aberlour
go
sp_addserver tomintoul
go
```

aberlour:

```
sp_addserver aberlour, local
go
sp_addserver glenlivet
go
sp_addserver tomintoul
go
```

tomintoul:

```
sp_addserver tomintoul, local
go
sp_addserver aberlour
go
sp_addserver glenlivet
go
```

Note that each server must also have all of the servers defined in the interfaces file. This is not done automatically. You will need to edit the individual interfaces files or create one with all servers in it and copy it around; the latter is a more reasonable approach once the network configuration is settled.

Having defined the servers in the network, the login IDs which will be checked when a remote call is executed are defined using the system procedure **sp_addremotelogin**. These are defined on each called server (the remote servers).

sp_addremotelogin

```
sp_addremotelogin server_name [, local_login [, remote_login]]
```

where:

server_name	the server name on which the remote logins are being defined (the server you are currently working in);
local_login	the login name on the called server (the server you are currently working in);
remote_login	the login name on the calling server (the login you are mapping to local_login).

Each server must have the standard logins/users defined using sp_addlogin and sp_adduser. The sp_addremotelogin simply defines the mapping of the remote logins to the local logins. This mapping may be done in one of three ways.

1. Use the remote login as the local login.

   ```
   sp_addremotelogin tomintoul
   ```

   This is not a particularly sensible option as it requires an exact match of IDs and names between the servers, which is not easy to maintain, as described earlier. It is easier in System 10 as you can lock logins instead of having to drop them.

2. Set all remote logins to a single local login.

```
sp_addremotelogin tomintoul, fred_rem
```

This is a common approach as it requires least work by the SA and it is not unreasonable to treat all remote logins as the same for security and privilege checking. It does of course lose the strict audit control of who is doing what, for which you need the third option.

3. Set a one-to-one remote to local mapping.

```
sp_addremotelogin tomintoul, john_rem, john
```

6.11.1 Password Checking

When a remote login is made to a local server, the default is to request password verification. This may be overridden for specific remote logins using the system procedure sp_remoteoption to treat the remote login as "trusted" and not request password verification.

sp_remoteoption

```
sp_remoteoption  remote_server,
                 login_name,
                 remote_login,
                 option,
                 {true | false}
```

where

remote_server	the remote server name;
login_name	the login on the local server;
remote_login	the login on the remote server;
option	"trusted" is currently the only option;
true|false	the default is false, i.e., password verification.

```
sp_remoteoption tomintoul, sa, sa, "trusted", true
```

In general, it is easiest for the one login to have the same password on every server but you need to be careful when changing password. It is best to change the password on all remote servers—using a remote procedure call (rpc)—before you change it on the local server.

```
exec tomintoul.fred.dbo.sp_password cyclops, phoenix
go
exec aberlour.fred.dbo.sp_password cyclops, phoenix
go
exec sp_password cyclops, phoenix
go
```

6.11.2 Timeout

The site connection handler automatically drops any physical connections which have not had a logical connection for over one minute. To avoid this happening, the "timeouts" option of the system procedure **sp_serveroption** may be set on to maintain all connections until one of the servers is shutdown. When the server is restarted, the option remains true and the site connection handler automatically reestablishes a connection when a remote procedure call is made.

sp_serveroption

```
sp_serveroption [server_name, option, {true | false}]
```

where

option	timeouts	Default is false which disconnects physical connections after one minute of no logical connection;
	net password encryption	Indicates if remote server connections are to be initiated with client-side password encryption. Default is false, which is the normal password encryption (see 6.3.3).

```
sp_serveroption aberlour, "timeouts", true
```

6.11.3 Procedure Calls

If the servers have been set up as above, then stored procedure calls may be executed from one server to another simply by qualifying the procedure name with the server name.

```
exec  glenlivet.malt_db.dbo.show_prices
```

This is the only method in current SQL Server versions of remote access to other servers. Only the procedure name may be qualified with the server name. It is not possible to write a single SQL command where the tables reside on different servers; that is, it is not possible to qualify a table name with the server name. So:

```
SELECT c.name, o.ord_no
       FROM glenlivet.cust_db.dbo.customer c,
            aberlour.order_db.dbo.orders o
       WHERE c.cust_no = o.cust_no
```

is not a valid command.

To access data from several servers in one command, you need to use the OmniSQL gateway server. (Of course, you could write an open server gateway yourself, but Sybase already provides one.)

6.11.4 System Tables

sysservers

sp_addserver updates sysservers in master.

```
select  *  from  sysservers
```

srvid	srvstatus	srvname	srvnetname
0	0	glenlivet	glenlivet
1	0	SYB_BACKUP	syb_backup
2	0	aberlour	aberlour
3	0	tomintoul	tomintoul

This is simply displayed using the system procedure **sp_helpserver**.

sp_helpserver

```
sp_helpserver [server_name]
```

```
sp_helpserver

name          network_name   status                                    id
glenlivet     glenlivet      timeouts, no net password encryption 0
SYB_BACKUP    syb_backup     timeouts, no net password encryption 1
tomintoul     tomintoul      timeouts, no net password encryption 3
aberlour      aberlour       timeouts, no net password encryption 2
```

where 0 is the local server.

```
sp_helpserver  glenlivet

name          network_name   status                                    id
glenlivet     glenlivet      timeouts, no net password encryption 0
```

sysremotelogins

sp_addremotelogin updates the system table sysremotelogins in master.

```
select  *  from  sysremotelogins

remoteserverid remoteusername suid   status
1              NULL           -1     0
```

This is displayed using the system procedure **sp_helpremotelogin**.

sp_helpremotelogin

```
      sp_helpremotelogin [remote_server [, remote_name]]

sp_helpremotelogin   tomintoul

server        remote_user_name              local_user_name       options
tomintoul     john                          fred
```

6.12 Summary

Access to the server is allowed by adding a login to the server using sp_addlogin. This login is unique to the server and does no more than allow password protected access and, optionally, attach the user to a database. Although attached to a database by the login, the user has no access rights in this database until a user name is defined in the database using sp_adduser. To use several databases, a user name must be defined in each of the databases. The login name need not match with the user names and the relationship need not be one-to-one, as several logins may be aliased to one user name. This is particularly useful in a test/development environment where all logins may be aliased to the DBO.

The administration commands of the SA login may be split between three roles: sa_role, sso_role and oper_role, which allow named logins to carry out administration, security and dump/load operations. This removes the need for the superuser SA and increases accountability when several logins require system administration capability, as the server user ID of each login is now known.

Once defined as a user in a database, a set of command and/or object privileges may be set up for each user using the grant and revoke commands. This privilege definition may be made easier by forming the users into groups using sp_addgroup and defining the privileges against the groups. SQL Server has two privilege hierarchies: users and objects. The user hierarchy defines the sequence of checking—user, group, public—which is useful in allowing individual user exceptions to take precedence. Thus, a single user in a group may be given special privileges as the user is checked before the group. The object hierarchy reduces the amount of checking that has to be carried out by not rechecking privileges if the object ownership does not change. Thus, the privileges on a table in a procedure will not be rechecked when the procedure is executed, if the procedure and the table are owned by the same user. This object hierarchy is one of the most important reasons for keeping the object ownership chains simple.

Access between servers using remote procedure calls requires the servers to have the remote access configuration option set using the system procedure sp_configure, as described in Chapter 11. Access between the servers is then achieved by defining the servers in the network using sp_addserver and by defining logins from the remote servers using sp_addremotelogin.

7
Miscellaneous New Sybase System 10 Features

This chapter describes a collection of new features added by Sybase. these include transaction status, rollback trigger, trigger self-recursion, sort timing parameters, join density and customized error messages. I have also included the SET command options here.

Chapter 12 details the System 11 changes from System 10. System 11 has dropped support for the set dup_in_subquery option and replaced the use of dbcc tune with sp_configure options for sort buffer size and sort page count.

COMMAND SYNTAX

```
rollback trigger
save transaction
raiserror
set
```

SYSTEM PROCEDURE SYNTAX

```
sp_addmessage
sp_bindmsg
sp_getmessage
```

7.1 Installation

Installation is carried out with a new command **sybinit** but, as with version 4.x, you simply answer the questions.

A major difference is that the system procedures are no longer in master but have their own database **sybsystemprocs** which you can install on a separate device if you wish. A reasonable size for sybsystemprocs is 10 MB, of which about 7 MB will be reserved after installation.

You can upgrade directly from 4.9.x to 11.0. The upgrade effectively does a System 10 upgrade first and then a 10 to 11 upgrade. The principal problems are with the upgrade to System 10. Most of the new reserved words and the functional and optimization changes to query execution are in System 10.

7.2 Transaction Status

Prior to System 10, it was rather awkward to detect the DML statement error. A new global variable **@@transtate** indicates if the statement—actually the transaction—has succeeded or failed. The values for @@transtate are:

0 transaction in progress
Returned when in a transaction and the last DML statement has succeeded.

1 transaction succeeded
Returned after a successful commit tran or after each stand-alone T-SQL command that succeeds. If you are in chained mode, there is no such concept as a stand-alone command and @@transtate is set to 0 after each successful command until the commit tran when it goes to 1.

2 statement aborted
Returned within a transaction when an error occurs that aborts the DML command but not the overall transaction. For example, an insert which finds a duplicate key will abort the insert but continue the transaction.

3 transaction aborted
Returned after a rollback tran or after an unchained mode stand-alone T-SQL command fails. Also returned after an error that aborts the transaction, such as permission errors.

Use of @@transtate gives us the construct for handling errors:

```
INSERT INTO tab_1 VALUES (1, 2, 3)
IF (@@transtate = 1)
        PRINT 'record inserted'
ELSE
        print 'insert failure please resubmit'
```

which replaces the test of all the error conditions.

```
INSERT INTO tab_1 VALUES (1, 2, 3)
IF (@@error in ('list of fatal error codes'))
        PRINT 'insert failure please resubmit'
ELSE
        PRINT 'record inserted'
```

It's not perfect, as you still get the regular error message with the above and you still need to test for individual errors to make the error message specific. However, it does provide a "catch-all" ability so that command errors do not abort the code months after the application was implemented.

```
IF EXISTS (SELECT 1 FROM tab_1 WHERE a = 'pkey value')
BEGIN
        PRINT 'record exists'
END
ELSE
BEGIN
        INSERT INTO tab_1 VALUES (1, 2, 3)
        IF (@@transtate = 1)
                PRINT 'record inserted'
        ELSE
                PRINT 'insert failure please resubmit'
END
```

Note that the above means that the @@transtate value is not altered by any triggers which the command fires. So the above test immediately after the insert is not effected by any commands executed by any insert trigger.

7.3 Rollback Trigger

Within a trigger, the command **rollback tran** rolls back to the beginning of the outer transaction. A new command **rollback trigger** simply rolls back to the beginning of the command which invoked the trigger.

rollback trigger

```
        ROLLBACK TRIGGER [WITH raiserror_statement]
```

```
CREATE TRIGGER trig_1 FOR INSERT ON tab_1
AS
BEGIN
UPDATE ctrl_tab
        SET tot_col = tot_col + 1
        WHERE pkey = 999
IF @@transtate = 1
        RETURN
ELSE
ROLLBACK TRIGGER
END
GO
BEGIN TRAN
INSERT INTO tab_2 VALUES ('a', 'b', 'c')
INSERT INTO tab_1 VALUES (1, 2, 3)
UPDATE tab_3
        SET a=5
        WHERE pkey = 50
COMMIT TRAN
```

If the insert to tab_1 fails in the trigger, the insert to tab_2 will not be rolled back and execution will continue with the update statement. A single rollback trigger will roll back any nested triggers to the beginning of the command which initiated the triggers.

7.3.1 Transaction Boundaries

The difference between the rollback trigger and a standard rollback tran is best appreciated with a fuller discussion of transaction boundaries and the effect of a rollback. (This discusses default SQL Server transactions—transaction mode unchained. The difference between this and the ANSI standard—transaction mode chained—is discussed in section 8.1.)

Statements in SQL Server may be grouped together in transactions so that they are committed together and all inserts/updates/deletes in the transaction are treated as one unit of work for recovery purposes. These transactions may be defined in triggers and/or procedures and, as these program objects may be invoked from within a transaction, SQL Server supports the concept of transaction nesting. However, the nested transactions are not real transactions and have no effect on the committing of statements; the boundaries and commit point of all statements are the outer begin and commit statements.

Therefore, any rollback in a nested transaction or in a procedure/trigger causes a rollback to the beginning of the outer transaction.

```
BEGIN TRAN
        UPDATE tab_1 SET col_1 = 20 WHERE pkey = 30
        INSERT INTO tab_2 VALUES (1, 1, 1)
        BEGIN TRAN
                DELETE tab_3 WHERE pkey = 100
                ROLLBACK TRAN
        COMMIT TRAN
COMMIT TRAN
```

The rollback in the nested transaction rolls back the delete, the insert and the update.

save transaction

You can limit the rollback in a transaction with **save transaction**:

```
        SAVE TRANSACTION savepoint_name
```

so that rollback of the transaction_name causes rollback to the savepoint only.

```
BEGIN TRAN
        UPDATE tab_1 SET col_1 = 20 WHERE pkey = 30
        INSERT INTO tab_2 VALUES (1, 1, 1)
        SAVE TRAN del_tran
                DELETE tab_3 WHERE pkey = 100
        ROLLBACK TRAN del_tran
COMMIT TRAN
```

The named transaction rollback rolls back only the delete retaining the update and insert to be committed by the outer transaction. However, transaction names can cause errors when used in nested transactions, so this is not a solution to procedure- or trigger-based transactions. It is not recommended that named transaction savepoints be used in procedures or triggers.

Also be careful of the next statement executed after the rollback statement. The rollback tran is just another T-SQL statement and once the effect of the transaction has been rolled back, execution continues with the next sequential statement after the rollback tran. So a rollback in a procedure or trigger continues with the next statement in the procedure or trigger. The rollback from the trigger will abort the batch so that no further commands in the batch are executed but the rollback from the procedure will continue to execute subsequent statements in the batch.

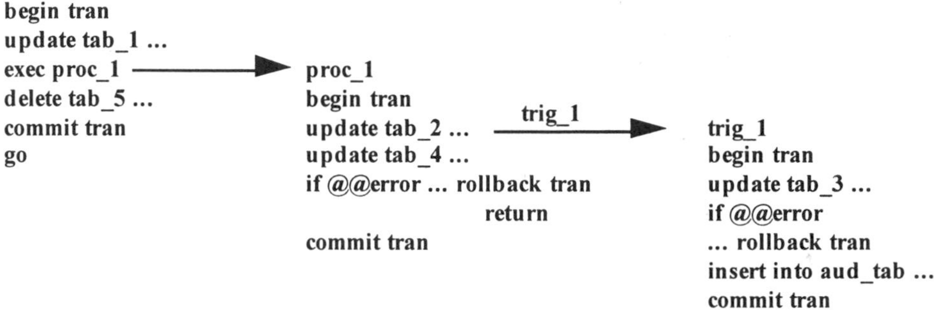

Figure 7.1 *Nested procedure and trigger.*

We have two rollback scenarios in the nested procedure and trigger of Figure 7.1.

Rollback from trigger rolls back the:

- trigger update tab_3
- procedure update tab_2
- calling batch update tab_1

then executes the insert to aud_tab and aborts the batch not executing the delete of tab_5.

Rollback from procedure rolls back the:

- procedure update tab_4
- trigger insert aud_tab
- trigger update tab_3
- procedure update tab_2
- calling batch update tab_1

and continues with the delete of tab_5.

Note the difference with the **rollback trigger** command, which does not complete the execution of any subsequent statements in the trigger. If the above trigger statement had been a rollback trigger, we would have had:

- rollback trigger update tab_3
- rollback calling update tab_2
- do NOT insert aud_tab

and continue with the execution of the procedure and the batch to update tab_4 and delete tab_5.

Be very careful with all of this as the most common default action is for the statements after a rollback to be executed. In most cases, you will not want this to happen so remember to place a **return** immediately after rollback statements. There are perfectly valid occasions when you wish to continue execution, but be careful, especially of the rollback trigger which does not execute the next sequential statement.

7.4 Extended Error Information

This is really an Open Client feature, available via ct-library. Therefore, I am not going to go into it in great detail, as the emphasis is on the server features of System 10.

The full format of the extended error data feature allows the client to determine which columns caused the error via the **raiserror** command. This command has been extended to contain the extended error data such as column name and the @@transtate global variable.

raiserror

```
RAISERROR error_number
          [{format_string|@variable}]
          [, arg_list]
          [extended_value = extended_value
          [, extended_value = extended_value]...]
```

Hmm! However, in its simpler form, it is just an extension of the raiserror command to allow parameterized user error messages. The format of the extended error data has changed in System 11 (see Chapter 12).

The simplest case is the default of an error number.

```
RAISERROR 30000
```

For error numbers greater than 20,000 the message text is retrieved from sysusermessages. If the message is not in sysusermessages, you get the error message:

```
Message number nnnnn, passed to RAISERROR, does not exist in sysmessages."
```

(No, I did not mistype it.)

These messages are added with **sp_addmessage** (section 7.10).

```
sp_addmessage 30000, 'john k error'
go
raiserror 30000
go

Msg 30000, level 16, state 1
Line 1          john k error
```

This is the most sensible way to deal with user error messages, but if you want the message to be hard coded, the format string may be used.

```
RAISERROR 30001 "hard coded error message"
go

Msg 30001, level 16, state 1
hard coded error message
```

Including the format string will override the sysusermessages message.
The error text string may contain argument substitutions.

```
RAISERROR 30002 "table %1! does not exist", @tab_name
go
```

where %n! matches the nth parameter in the argument list.
This argument substitution may be used from sysusermessages.

```
sp_addmessage 30003, "column %1! does not exist for table %2!"
go
RAISERROR 30003, @col_name, @tab_name
go
```

The extended value allows certain data values to be passed back to the client program. Such data as the table name, the column name and the user name are common.

```
RAISERROR 30004 "login name too short", "column" = "login",
                 "server" = @@servername
go
```

The contents of sysusermessages is quite straightforward.

```
select * from sysusermessages

error          uid     description           langid
30000          1       john k error          0
```

7.5 Network Connections System Table

A new system **table syslisteners** contains the network address for which the server is accepting connections.

```
select * from syslisteners

nettype address info
tcp     glenlivet 1234
```

7.6 Trigger Self-Recursion

Prior to System 10, there was no trigger self-recursion. In other words, a trigger could not fire itself. So:

```
CREATE TRIGGER trig_1 FOR UPDATE ON tab_1
AS
BEGIN
        UPDATE tab_1
                SET ctrl_col = ctrl_col + 1
                WHERE pkey = 'ZZZZZ'
END
```

would not fire the update trigger for the update of the control record 'ZZZZZ' even though it was on the same table.

This is still the default in System 10 but a new set option:

```
set self_recursion on
```

allows a trigger to fire itself.

I had to think quite a bit about when this would be useful until I realized that it is the answer to the "bill of material" type self-recursive structure. When we update values at a low level in the hierarchy, a self-recursive trigger will reflect the update at each level in turn until the top of the hierarchy, or until stopped by the application.

Consider a three-level hierarchy of parts:

part number	parent part number	price
AB123	AB12	100
AB12	AB	400
AB	null	2400

If we increase the component prices (such as AB123 by 10%), we may want to increase the subassembly and assembly prices by a related amount. For simplicity, I'll increase all of the prices by 10%.

```
CREATE TRIGGER upd_assy_trig
        ON part_tab FOR UPDATE
AS
BEGIN
UPDATE part_tab
        SET part_tab.price = part_tab.price * 1.10
        FROM inserted i, part_tab p
        WHERE p.part_number = i.parent_part_number
END
GO
```

When we issue the command:

```
UPDATE part_tab
        SET price = price * 1.10
        WHERE part_number = 'AB123'
```

the following actions take place.

- Update to AB123 sets the price to 110.
- Trigger fires to update AB12 and set price to 440.
- Trigger fires to update AB and set price to 2640.
- Trigger fires but the inserted.parent_part_number is null which means that no rows are updated and the trigger does not fire again.

7.7 Sort Tuning

The existing SQL Server sort algorithm has three principal bottlenecks:

1. one page read at a time;
2. 50 buffer limit for processing input data;
3. 100 page limit for internal dynamic data structure.

Some of these can be tuned using parameters to buildmaster but this is a little cumbersome and not the most convenient approach. It is also undocumented.

The above restrictions—especially the first two—can lead to a large number of passes in the sort, which increases the writes and reads to disk. System 10 has several new options to alter these limitations. Do not alter them without first discussing the situation with Sybase.

7.7.1 Create Index Sort

The number of buffers used during the sort phase of the create index—the extent I/O buffers—can be configured using sp_configure.

```
sp_configure "extent i/o buffers (for sort)", nn
```

where

nn is 0 to 2,147,483,647 with default of 0.

The create index uses these extent buffers which are the usual extent size of eight pages. So the default of zero is actually eight pages. More specifically, if more than one user is running a create index, all of the extent I/O buffers are assigned to the first user and the others use normal page I/O. So the most effective use will be for large indexes with the index creation being done by one user (administrator).

This value is server-wide and is not reset until the server is rebooted, so aim to improve the largest index builds. The optimum value will be implementation dependent but the suggestion is to try a value of 10 and see how much improvement is achieved. Of course, you get nothing for nothing and the additional pages used by the extent I/O buffers come from the data and procedure cache allocation. However, as you really should not be creating indexes during high user activity, this is not too significant.

To display the current value of extent I/O buffers, use sp_configure.

7.7.2 Sort Buffer Size

The number of buffers used during a sort can be tuned using the **dbcc tune** command.

```
dbcc tune ("sort bufsize", nn)
```

where

nn	Up to half the number of buffers available. SQL Server does not allow any single process to reserve more than half the total number of buffers, so this is the practical limit. A reasonable value is 10-15% of the total number of buffers.

The new value takes effect immediately and the current value may be displayed using dbcc resource. (It's at the end of the output of dbcc resource in the field csortbufsize.)

System 11 has replaced this with the sp_configure option **number of sort buffers**.

```
sp_configure "number of sort buffers", 100
```

7.7.3 Sort Memory Usage

A sort requires about 50 bytes of memory for each input row and the current version has a limit of 200 K. When using only 50 sort buffers, this is not usually a problem as the 200 K is almost sufficient for 50 buffers. In fact, you should not find much need to increase the 200 K memory limit for a sort buffer size of less than 100, so this is a configuration parameter which you should change only if you are experiencing trouble with sorts frequently running out of memory. There is no performance implication to the size of this parameter. It will give you a problem only if it is too small.

To alter the memory allocation for a sort, use dbcc tune.

```
dbcc tune ("sortpgcount", nn)
```

The new value goes into effect immediately, although sorts already in progress are not effected.

The rule of thumb for sort memory is 200 K for a sort buffer size of less than 100, otherwise two times the sort buffer size. More accurately, the optimum size may be calculated as:

sort buffer size * average rows per page ÷ 50

As I have said, do not increase this value unless you need to as the number of pages used by sorts will effect other users. In a multiuser environment, the above calculations are approximate as the optimum value is dependent on the number of users and the application mix. As an upper limit, it is not recommended that you exceed 30% of the total available proc headers (the value can be shown with dbcc memusage).

If you do increase sort parameters, be aware that the same values are used when the sort is redone. The most important occasion when this happens is a load transaction of the log dump that includes a create index. The log entry of a create index is simply the create index command; it is reexecuted by the load transaction causing a sort to be done. If this sort has large buffer and memory parameters and you are trying to reload to a smaller configuration, you may find yourself in serious trouble.

System 11 has replaced this with the sp_configure parameter **sort page count**.

```
sp_configure "sort page count", 100
```

7.8 Join Optimization

When joining two tables together, the optimizer has to consider how many rows it will retrieve for each join value to determine which index—if any—is the most useful. The basic approach to this is to divide the number of records in each table.

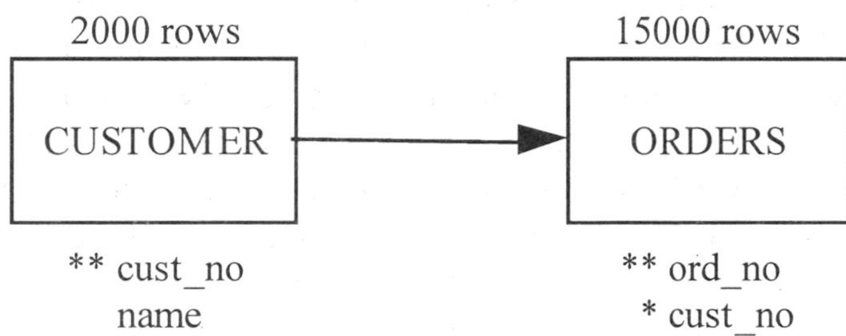

Figure 7.2 *Join optimization.*

In the example of Figure 7.2, the simple calculation for the join on cust_no between CUSTOMER and ORDERS is the number of rows in ORDERS divided by the number of rows in CUSTOMER; that is, 15,000÷2,000 = 7.5 order rows per customer. This simple calculation by the optimizer would normally mean that the cust_no index on ORDERS would be useful for the join.

When SQL Server builds statistics on an index, it calculates a figure called the density, which is the percentage of duplication in the table for the index values. When these statistics are available for an index, the SQL Server optimizer will use the density to determine the number of records per join value. In the example above, if the cust_no index had a density of 0.1% then the average number of orders per cust_no would be 15,000*0.1÷100 = 15. This is a more useful value as it is based on the data values and is more likely to give a good execution plan.

However, there is a problem with this when the index is a composite index of several columns in the table but the join is not made on all of the index columns. When SQL Server creates a density value, it uses all columns of the index; therefore, only a join which uses all of the index columns will have an accurate figure for the number of rows per join value.

Consider an index:

```
CREATE UNIQUE INDEX idx_1 ON tab_1(col_1, col_2, col_3)
```

on a table of 10,000 rows. Because the index is unique, the density will be (1÷10,000)*100 = 0.01%. This means that the optimizer will assume one row per join value and always use this index for a join.

However, if col_1 is not very selective and has only four unique values, then the join:

```
SELECT tab_1.col_4, tab_2.col_5
       FROM tab_1, tab_2
       WHERE tab_1.col_1 = tab_2.col_2
       AND tab_1.col_1 = 40
```

is liable to use the index because of the 0.01% density but will make 2,500 indexed accesses to tab_1 instead of a table scan. I have exaggerated this to illustrate the point but it can cause severe join performance problems.

To resolve this problem, System 10 now calculates the density for each combination of columns which may use the index. In our above example, the density would be calculated for:

col_1, col_2, col_3
col_1, col_2
col_1

None of the other combinations are relevant as the index will not be considered if col_1 is not in a where clause and the combination col_1, col_3 looks like the col_1 density, as all values of col_2 would have to be searched for each col_1 value to locate the col_3 value.

This means that our example:

```
SELECT tab_1.col_4, tab_2.col_5
       FROM tab_1, tab_2
       WHERE tab_1.col_1 = tab_2.col_2
       AND tab_1.col_1 = 40
```

will examine the col_1 density and see that it is 25%, which will give 2,500 rows per join value. This will undoubtedly cause the optimizer to choose another option as more efficient (assuming a nonclustered index, of course).

As before, the density is maintained by create index and update statistics. There is no need to rush to upgrade the statistics, as the 4.x and 10.x distribution pages are compatible. However, I see no reason why you should not reinitialize the statistics as part of your upgrade.

7.9 set Command Options

There are several new options available with the set command and some changes to the existing options. These new/changed features are covered in detail in the appropriate section to which the set option applies. This section is a summary with the important aspects discussed again.

set

set ansinull

```
set ansinull {on|off}
```

The default of off retains the normal SQL Server operation where a null value may be retrieved using the equality operator and does not require the special is (not) null test. Set to on, it enforces the ANSI standard which requires is (not) null to test for null values.

set Ansi_Permissions

```
set ansi_permissions {on|off}
```

The default of off retains the normal SQL Server update and delete permission checks of update permission on the columns being changed and delete permission on the table. Set to on, it enforces the ANSI standard of the above plus:

update: select permission on all columns in any where clause and select permission on any column on the right hand side of the set clause;

delete: select permission on all columns in any where clause.

set Arithabort

```
set arithabort [arith_overflow|numeric_truncation] {on|off}
```

The default of on aborts a query with an error message when arithmetic overflow or truncation occurs. Prior to this, the error message was produced but the transaction continued, which could produce quite a few error messages. However, the statement might have continued quite happily after the first occurrence, so be aware of this change to error detection. Set to off, it suppresses the error message; the command still aborts.

set Arithignore

```
set arithignore [arith_overflow] {on|off}
```

The default of off displays warning messages when arithmetic overflow occurs.

set Chained

```
set chained {on|off}
```

This toggles the chained transaction mode. The default of off operates in unchained mode, which is the normal SQL Server operating mode, where each stand-alone SQL command is an implicit transaction. To group multiple commands into a transaction in unchained mode, they must be bounded by a begin tran...commit (rollback) tran pairing. In chained mode, which is the ANSI standard, an SQL command automatically starts a transaction if none is active. This transaction continues until explicitly committed or rolled back. This is covered in detail in section 8.1.

set Close on Endtran

```
set close on endtran {on|off}
```

When set to on, this option forces all cursors opened within a transaction to be closed on end of the transaction. When set to off (the default), the cursor remains open across the transaction until explicitly closed. Cursor scope is discussed in detail in section 2.3.1.

set Cursor Rows

```
set cursor rows number for cursor_name
```

This sets the number of rows returned by each fetch within a cursor. The default is one. If the fetch is made to a list of variables, the number of rows fetched is always one, regardless of this setting. This is covered in detail in section 2.3.

set dup_in_subquery

```
set dup_in_subquery {on|off}
```

The default of off does not return duplicate rows from a nested query which is flattened into a join. Prior to System 10, SQL Server did a normal equality join when it flattened nested queries, which could display duplicate results. This no longer occurs as ANSI standard requires an existence join to be done and duplicate output results to be suppressed. This is explained in detail in section 10.4.2. This is no longer supported in System 11.

set Fipsflagger

```
set fipsflagger {on|off}
```

The default of off does not display a message when a non-ANSI standard T-SQL command is used. If you need to know when such a command is executed, set this option to on. (Federal Information Processing Standard (FIPS) is explained in section 8.3.3.)

set Identity_Insert

```
set identity_insert table_name {on|off}
```

The default of off does not allow inserts to the identity column of a table. In this mode, the identity column starts at 1 and increases numerically. When the option is on, the table owner may insert a record with identity set to the supplied value. This allows a "seed" value to be used for a table or allows accidentally deleted records to be recreated. When a value is supplied in an insert, the numeric sequence for the identity column starts from the maximum of the next value or the highest value in the table +1. This is covered in detail in section 1.1.3.

set Role

```
set role {'sa_role'|'sso_role'|'oper_role'} {on|off}
```

This turns the specified administration role on or off. You must enter the quotes. SQL Server now allows server logins to be assigned to administration roles. This allows tracking of individuals in the server so that you can tell which user with the appropriate permission; for example, sa_role, carried out a specific command. All roles which have been assigned to a login are automatically turned on when the user logs in. Use this option to turn them off if you need to.

set Self_Recursion

```
set self_recursion {on|off}
```

This determines whether a trigger can fire itself, such that an update trigger which updated a record on the same table would fire the trigger again. The SQL Server default is off, which does not allow self-recursion in trigger firing. If you set self-recursion on in a trigger, then it is automatically set off when the trigger ends or when the trigger causes another trigger to fire. This is discussed in detail in section 7.6.

set Statistics Subquerycache

```
set statistics subquerycache {on|off}
```

This System 11 set statistics option displays the number of cache hits and misses and the number of rows in cache.

set Transaction Isolation Level

```
set transaction isolation level {1|3}
```

The default, level 1, does not retain shared locks on data. By setting level 3, a holdlock is automatically applied to all select operations in a transaction. This is covered in detail in section 8.2.

Just in case you missed some of the later version 4 changes, here is a summary of the other options.

---

set Char_Convert

```
set char_convert {off|on [with {error|no_error}]
                          | charset [with {error|no_error}]}
```

This turns character set conversion off|on between SQL server and a client. If the client and server are using different character sets, conversion is automatically turned on during login. The with no_error option does not report when server characters cannot be converted to client characters.

set Datefirst

```
set datefirst number
```

This sets first day of the week. The default is 1: Sunday.

set Dateformat

```
set dateformat format
```

This option sets the ordering for entering dates. The default is mdy.

set Flushmessage

```
set flushmessage {on|off}
```

This determines when messages are returned to the user. The default of off stores the messages in a buffer until the query is complete or the buffer fills up. Set to on flushes the messages immediately to the user.

set Forceplan

```
set forceplan {on|off}
```

Now documented in System 11, if set to on, it allows you to force the optimizer to choose an index which it might not normally use for the query, or to force the optimizer to join the tables in the sequence of the from clause (from the left).

```
SET forceplan on
go
SELECT * FROM tab_1(2)
        WHERE col_1 BETWEEN 10 AND 100
        AND col_2 LIKE "AB%"
```

This forces the tab_1 index with indid 2 to be used to evaluate the command. This is obviously a dangerous thing to do as a drop and rebuild of the indexes may rebuild them in a different sequence.

It is more useful to force a table scan when the optimizer refuses to consider it:

```
SELECT * FROM tab_1(0)
        WHERE col_1 BETWEEN 10 AND 100
        OR col_2 LIKE "AB%"
```

as the table always has an indid of 0. It may be easier to force a table scan by altering the where clauses so that they are not search arguments (see Chapter 10).

```
SELECT * FROM tab_1
        WHERE col_1 + 0 BETWEEN 10 AND 100
        OR col_2 + " " like "AB%"
```

In some cases, the optimizer can get the sequence of the join tables wrong, especially when there are many tables in the join and some of them are very small. set forceplan can help here.

```
set forceplan on
go
SELECT * FROM tab_1, tab_2, tab_4, tab_3, tab_5, tab_7, tab_6
        WHERE tab_2.col_1 = tab_1.col_1
        AND tab_2.col_2 = tab_4.col_2
        AND tab_1.col_3 = tab_3.col_3
        AND tab_3.col_1 = tab_5.col_1
        AND tab_5.col_1 = tab_7.col_1
        AND tab_7.col_4 = tab_6.col_4
```

This will be evaluated with the tables nested in the sequence of tab_1, tab_2, tab_4, tab_3, tab_5, tab_7, tab_6. (There are many more join clauses that should be supplied to help the optimizer. This is only an example.)

set Language

```
set language lang_name
```

This option sets the language name for system messages.

set Nocount

```
set nocount {on|off}
```

Set to on, this option turns off the display message of "rows affected" after a SQL statement.

set Noexec

```
set noexec {on|off}
```

Set to on, this option compiles a query but does not execute it. It is used with showplan to see the optimizer plan but not execute the command.

set Offsets Keyword_List

```
set offsets keyword_list {on|off}
```

This option is used on Open Client db_library to return the position of a keyword in an SQL statement. Valid keywords are select, from, compute, order, table, procedure, statement, param, execute.

set Parseonly

```
set parseonly {on|off}
```

Set to on, this option checks the syntax without compiling or executing the statement.

set Procid

```
set procid {on|off}
```

This option is used in Open Client db_library to return the procedure ID before returning the rows.

set Quoted_Identifier

```
set quoted_identifier {on|off}
```

Set to on, this option allows double quoted strings to be used as identifiers; for example, "fred". This allows the use of non-alphabetic first characters and the inclusion of special characters in the identifier names.

set Rowcount

```
set rowcount number
```

This option stops statement processing after the specified number of rows are displayed. Zero displays all rows. Note that this is displayed rows, so "set rowcount 1" will read all 1,000,000,000 rows if none qualify.

set Showplan

```
set showplan {on|off}
```

Set to on, this option displays the optimizer plan for a SQL statement.

set Statistics I/O

```
set statistics io {on|off}
```

Set to on, this option displays the reads/writes for a statement.

set Statistics Time

```
set statistics time {on|off}
```

Set to on, this option displays parse, compile and execute time.

set String_Rtruncation

```
set string_rtruncation {on|off}
```

Set to on, this option raises a SQLSTATE exception when insert or update truncates a character string.

set Textsize

```
set textsize number
```

This option specifies the number of bytes to display from text datatypes. Zero defaults to 32 K.

7.10 Customized Error Messages

In System 10, you can customize the error messages produced by the server using **sp_addmessage** and **sp_bindmsg**. The user-defined error message is added to sysusermessages by sp_addmessage for use by the print and raiserror commands and to be bound to constraints by sp_bindmsg.

sp_addmessage

```
sp_addmessage  message_number, message_text [, language]
```

```
sp_addmessage 30001, "incorrect value check on the %1! table"
```

where

message_number	must be greater than 20,000.
message_text	message text of up to 255 bytes which may contain place holders of the format %n!. A special placeholder is %OP, which is replaced by the name of the operation (insert, etc.) that invoked the message. Use of the placeholders is also illustrated in section 7.4.

This adds the message to sysusermessages where it may be accessed by message_number for the print or raiserror commands or bound to a constraint by sp_bindmsg.

sp_bindmsg

```
sp_bindmsg constraint_name, message_number
```

```
sp_bindmsg item_value_chk, 30001
```

This is a good idea for integrity checks, as the default error message is of the form:

```
"Foreign key constraint violation occurred, db_name =''jk_db', table_name =
'orders', constraint_name = 'orders_cust_n176003658'"'"
```

The raiserror is straightforward as it retrieves the error message by number:

```
sp_addmessage 30000, "john kirkwood"
go
RAISERROR 30000
go

________

john kirkwood

sp_addmessage 40000, "user %1! has no access to table %2!"
go
RAISERROR 40000, @user_name, @tab_name
go

________

user fred has no access to table employee
```

The print statement does not have this facility and the message must be retrieved into a variable before use, using **sp_getmessage**.

sp_getmessage

```
DECLARE @msg char(30)
EXEC sp_getmessage 30000, @msg output
PRINT @msg
go

________

john kirkwood
```

Remember the exec or you get an error message.

The full syntax of the sp_getmessage is:

```
sp_getmessage message_number, @msg_var output [, language]
```

```
sp_getmessage  30001, @chk_var output
```

where

@msg_var	a local variable to receive the message text. The variable datatype must be character (char, varchar, nchar, nvarchar).

7.11 Summary

This chapter covered a collection of useful features, some of which we have been waiting a long time for.

8
Miscellaneous New ANSI Features

This chapter describes a collection of new features added to comply with ANSI 89. In general, these are switchable among the version 4.x settings, which are usually the default settings. The principal features are chained transaction mode, locking isolation levels, view with check option, null testing, a schema definition and subquery changes.

System 11 has introduced isolation level 0 to the locking mechanism.

COMMAND SYNTAX

```
create view
create schema authorization
```

SYSTEM PROCEDURE SYNTAX

```
sp_procxmode
```

8.1 Transaction Modes

Prior to System 10, SQL Server's concept of a transaction was not ANSI 89 standard. To conform to the ANSI standard, SQL Server now has a new mode for transaction operation:

unchained   the SQL Server standard mode and the default;

chained   the ANSI standard mode.

8.1.1 Unchained

The standard SQL Server implementation of a transaction is that it is bounded by a **begin tran** and a **commit tran** or **rollback tran**. If there is no **begin tran** ... **commit tran**, then every individual maintenance statement (insert/update/delete) is a separate transaction.

So:

```
UPDATE tab_1 SET x = 5 WHERE pkey = 10
UPDATE ctrl_tab SET tot_recs = tot_recs + 1
```

are two transactions in unchained mode. As such, they are committed separately and a rollback during the second update will not cause the first update to roll back.

To cause these two updates to be related for recovery purposes, an explicit transaction is required.

```
BEGIN TRAN
        UPDATE tab_1 SET x = 5 WHERE pkey = 10
        UPDATE ctrl_tab SET tot_recs = tot_recs + 1
COMMIT TRAN
```

By the same logic, a mixture of implicit and explicit transactions rolls back to the transaction boundaries.

```
UPDATE tab_1 SET x = 10 WHERE pkey = 30
BEGIN TRAN
        DECLARE @var_1 int
        SELECT @var_1 = count(*) FROM ctrl_tab
        IF @var_1 = 0
        BEGIN
                INSERT INTO ctrl_tab VALUES ('zzzz')
        END
        ELSE
        BEGIN
                ROLLBACK TRAN
        END
COMMIT TRAN
```

The rollback tran does not roll back the update of tab_1 before the begin tran when in unchained mode.

8.1.2 Chained

This is the mode required for ANSI compatibility and dictates that all DML is done within a transaction. Therefore, a statement automatically starts a transaction if no transaction is active.

In chained mode, a transaction is started implicitly by one of the following statements:

- select
- insert
- delete
- update
- open cursor
- fetch

and does not finish until an explicit commit tran. Because of this, there is no need to match a commit tran with a begin tran. Once a transaction is started, any begin tran ... commit tran block is treated as a nested transaction.

Taking the previous update statements, these are a single transaction in chained mode by issuing a commit tran as:

```
UPDATE tab_1 SET x = 5 WHERE pkey = 10
UPDATE ctrl_tab SET tot_recs = tot_recs + 1
COMMIT TRAN
```

The first update starts the transaction, which remains in effect until the commit tran. This means that all locks are held until the commit. So, if using chained mode, take care how long the locks are held as the longer a lock is held, the greater the contention.

In chained mode, our second example:

```
UPDATE tab_1 SET x = 10 WHERE pkey = 30
BEGIN TRAN
        DECLARE @var_1 int
        SELECT @var_1 = count(*) FROM ctrl_tab
        IF @var_1 = 0
        BEGIN
```

```
                INSERT INTO ctrl_tab VALUES ('zzzz')
        END
        ELSE
        BEGIN
                ROLLBACK TRAN
        END
COMMIT TRAN
```

will now roll back the initial update of tab_1 as it started the transaction and the begin tran ... commit tran block is a nested transaction of this. Even if the first update is in its own batch:

```
UPDATE tab_1 SET x = 10 WHERE pkey = 30
GO
BEGIN TRAN
        DECLARE @var_1 int
        SELECT @var_1 = count(*) FROM ctrl_tab
        IF @var_1 = 0
        BEGIN
                INSERT INTO ctrl_tab VALUES ('zzzz')
        END
        ELSE
        BEGIN
                ROLLBACK TRAN
        END
COMMIT TRAN
GO
```

there is still a nested transaction situation and the rollback will roll back the initial update. To make them separate we need to commit the first update before starting the second transaction.

```
UPDATE tab_1 SET x = 10 WHERE pkey = 30
GO
COMMIT TRAN
GO
BEGIN TRAN
        DECLARE @var_1 int
                SELECT @var_1 = count(*) FROM ctrl_tab
        IF @var_1 = 0
        BEGIN
                INSERT INTO ctrl_tab VALUES ('zzzz')
        END
        ELSE
        BEGIN
                ROLLBACK TRAN
        END
COMMIT TRAN
GO
```

Now the rollback tran cannot roll back the update of tab_1, as it has been committed with an explicit commit tran.

Be careful if you are used to working with SQL Server and start using chained mode, as each command is no longer a transaction and nothing is permanent until you have issued a commit tran.

```
INSERT INTO tab_1 VALUES (6)
GO
SELECT * FROM tab_1
GO

pkey
----
1
2
3
4
5
6

ROLLBACK TRAN
GO
SELECT * FROM tab_1
GO

pkey
----
1
2
3
4
5
```

Be warned, exiting from the session without issuing a commit tran does an automatic rollback tran, which can be a lot of work in chained mode.

Switching between transaction modes is done using the **set chained** command.

```
set chained {on|off}
```

To protect transaction consistency, this cannot be used inside a transaction, so you need to commit before using set chained. To check the current mode, query the global variable **@@tranchained**.

```
SELECT @@tranchained

0       unchained (default)
1       chained
```

8.1.3 Stored Procedures and Transaction Mode

The mode in which stored procedures execute is the mode in which they were created. If you create a procedure in unchained mode, then it may be executed in unchained mode only. If you create a procedure in chained mode, then it may be executed in chained mode only. When the procedure is created, the sysobjects entry is flagged with the transaction mode at creation. An attempt to execute in the opposite mode results in an error. This can cause some problems if you are in the habit of mixing modes. There is a system procedure **sp_procxmode** to reset the transaction mode of a stored procedure by updating the transaction mode setting in sysobjects.

To use sp_procxmode you need to be in unchained mode.

sp_procxmode

```
sp_procxmode   [proc_name [, transaction_mode]]
```

where

transaction_mode	chained; unchained; anymode.

```
sp_procxmode jk1_proc, chained
```

The anymode is the useful mode if you are in the habit of mixing modes and want the procedure to execute in both modes without having continually to change the mode of the procedure.

```
sp_procxmode jk2_proc, anymode
go
```

Almost all of the system procedures have been created in anymode. The exceptions I found were sp_addlanguage, sp_droplanguage, sp_fixindex, sp_fkeys, sp_loaddbupgrade, sp_monitor and sp_setlangalias, which were all in unchained mode. It's easy to check. Simply use sybsystemprocs database and issue sp_procxmode with no parameters, which displays the transaction mode of all procedures in the database.

```
USE sybsystemprocs
GO
EXEC sp_procxmode
GO
```

```
procedure_name user_name            transaction_mode
sp_addlogin    dbo                  anymode
sp_adduser     dbo                  anymode
sp_addlanguage dbo                  unchained
etc
```

8.2 Isolation Levels

ANSI 89 requires that transactions operate independently of each other (that is, in isolation), as if each transaction is the only transaction currently executing in the system. This is reasonable with insert/update/delete as the locking mechanism does not allow transactions to interfere with each other. However, the ANSI requirement means that all select commands must be repeatable if there is a problem during their execution.

This type of execution of a select is achieved in SQL Server by using the HOLDLOCK keyword in the select statement.

```
SELECT a, b FROM tab_1 HOLDLOCK
```

This takes a shared lock on the table before the command executes and retains it until the command is complete. Note that a table scan command is the only way to guarantee read consistency using holdlock, as any index access takes page locks until the escalation point of 200 locks is reached when a table lock is requested. (Locking strategies are explained in Appendix F.)

To support the ANSI standard automatically, System 10 has a **set transaction isolation level** command.

```
set transaction isolation level level_value
```

where

level_value		
	0	reads do not apply locks and therefore can access any data whether it is locked or not;
	1	default SQL Server non-repeatable read;
	3	ANSI standard repeatable read.

Isolation level 0 is a System 11 extension.

The effect of isolation level 3 is to automatically place a HOLDLOCK on each table in every select.

```
set transaction isolation level 3
go
BEGIN TRAN
        SELECT tab_1.a, tab_2.b
                FROM tab_1, tab_2
                WHERE tab_1.c = tab_2.c
                AND tab_1.a > 20
        SELECT x, sum(y) FROM tab_3
                WHERE x like 'K%'
                GROUP BY x
COMMIT TRAN
```

This will retain SLOCKs on all pages read by both selects until the commit tran. (I'm not recommending this, only telling you about it. The concurrency problems are horrendous.)

To provide complete flexibility in this new repeatable read environment, there is a new keyword NOHOLDLOCK, which does not hold SLOCKs for a specific table in isolation level 3.

```
SET transaction isolation level 3
GO
BEGIN TRAN
        SELECT tab_1.a, tab_2.b
                FROM tab_1, tab_2 NOHOLDLOCK
                WHERE tab_1.c = tab_2.c
                AND tab_1.a > 20
        SELECT x, sum(y) FROM tab_3
                WHERE x like 'K%'
                GROUP BY x
COMMIT TRAN
```

In this, the pages read from tab_1 and tab_3 will remain SLOCKed until the commit tran, but the pages read in tab_2 will be SLOCKed only for as long as the select requires to read the records in the page.

The System 11 isolation level 0 means that a select statement does not try to set any locks on the data and does not check any current locks when it tries to read data. Therefore, access is never denied even if the data is currently exclusively locked for update. This means that that the value read may not be the value that the data actually acquires as the update may be rolled back. This is not the isolation level to use if you need to bet the business on the value returned, but it takes a minimum of overhead if all you want is a current snapshot of the data.

If you have set isolation level 0, then maintenance commands and other statements such as DBCC still take their normal locks, even shared locks, as they must ensure data integrity.

A new global variable **@@isolation** gives the current value of the isolation level.

```
SELECT @@isolation

-----
   1
```

If you are wondering what isolation level 2 is in the grand scheme of things, wonder no longer. Here are the ANSI definitions of isolation levels that are followed by Sybase.

level 0 a write protection which prevents other updates to a piece of data that is currently being modified until the current transaction has committed. Reads are allowed at all times, even to data which is currently being modified.

level 1 a guarantee that data is not corrupted by two updaters, as in level 0 plus read consistency, which does not allow a read on data currently being updated. This is the SQL Server default isolation level.

level 2 a guarantee that a transaction will have **repeatable** reads on a row. A row read by a transaction may not be updated by another transaction until the read transaction has finished. Therefore, if the read transaction rereads the row, it gets the same data as when it read the row the first time.

level 3 a prevention of **phantoms** in a read transaction. This is subtly different from level 2 in that it encompasses the full set of rows being read by a transaction. All rows must reflect their start state at the beginning of the transaction until the transaction finishes. Therefore, any modifications by other transactions to the data set being processed must not be visible to the current transaction.

Isolation level 0 is achieved by the **set isolation level 0** command.

Isolation level 1 is the SQL Server default. Exclusive locks are set by maintenance statements and retained until the end of the transaction. Shared locks are set by read statements and released after the data page has been read.

Isolation level 2 is achieved by **holdlock** in the **select** statement so that the shared locks on pages read are retained until the end of the transaction. This may cause lock escalation to the table level.

Isolation level 3 is achieved by the **set isolation level 3** command or by **holdlock** in a **select** statement, which acquires a table lock at the start of the transaction. In this case, a shared lock is set on the table at the start of the transaction and retained until the end of the transaction. The acquiring of a table lock is determined by the optimizer and is achieved by a **select**, which does not use an index on the table but requires a table scan.

Be careful here. If you are operating in chained transaction mode, the SLOCKs will be retained until the end of the transaction. In chained mode, each select is not an implicit transaction so the concurrency effect of a HOLDLOCK in chained transaction mode can be severe (which is a euphemism for disastrous).

```
SET transaction isolation level 3
GO
SET chained on
GO
SELECT * FROM tab_1
GO

pkey
----
1
2
3
4
4
6
10
11
12
20
15

EXEC sp_lock
go

sp_id   lock_type      table_id      page   db_name      class
5       sh_table       320004171     0      jk_db        Non cursor lock
5       sh_intent      36            0      master       Non cursor lock
5       sh_page        36            0      master       Non cursor lock
5       sh_intent      384004399     0      master       Non cursor lock
```

Be very careful here as the concurrency problems are horrendous. The class column will display the cursor name for locks associated with a cursor for the current user and the cursor ID for other users.

8.3 ANSI Compatibility

A large number of ANSI features do not come under a specific heading, so I have grouped them together here.

8.3.1 Between

The BETWEEN clause now conforms to ANSI 89, which means that the values in the between clause must be in ascending sequence.

```
BETWEEN 50 AND 100
```

In System 10, the reverse no longer works.

```
BETWEEN 100 AND 50
```

will not return any rows. SQL Server used to switch the values to the correct sequence but no longer does, so watch your SQL for this change to the between processing. This is most important when you are using variables:

```
BETWEEN @var_1 AND @var_2
```

You will now need to check which of them is the lower so that you always put it first in the clause. Aren't standards wonderful?

8.3.2 Comments

System 10 supports ANSI standard comments which begin with two or more consecutive hyphens "--" and end with a <newline>. Note that this means that there are no multiline comments in ANSI and each comment line must begin with the comment start notation "--".

```
-- line 1 of the comment
-- line 2 of the comment
-- etc
```

These coexist with the current SQL Server /* comment */ style comments so you do not need to make any changes here. But be careful of some of your arithmetic if you have been in the habit of using unary minus.

4+-2 is OK and = 2

4--2 is not OK as it sees the --2 as a comment returning 4.

You need 4-(-2) or spaces such as 4 --2 to retain the arithmetic.

8.3.3 FIPS Flagger

As well as conforming to ANSI standards in System 10, SQL Server is also supporting the Federal Information Processing Standard 127–1, which states:

An implementation that provides facilities not specified by the standard (ANSI 89) shall also provide an option to flag nonconforming SQL language or conforming SQL language that may be processed in a nonconforming manner.There is no requirement to detect extensions that cannot be determined until execution time.

The FIPS flagger is the System 10 option that supports this requirement. It is set using the set command option:

```
SET fipsflagger {on|off}
```

When it is on, warning messages are displayed for any statements which do not conform to the ANSI 89 standard. For example:

```
Error 7309     SQL, statement in line number nn contains non ANSI text. This
error is caused due to the use of a DUMP command.
```

Although it says "error," it is just a warning and has no effect on the execution of the command or subsequent commands. Amusingly, the set command is not ANSI standard so set fipsflagger off generates the warning message.

What qualifies as non-ANSI standard SQL is surprising. It can be classified as:

- necessary administration/performance related commands such as truncate table;
- useful additional features such as text manipulation;
- management systems management such as disk space monitoring;
- procedural language extensions such as stored procedures and triggers;

and therefore includes such commands as:

- alter, drop, truncate;
- dbcc;
- dump, load;
- create default, proc, trigger.

So you will not see many warnings during normal execution of DML commands but it gets very annoying when you are working as the administrator using data definition language (DDL).

8.3.4 NULL Testing

ANSI is very specific about testing for null. If the value of at least one of the operands is null, then the result is unknown; that is, null and not true or false.

SQL Server was always a little more relaxed when testing equality/inequality and returned true/false if one of the operands was a column, parameter or variable. If you always used the **is null** test just in case, you will have no problems, but if you used equals, the test now returns different answers.

ANSI standard:

```
SELECT * FROM tab_1 WHERE col_1 = NULL
```

returns no rows.

SQL Server default:

```
SELECT * FROM tab_1 WHERE col_1 = NULL
```

returns the rows where col_1 is null.

System 10 retains backwards compatibility in this situation with a set command option:

```
SET ansinull {on|off}
```

where the default is off, which retains the existing null testing condition.

8.3.5 Views

Select Distinct

You can now use select distinct in a view.

create view

```
CREATE VIEW view_1
AS
        SELECT DISTINCT a FROM tab_1
```

As with any distinct, the uniqueness of the output applies to all columns in the column list. For example:

```
tab_1          a    b    c
               1    1    1
               1    1    2
               1    2    1
               1    2    2
               1    2    3
               2    1    1

CREATE VIEW view_2 AS
        SELECT DISTINCT a, b FROM tab_1
```

creates:

```
view_2         a    b
               1    1
               1    2
               2    1
```

So the command:

```
SELECT a FROM view_2
```

will still display duplicate values for a of 1 and 1.

Views which are created with a distinct in the select clause are read only. This is perfectly reasonable as there is no one-to-one row relationship between the view and the table so you could not maintain the table via this view.

This type of view is not the most efficient performer because it requires two separate executions when it is used. When the view is used in a select, it is fully evaluated before the select is performed on it with no merging of the SQL before optimization. You get the performance overhead of the view execution followed by the select execution. (This is a general aspect of views. You should always beware of a view which is not a row-by-row mapping from the table to the view. In general, joins may be excluded from this problem but watch out for GROUP BY and complicated nestings.)

With Check Option

The **with check option** in a view ensures that the data maintained via the view conforms to any restrictions placed on data in the view. You may only insert/update data in a **with check option** view if the new data may appear in the view; that is, it satisfies the check.

If a view holds data only for price in (10, 20) then you may insert only prices of 10 or 20 and update other prices only to 10 or 20.
For example:

```
CREATE VIEW view_3 AS
       SELECT pkey, description, price FROM tab_3
              WHERE price > 1000
       WITH CHECK OPTION
```

These commands are allowed:

```
INSERT INTO view_3 (pkey, description, price)
       VALUES (1, 'resistor', 2000)
UPDATE view_3
       SET price = 5000
       WHERE pkey = 20
```

These commands are not allowed, producing error messages:

```
INSERT INTO view_3 (pkey, description, price)
       VALUES (2, 'transistor', 50)
UPDATE view_3
       SET price = 900
       WHERE pkey = 12
```

And what an error message it is:

```
The attempted insert or update failed because the target view was either created
WITH CHECK OPTION or spans another view created WITH CHECK OPTION. At least one
resultant row would not qualify under the CHECK OPTION constraint."
```

Similarly:

```
UPDATE view_3
       SET price = price * 1.10
```

is allowed but:

```
UPDATE view_3
       SET price = price * 0.90
```

may not be allowed.

The last example is a multiple record update and is aborted if one of the records fails the check constraint; that is, updates the price out of range of the view. This will cause all of the updates to be rolled back, so be careful as the multiple record rollback can take some time. There is no warning that it might happen.

If you have a hierarchy of views, the **with check option** is inherited.

```
CREATE VIEW check_view_1
AS
        SELECT * FROM tab_1 WHERE price > 50
        WITH CHECK OPTION
go
CREATE VIEW nocheck_view_1
AS
        SELECT * FROM check_view_1 WHERE qty > 10
go
```

The view nocheck_view_1 inherits the check option "price > 50" and any rows inserted or updated via nocheck_view_1 must have the price greater than 50.

```
UPDATE nocheck_view_1
        SET price = 100,
                qty = 2
        WHERE pkey = 123
```

is allowed but:

```
UPDATE nocheck_view_1
        SET price = 20
        WHERE pkey = 123
```

is not allowed.

View Updating Rules

SQL Server will allow insert/update/delete to a view if it is a one-to-one mapping of rows from the base table to the view. Obviously, insert will also require the view to contain all of the mandatory columns.

When the view contains a join and the **with check option**, the rules for inserting/updating are changed from the normal SQL Server ones.

Inserts are not allowed to a join view with check option in any circumstances.

Updates are not allowed to a join view with check option if a column being updated appears in a where clause that contains columns from more than one table. This always includes the join fields.

```
CREATE VIEW join_check
AS
        SELECT a.*, b.* FROM tab_1 a, tab_2 b
                WHERE a.col_1 = b.col_1
                AND a.col_3 = 40
                AND b.col_2 = 100
                AND a.col_4 + b.col_4 > 60
        WITH CHECK OPTION
```

Updates are not allowed to the view join_check if the update command attempts to update col_1 or col_4 from either table.

Again, it's a beauty of an error message:

```
View 'join_check' does not allow this update because either it was created WITH
CHECK OPTION or it spans a view created WITH CHECK OPTION, and one of the update
columns appears in a multi-table expression in the WHERE clause of a CHECK OPTION
view."
```

In summary, the update/insert rules for views are:

- insert is not allowed on views created with distinct or with check option;
- insert is not allowed if it does not contain all mandatory columns;
- insert is not allowed on a view containing a computed column;
- all columns of insert/update statement to join view must belong to one table;
- delete is not allowed on join views;
- update is not allowed on a view containing the distinct operator;
- update is not allowed on join views with check option if any updated column appears in a multitable where clause;
- update is not allowed on a view containing an aggregate;
- update cannot change a column in a view which is in a computation.

Finally, there is a change to the creation syntax in using column names. In System 10, you must supply a column name if the column in the view is not a simple heading mapping; that is, a default column name cannot be derived in the select command of the view. This normally means that a column name must be supplied if the column of the select command is involved in an expression such as arithmetic, but also includes when two columns have the same name because of a join.

```
CREATE VIEW jk_view ( pkey, ave_price) AS
SELECT pkey, avg(price)
       FROM tab_1
       GROUP BY pkey
go
```

8.4 Schemas

System 10 supports the DDL concept of a schema, which in SQL Server terms is a collection of tables, views and privileges. A schema is defined by the **create schema** command and can contain any mixture of the three statements:

- create table
- create view
- grant.

create schema authorization

```
CREATE SCHEMA AUTHORIZATION user_name
        create_statement
        [create_statement...]
        [permission_statement...]
```

For example:

```
CREATE SCHEMA AUTHORIZATION fred
CREATE TABLE tab_1 (a int primary key,
                    b char(10),
                    c varchar(30) null)

CREATE VIEW view_1
       AS
       SELECT a, c FROM tab_1
GO
```

The current implementation restricts the user_name to the current user in the database (that is, yourself), so you can really only create schemas for yourself at the moment. The DBO can always setuser to anyone in the database but the user_name restriction is not really important as most production environments will be created by the DBO anyway.

However, the schema is not named and therefore it cannot be addressed as an independent object. Thus there is no ability to reference the collection of schema objects and assign access rights to it. We can hope that this is the first step by Sybase in the use of schemas because, at the moment, it does not accomplish anything. What the DBA wants from a schema (well, what I always wanted) is the ability to assign any object to it—table, view, rule, default, procedure, trigger—and then to assign users and privileges to the schema. Used with groups this is the simplest way to restrict access in a database. I really cannot see a great deal of use for schemas in SQL Server at the moment; they need to be independent named objects which can encompass all objects, including subschemas, and to which users and privileges can be assigned.

The schema definition consists of all schema statements—create table, create view, grant—after the create schema statement, until the end of the batch or the first non-schema statement. (Wouldn't a begin ... end be helpful?)

```
CREATE SCHEMA AUTHORIZATION fred
CREATE TABLE tab_1 (a int primary key,
                    b char(10),
                    c varchar(20) null,
                    d int references tab_2(d))
CREATE TABLE tab_2 (d int primary key,
                    e varchar(50))
CREATE VIEW view_1
AS
SELECT * FROM tab_1
CREATE VIEW view_2
AS
SELECT tab_1.a, tab_2.d, tab_2.e
       FROM tab_1, tab_2
       WHERE tab_1.d = tab_2.d
GO
```

or

```
CREATE SCHEMA AUTHORIZATION fred
CREATE TABLE tab_1 (a int primary key,
                    b char(10),
                    c varchar(20) null,
                    d int references tab_2(d))
CREATE TABLE tab_2 (d int primary key,
                    e varchar(50))
CREATE VIEW view_1
AS
SELECT * FROM tab_1
CREATE VIEW view_2
AS
SELECT tab_1.a, tab_2.d, tab_2.e
       FROM tab_1, tab_2
       WHERE tab_1.d = tab_2.d
SELECT * FROM view_2
```

Both the go and the command select * from view_2 terminate the definition of the schema.

Three points to note are as follows.

- All commands which are part of the schema definition are single transactions.
- The schema definition may contain multiple view statements (as above).
- The schema definition may define a referential integrity references constraint on a table which has not yet been defined in the schema (as above). Outside of a schema definition you must define the referenced table before referencing it. You cannot define a referential integrity constraint to a table which will not be in the schema.

The latter two points stem from the single transaction nature of the create schema statement, as the complete syntax and dependencies are not checked until the end of the transaction.

8.5 Subquery Changes

8.5.1 Duplicate Returns from a Subquery

The simple subquery syntax using in (or = any) did not conform to the ANSI standard in version 4.x, as it displayed duplicate rows if the subquery contained duplicates. Consider the following.

```
tab_1          a     b                  tab_2          a     b
               1     2                                 1     1
               2     1                                 1     4
                                                       2     6
```

```
SELECT tab_1.a FROM tab_1
      WHERE tab_1.a IN (SELECT a FROM tab_2)
```

displayed:

```
a
1
1
2
```

This occurred because SQL Server evaluated the subquery as a join.

```
SELECT tab_1.a FROM tab_1, tab_2
      WHERE tab_1.a = tab_2.a
```

ANSI requires that the in operates as an existence check regardless of the existence of duplicates in the subquery list, so System 10 will display two results, a=1 and a=2, from the above subquery. This is accomplished by a special "existence join" which stops looking for a match on the inner table once it finds the first match for each value. This requires the System 10 optimizer to predefine the join order as the inner table being the subquery table, which may not be the most efficient order for the join. If you do not want to rewrite some logic, or if performance is a problem and you know that there are no duplicates, you can resort to the old SQL Server join optimization of the subquery using a set command option.

```
set dup_in_subquery on
```

If the subquery is in a stored procedure, run the set command before you create the stored procedure.

The dup_in_subquery option is no longer supported in System 11.

8.5.2 Null in Subquery Returning True for "Not In"

```
SELECT a FROM tab_1
       WHERE 20 NOT IN (SELECT c FROM tab_2
                              WHERE tab_1.a = tab_2.a)
```

In version 4.x, if the subquery returned a null value, a true result was returned. ANSI says that this is incorrect as the presence of a null in the subquery indicates an unknown value; therefore, the "not in" test cannot determine if the value being tested does or does not match, so no output is displayed. For that reason, a null or a false result must be returned when the subquery returns a null value.

This is now the result in System 10. A null returned by a subquery will cause a "not in" test not to return the row in the outer query.

For example:

```
tab_1          col_1          col_2
               1              1
               2              2
               3              3

tab_2          col_1          col_2          col_3
               1              1              1
               2              2              10
               3              3              null
               4              4              20

SELECT col_1, col_2 FROM tab_1
       WHERE 20 NOT IN (SELECT col_3 FROM tab_2
                              WHERE tab_1.col_1 = tab_2.col_2)
```

col_1	col_2
1	1
2	2

8.5.3 Empty Table Subquery and OR Returning No Rows

In version 4.x, an exists, in, or any subquery which contained an empty table did not return any rows, even if combined with a true OR clause.

```
SELECT a FROM tab_1
       WHERE b IN (SELECT c FROM tab_2)
       OR d = 10
```

returned no rows when tab_2 was empty, even if d = 10 was true.

This was caused by SQL Server flattening the query to a join:

```
SELECT tab_1.a FROM tab_1, tab_2
       WHERE tab_1.b = tab_2.c
       OR tab_1.d = 10
```

and the join of tab_1 with the empty tab_2 never returns any rows, regardless of what the rest of the query does. (This is actually an ANSI standard based on the unknown nature of null.)

This problem has been resolved by SQL Server by not flattening the subquery to a join when it consists of exists, in or any. However, if you write them as joins, you will still get no rows returned, so make sure that your SQL standards state how to write this type of command.

For example:

tab_2

col_1	col_2	col_3
1	1	1
2	2	10
3	3	null
4	4	20

tab_3 no data

```
Select col_1 FROM tab_2
       WHERE col_2 IN (SELECT col_2 FROM tab_3)
       OR col_3 = 20
```

```
col_1
4

SELECT tab_2.col_1 FROM tab_2, tab_3
       WHERE tab_2.col_2 = tab_3.col_2
       OR tab_2.col_3
```

returns no data

8.5.4 <ALL and >ALL when the Subquery Returned No Rows

```
SELECT a FROM tab_1
       WHERE b >ALL (SELECT c FROM tab_2
                            WHERE c = 'nonexistent value')
```

In version 4.x, the above would return no rows because the subquery returned no rows. In other words, the >ALL test returned false. The ANSI standard says that the >ALL should return true in this situation and the above command should return all rows from the outer table. I find this incomprehensible but this is how it works now to conform to the ANSI standard.

This was caused by SQL Server converting the >ALL and <ALL to MAX and MIN. The above becoming:

```
SELECT a FROM tab_1
       WHERE b >= (SELECT max(c) FROM tab_2
                         WHERE c = 'nonexistent value')
```

which returned no rows if the subquery returned null, as no value is >= null.

This is resolved by converting the >ALL and <ALL to NOT IN.

For example (using the same tables as before):

```
SELECT col_1 FROM tab_1
       WHERE 100 > all (SELECT col_3 FROM tab_2
                              WHERE col_3 = 30000)

col_1
1
2
3
```

8.5.5 Aggregates in Subquery Where Clauses

In general, aggregates are not allowed in where clauses but ANSI states that it is permissible when:

- the where clause is in a subquery;
- the subquery is in a having clause;
- the column is in the aggregate clause of the outer query.

So, System 10 supports:

```
SELECT tab_1.a, sum(tab_1.b)
       FROM tab_1
       GROUP BY tab_1.a
       HAVING tab_1.c IN
              (SELECT tab_2.c FROM tab_2
                             WHERE tab_2.d = sum(tab_1.b))
```

8.6 Summary

I recommend avoiding the chained transaction mode and isolation level 3 and sticking to the default SQL Server operation, which I happen to believe is the optimum for client/server operation.

This is based on the increased concurrency of not retaining locks for long periods of time. It is not so important with the exclusive lock, as you can always issue commit tran after each update. However, the retention of shared locks during the transaction is simply asking for serious contention problems in a mixed read/update environment. Most ANSI standard implementations will use a nolock situation on the read to allow update transactions to proceed, as in System 11 with isolation level 0.

The null checking and sequence of parameters in the between clause are simple examples of changes which may cause problems with existing code. The changes to subquery execution are more serious with particular attention to the simple existence subquery, which may degrade quite significantly in performance. The other subquery situations are special nesting conditions which you have probably had to work around already anyway so you will be more aware of them.

9

Backup and Recovery

This chapter discusses System 10/11 backup and recovery. Transaction management is discussed first, covering the transaction log entries and the actions taken to recover from media and system failures. This if followed by a detailed description of the commands and procedures necessary to enable the dump and restoration of databases and transaction logs to ensure full recovery from failure. We deal with recovery of the master database and how to achieve a full system rebuild in Appendix D.

System 11 introduced private transaction log caches to reduce the write contention on the log.

COMMAND SYNTAX

```
begin tran
rollback tran
commit tran
checkpoint
dump database
dump transaction
load database
load transaction
dbcc dbrepair
```

SYSTEM PROCEDURE SYNTAX

```
sp_configure
sp_helplog
sp_addumpdevice
sp_dropdevice
sp_volchanged
```

9.1 Introduction

There are two aspects to backup and recovery: the run-time management of the transaction to enable recovery and the procedures to carry out the recovery. The transaction management involves copying the effects of each transaction to a log so that the transactions may be repeated or any erroneous actions may be removed. The backup procedures involve the commands to dump and restore the database and the transaction log, and the recovery processing to repeat the transactions against the data.

There are several options to repeat the transactions: from application specific code which reprocesses the transactions, to application-independent automatic software to rewrite data updates to the database. It is the latter that interests us; that is, how SQL Server performs transaction management and recovery to provide a transparent ability to recover a database after a failure.

There are two types of failure that the recovery management and procedures must be able to deal with: system failure, where the currently executing transactions have not completed properly but the data on the database is intact, and media failure, where the database has been damaged and is no longer usable.

SQL Server supports fully automatic recovery using a transaction log containing images of the data updates and checkpoints to synchronize the flushing of cache to disk. This by itself permits recovery from system failure by applying the before images of the uncompleted transactions. With the addition of a database dump and transaction log dumps, recovery may be made from a media failure by rolling forward the after images of completed transactions from the last database dump.

SQL Server provides 100% recovery from a failure up to the last completed transaction. This requires dumping all transaction records, which may be difficult if the media failure loses the only copy of the current disk log. However, such combinations of sloppy system administration and capricious acts of God are beyond any vendor's foresight.

So far, I have been loose with the terminology and lacking in definition, so let's define a few terms.

system failure	an event that requires one or more executing transactions to go back to their start point. The event may range from a loss of data cache to an application error. The important aspect of a system failure is that the database is intact and not damaged or corrupted.
media failure	an event that causes the database to be damaged and unusable.

database dump — a copy of the database at a point in time.

transaction dump — a copy of the current transaction log. This dump will normally clear out the completed transaction information once the dump has completed.

rollback — a recovery process that recovers from a system failure by reversing the effects of uncompleted transactions on the database.

roll forward — a recovery process that recovers from a media failure by posting the completed transactions in the transaction log dumps to the database dump.

before image — a logical description of the information on the log which reflects the position of the relevant record immediately before it is updated by the transaction.

after image — a logical description of the information on the log which reflects the position of the relevant record immediately after it has been updated by the transaction.

SQL Server backs up the database and the associated transaction log to ensure that the database may be recovered from a media failure by loading the last database dump and rolling forward the transaction log dumps from the time of the database dump until the last completed transaction. The transaction log is crucial to this roll forward as it contains a record of every change to the database pages. Every transaction has the updated version of the data written to the transaction log and these are reposted to the database to bring it up-to-date. A checkpoint process is also involved to flush the "dirty" pages to disk. This ensures that rollback recovery from a system failure does not take too long.

System 10 has significantly augmented the backup facilities and speed of both backup and restore by introducing a backup server. Life with the backup server is much the same as it was previously. The major operating differences are that you no longer require the console program and that the backup server must be configured as a remote server. If you do not use any of the new striping, remote backup and multiple files per backup device, there is no difference to the commands and the backup strategy. The current syntax of the dump and load will run unchanged. Unfortunately, the actual format of the dump has changed in System 10 and previous 4.9.X dumps are not compatible with a System 10 dump. There is no problem between System 10 and System 11.

However, what the backup server really gives you is a significant increase in dump/load speed in the order of gigabytes per hour using Exabyte 8mm tape. As with any piece of software, there are overheads, which means that the performance is not much better in some instances. In general, the small databases dump/load is no faster because of the amount of rpc traffic between the SQL Server and the backup server just to get the dump/load started. Figures I have seen for tens of megabytes of data show only modest improvement in the region of 10-20%. However, for large databases, the backup server will show improvement by factors of ten. My own experience of performance was a 350 MB database dump to disk in ten minutes and a similar time to load on a VAX 9000/40 workstation.

The backup server allows you to do the following.

- Dump and load across the network to another backup server running on a remote machine. From the performance viewpoint, the bottleneck will be the network.
- Stripe the dump across up to 32 dump devices in parallel.
- Dump across several tapes.
- Dump several dumps to the same tape. The load will load a single dump from the multidump tape.
- Support platform-specific tape handling characteristics.
- Replace the console program with sp_volchanged, making all facilities available from isql.

9.2 Installation

The backup server is installed when you install SQL Server. The entry SYB_BACKUP is created in sysservers and the interfaces file. As with any remote operation, if you are dumping to a remote backup server you need to copy its local interfaces entry to every interfaces file in the network. I always recommend that every interfaces file on each server is the same anyway, even if you are not interested in remote connections at present. If you want to share a backup server between SQL Servers, then share the interfaces file; do not modify sysservers.

Installation does not automatically start the backup server; you need to issue a startserver for the backup server. For simplicity, make sure that the same user starts the backup server and the SQL Server. At the least, make sure that the user who starts the backup server has write permission to the dump devices.

The SQL Server and the backup server communicate via remote procedure calls so, even on the same machine, you need to configure SQL Server for remote access to carry out dumps and loads. I see no problem in having it configured for remote access all of the time but if this is a problem for you, you can use **sp_configure** before and after the dump/load.

sp_configure

```
sp_configure "remote access", 1
go
reconfigure
go
dump/load
go
sp_configure "remote access", 0
go
reconfigure
go
```

Note that even if you are dumping to a remote backup server, you need to have a backup server running on the same machine as the SQL Server although the remote backup server does not need a SQL server on its machine. (Sybase licenses the backup server separately when it is functioning as a remote backup server.) The dump/load command must be made to a SQL server, which communicates with a local backup server to pass information on the dump/load. The local backup server then communicates directly with any remote backup servers.

9.3 Transaction Management

SQL Server operates a changes log, which means it records only the changes to each data page made by the transaction. The insert and delete are easy to visualize as they need to record the complete record in the log. The update is not as simple since most SQL Server updates are actioned as a delete followed by an insert. When the update is done "in place" so that the record does not physically move in the page, the log entry is a changes entry of the updated data only. If the update causes the record to move physically, there are two log entries for an update: the insert change and the delete change. The occasions when an update causes the record to move are covered in Appendix E.

9.3.1 Transaction

A transaction is a single unit of work in regards to modification to the database. It has a finite start and end point and may contain one or more commands against one or more databases. A single, stand-alone command is automatically a transaction in SQL Server. If you wish several such commands to be treated as a single transaction, you must enclose the commands in a transaction block.

begin tran, rollback tran, commit tran

```
UPDATE tab_1 SET col_1 = 15
BEGIN TRANSACTION
        INSERT INTO tab_2 VALUES (1, 5, 10)
        INSERT INTO tab_2 VALUES (2, 8, 10)
        UPDATE tab_3 SET ctrl = ctrl + 2
                WHERE key_col = 999
COMMIT TRANSACTION
```

The above shows two transactions: a stand-alone update and a multiple insert and update. The single statement transaction has an implicit begin/commit. For clarity, I shall continue the discussion by always showing the begin/commit block. The transaction management always records a begin and commit entry on the log so it helps to show them in the discussion.

So:

```
BEGIN TRAN
        UPDATE tab_1 SET x = 15
COMMIT TRAN
```

and

```
UPDATE tab_1 SET x = 15
```

are executed and logged identically. Of course, this applies to SQL Server transactions only (unchained transactions as discussed in section 8.1) as the ANSI standard transactions (chained transactions) do not require the explicit begin transaction and do not terminate until an explicit commit transaction. However, the log entries are the same regardless of the transaction mode and I will use the SQL Server transaction mode throughout this chapter.

A transaction may have two outcomes: it may complete correctly with a commit or it may meet a condition which requires it to go back to the beginning with a rollback. The rollback situation may occur as an abort because of external system failure or may be deliberately requested by the transaction because of an error condition.

```
BEGIN TRAN
        DECLARE @var_1 int
        UPDATE tab_2 SET entry = entry + 1
        SELECT @var_1 = count(*) FROM tab_1
        IF @var_1 = 0
        BEGIN
                PRINT 'no records'
                ROLLBACK TRAN
                RETURN
        END
COMMIT TRAN
```

The above transaction checks to see if there are records on the table. If not, it rolls the transaction back reversing the update at the beginning of the transaction. (I know that it's a foolish place to put the update, but it's only an example.) Note the return after the rollback to stop the transaction continuing processing. In this case, it does matter but rollback tran is simply another SQL command and execution continues with the next statement. This means that if you do not wish the rest of the transaction code to execute, you must put a return after the rollback.

The purpose of fixing the start and end of the transaction is to ensure that the effects of the transaction may be repeated or reversed if there is a failure. A transaction is an "atomic" event, which means that there is no in-between state with a transaction. It is all or nothing: either it happens or it does not.

```
BEGIN TRAN
        UPDATE tab_1 SET x = 15
                WHERE p_key = 123
        UPDATE tab_2 SET y = 20
                WHERE p_key = 687
        UPDATE tab_3 SET a = 157
                WHERE p_key = 10
COMMIT TRAN
```

During the transaction, none of the updates are made to the database and none of the updated pages are available to other transactions once each update has started. Each update takes an exclusive lock (XLOCK) on the data page in cache. This is retained until the commit so that no other transaction can have access to the page until the updating transaction has completed. (We will look at locking in more detail in Appendix F, but quite simply, we must lock until the commit as we have no guarantee that the transaction will not roll back and restore updated values back to their original state. Therefore, once XLOCKed, no other transaction gets to the data until the locking transaction has completed—commit or rollback.)

9.3.2 Log Records

Each update makes an entry in the transaction log and, at the commit, the log is flushed to disk before the data updates are written to disk. The log write is a force write to disk to guarantee that it gets there immediately, but the data writes are logical and are made under the control of the cache manager. Therefore, in normal circumstances, the only disk writes during the transaction are the forced log writes, as the data page updates occur whenever the cache manager (or checkpoint) requires them to. This normally will be outside the transaction boundary.

This sequence of events ensures that every completed transaction is logged to disk regardless of what happens in cache. Therefore, if recovery is required, the disk log may be used to roll back or roll forward, depending on the action of the transaction.

The sequence of events is:

1. log a BEGIN TRAN record;
2. for every modification to a page:
   log the modification;
   modify the page in cache;
3. log the COMMIT/ROLLBACK TRAN record
4. flush the log to disk;
5. release the locks on the cache pages.

Remember that in Unix, the only guarantee that a write reaches the disk immediately is when the device is defined as a raw partition, to prevent the Unix cache manager intercepting the write request. So if you want to be able to guarantee 100% recovery, make sure that you create the log device(s) as raw partitions.

The log information is written to the system table syslogs, which is a heap storage structure with no index. Therefore, all log records are written to the last page of syslogs. With multiple update transactions writing to syslogs, this creates "hot spot" contention on the transaction log. System 11 hase reduced this by creating private log caches per connection, which buffer the transaction log activity before it is written to the database transaction log. The log entries are classified as data rows by SQL Server but they do not have the same structure, as shown in Figure 9.1.

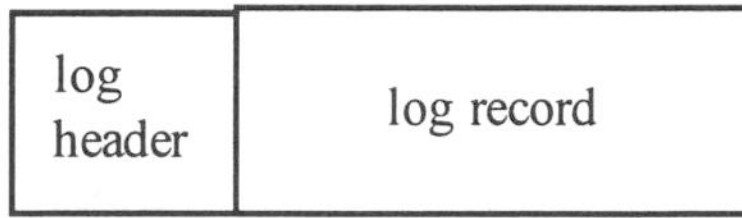

Figure 9.1 *Log record layout.*

where

log header	a 12 byte header containing: row number; log record type; transaction_id; length of row;
log record	a variable number of bytes containing the modified data. The SQL Server log is a logical log of what the change was and where it occurred. So a minimum of changed data with a page offset is recorded in the log record. This functions as both a before image (BI) for rollback and an after image (AI) for roll forward.

The various log records for a transaction are related by the transaction_id, which is the record_id of the begin tran log record. Because the records in syslogs are not like other data rows, you will not get readable output from a select statement. Although regular "select count(*) from syslogs" will give you a good idea of how the log is growing, the recommended method of getting an accurate log size is DBCC:

```
dbcc checktable(syslogs)

Checking syslogs
The total number of pages in this table is 3.
*** NOTICE:  Space used on the log segment is 0.01 Mbytes, 0.29%.
*** NOTICE:  Space free on the log segment is 1.99 Mbytes, 99.71%
Table has 65 data rows.
DBCC execution completed. If DBCC printed error messages, contact a user with
System Administrator (SA) role.
```

Note that space used information is presented only if the log is defined on its own device.

Using sp_spaceused also gives a reasonably accurate size but this has a history of low accuracy on syslogs unless you have just done a checkpoint. A dbcc checktable is the more common approach although in System 10 I have found that **sp_helpsegment** on the logsegment gives an accurate indication of the log usage.

sp_helpsegment

```
sp_helpsegment logsegment
```

```
segment name                    status
2       logsegment              0

device                  size                    free_pages
data2_log               18.0MB                  9216
data_log                50.0MB                  24760
table_name              index_name              indid
syslogs                 syslogs                 0
```

The name of the device which contains the first page of the log is displayed using **sp_helplog**.

sp_helplog

```
sp_helplog
```

```
sp_helplog
In database "fred_db", the log starts on device "data_dev1".
```

Note that all page modifications are logged, which includes not only the data pages but any associated index updates.

Consider the tables:

```
CREATE TABLE tab_1 ( a int, b int, c int )
CREATE INDEX ind_1 on tab_1(a)
CREATE INDEX ind_2 on tab_1(c, b)
```

The insert:

```
INSERT INTO tab_1 VALUES (1, 2, 3)
```

will create the log records:

- begin tran
- index page ind_1
- index page ind_2
- data page tab_1
- commit tran.

Of course, if the index updates caused node splitting, there would be other index log records. These log records are then used by the recovery mechanism to recover the database from a failure.

9.4 Recovery

Consider the transaction of Figure 9.2 which inserts three records with the appropriate data log records.

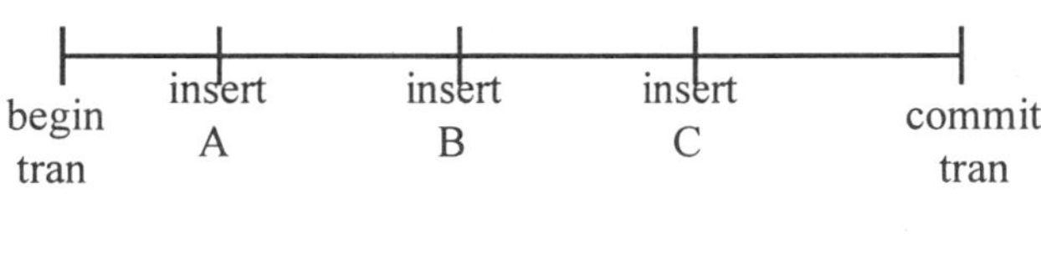

log records	begin tran	insert A log	insert B log	insert C log	commit tran

Figure 9.2 *Transaction log records.*

9.4.1 Media Failure

If we have a media failure and need to restore the effect of this transaction, we simply redo the logs of the inserts; that is, post the page changes to the appropriate page offsets. This roll forward is the recovery used when there has been a media failure that has lost the current version of the database. A previous database dump is reloaded and the completed transactions from the transaction log reposted to this dump. In logical terms, we post the after images of the changes from the transaction log. This brings the restored dump up to the state of the last completed transaction written to the log.

9.4.2 System Failure

When a system failure occurs, the transactions currently executing cannot complete and any information in cache may be lost. Because the transaction has not completed, we do not know what stage the transaction has reached and what effect the transaction has had on the data. The safest thing is to roll the transaction back to the start, restoring the database to its state prior to the start of the transaction, as if it had not taken place.

When a system failure occurs, the rollback procedure is invoked for each currently executing transaction. and the log records posted to the database to restore it to its state prior to the start of the transaction. In logical terms, we post the before image of the changes from the transaction log.

The combination of dumps and log records allows roll forward from a media failure that has corrupted the database or roll back from a system failure that has not damaged the database but has lost the currently executing transactions.

9.4.3 Deferred Updating

Additional log activity occurs when a long-running transaction updates many records. The simple update command:

```
UPDATE CUSTOMER SET X = X + 5
```

will change every record in the CUSTOMER table. This is handled by not actioning the updates immediately but deferring them to the commit time. Deferred updating writes the row IDs of the records to be updated to the log instead of directly updating the data record in the page. The log is then reread at the commit and the records updated. A more complete explanation of deferred updating is given in section 12.4

9.4.4 Checkpoint

At first glance, everything appears OK but an important fact of the system failure is that the data cache is lost. This can contain several of the data record updates which completed transactions have issued. Remember that at the commit point, the log is flushed from cache to disk but the data record updates are deliberately left in cache to be paged out as required by the cache manager. We do this to save physical disk access to improve performance. Unfortunately, it complicates our recovery.

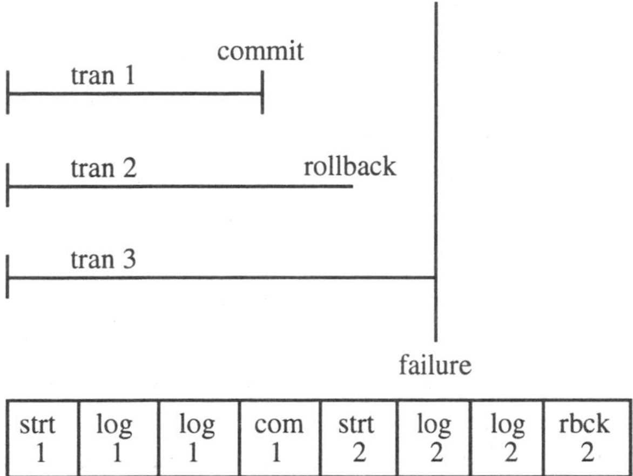

***Figure 9.3** Disk log at failure point.*

In the scenario shown in Figure 9.3, the recovery system can only assume that no action is required for transactions 1 and 2 as they have been completed and written to disk. However, although the log records have been written to disk, the efficient cache management system has not yet identified all of the updates or before images of transactions 1 and 2 as needing to be paged out of cache yet. So the database does not accurately reflect the updated versions of transactions 1 and 2. In fact, we do not know what the state of the database is as we do not know which pages have been written to disk. Consequently, the recovery system needs a point in time at which it can be sure that all updated cache pages have been flushed to disk. This is called a **checkpoint**.

At a checkpoint, the buffer manager flushes all "dirty" pages in the cache to disk and writes a checkpoint record to the log. When a system failure occurs now, the recovery routine knows that any updates before the last checkpoint entry in the log have been actioned and it need take action on only those transactions after the checkpoint. System 11 has introduced a "housekeeping task" that uses system interactivity periods to write "dirty" pages to disk. This can help reduce the disk activity at a checkpoint.

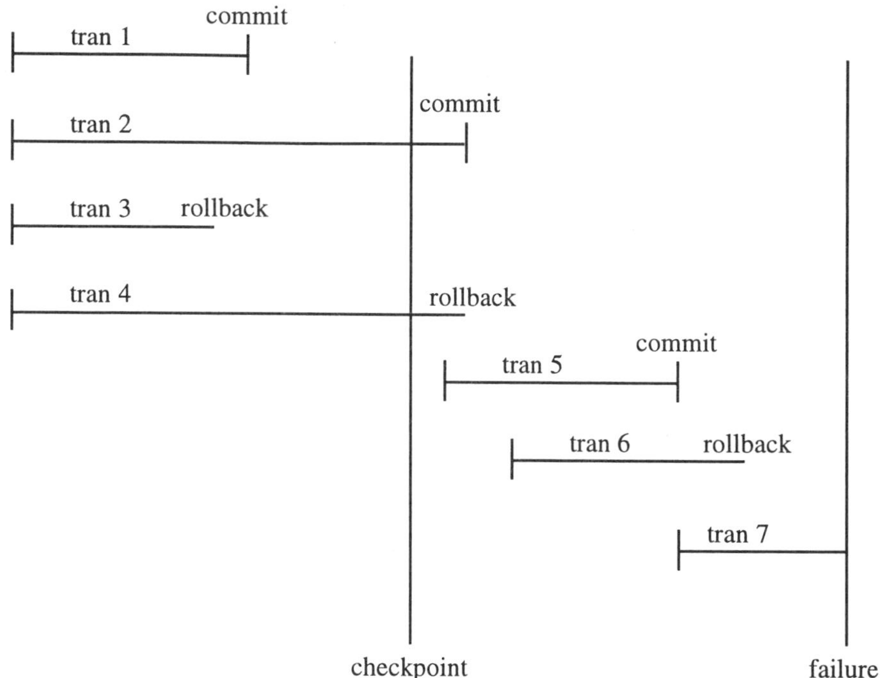

Figure 9.4 *Checkpoint recovery.*

If we consider the situation shown in Figure 9.4, transactions 1 and 3 completed before the checkpoint and therefore no recovery action is necessary.

Transaction 2 committed after the checkpoint and we are not sure if all the updates reached the disk, so we roll it forward after the checkpoint. SQL Server does not duplicate writes as the internal mechanism checks to see if the write for that log record made it to disk.

Transactions 5, 6 and 7 started and ended after the checkpoint, so the system will roll forward and roll back respectively.

Transaction 4 completed after the checkpoint but there is no guarantee that the posting initiated by the rollback reached the disk, so roll it back again. The complete transaction needs to be rolled back in this case because the rollback action occurred after the checkpoint, so there is no guarantee that any of the original rolled back pages reached the disk. No data page updates go to disk directly; they all go via the cache manager.

Let's look at this one in a bit more detail as in Figure 9.5.

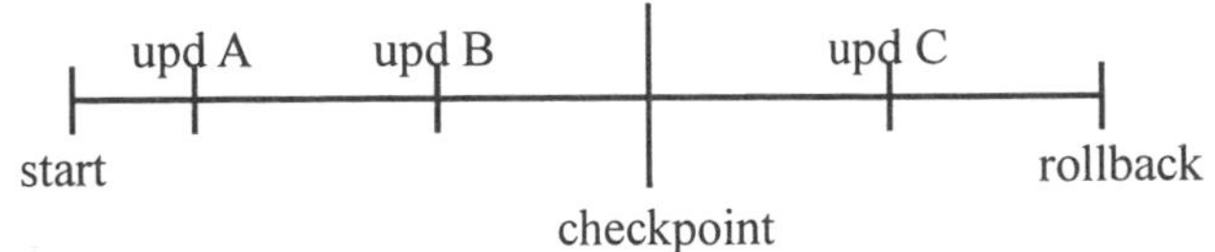

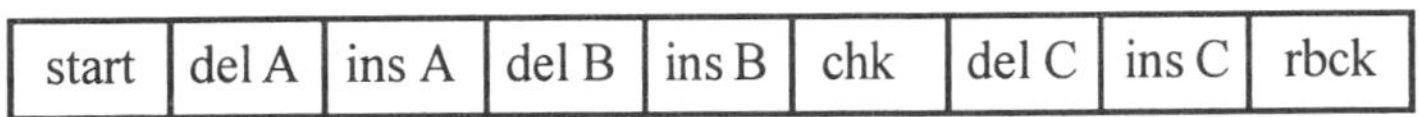

Figure 9.5 *Backup Procedures.*

The only guarantee that something is on disk is before the checkpoint, which means that the only guarantee of the data on disk is the updated versions of A and B. Because the rollback portion of the transactions occurred after the checkpoint, all of the rollback pages may still be sitting in cache. So this transaction must be rolled back to the beginning.

The actual mechanics of recovery are a little more complicated than simply rolling forward or back based on relative position to the checkpoint record. Such a recovery scenario is valid only for a BI/AI style log, which is not the case in SQL Server. Therefore, additional checks—mainly based on timestamp checks—are required for the relevant log records to determine if they should be applied to disk.

The checkpoint takes place at a regular interval, as defined by the recovery interval set by sp_configure. The default interval is five minutes and the server uses this as the amount of time it should take to recover. After the server accumulates five minutes of data to recover, a checkpoint is taken. The checkpoint process is invoked once a minute to check how much work is required to recover each database. If this is greater than the recovery interval, a checkpoint is initiated for the database. The calculation is based on the number of log records since the last checkpoint multiplied by 10 msecs.

Note that the recovery interval is not a maximum figure for recovery. If you create update transactions which run for hours, then they will take a long time to roll back if they fail just before they are finished. The recovery interval is set using sp_configure:

```
sp_configure "recovery interval", 3
go
```

The SA or DBO can issue a checkpoint at any time.

```
go
CHECKPOINT
go
```

9.4.5 Page Locking

Since the log record is the changed bytes in the page as an offset from the start of the page, this means that page level locking is crucial to the SQL Server recovery. In a page with two records, if we delete the second and add a new record, the third record takes the place of the deleted one and now starts at the same offset as the record just deleted. As long as the page is locked while the deletion takes place, everything is OK because the actions are serial, so any recovery is serial in the same sequence. But if we allow the insert of the new record to take place before the delete completes—as in record level locking—a rollback of the delete will corrupt the data in the page because the deleted record will replace valid data.

This is similar to the standard uncommitted dependency problem of concurrency but the effect is different. We do not just lose data updates in a record but actually corrupt the page contents, which are now attempting to start two records at the same offset in the page.

Sybase gives many reasons for not implementing record level locking but this is one that they do not discuss often; it will make it difficult and costly to change from page level locking.

9.5 Backup Procedures

The transaction log, checkpoint and rollback guarantee recovery and data integrity when there is a system failure that does not destroy any data. We now need to have a set of procedures which will guarantee recovery and data integrity when there is a media failure that destroys data on the disk.

To do this, we require a dump of the database at a point in time and a dump of the transaction log records since that point in time. The recovery mechanism can then reload the database dump and roll forward the completed transactions from the dump of the transaction log in order to restore the data in the database to the last completed transaction before the failure.

9.5.1 Backup Server Operation

Figure 9.6 illustrates the local communication between SQL Server and backup server.

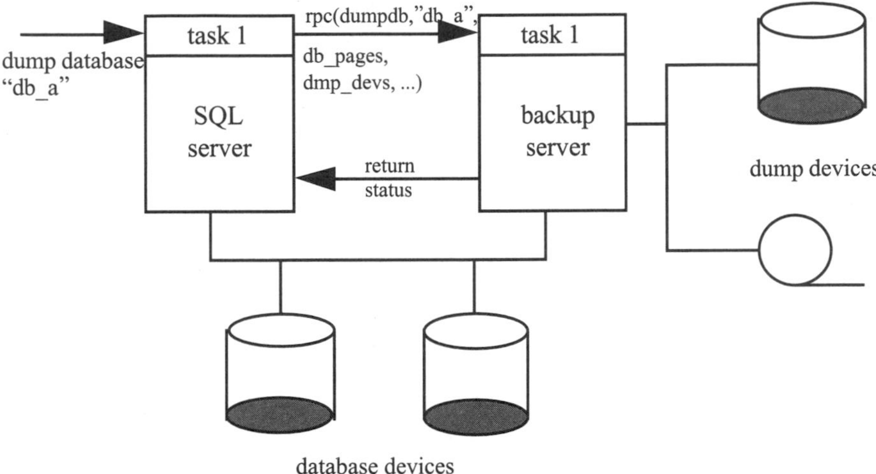

Figure 9.6 *SQL Server to backup server communication.*

A user issues a **dump database** in isql causing SQL Server to issue rpcs to the local backup server, telling it (among other information):

- action of dump or load;
- which database;
- the dump devices involved.

The local backup server then reads the database pages from the database devices and writes them to the dump devices or sends them across the network to a remote backup server which writes them to the dump devices. The reverse is actioned for load. The SQL server no longer has any involvement in the disk activity associated with the dump/load; everything is carried out by the backup server. The rpc approach means that the dump is now doing the disk I/O asynchronously and not blocking out any other SQL Server tasks.

9.5.2 Dump Devices

Dump devices are defined using the system procedure **sp_addumpdevice** and create an entry in sysdevices in master.

sp_addumpdevice

```
sp_addumpdevice        type,
                       logical_name,
                       physical_name
                       [, tape_capacity]
```

where

type	specifies if the dump device is "tape" or "disk" (the quotes are necessary);
tape_capacity	a value in megabytes to indicate multivolume tapes for some operating systems such as Unix;

To define a tape dump device:

```
sp_addumpdevice "tape", "tape_1", "/dev/rmt4", 100
```

To define a disk dump device:

```
sp_addumpdevice, "disk", "disk_1",
          "/usr/u/dump.dir/disk.dump"
```

To drop a dump device, use the system procedure **sp_dropdevice** as for any device.

sp_dropdevice

```
sp_dropdevice logical_name
```

This simply removes the pointer to an operating system file; it does not delete the physical file. You need to delete this from the operating system to free up the disk space.

If you have more than one tape drive and you would like to dump to multiple devices, you need to define the separate tape dump devices with unique controller types.

```
sp_addumpdevice "tape", "tape_2", "/dev/rmt4", 3, 100
go
sp_addumpdevice 'tape", "tape_3", "/dev/rmt5", 4, 100
go
```

9.5.3 Dump Database

We can now use the dump device to dump the database and/or the transaction log. The database is dumped using the command **dump database**. This is now a very involved command, so I shall discuss the syntax in stages relevant to the new features. The basic:

dump database

```
DUMP DATABASE db_name TO dump_device_name
```

causes SQL Server to:

- instruct the backup server to dump the database: data and log;
- send the backup server a list of pages changed by transactions since the dump started to enable backup server to dump these pages;
- instructs the backup server to dump any log pages written during the dump.

```
DUMP DATABASE fred TO "/dev/rmtln"
```

This also illustrates that you may use the logical or physical device name in the dump and load commands. When dumping to a remote backup server, you must use the operating system file name.

```
DUMP DATABASE fred_db TO diskdumpl_dev

Backup Server session id: 15. Use this value when executing the sp_volchanged
system stored procedure after fulfilling any volume change request from the back-
up server.
Backup Server: 6.28.1.1: Dump file name 'mark_db94255AB650'
section number 0001 mounted on disk dka500:[testdir]diskdumpdev.dat

Backup server: 4.58.1.1: Database fred_db: 4716 Kilobytes DUMPed
Backup server: 4.58.1.1: Database fred_db: 16942 Kilobytes DUMPed
Backup server: 4.58.1.1: Database fred_db: 36542 Kilobytes DUMPed
.
.
.
Backup server: 4.58.1.1: Database fred_db: 193298 Kilobytes DUMPed

Backup server: 3.43.1.1: Dump phase number 1 completed.
Backup server: 3.43.1.1: Dump phase number 2 completed.
Backup server: 3.43.1.1: Dump phase number 3 completed.
```

```
Backup server: 4.58.1.1: Database fred_db: 193428 Kilobytes DUMPed.
Backup server: 3.42.1.1: DUMP is complete (database fred_db).
```

When a dump command is issued, SQL Server sends rpcs to:

- obtain the session ID;
- announce the dump;
- send each logical to physical database mapping;
- send details of each dump device;
- write the dump header;
- begin the dump;
- end the dump;
- send flushed pages.

During the dump, the memory resident list of flush pages is checked periodically. If it is full, the contents are sent to the backup server to dump these pages. When a flush list becomes full, the server starts another one.

One aspect of the dump has changed: the dump instance is now at the end of the dump. In version 4.x, the dump instance was at the beginning of the dump. This means that there is less blocking of transactions while the dump is running and the dump is more up-to-date as a long-running dump now reflects the database at the end of the dump, not as it was when the dump started (which may have been several hours earlier). However, as useful as this is, changing the dump instance time still does not provide any synchronization of multiple database dumps.

Note that the backup server requires nonrewinding tape devices, which is specified in Unix with a "n" after "/dev"

The SQL Server dump is a logical dump, which means that it dumps used pages only. So in a 100 MB database, if only 60 MB are used, the dump is only of that 60 MB. (These arbitrary figures interest you? You are an SA. Think problems when you see anything on databases. If there is a table of 30 MB in this database, we are running close to not being able to create a clustered index because of the free space figure.) This may seem like a useful feature but it means that the restore of the dump is not writing every page of the database space. Therefore, the unused pages that are not overwritten by the restore must be initialized.

This also means that you cannot reduce the size of a database using dump and load. In an active database there is no guarantee where the unused pages occur, so you cannot restore a dump onto a smaller database.

You can, of course, use the operating system disk backup utilities to back up every disk that the database resides on. You must dump the complete disk space but with a database using the majority of its disk space, this is not a problem. Operating system backups need the database to be off-line but often the speed benefit can justify this.

9.5.4 Dump Striping

```
DUMP DATABASE   db_name
                TO dev_name
                [ STRIPE ON stripe_devname
                [ STRIPE ON stripe_devname]...]
```

```
DUMP DATABASE fred
        TO disk_dump_1
        STRIPE ON disk_dump_2
        STRIPE ON disk_dump_3
```

The database is divided into the appropriate portions (as equally as possible) and each portion is dumped to the named dump device. This speeds up the dump (and load) by introducing an element of parallelism into the dump activity and reduces the number of tape changes required during a large dump. You can stripe the dump across different device types. These may be a mixture of local and remote if you so wish. Up to 32 devices may be used and the load may be made from a different number of devices than the dump was striped on. The same device types are needed for each stripe, of course, but the use of ANSI format volume headers means that the system prompts for the correct tapes.

The backup server spawns an open server thread for each dump device so a few large, fast devices are recommended for optimum backup server performance.

9.5.5 Remote Backup

```
DUMP DATABASE   db_name
                TO dev_name [AT rem_serv_name]
                [ STRIPE ON stripe_devname [AT rem_serv_name]
                [ STRIPE ON stripe_devname [AT rem_serv_name]...]]
```

```
DUMP DATABASE fred_db
        TO "/dev/rmt1" AT glenlivet
        STRIPE ON "/dev/rmt2" AT glenlivet
        STRIPE ON "/dev/rmt3" AT lagavulin
```

The backup server sends the pages across the network to a remote backup server, which dumps the pages to the named dump device. When striping the dump as above, every device must quote the server name. If you omit the remote server name, the backup server will attempt to locate the dump device at the local server. As mentioned above, you must use the operating system file name when dumping to a remote backup server.

Any messages (such as volume change) during a dump/load are sent to the client or terminal session which issued the dump/load command. This may not be the best place to send such messages when dumping remotely, so a notify clause is used to specify the destination of messages during the dump/load.

```
DUMP DATABASE  db_name
        TO dev_name
        WITH NOTIFY = {client|operator_console}
```

where

client	the default of the originating client/terminal;
operator_console	the terminal or workstation where the remote backup server is running.

9.5.6 Platform-specific Options

Density, Blocksize and Capacity

```
DUMP DATABASE  db_name
        TO dev_name
               [DENSITY = value,
                BLOCKSIZE = value,
                CAPACITY = value]
```

where

density	the recording density of a tape dump device;
blocksize	any blocksize accepted by the device;
capacity	kilobyte value indicating the maximum amount of data that can be written to a tape. Used for systems that cannot recognize end of tape markers. The backup server will request a volume change when it reaches the specified capacity value.
These may be specified separately for each stripe device.	

Except for special dump devices, you should not really need to specify any of these values. SQL Server will automatically use the operating system defaults and, in the case of blocksize, it will choose what it considers to be the optimum value.

9.5.7 Tape Handling Options

```
DUMP DATABASE db_name
        TO dev_name
                [dumpvolume = volume_name]
        [WITH{[dismount|nodismount],
                [nounload|unload],
                retaindays = value,
                [noinit|init],
                file = file_name,
                [notify = {client|operator_console}]}]
```

where

dumpvolume = volume_name	assigns a volume name to the tape label which is checked at load. Try to assign this, as the default volume name contains hexadecimal characters and is not particularly readable. This value is checked by the load database.
dismount|nodismount	the use of nodismount on systems such as VMS which support logical dismount leaves the tape mounted for further dumping. Default is dismount. This parameter has no effect in Unix.
nounload|unload	unload rewinds and unloads the tape. The default is nounload.

retaindays=value	specifies the number of days which must elapse before the tape may be overwritten. The default is the tape retention set by sp_configure.
noinit|init	specifies whether the volume should be overwritten. The default is noinit, which appends to the end of the tape.
file = file_name	the name of the dump file. Default is the concatenation of: last 7 characters of database name; 2 digit year number; 3 digit day of year; hex dump file create time.

The initialization and unload options allow multiple dumps to the same tape volume. The steps are:

1. first dump with init option (default is nounload);
2. subsequent dumps with defaults (noinit and nounload);
3. last dump with unload option.

The full dump database syntax is:

```
DUMP DATABASE db_name
        TO device_name [at server_name]
                [DENSITY = value,
                BLOCKSIZE = value,
                CAPACITY = value,
                DUMPVOLUME = vol_name]
        [, STRIPE ON device_name [at server_name]
                [DENSITY = value,
                BLOCKSIZE = value,
                CAPACITY = value,
                DUMPVOLUME = vol_name]
        [, STRIPE ON device_name [at server_name]
                [DENSITY = value,
                BLOCKSIZE = value,
                CAPACITY = value,
                DUMPVOLUME = vol_name]...]]
        [WITH {[dismount|nodismount],
                        [nounload|unload],
                        retaindays = value,
                        [noinit|init],
                        file = file_name
                        [notify = {client|oper_console}]}]
```

Note that the device name may be physical device names as well as logical names.

The database name in dump/load may be supplied as the contents of a variable. This was implemented to allow a parameterized dump tran in the threshold procedures. This is excellent news but one may wonder why Sybase has not extended this to the DML statements to make life easier in generic procedures that are not sure of the database/table/column names until the procedure executes.

9.5.8 Dump Transaction

Dumping a large database frequently is a significant overhead so you do not want to dump the database too often. However, you do not want to leave the system running for too long before taking some sort of security dump. If you dump the database every morning, the last thing the user wants to hear when the system crashes at 16:00 hours is that you can bring back the database only as at the start of the day.

We need to dump the transaction log regularly so that the possible unrecoverable period is minimized. Because the transaction log is smaller than the database, it does not take as long to dump and does not interfere with the transactions as it is unconcerned with the data pages. There is still a disk activity overhead but this is one that you will have to suffer. Keep the log and dump devices on physical disks that are not used by the rest of the system in order to avoid the increased disk activity having a direct effect on data access. And if peak activity is 10:00 to 11:00, dump the log at 09:30 and 11:30.

The transaction log is dumped using the **dump transaction** command, which uses the same clauses as dump database. Striping, remote dumping and tape handling are all available.

dump transaction

```
DUMP TRAN db_name
        {WITH truncate_only|no_log}|
        TO device_name [at server_name]
                [DENSITY = value,
                BLOCKSIZE = value,
                CAPACITY = value,
                DUMPVOLUME = vol_name]
        [, STRIPE ON device_name [at server_name]
```

```
        [DENSITY = value,
        BLOCKSIZE = value,
        CAPACITY = value,
        DUMPVOLUME = vol_name]
[, STRIPE ON device_name [at server_name]
        [DENSITY = value,
        BLOCKSIZE = value,
        CAPACITY = value,
        DUMPVOLUME = vol_name]...]]
[WITH   {[dismount|nodismount],
               [nounload|unload],
               retaindays = value,
               [noinit|init],
               file = file_name,
               no_truncate
               [, notify = {client|oper_console}]}]
```

There are two differences between the dump transaction and the dump database SQL Server uses to back up server communication. The dump tran has only one connection to the backup server and there is only one dump phase. The difference is simply that there is no need for the flush list pages, so the additional connection/dump phase is not necessary.

9.5.9 Dump Transaction Options

The regular dump transaction:

```
DUMP TRANSACTION fred TO dump_dev
```

dumps the complete transaction log, clears out all transactions which finished before the oldest open transaction, and checkpoints the database. Regular transaction dumping keeps the log tidy and keeps its size down. This stops the log filling up, which is an excellent reason for regular transaction dumps. Note that because open transactions cannot be cleared out, a long-running maintenance transaction can fill the log. You will not be able to clear out transactions which completed after the start of the long-running transaction.

Dump transaction has three additional options which offer variations on this, depending on the circumstances of the dump.

with truncate_only

This option does not dump the log to the dump device but simply clears out the log and takes a checkpoint. This is the option you use if you have a small database for which you are dumping the database only. Doing a dump transaction immediately before the dump database will make the database dump go faster because the log is nearly empty. You are not allowed to run a database without a log but, in this case, you are not interested in the contents of the log and do not intend to use the recovery system to restore from a log, so use this option to purge the log.

with no_log

You do not want to be in the position to have to use this option. This is the option to use when the log has filled up and there is no more space to continue working. When the log is full, no more work can be done against the database and the system using the database stops. You need to dump the log to clear it out so that work may continue but unfortunately the dump tran tries to write a record to the log. The no_log option simply dumps and clears the log without writing a dump tran record. Unfortunately, because the transaction log dump does not have a dump tran record, it cannot be used in a recovery sequence. Therefore, normal roll forward from the transaction log is not possible after a dump tran with no_log and you need to take an immediate dump database to guarantee full recovery.

with no_truncate

The regular dump transaction requires the database to be intact. Unfortunately, when the database fail, there will be a portion of the log still on disk but not dumped. The no_truncate option does not need the database to be intact and allows you to dump the current log of a damaged database. It does need the log to be on a separate device from the database and you must run it before you drop the faulty database. If this dump is successful—and there is no guarantee as you are in an error situation—you will be able to recover the database up to the last completed transaction. If the no_truncate dump is not successful, you will be able to recover only up to the last transaction in the previous transaction dump. This is another reason for keeping the interval between transaction dumps as short as you can.

After using dump tran with the no_log or truncate_only options, any subsequent changes cannot be used to recover from a media failure since a portion of the log has been discarded or has no dump checkpoint record. You must dump the database after using these options, so do not let the operational log fill up.

Some commands (high speed bulk copy, select into and truncate) do not write page modifications to the log. In general, a command that operates at the page level instead of the record level is not logged. A dump database is necessary after these commands. A dump transaction to archive will be disallowed and similarly any automatic dump script which contains a dump transaction will fail. Keep "select into" away from users in the operational databases, as it will cause the regular dump transaction to archive to fail. Not a good idea.

Create index is special as far as recovery is concerned. Because the command causes a large number of modifications, these are not logged but the actual command is. This means that the load transaction recovery can take as long to reconstruct the index as the original create index took to build it. This can take a long time, which you probably want to avoid during recovery. Dump the database after large index builds, not because the index cannot be recovered but because it may take a long time.

9.6 Volume Handling Requirements

When volumes need to be changed, the backup server sends messages to the terminal specified in the "with notify" clause to indicate that the volume needs to be changed.

The system procedure **sp_volchanged** is used to indicate to backup server that the volume has been changed.

sp_volchanged

```
sp_volchanged         session_id,
                      device_name,
                      action
                      [, file_name
                      [, volume_name]]
```

where

session_id	the backup server session which requested the volume change;
device_name	the name of the device that is to receive the volume change. If the backup server is not on the same machine as the SQL Server, you must use the format **device_name at backup_server_name**.
action	specifies how the backup server should proceed. The accepted actions—proceed, retry, abort—are listed in the message which requested the volume change.

file_name	specifies the file on the tape to be used by backup server;
volume_name	specifies the volume name field of the ANSI tape label.

The session ID and device name are contained in the message sent by the backup server.

When the sp_volchanged has to be run by the same user who initiated the dump/load, another isql session will have to be started as the original session is tied up with the dump/load command.

When dumping the sybsystemprocs database, make sure that it can be contained in a single dump device. This means that you do not need to change a volume as you cannot use sp_volchanged while loading the sybsystemprocs dump. (Or keep a copy of sp_volchanged in master.)

9.7 Restore Procedures

9.7.1 Load Database

When a media failure occurs, the database is unusable and needs to be restored to its current status from the database and transaction dumps. The first step is to load the latest dump of the database using **load database**.

load database

```
LOAD DATABASE db_name
        FROM device_name [at server_name]
                [DENSITY = value,
                BLOCKSIZE = value,
                DUMPVOLUME = vol_name]
        [, STRIPE ON device_name [at server_name]
                [DENSITY = value,
                BLOCKSIZE = value,
                DUMPVOLUME = vol_name]
        [, STRIPE ON device_name [at server_name]
                [DENSITY = value,
                BLOCKSIZE = value,
                DUMPVOLUME = vol_name]...]]
        [WITH   {[dismount|nodismount],
                        [nounload|unload],
                        file = file_name,
                        listonly [= full],
                        headeronly,
                        notify = {client|oper_console}}]
```

where

listonly [= full]	displays dump file information but does not load the data base. Information displayed without the full option is data base, device, dump date/time and overwrite date/time.
headeronly	displays header information about the first dump file, or the named file, but does not load the database. Information dis played is database or log dump, database ID, file name, dump date, character set, sort order, page count and next object ID.

The load is the simplest of them all as no phase logic applies. The dump has written all the most up-to-date versions of the pages to the dump device, so the load simply writes them back to the disk. Because the tapes are using standard ANSI headers, the load will prompt for the tapes in the correct sequence.

The database that is being restored with load database cannot be in use by any users. This includes yourself so make sure that you are in master when you issue this command.

```
LOAD DATABASE fred_db FROM diskdump2_dev

Backup server session ID is: 30 Use this value when executing the 'sp_volchanged'
system stored procedure after fulfilling any volume change request from Backup
Server.

Backup server: 6.28.1.1 Dump file name 'mark_db94270c2d90'
section number 0001 mounted on 'dka500:[testdir]diskdump2_dev.dat

Backup server: 4.58.1.1 Database fred_db: 6114 Kilobytes loaded
Backup server: 4.58.1.1 Database fred_db: 34832 Kilobytes loaded
.
.
Backup server: 4.58.1.1 Database fred_db: 389122 Kilobytes loaded

Backup server 3.42.1.1 LOAD is complete (database fred_db)
```

When a media failure occurs, you may not be able to load the database from the dump because the database is marked as suspect by the server. In this case, you need to drop the database and recreate it before you can run load database. The create should use the **for load** option to save you time. Both the create database and load database initialize the data pages; the use of the for load option in create database suppresses this and saves the page initialization being done twice. However, the standard drop database command may not execute because the database is marked as suspect so you may need to use **dbcc dbrepair**.

dbcc dbrepair

```
dbcc dbrepair(db_name, dropdb)
```

Be careful when you recreate the database in this sequence as the database definition in the system tables must be as it was when the database was dumped. If the initial allocation was:

```
CREATE DATABASE fred ON dev_1 = 6 LOG ON dev_1 = 2
WITH OVERRIDE
```

and then altered as:

```
ALTER DATABASE fred ON dev_1 = 4
WITH OVERRIDE
```

the allocation of the database will be as in Figure 9.7.

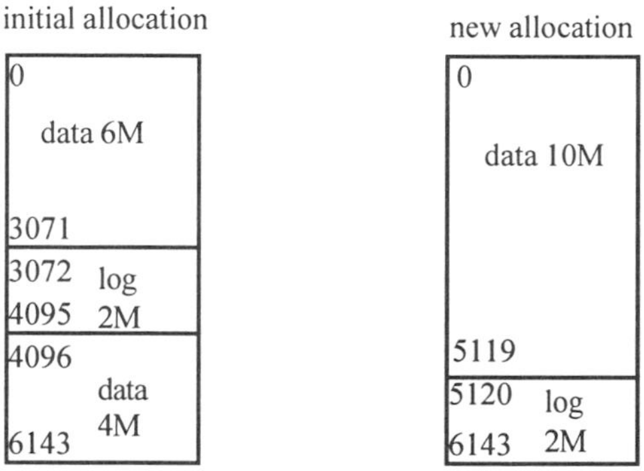

initial allocation
0 data 6M 3071
3072 log 4095 2M
4096 data 4M 6143

new allocation
0 data 10M 5119
5120 log 6143 2M

Figure 9.7 *Incorrect load allocations.*

If we recreate the database as:

```
CREATE DATABASE fred ON dev_1 = 10 LOGON dev_1 = 2
WITH OVERRIDE
```

loading the logical page numbers of the initial allocation into the new allocation will give errors because log pages and data pages are being misplaced. This also applies to user-defined segments on the database. Make sure that the definition of the recreated database matches the definition of the dump. This is an excellent reason for dumps of master and the relevant database after altering a database allocation of devices or segments.

Unfortunately, SQL Server does not tell you during the load that this mismatch of data and log pages is happening (to be fair, it does not know without checking the allocations and the page contents). It is only reported when you run a dbcc checkalloc, so make sure that any create before a load specifies the same allocations as the dump.

9.7.2 Load Transaction

Having restored the latest dump of the database, it will be out-of-date as it does not include all of the transactions which took place from the last dump database. This is unavoidable and is catered for by regular transaction log dumps, which can then be recovered in sequence against the reloaded database. This is done with the **load transaction** command.

load transaction

```
LOAD TRANSACTION db_name
       FROM device_name [at server_name]
              [DENSITY = value,
              BLOCKSIZE = value,
              DUMPVOLUME = vol_name]
       [ STRIPE ON device_name [at server_name]
              [DENSITY = value,
              BLOCKSIZE = value,
              DUMPVOLUME = vol_name]
       [ STRIPE ON device_name [at server_name]
              [DENSITY = value,
              BLOCKSIZE = value,
              DUMPVOLUME = vol_name]...]]
       [WITH  {[dismount|nodismount],
                     [nounload|unload],
                     file = file_name,
                     listonly [= full],
                     headeronly,
                     notify = {client|oper_console}}]
```

The transaction log dumps since the last database dump must be loaded in sequence against the loaded database with no gaps. SQL Server helps as it checks the sequence of the reloaded transaction logs but it will not recover without all of the transactions logs, so do not lose one. Make sure that your operations staff label the tapes in such a manner that it is obvious which transaction dumps are linked with which database dumps and what the sequence of transaction dumps is.

Of course, failure always occurs at the most awkward moment. You must make use of the **with no_truncate** option of the dump transaction command to ensure that you can restore up to the last completed transaction. A dump scenario of:

- dump database at 6:00 am;
- dump transaction every two hours during on-line system;
- dump database at 6:00 pm;
- carry out overnight batch processing;
  will give you a distinct problem when the media failure occurs at 5:50 pm. There will be a valid database dump at 6:00 am with transaction dumps every two hours until 4:00 pm, but the period between 4:00 pm and 5:50 pm has not been dumped and therefore cannot be used in the recovery which will leave about two hours of transactions unrecovered. As discussed, the dump transaction has an option **with no_truncate** which does no checking with the database but simply dumps the current transaction log. This option of dump transaction is essential to ensure that recovery can be made up to the last completed transaction. This should be the first thing that you do when a media failure occurs. The whole server is in an unstable condition—some of the disks are unusable—so do not get clever. Dump transaction with no_truncate and then you can mess about to see if you can ascertain what is wrong.

The sequence on media failure is:

```
DUMP TRANSACTION db_name
        TO log_dev_dump with no_truncate
LOAD DATABASE db_name FROM db_dump_device
LOAD TRANSACTION db_name FROM log_dev_dump
repeat the load transaction
until all transaction logs restored
```

If the dump transaction with no_truncate is successful, the database will be restored up to the last completed transaction. If the dump transaction with no_truncate fails—and you have no guarantee that it will work as the database is not intact—the database will be restored up to the end of the last regular transaction dump.

9.8 Summary

Backup and recovery in System 10/11 has been significantly improved with the introduction of the backup server. The backup server has removed all of the timing problems of database dumps and loads. In general, you can now dump as fast as the physical devices will allow you to. With the ability to stripe the dump in parallel across multiple physical devices, you no longer need to lose any sleep about how long it takes—just ask the boss for more dump devices. Of course, the load is not quite as fast as the dump as it still has to initialize the unused pages, but there is no way around this and you will be pleasantly surprised by the speed improvements.

Moving the dump instance to be the end of the dump is also beneficial as more currently executing transactions can be included in the dump, which reduces the amount of blocking when you need to run an on-line dump.

10

The Optimizer

This chapter describes the System 10 optimizer. Because of the number of changes, and the importance of this topic, I have not just listed the System 10 features but have given a full treatment of the subject. The chapter first gives a definition of the various terms and explanations of how they effect the optimization. This is followed by two detailed optimization sections: one on the simpler optimization plans of single tables and joins and the other on the more complicated plans of nested statements.

Changes in the System 11 optimizer—mainly presentation of the showplan and subquery optimization—are detailed in Chapter 12.

COMMAND SYNTAX

```
update statistics
```

SYSTEM PROCEDURE SYNTAX

```
sp_recompile
```

10.1 Introduction

There have been many changes and improvements in the System 10 optimizer—some of which have been fitted to 4.9.2—so I have treated this subject from scratch and given a full description of all of the optimization plans. This means that a lot of the material is a duplication of my previous book on version 4, but I think it would have been rather disjointed to simply list the changes. Also, I believe it will be worthwhile to suffer the repetition as System 10 has several useful improvements, especially in the use of covered indexes, which will prove interesting.

The optimizer is that extremely useful piece of server software which decides how to access the data to retrieve the records that satisfy the SQL statement. This decision is based on the available methods of accessing the data, such as the presence of indexes, and the "cost" of each access route based on estimates of the disk activity and CPU time.

There are three types of optimizer in general use.

1. positional — where the position of the selection criteria is used to choose the optimum execution plan. The assumption here is that the writer of the command will put the most selective criteria first in the command. This is usually true but open to error.

2. syntactical — where the optimizer uses the syntax of the selection criteria to choose the optimum execution plan. Each operator (=, >, between, etc.) is given a fixed percentage of records that will be retrieved, with equality being the most selective, a closed limit next, less than, greater than next and so on. This is not an unreasonable assumption but still liable to give a poor execution plan.

3. statistical — where the optimizer uses the statistics of the record distribution for the index to choose the optimum execution plan.This is the best option as it uses actual record distribution but is still incomplete in its implementation as the statistics are not dynamically updated and, on occasion, the statistical optimizer will revert to its roots of syntactical or positional.

SQL Server operates a statistical optimizer except when there are no available statistics for it to use, in which case it reverts to syntactical optimization.

10.2 Basic Terminology

10.2.1 Search Argument (sarg)

The format of the where clause search condition is crucial to the optimizer when it is deciding which indexes may be used to execute the SQL command. If the where clause search condition is not in the format called a **search argument** (sarg) then the index will not be considered, even if it is the most useful index for the command; that is, the least cost method of retrieving the records. There are a few exceptions to this, which I discuss later, but the general rule is: before the optimizer will even consider an index, the search condition must be in the format of a search argument.

The definition of a **search argument** is very specific.

	column	operator	expression
eg	VALUE	=	1500
	LIMIT	>	1200
	SALARY	>	1000 * 12

This is the only format which the optimizer will recognize as a search argument and attempt to look at an index. The valid operators are:

=	equals
>	greater than
<	less than
>=	greater than or equal to
<=	less than or equal to

like

between.

Note that != (not equal) is not considered a search argument operator and will always cause a table scan. In general, any use of a not operator causes a table scan as the optimizer assumes a nonselective match with the data; that is, a lot of records returned. If a search argument is not found in the selection clause, the optimizer will not use the index. (There are a few exceptions to this, such as min/max, order by, and count(*), which I deal with later.)

So:

```
salary * 12 > 12000
```

will not use an index on salary because salary * 12 is an expression, not a column.

```
SUBSTRING(name, 1, 4) = 'KIRK'
```

will not use an index on name because SUBSTRING(name, 1, 4) is an expression, not a column.

In the following table, the left hand column are not search arguments and, if you want an index to be used, you should write them as shown in the right hand column (although you may have no choice).

NOT search arguments	**search arguments**
150 = price * 12	150 / 12 = price
upper(name) = 'KIRKWOOD'	no equivalent: be careful with upper- and lowercase. If possible you can improve performance by converting on input.
qty + 10 > 200	qty > 200 - 10
firstname + ' ' + surname = "john kirkwood"	firstname = "john" and surname = "kirkwood"
ltrim(name) = 'kirkwood'	no equivalent: be careful with leading spaces. Always worth removing any possible leading spaces on input.

10.2.2 Statistics

Having decided that there is a valid search argument, the optimizer then has to evaluate the cost of using any available indexes. The estimate of the disk activity is based on the distribution statistics for the index. The index statistics provide the optimizer with the estimated number of records which will be retrieved for specific index values.

SQL Server keeps the statistics in a single page (often called the distribution page) which means that there is 2 K available to retain the statistics figures. Each entry in the page is an index key value so the number of entries is:

number of distribution steps (n) = page size ÷ key size.

The value of the index key at each nth position is then recorded in the distribution page. The maximum number of rows per step is:

number of rows per step = (number of rows - 1) ÷ number of steps.

If we are indexing on an alphabetic field for a table of 20 rows and six distribution steps, we have:

index field	rec id	statistics page	
		step	key value
A	1		
A	10	0	A
A	40	1	C
B	12	2	F
C	18	3	N
D	7	4	S
E	6	5	W
E	35		
F	21		
G	23		
H	9		
M	8		
N	64		
S	68		
S	73		
S	75		
S	108		
S	100		
T	25		
W	21		

Since we know that there are four keys in each row, we can now estimate that there are four steps fewer than F (eight records); one step between S and W (four records); and so on.

Notice the importance of the key size, which not only means a larger index but will give less accurate statistics. Because of this, the statistics are held on the first field only of a composite index. This means that the sequence of fields when you define the index is very important as it determines the field that the statistics will be collected on. To get the most useful statistics, it is important to place the field with the most distinct values as the first field in the index definition. At a very detailed level, it is worth noting that variable length columns are held as variable length in the distribution page, so the statistics for a large char column might be improved by defining it as varchar. Do not dash out and change all your char columns because of this; it's only if you are having serious problems with an index not being used on a large character column which you have defined as char(n).

So if you have nothing in the statement to determine the field significance, put the one with the most values as the most significant. In the extreme, if I wish to index on:

marital_status, name

the composite index (marital_status, name) will collect statistics against marital_status. As there are only a few values of marital_status, the statistics distribution will be close to useless and the index will look like an index on a field with few values. Such an index, when nonclustered, will normally do a table scan regardless of the selectivity of the enquiry because of the expected number of records to be accessed. (This is discussed in more detail in section 10.2.5.)

However, the statistics on (name, marital_status) will be collected on name, giving a good, useful distribution.

If the number of distinct values per field of a composite index is about the same, the field sequence in the index create is not that significant. However you can still improve the use of the index if you know that one of the fields is used more often for restrictive selections such as equality. If a composite key on (first_name, last_name) has about the same distribution of values on each field but the where clauses more often use equality on the last_name, then it is better to index as (last_name, first_name). Of course if there are a number of SQL commands which use the first_name only, you will have to review this decision as the index (last_name, first_name) is not used for enquiries that do not quote the most significant field of the index. Nobody said that index choice was easy.

The index key values distribution is created by the create index command and kept up-to-date using the command **update statistics**. Index statistics are not maintained dynamically as records are deleted and inserted; the only method is to execute update statistics.

update statistics

```
update statistics table_name [index_name]
```

Omission of the index name updates every index on the table.

This command should be run as often as you can on every index which has its distribution changed by deletion and/or insertion. This does not apply to every table. A table which is simply updated with little insert/delete activity does not need the statistics updated as the distribution of the key values does not change (as long as you are not updating the index key field).

The statistics are initialized when the index is created. This means that an index created on an empty table does not have any statistics as there is no data to build the statistics on. Therefore, the optimizer will still have no statistics on this index and will be using syntactical optimization on this index until you run update statistics. Try to keep to the sequence of:

1. create the table;
2. load the data;
3. create the indexes.

Statistics are more important for nonclustered indexes than for clustered indexes because of the manner in which the records are stored. The clustered index is a sparse B-tree with the data records being held in sequence of the index key values. The nonclustered index is a dense B-tree where the records are in no predetermined sequence but the index contains a set of pointers to the records and these pointers are in sequence of the index key values. To find several records in sequence in a clustered index, the index tree is used to locate the first record and then the data pages are browsed, which requires no further index access and gives a maximum number of data page reads equal to the pages in the table. Therefore, in practice, a full clustered index scan is no less efficient than a full table scan. SQL Server will always use a clustered index if it is available except when very close to reading all of the records in the table when it reverts to a table scan. (Section 10.2.5 describes the indexes in detail.)

However having located the first record in a nonclustered index, the next record is, most likely, going to be in a different data page. Therefore, the number of disk accesses required to read records from a nonclustered index is approximately equal to the number of records to be read. When this value exceeds the total number of data pages in the table, the optimizer will take the table scan as more efficient and not use the index. Consequently, it is important to have an accurate estimate of how many records are expected from a nonclustered index access. This is best provided by collecting statistics on the key value distribution.

The System 10/11 optimizer takes more account of the physical accesses involved in reading records from the nonclustered index, so the above rule of thumb for use of a nonclustered index—the number of records less than the number of data pages—is not quite accurate. The costing of nonclustered indexes now uses a cost formula which involves the probability of a page being read to estimate the physical reads associated with a number of logical reads. The formula is:

probability of reading a single page:

$$p = 1 - (1 - 1/n)^{(L*S)}$$

where

---

n = number of data pages;
L = logical reads per scan;
s = number of scans.

---

total number of distinct pages read:

$$d = p * n$$

physical reads:

d if d is smaller than the available cache size (c)

c + (L*s-c) * (1 - c ÷d) if d is greater than the available cache

I do not really understand it either but an example of the calculation provided by Sybase is:

20,000 row table
2,000 data pages
100 leaf pages in nonclustered index
1,500 page cache
10% selectivity
2 scans of the index.
Old model of records versus pages read:

2,000 logical reads per scan for full table scan
10% * 100 + 10% * 2,000
= 2,010 logical reads per scan to read the index.

Optimizer chooses a full table scan.

New model considering physical reads:

p = 1 - (1 - 1÷2,000) (2010*2) = 0.866

d = 0.866 * 2,000 = 1,732

physical reads = 1,500 + (2,010 * 2 - 1,500) * (1 - 1,500÷1,732)
= 1,837

full table scan: 4,000 logical + 4,000 physical
which requires 80,000 ms
(@ 2ms per logical and 18ms per physical)

index scan: 4,020 logical + 1,837 physical
which requires 41,106 ms.

The optimizer chooses the nonclustered index.

10.2.3 Density

In addition to the statistics on the index key values distribution, the distribution page holds density figures on the index fields, which indicate the amount of replication in the field values. These density figures are used by the optimizer to estimate the number of records which will be retrieved in a join for each join field value. They are also used when the statistics are available but cannot be used because of datatype mismatches or unknown data values.

The density is the average percentage of duplicate keys for the index. The smaller this is, the more unique the data. A density of 100% means that all keys have the same value. If we have a 1,000 row table with 25% density then we expect to get back, on average, 250 rows per index value. The best density is 100/n% where n is the number of records in the table, which means that we expect one record per key value.

The density is used in the join strategy to estimate the number of records per join. If there are no statistics for the index, the intuitive approach used is simply to divide the number of records in each table. The average records per join between CUSTOMER and ORDER on cust_no is intuitively determined as:

number of records in ORDER ÷ number of records in CUSTOMER

for 1,000 CUSTOMER records and 20,000 ORDER records, the simple calculation is that every customer will have an average of 20 order records.

This obvious, but rather average, figure is replaced by the optimizer based on the index statistics using the density. The average records per join is obtained by multiplying the number of records in the table which contains the join key index by the density.

average records per join = records in table * index density.

So in the above example, if the density of the cust_no index on the ORDER table is 1%:

average order records per customer = 20,000 * 1 ÷ 100 = 200.

Prior to System 10, there was only one density for the index that indicated the percentage of replication for all the fields in the index; that is, the complete composite value. This has been changed in System 10 and there is now one density for each meaningful composite index field combination.

So the index:

(a, b, c)

will have densities for:

a, b, c
a, b
a

(The combinations (b, c); (b); (c) are not meaningful as the index is used only if the most meaningful field—a—is in the where clause. The combination (a, c) looks like (a) as all values of b have to be searched to retrieve the row.)

This may now provide different execution plans from version 4.9.1 when not all of the columns are used in a join clause.

Consider a table of 20,000 records of 200 bytes (that is, 2,500 pages at 75% fillfactor) with an index (a, b) that has a density of 0.02%. This means that there is an average of four rows per value. A join on this index will always use the index as the number of rows per value is less than the number of pages in the table. Consider the two joins:

```
SELECT tab_1.*, tab_2.* FROM tab_1, tab_2
       WHERE tab_2.x = tab_1.a
       AND tab_2.y = tab_1.b
```

and

```
SELECT tab_1.*, tab_3.* FROM tab_1, tab_3
       WHERE tab_3.x = tab_1.a
```

In the first case, the density figures for the index (a, b) on tab_1 indicate a useful index and the join will be done as a nested iteration using the index (a, b) to retrieve the records from tab_1.

In the second case, the index (a, b) on tab_1 may be used for the join, as column "a" has been supplied in a search argument and the density indicates that it is a useful index. However, the density is on both columns "a" and "b" and if column "a" by itself is not very selective—say five distinct values—then each index access to tab_1 will generate about 4,000 record accesses, which is more than the pages in the table. In other words, an indexed-based nested iteration would be done because the density of the index being used does not reflect the distribution of the column(s) being used for the join. A table scan based reformatting strategy looks much more suitable.

In System 10, the multiple densities avoid this because the density for the column "a" will inform the optimizer that a table scan is better for a join on column "a" only. (This is an exaggeration but it illustrates the point. This is a very useful change in System 10.)

10.2.4 Default Percentages

When the optimizer does not have any statistics available for an index, it uses a set of fixed percentages based on the where clause operator. These default percentages are:

exact match	10%
closed interval	25%
open interval	33%

As already mentioned, these values are important only for the nonclustered indexes and, in my opinion, are rather high.

The rule of thumb for the nonclustered index is that the index is used only when the number of records to be retrieved is less than the number of pages in the table. The important values in this ratio are the size of the record and the number of records. If there is one record per page then the percentages (and the statistics) will always return fewer rows than pages in the table. If there are many rows per page and not many pages, the percentages will always return more rows than pages in the table. The important times are in between these extremes.

The record size determines the number of pages in the table to give a breakeven percentage of:

p ÷ 100 = number of pages ÷ number of records

Consider the following cases (I have used a 75% fillfactor when calculating the sizes).

number of records	record size	number of pages	breakeven percentage
50000	150	5000	10
1000000	250	142858	15
50000	300	10000	20
10000	100	667	7
10000000	400	2500000	25
10000	500	3334	33

The larger the record size, the larger the number of pages and the larger the breakeven percentage. In my opinion the average table does not have 400–500 byte records and therefore, you will usually find that the breakeven percentage is lower than this, often as low as 5% and often in single figures. As a result, you will often find that no statistics means that equality in where clauses is table scanning. So make sure that the statistics are initialized and used. So when are the default percentages used? The question is really: when are the statistics not available or not used? There are three occasions.

No Statistics Available

This has already been covered in section 10.2.2. The statistics are initialized by the **create index** command and updated by the **update statistics** command. They are not dynamically maintained. Therefore, if you create the index before you load in the data, there are no statistics for the index. If the value of the column distribution in sysindexes is zero, there are no statistics for the index.

Statistics Not Used

The documentation states that the statistics are accessed on a look-up basis only and no conversion of datatypes is made in the comparison with the search argument value. Therefore, if the value in the where clause is not the same datatype as the column the statistics are collected on, the statistics will not be used. Although the index key values distribution statistics cannot be used in this situation, the statistics have been created and the optimizer does use the density values instead of the fixed percentages. Be careful with null and not null datatypes as SQL Server treats these as different datatypes and so (char not null and char null) or (char not null and varchar—null or not null) are different datatypes. Interestingly, the only exception to this is int not null and int null, which are treated as the same datatype. In addition, this does not apply to variables that, although they default to null, still use the statistics when compared with not null datatypes.

Be very careful with the numeric datatype. In general, numbers do not give a problem and the statistics will be used when comparing mismatching number datatypes. So:

```
int_col = 20
int_col = 20.0
int_col = 2e+1
float_col = 20
float_col = 20.0
float_col = 2e+1
```

will all use the statistics. However, with the numeric datatype, you must get the scale the same or the statistics will not be used.

```
num_6_1_col = 20      not use statistics
num_6_1_col = 20.0    use statistics
num_6_1_col = 2e+1    use statistics
num_6_1_col = 20.12   not use statistics
num_6_1_col = 2e+2    not use statistics
```

This is actually an example of the next point—unknown value at optimization time—as the mismatching scale literal has to be converted to make the scale match and the optimizer will not know the result value at optimization time and cannot use the statistics. Be very careful.

Optimizer Does Not Know Value in Search Argument

Although a search argument is present, the structure of the command batch may not allow the optimizer to know the value of the column being tested so the statistics cannot be used. The most common occurrence of this is variable values:

```
DECLARE @var_1 int
SELECT @var_1 = 50
SELECT * FROM tab_1 WHERE pkey = @var_1
```

At the time the SQL is optimized, the variable does not have a value, so the statistics cannot be used. However, the statistics have been created and the optimizer will use the density values.

This example can be overcome with a procedure to execute the select command, in which case the procedure is optimized when a value is supplied for the parameter.

```
CREATE PROC proc_1 (@par_1 int) AS
SELECT * FROM tab_1 WHERE pkey = @par_1
go
DECLARE @var_1
SELECT @var_1 = 50
EXEC proc_1 @par_1 = @var_1
```

Another common occurrence of this is equality on a nested value—most often used with aggregates:

```
SELECT a FROM tab_1
       WHERE b = (SELECT avg(b) FROM tab_2)
```

Again, the optimizer does not know the value of the nested aggregate when the SQL is optimized, so the default percentages will be used. A combination of assigning the nested value to a variable and using the above procedure approach is needed to allow the optimizer to access the statistics.

```
CREATE PROC jk_prc (@par_1 float = 0.0) AS
SELECT a FROM tab_1 WHERE b = @par_1
go
DECLARE @var_1 float
SELECT @var_1 = avg(b) FROM tab_2
EXEC jk_prc @par_1 = @var_1
go
```

10.2.5 Index Structures

SQL Server has two B-tree index structures: nonclustered and clustered.

Nonclustered

The nonclustered index is a standard implementation of a dense B-tree where every data record has an entry in the B-tree index, which points to the location of the record. These record pointers are held in sequence of the index key values and an access tree is built to reach these record pointers as efficiently as possible. This is illustrated in Figure 10.1, which shows a nonclustered index on an alphabetic field.

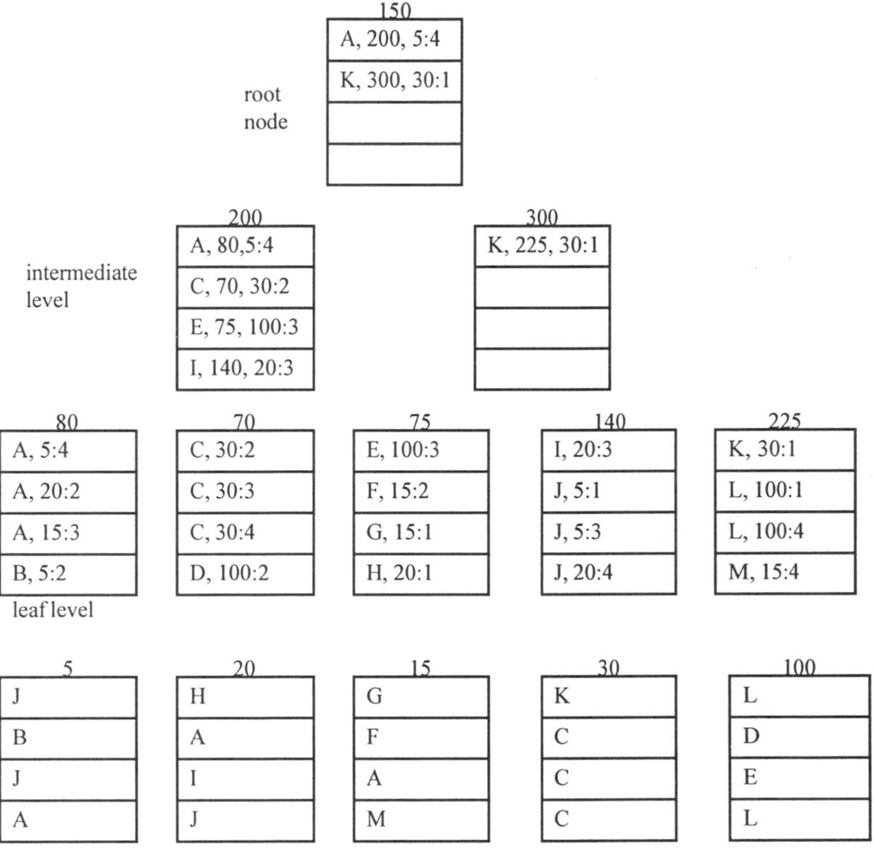

Figure 10.1 *Nonclustered index.*

The record pointers are a combination of page number and record number in the page. (An offset table in the footer of the data page uses the record number to provide the location of the record in the page—see Appendix E. The diagram simplification of the record position being the same as the record number is not necessarily the case. The record number is the address to the offset table entry that points to the record location in the page.)

The record pointers are held in the leaf level (or sequence set) of the index in sequence of the index key. The subsequent levels of the index then need to index only the first entry in each page of the leaf level. The tree is constructed until the level contains only one index node—the root node. To locate records, the index is accessed vertically from the root node until the first leaf level entry that satisfies the selection criteria is located. This provides the record location. The leaf level is then browsed horizontally and each record accessed until the selection criteria is invalid. To locate index values of "L" in our example, the root node indicates that "L" is in the right hand branch, the intermediate level indicates that "L" is in page 225 beginning with "K," and the leaf level indicates that there are two records with key value "L" in page 100.

As the number of records retrieved increases, the number of data pages read increases and becomes the important factor in the total number of accesses to read the required records from the nonclustered index. If we retrieve records between "C" and "K," we would need 13 data page accesses. Therefore there is a cut-off point for a nonclustered index when the number of data page reads exceeds the number of pages in the table. The optimizer equates this to the number of records retrieved being greater than the number of pages in the table (although as we have seen above with "L" there is an element of sequential reads to the same data page which the System 10 optimizer makes allowance for, so this rule of thumb is a little pessimistic, but still a good rule). When the number of records retrieved exceeds the number of pages in the table, the index is less efficient than a table scan and the optimizer will not use the index but will default to the table scan.

The optimizer uses the index statistics to estimate the number of records to be retrieved for the supplied index key values. If this exceeds the number of pages in data_pgs(id, doampg) from sysindexes, the optimizer will not use the index.

This has several important administration aspects:

Make sure that the statistics are initialized.

This is dealt with in section 10.2.2. Statistics are initialized with create index or update statistics.

Make sure that the statistics are accurate.

The index statistics are not maintained dynamically by insert/update/delete but require a separate run of update statistics. Do this regularly when the maintenance activity alters the index key value distribution; that is, after large insert/delete commands.

Make sure the statistics are used.

This has already been covered in section 10.2.4 but the statistics are look-up only with no conversion of datatype carried out. Be careful of null/not null and numeric datatypes.

Make sure the statistics are useful.

This is dealt with in section 10.2.2. Statistics are collected on the first column only of a composite index, so make sure that it is selective enough; that is, it has sufficient distinct values to make it return few enough rows to use the index and not table scan.

Clustered

The SQL Server clustered index is an example of a sparse B-tree index. In this case, the data records themselves are in sequence of the index values and the data pages become the leaf level of the dense B-tree index, as in Figure 10.2.

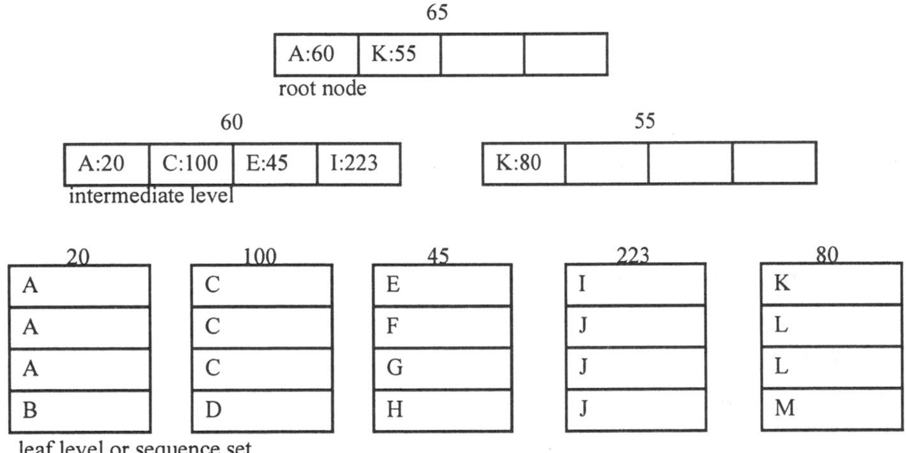

Figure 10.2 *Clustered index.*

To access records between "C" and "K" we access vertically from the root node until we locate the first record and browse the data pages until the last qualifying record is retrieved. We now have the situation where the maximum number of data pages read is never greater than a complete table scan. This makes the clustered index very efficient for sequential retrieval and it will be used almost automatically by the optimizer.

It is a reasonable rule of thumb to assume that a clustered index will always be used. However the optimizer is still making its own cost comparisons and will table scan when very close to reading all the pages anyway. Also, when the query is complex or involves many joins, the optimizer cost equations may not choose the clustered index. This is not common but be aware that it can happen. In general, when an index is clustered, it will be used for access on the index field.

10.2.6 Covered index

A special case of a nonclustered index is when it is covered. This means that the fields quoted in the select command are all contained in the index: so the index covers the query. The optimizer recognizes this situation and does not access the data records but stops at the leaf level of the nonclustered index, as this contains all of the information that is required to satisfy the query. The nonclustered index is actually functioning as a clustered index in this special case, with the additional advantage that the index entries are usually smaller than the data record, so there are fewer leaf level index pages to read. This usually makes the covered index the most efficient strategy for retrieval of several records (though not for maintenance as insert/update/delete commands must access the data page).

Comparing each index strategy, the dominant factor in the number of accesses is:

clustered number of data pages;

nonclustered number of data records;

covered number of leaf level index pages.

The covered index is therefore always better than the nonclustered index. (There is an extreme case when all fields are in the index when a table scan is better but this is rarely of practical interest.)

Compared to the clustered index, the covered index advantage is based on the ratio of number of leaf level pages to number of data pages, which reduces to size of index record compared to size of data record. Again, it is an extreme case when the index entry is greater than the data record, so the covered index will almost always be more efficient than the clustered index. The performance advantage is given by the ratio of size of index record to size of data record.

So the query:

```
SELECT a, b, c FROM tab_1
       WHERE a = 20
       AND b > 50
```

is best indexed as nonclustered (a, b, c). Why (a, b, c) and not (b, a, c) or (b, c, a)? Because the index is most efficient if it starts with column a, which has an equality search argument, and then followed by column b, which is also present in a where clause search argument. The indexes (c, a, b), (b, c, a), (c, a, b), (c, b, a) would all be used by the above query as the index is still covered. However, an index scan would be required as the most restrictive column (a) is not the first column in the index. An interesting aspect of System 10 index covering is that a search argument is not required. The query:

```
SELECT a FROM tab_1
```

will do an index scan on a nonclustered index containing the column a.

10.2.7 Viewing the Execution Plan

To see the plan that the optimizer has chosen, you set the showplan environment variable.

```
set showplan on
go
```

If testing against the operational database, you will usually not want to wait for the command to execute so you will also set the noexec environment variable.

```
set noexec on
go
```

Make sure that you do this in the above sequence, as the only command which executes under noexec is "set noexec off."

10.2.8 Index Ranking

The SQL Server optimizer does not rank indexes in order of usefulness but uses cost formulas which include both logical and physical disk access considerations. The overall effect is a prioritization sequence of:

- equality on uniqueness
- covered

- clustered
- nonclustered
- table scan.

Browsing of the data pages means that the maximum number of pages is equivalent to a table scan, so the clustered is favored.

Nonclustered

This is used only if the number of records retrieved is less than the number of data pages in the table. If not, the table scan is preferred.

Table Scan

This is the default plan if no better is available.

Remember that this is only the effect of the optimizer and is a good rule of thumb to use when creating the indexes, but do not be surprised if the execution of the command is not what you expected. As mentioned already, when the query is complex —by which I mean many tables, many joins and many nestings—the cost formula of the optimizer may not use the indexes in the above sequence.

10.3 Basic Optimization Plans

10.3.1 DBCC Settings

There are some DBCC settings which effect the display of the optimization plan. In general, these produce volumes of output and do not add enough to the basic plan to make it worthwhile to replace the basic plan with them. Also be aware that they tend to be global settings and, if you have several people working as DBAs, it can come as a shock when a simple showplan creates rather a large amount of output.

The three trace flags which I use are 302, 310 and 311. The 302 and 310 settings require the 3604 setting to display the output on the terminal.

```
dbcc traceon(3604)
go
```

In reverse order of preference (310, 302, 311), the output associated with each of these is:

```
dbcc traceon(310)
go
set showplan on
go
set noexec on
go
SELECT * FROM jk1_tab
go

QUERY IS CONNECTED

0-
NEW PLAN (total cost = 5120);

varno=0 indexid=0 path=0x4018f6 pathtype=sclause method=NESTED ITERATION
outerrows=1 rows=512 joinsel=1 cpages=256 lp=256 pp=256 corder=1
TOTAL # PERMUTATIONS: 1
TOTAL # OF PLANS CONSIDERED: 1

FINAL PLAN (total cost = 5120);

varno=0 indexid=0 path=0x4018f6 pathtype=sclause method=NESTED ITERATION
outerrows=1 rows=512 joinsel=1 cpages=256 lp=256 pp=256 corder=1
Table: jk1_tab scan count 1, logical reads: 256, physical reads: 256
```

This indicates the plans considered, with the appropriate index ID, and the one selected with the amount of expected logical and physical I/O. I think that this one is rather difficult to read and I prefer the 302 setting, although if I am trying to work out what is going on, I usually set both of them on.

```
dbcc traceon(302)
go
set showplan on
go
set noexec on
go
SELECT a.col_1, b.col_2 FROM tab_1 a, tab_2 b
        WHERE a.pkey = b.pkey
go

Entering q_score_index() for table 'tab_1' (objectid 16003088)
Cheapest index is index 2, costing 2 pages and generating 7 rows per scan.
Index covers query.
Search argument selectivity is 1.000000
***************************

***************************
Entering q_score_index() for table 'tab_1' (objectid 16003088)
The table has 7 rows and 1 pages
```

```
Scoring the JOIN CLAUSE
       pkey EQ pkey

Base cost: indid: 0  rows: 7  pages: 1
Relop bits are: 5
Estimate: indid: 1  selectivity 9.090909e-02,  rows 1,  pages 2

Cheapest index is index 1, costing 2 pages and generating 1 rows per scan.
Join selectivity is 11
***************************

***************************
Entering q_score_index() for table 'tab_2' (objectid 48003202)
The table has 25 rows and 1 pages.
Scoring the JOIN CLAUSE
       pkey EQ pkey
Base cost: indid: 0  rows: 25  pages: 1

Cheapest index is index 0, costing 1 pages and generating 3 rows per scan.
Join selectivity is 7.
***************************
```

This is useful stuff because you see the index selectivity and, for where clauses, the number of steps of the statistics. These values can be surprising and indicate why your beautiful index is not being used. You may think that the key value distribution is uniform but the statistics index selectivity may show different.

```
dbcc traceon(302)
go
set showplan on
go
set noexec on
go
SELECT col_1, col_2 FROM tab_1 WHERE col_1 LIKE "AB%"
go

Entering q_score_index() for table 'tab_1' (objectid 48003202)
The table has 7 rows and 1 pages.
Scoring the SEARCH CLAUSE:
              col_1 LT
              col_1 GE

Base cost: indid: 0  rows: 8  pages: 1
Relop bits are: d
Qualifying stat page; pgno: 633  steps: 13
Search value: B
No steps for search value – qual page for LT search value finds value < first
step – use outside sc
Net selectivity of interval: 0.000000e+00
```

```
Estimate: indid: 1, selectivity 0.000000e+00, rows 1, pages 2
Cheapest index is indid 1, costing 2 pages and generating 1 rows per scan
Search argument selectivity 0.000000e+00
************************
```

Note the interesting output of the statistics page number, which you can then look at using **dbcc page** (see Chapter 11).

These two settings (310 and 302) are very useful for troubleshooting but are not the sort of output you will want to use on a regular basis. In practice, you will find them useful only when you cannot understand why a particular plan has (or has not) been chosen.

However, the 311 trace setting is extremely useful and worth using as standard.

```
dbcc traceon(311)
go
set showplan on
go
set noexec on
go
SELECT * FROM jkl_tab
go
```

This produces output which looks like a set statistics io on, showing the estimated number of logical and physical reads. A major difference between these and the actual set statistics io on figures can indicate that the optimizer is looking at inconsistent index statistics and that you need to run update statistics.

```
Table: jkl_tab scan count 1, log reads = 1793, phys reads = 1793
STEP 1
The type of query is SELECT
FROM TABLE
jkl_tab
Nested Iteration
Table scan
```

I employ the basic display in my examples because this is the most common use and employ the 311 setting occasionally when it is useful to see the estimated accesses. Bear in mind that the optimizer figures are estimates and the only accurate data on disk accesses is obtained by executing the command with set statistics io on. This can be tiresome on a long-running command but remember that by this stage you are only checking for refinements in one or two optimum execution plans.

10.3.2 Table Scan

The basic execution plan is the table scan.

```
SELECT * FROM tab_1

STEP 1
The type of query is SELECT
FROM TABLE
tab_1
Nested iteration
Table scan
```

This is not too bad a display of the execution plan and it is quite readable. Notice also that SQL Server uses the term "nested iteration" throughout the showplan output. This is best treated as noise in the output as it contributes nothing to the meaning of the plan. The only time that it means anything useful is for the indexed join strategy, which is called a nested iteration.

10.3.3 Clustered Index

```
SELECT ord_no, cust_no, price
       FROM customer
       WHERE name = 'KIRKWOOD'
```

Clustered Index on Name

```
STEP 1
The type of query is SELECT
FROM TABLE
customer
Nested iteration
Using clustered index
```

Note that the execution plan does not name the clustered index or show what the columns of the index are. This is extremely annoying as it is unlikely that you will remember the composition of the index. It is easy in the above example, but a multi-table join with several where clauses could do with the clustered index columns being named.

10.3.4 Nonclustered Index

```
SELECT name, address, tel_no FROM customer
       WHERE cust_no = '100'
```

Nonclustered Index on cust_no

```
STEP 1
The type of query is SELECT
FROM TABLE
customer
Nested iteration
Index:  cust_no
```

Again, there is no statement of the index columns, so you may find it useful to name the indexes carefully.

Note that the plan for a covered index retrieval is the same.

```
SELECT cust_no FROM orders
       WHERE cust_no = "100"
```

```
STEP 1
The type of query is SELECT
FROM TABLE
customer
Nested iteration
Index:  cust_no
```

However, the covered index plan is much more efficient and, as this is not highlighted in the optimizer plan, it makes it an obvious candidate for using the 311 trace flag.

```
dbcc traceon(311)
go
SELECT * FROM orders
       WHERE cust_no = "100"
go

Table: orders scan count 1, log reads  = 134, phys reads = 134
STEP 1
The type of query is SELECT
FROM TABLE
customer
Nested iteration
Index:  cust_no

SELECT cust_no FROM orders
       WHERE cust_no = "100"
```

```
Table: orders scan count 1, log reads = 25, phys reads = 25
STEP 1
The type of query is SELECT
FROM TABLE
customer
Nested iteration
Index: cust_no
```

10.3.5 Covered Index Use Without a Search Argument

System 10 will use a covered index whenever it can. Some particularly useful examples are the aggregate functions and order by.

Min/Max

Because these need the information from one record only, the presence of an index on the field will cause the index to be used without a where clause being necessary.

```
SELECT min(qty) FROM order_item
```

```
STEP 1
The type of query is SELECT
Scalar aggregate
FROM TABLE
order_item
Nested iteration
Index: qty_idx
STEP 2
The type of query is SELECT
Table scan
```

Don't worry about the STEP2 table scan; it is on the tempdb worktable, which I explain fully in 10.3.8.

Either a clustered or nonclustered index will be used for min and max. Note that the nonclustered index has the query covered (that is, all the information is in the index) and therefore would appear to provide a faster solution. However, the difference in levels between a nonclustered and a clustered index is normally one level. As only one record is being read, there is no difference between the covered nonclustered index and the clustered index in regards to disk access. Remember that covering is effective when several records are being retrieved; it has no advantage over clustering for single record retrieval.

Prior to System 10, the combination of both min and max in the same select statement caused a table scan instead of using the index. This has been fixed in System

10 and the index is used when both min and max are requested in the same select statement.

```
SELECT min(qty), max(qty) FROM order_item

STEP 1
The type of query is SELECT
Scalar aggregate
FROM TABLE
order_item
Nested iteration
Index: qty_idx
STEP 2
The type of query is SELECT
Table Scan
```

Count

If a nonclustered index is available, it is used to evaluate count(*) or count(index_col) without the need for a where clause. The count is treated as a covered query and only the index is scanned to determine the number of records. Clearly, this needs to be a nonclustered index as this has one entry for every record in the table.

```
SELECT count(*) FROM orders

STEP 1
The type of query is SELECT
Scalar aggregate
From Table
orders
Nested Iteration
Index: jk1_idx
STEP 2
The type of query is SELECT
Table scan
```

Order By

The order by clause in a select statement requests the output in sequence of the order by field(s). If any of these are requested in descending sequence, there is little we can do about it. If it is in ascending sequence, the indexes may be used.

SQL Server will use a clustered index if available, even without a search argument.

```
SELECT name, tel_no FROM customer
       ORDER BY name
```

```
STEP 1
The type of query is SELECT
FROM TABLE
customer
Nested Iteration
Table Scan
```

This says it is a table scan but remember that a scan of the data pages of the clustered index is the same as a table scan. As you can see from the sort plan below, the clustered index is being used although the plan does not make this clear.

If we have a nonclustered index that covers the query, System 10 will use the index without the need for a where clause or a search argument.

```
SELECT ord_no, ord_date, name FROM orders
       ORDER BY ord_no
```

```
STEP 1
The type of query is SELECT
FROM TABLE
orders
Nested iteration
Index: ordno_idx
```

As with any covered index execution, this can be a significant saving for order by statements and is always worth considering.

If there is no index that the order by can use, the standard sort plan is used.

```
SELECT ord_date, name FROM orders
       ORDER BY ord_date
```

```
STEP 1
The type of query is INSERT
The update mode is direct
Worktable created for ORDER BY
FROM TABLE
orders
FROM TABLE
orders
Nested Iteration
Table Scan
TO TABLE
Worktable                (creation of worktable from table scan of orders)
STEP 2
The type of query is SELECT
This step involves sorting
FROM TABLE
Worktable
Using GETSORTED
Table Scan                        (worktable sort)
```

This is the standard **order by** sort plan when no clustered or covered index is available. The stutter FROM TABLE orders is not mine but an actual example from SQL Server. (The comments are my additions; they are not part of the showplan output.)

Notice the initial creation of a temporary table before the sort is done. This means that the order by does an initial projection (and restriction if there is a where clause) to sort only the columns (and records) which are necessary (as explained in the reformatting join strategy in section 10.3.7). So try not to write select * with order by.

10.3.6 OR Strategy: Dynamic Index

An OR is quite simply a merge, or combination, of more than one query. The principal complication is that a record may qualify in more than one of the selection clauses but it must be shown only once.

Therefore, the or strategy involves the creation of an internal work table of row IDs which can be used to check for and eliminate duplicates. The simple internal approach to this is to create a work table of all row IDs satisfying any of the selection criteria, sort the work table to eliminate duplicates and use the sorted work table to retrieve the rows from the data table.

So if we have the query:

```
SELECT name, address, salary FROM employee
       WHERE name LIKE 'Kirk%'
       OR salary > 1200
```

with indexes on name and salary, the or clause will be evaluated as two separate queries and the results sort/merged to eliminate the duplicate rows. If the results of name LIKE 'Kirk%' are rows 1, 5, 7, 9, 10, 11 and of salary > 1200 are 2, 4, 5, 10, 12, we get a work table as shown in Figure 10.3.

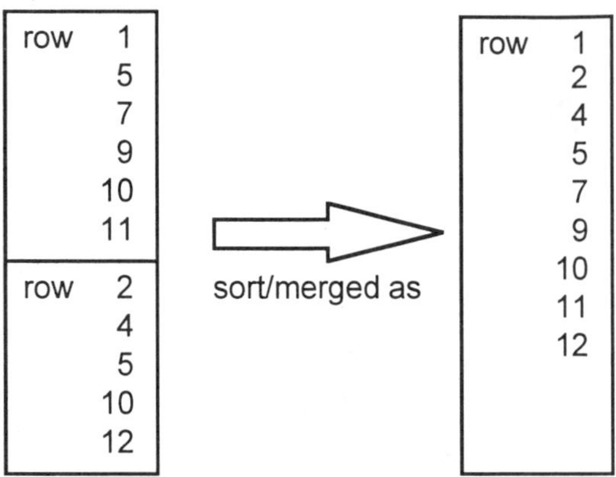

Figure 10.3 *OR strategy internal sort/merge.*

These row IDs are then used to read the records directly from the data pages. The execution plan is:

```
STEP 1
The type of query is SELECT
FROM TABLE
employee
Nested iteration
Using clustered index   (first pass through employee on name index)
FROM TABLE
employee
Nested iteration
Index: sal_ind          (second pass through employee on salary index)
FROM TABLE
employee
Nested iteration
Using Dynamic Index     (final pass through employee to retrieve records)
```

This plan is a little difficult to identify at first glance because it is not until you get to the end of the plan that you see the important words **dynamic index**, which means that the two previous index accesses were to create the internal lists of row IDs that are then merged into the dynamic index to read the qualifying employee records.

The simple rule of thumb is that if one of the selection criteria does not use an index and causes a table scan, the whole of the query will be solved by a table scan.

```
SELECT name, address, salary FROM employee
       WHERE name LIKE 'Kirk%'
       OR tel_no LIKE '0734%'
```

```
STEP 1
The type of query is SELECT
FROM TABLE
employee
Nested iteration
Table scan
```

Because there is no index on tel_no, the second where clause will need to do a table scan so the whole command does a table scan. SQL Server is quite sophisticated in determining when to do a table scan and when to do a dynamic index strategy. Even when suitable indexes are available for each clause in the or, SQL Server will add up the expected number of records to read for each clause and if the total comes to more than the number of pages in the table, a table scan plan is chosen.

If there are indexes on custid (unique), name and salary, the dynamic index will be used for:

```
SELECT name FROM customer
       WHERE name LIKE 'Kirk%'
       OR salary > 12000
SELECT name, salary FROM customer
       WHERE custid IN (1234, 1235, 1236)
```

where the IN is treated like an OR.

Note that in the last example, it is intuitively obvious that, as the custid is unique, it is sufficient to access by this index and not carry out the OR strategy, which has the overhead of creating and sorting the dynamic index. Unfortunately, SQL Server does not recognize this and the OR strategy takes precedence.

10.3.7 Join

So far we have worked with single tables in seeing how the optimizer processes the query once the various clauses and indexes are determined. With a join of two or more tables via join clauses, the optimizer has to determine another strategy to handle the join.

SQL Server has two cases: nested iteration and reformatting. The former is used when indexes are available and the latter is used when table scans are required.

Nested Iteration

When suitable indexes are available to action the join clause, the optimizer will nest the tables. It will perform a search of the inner table for each qualifying row in the outer table.

To satisfy the query (assuming suitable indexes):

```
SELECT  emp.name, emp.deptno,
            job.jobno, job.jobdesc
        FROM emp, job
        WHERE emp.empno = 10
        AND emp.jobno = job.jobno
```

the optimizer has two choices.

The first is to nest emp as outer and job as inner, as in Figure 10.4, which has to retrieve qualifying rows from emp and for each of these to access job.

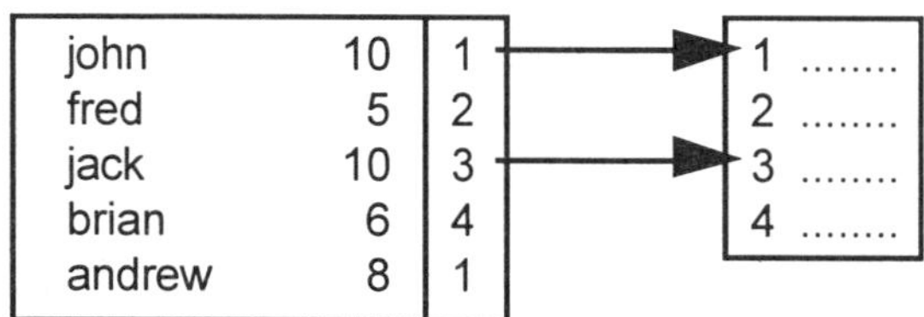

Figure 10.4 *Nested iteration—most selective as outer.*

The second option is to nest job as outer and emp as inner, as in Figure 10.5, which has to scan the job table and read each emp record for the jobno to see if they qualify.

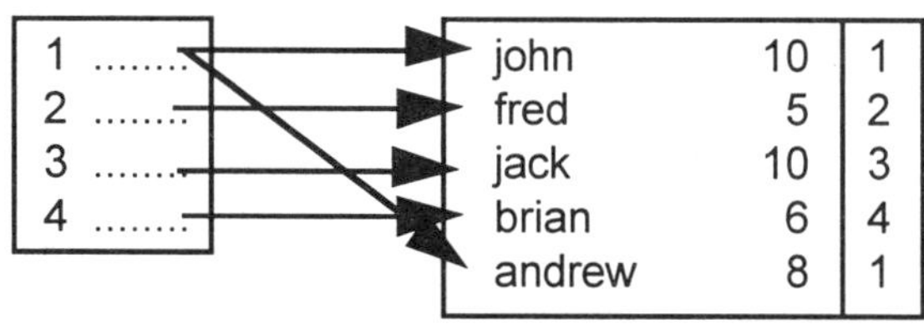

Figure 10.5 *Nested iteration—least selective as outer.*

In this case, the former requires two index accesses to emp plus two index accesses to job; the latter requires a table scan of job and five index accesses to emp. Clearly the former is preferable—assuming reasonably similar table sizes—but the optimizer needs to determine how to make the choice.

There are two criteria used in nested iteration to determine which table is the outer and which is the inner. The join densities are then used (as explained in 10.3.3) to determine the number of records from the inner table for each qualifying record from the outer table.

The criteria to determine the table sequence are:

- how selective are the criteria on each table? (most selective as outer);
- is a table small enough to be cache-resident? (smallest as inner).

The optimizer then tries to make the smaller table the inner table and the more selective table the outer table. Thus the selection criteria which returns the smaller number of records will be made the outer table and the smaller table will be made the inner table. The nested iteration strategy is always a balance between these two decisions and it is in this area that the optimizer will sometimes get it wrong. Putting the most selective table as the outer table is given most weight and this will sometimes give an incorrect strategy.

In the above example, the first approach of emp as outer and job as inner is preferable (four data record I/Os against table scan and five record I/Os) because the emp selection criteria is more selective.

So the command:

```
SELECT  emp.name, emp.deptno,
              job.jobno, job.jobdesc
        FROM emp, job
        WHERE emp.deptno = 10
        AND emp.jobno = job.jobno
```

gives the execution plan:

```
STEP 1
The type of query is SELECT
FROM TABLE
emp
nested iteration
Using clustered index          (emp as outer table, selection on dept_no)
FROM TABLE
job
Nested iteration
Using clustered index        (job as inner table, index access on job_no)
```

Notice how awkward the continued use of the term "nested iteration" is now that it is meaningful. It is actually meaningful in all cases, as a single table plan is simply a specific of the more general multitable plan, but it would be much clearer if the output of the plan did not use the same term for a single table plan as it does for a multitable plan.

Let's look at a three table join:

```
SELECT o.custno, p.prodno
       FROM orders o, item i, product p
       WHERE p.prodno = i.prodno
       AND i.ordno = o.ordno
       AND p.proddesc = 'RESISTOR'
```

Consider small tables of four orders, seven items and five products with the only RESISTOR being product 2. If we search in the sequence of orders, item, products, as in in Figure 10.6, we need to search the orders table and for each order, search the item table and for each item, search the product table.

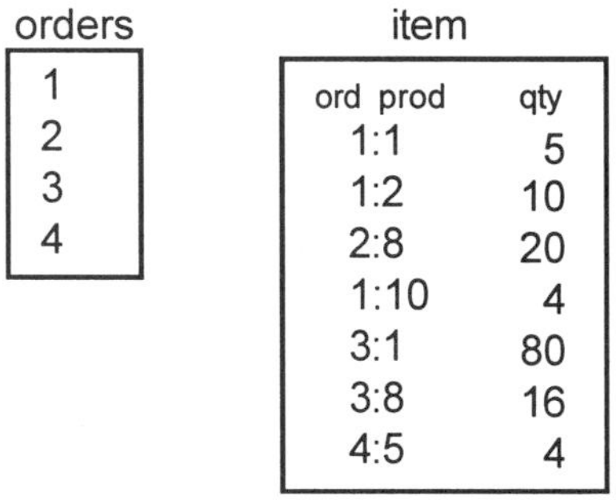

orders
1
2
3
4

item	
ord prod	qty
1:1	5
1:2	10
2:8	20
1:10	4
3:1	80
3:8	16
4:5	4

product
1
2
5
8
10

***Figure 10.6** Three table join: least selective as outer.*

This means that we need one table scan of orders, four table scans of item and seven record accesses of product.

The alternate nesting of product then item then orders is in Figure 10.7.

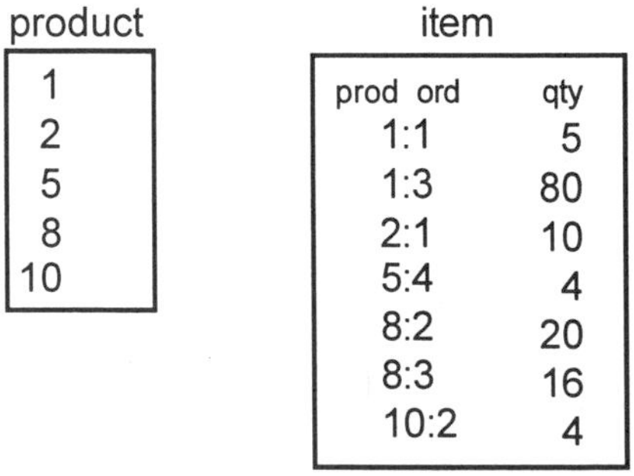

product
1
2
5
8
10

item	
prod ord	qty
1:1	5
1:3	80
2:1	10
5:4	4
8:2	20
8:3	16
10:2	4

orders
1
2
3
4

***Figure 10.7** Three table join: most selective as outer.*

Now we require one record access of product, which identifies one record—product 2—so we have only one access of item, which identifies two records. Therefore, we need to access orders only twice.

Again, putting the most selective criteria as the outer table is the better strategy. The command:

```
SELECT o.custno, p.prodno
       FROM orders o, item i, product p
       WHERE p.prodno = i.prodno
       AND i.ordno = o.ordno
       AND p.proddesc = 'RESISTOR'
```

gives the execution plan:

```
STEP 1
The type of query is SELECT
FROM TABLE
product
nested iteration
Index:  desc_idx            (product as outer, selection on proddesc index)
FROM TABLE
item
Nested iteration
Using clustered index      (item next in nesting, selection on prodno index)
FROM TABLE
orders
Nested iteration
Index: ord_idx              (orders as inner, selection on ordno index)
```

Reformatting

If there are no suitable indexes available, the optimizer will need to choose a table scan of the outer table and a table scan of the inner table for every qualifying row from the outer table.

This is likely to be an expensive strategy when no indexes are available. Therefore, when table scans are required in a join, the optimizer will evaluate the reformatting strategy, which takes the inner table and sorts it into a clustered index to avoid a table scan for every qualifying row from the outer table.

The sort on the inner table is done as a projected, restricted version of the table. Only those fields and those records which are necessary for the statement are put into the sort. This reduces the storage required and the sort effort. It also means that the normal reformatting tactic is to take the table which has a search criteria and make it the inner table. This is the opposite to the nested iteration, which puts a table with a search criteria as the outer table.

If I have two equal tables, tab_1 and tab_2, with no indexing:

```
SELECT tab_1.A, tab_2.B, tab_2.C
       FROM tab_1, tab_2
       WHERE tab_1.X = tab_2.X
       AND tab_2.B = 50
```

reformatting will create an internal work table of tab_2.B, tab_2.C for all records, with tab_2.B = 50 in the sequence of tab_2.X. The reformatting strategy, having created a work table, looks like a nested iteration.

The execution plan is:

```
STEP 1
The type of query is SELECT
The update mode is direct
Worktable created for REFORMATTING
FROM TABLE
tab_2
Nested iteration
Table scan               (tab_2 chosen as inner table, no index)
TO TABLE
Worktable                (Worktable create from tab_2)
STEP 2
The type of query is SELECT
FROM TABLE
tab_1
Nested iteration
Table scan               (tab_1 as outer table in nested iteration, no index)
FROM TABLE
Worktable
Nested iteration
Using clustered index    (clustered index access to worktable, index on X)
```

STEP 1 is the creation of the internal worktable and STEP 2 is then a nested iteration with tab_1 as the outer table and the clustered index worktable as the inner table.

Altering the above to read:

```
SELECT tab_1.A, tab_2.B, tab_2.C
       FROM tab_1, tab_2
       WHERE tab_1.X = tab_2.X
       AND tab_1.B = 50
```

will create a work table of tab_1.A for all records, with tab_1.B = 50 in the sequence of tab_1.X.

The execution plan is:

```
STEP 1
The type of query is SELECT
The update mode is direct
Worktable created for REFORMATTING
FROM TABLE
tab_1
Nested iteration
Table scan                    (tab_1 chosen as inner table, no index)
TO TABLE
Worktable                     (worktable create from tab_1)
STEP 2
The type of query is SELECT
FROM TABLE
tab_2
Nested iteration
Table scan                    (tab_2 as outer table in nested iteration)
FROM TABLE
Worktable
Nested iteration
Using clustered index         (clustered index access to worktable on X)
```

The number of logical I/Os for the nested iteration strategy is:

number of pages in outer table
+
(number of qualifying rows in outer table
*
number of pages in inner table)

If we take two tables: table 1 with 200 pages and 100 qualifying rows and table 2 with 100 pages, the maximum nested iteration cost of doing a table scan is:

200 + (100 * 100) i.e. 10,200 logical I/Os

The cost of reformatting is:

cost of a sort
+
number of pages in outer table
+
number of qualifying rows
*
1 (access to clustered index)

where

the cost of a sort is:	number of pages in the inner table + number of pages in the inner table * log2 (number of pages in the inner table)

For our example, this evaluates to:

100 + 100 * log(100) +
200 +
100 * 1

i.e. 1,100 logical I/Os

In effect, the sort is creating an internal clustered index of the inner table to minimize the number of accesses to retrieve the data. The formula assumes one access per qualifying row to the sorted table, which seems reasonable but see some of the practice versus theory in section 10.6. This is dependent on the size of cache and the sorted results but you have no choice if the practice is slower than the theory. The reformatting strategy will still produce better results over any other strategy when there are no useful indexes. If you have a serious performance problem with this strategy, try pre-sorting the outer table before you present it to the join.

Again, here is a chance to correct some information in the version 4 book about more than four table joins. When the statement has more than four tables in it, SQL Server does not check all possible permutations of the tables and optimizes the tables in groups of four. I said that SQL Server groups the tables from the left hand side. This is not correct. The optimizer only checks four table combinations to determine the table order.

If we take a simple example:

```
SELECT ......
        FROM A, B, C, D, E, F, G
        WHERE A.key = B.key
        AND B.key = C.key
        AND A.key = D.key
        AND D.key = G.key
        AND G.key = E.key
        AND E.key = F.key
```

(I have given only the minimum number of join clauses; you should always supply the optimizer with all possible join clauses.)

The optimizer will check only the valid four table combinations to decide on what is the best outer table. It will not look at five, six or seven table combinations. Having fixed the outer table, it then repeats the process with the remaining tables to fix the next table in the join sequence until only four tables remain when these are resolved.

This is the only time SQL Server exhibits any positional optimization. At all other times, the sequence of the tables or the where clauses has no effect on the execution plan.

On all occasions of more than four table joins, you should be aware that the best plan may have been missed. It is worth checking with the 311 trace flag and set forceplan on to force specific sequences. With forceplan on, the optimizer will join the tables in the sequence they occur in the **from** clause, left to right. This is not a large exercise as the choice is usually limited by the table relationships but it is often worthwhile because the optimizer can get it wrong with more than four tables in the join.

Cartesian Product

If you specify a join but do not provide any join clauses, the optimizer has no option but to do a cartesian product join, which takes each record in one table and joins it with every record in the other table. This gives a simple nested iteration plan without using any indexes.

```
dbcc traceon(311)
go
SELECT a.c, b.d FROM jk1_tab a, jk2_tab b
go

Table jk2_tab  scan count 1, log reads = 256, phys reads = 256
Table jk1_tab  scan count 1, log reads = 459008, phys reads 1793

STEP 1
The type of query is SELECT
From Table
jk2_tab
Nested Iteration
Table Scan
From Table
jk1_tab
Nested Iteration
Table Scan
```

This will try to use covered indexes if available, even without where clauses or search arguments.

```
Table: jk2_tab  Scan count 1, log reads = 256, phys reads = 256
Table: jk1_tab  Scan count 256, log reads 79872, phys reads 312

STEP 1
The type of query is SELECT
From Table
jk2_tab
Nested Iteration
Table scan
From Table
jk1_tab
Nested Iteration
Index: jka_idx                (a covered index on column a)
```

As seen from the 311 trace flag output, this can be a considerable saving, which emphasizes the need to avoid using select * in joins.

A cartesian product may be chosen by the optimizer if the tables are small and the cost of reformatting is high.

10.3.8 Aggregates

Scalar Aggregates

Aggregates in a select clause—count, avg, min, max, sum—use tempdb for working storage even if the result is one value. If customer has a clustered index on name:

```
SELECT count(*) FROM customer
       WHERE name LIKE 'K%'
```

gives an execution plan of:

```
STEP 1
The type of query is SELECT
Scalar aggregate
FROM TABLE
customer
Nested iteration
Using clustered index          (index access to customer on name)
STEP 2
The type of query is SELECT
Table scan                     (table scan of aggregate worktable in tempdb)
```

The first step is the actual optimization of the command, using the clustered index to create a temporary table in tempdb. The second step is a table scan of the temporary table in tempdb to retrieve the results for display. Although this is a scalar aggregate with only one result value and will be a cache page read, the optimizer treats it as a table which has to be scanned.

If no where clause is specified, the statement will table scan as always.

```
SELECT avg(qty) FROM order_item

STEP 1
The type of query is SELECT
Scalar aggregate
FROM TABLE
order_item
Nested iteration
Table scan
STEP 2
The type of query is SELECT
Table scan
```

Although, if there is a nonclustered index which covers the query, the covered index will be used without a where clause or a search argument.

```
SELECT avg(qty) FROM order_item

STEP 1
The type of query is SELECT
Scalar aggregate
FROM TABLE
order_item
Nested iteration
Index: qty_idx           a covered index on qty
STEP 2
The type of query is SELECT
Table scan
```

Vector Aggregates

The aggregate may be qualified by GROUP BY and HAVING clauses. The optimization effect of these is trivial as the tempdb table is not indexed and therefore is always table scanned. The use of group by does force the tempdb table to be held in sequence of the group by field(s), so clearly there is extra work involved. However, it is not an optimization overhead.

```
SELECT prod_no, sum(qty) FROM order_item
       GROUP BY prod_no

STEP 1
The type of query is SELECT (into a worktable)
GROUP BY
```

```
Vector aggregate
FROM TABLE
order_item
Nested Iteration
Table Scan
TO TABLE
Worktable   (GROUP BY worktable created from table scan of order_item)
STEP 2
The type of query is SELECT
FROM TABLE
Worktable
Nested Iteration
Table Scan                    (table scan of aggregate worktable in tempdb)
```

STEP 2 is identical to the scalar aggregate but STEP 1 now states that a vector aggregate is being done for the group by. This simply means that the results stored in tempdb are potentially made up of more than one value in more than one row. In effect, a temporary table of prod_no:sum(qty) is being created with one record per prod_no.

```
SELECT prod_no, sum(qty) FROM order_item
       WHERE prod_no LIKE 'ABC%'
       GROUP BY prod_no
       HAVING sum(qty) > 10

STEP 1
The type of query is SELECT (into a worktable)
GROUP BY
Vector aggregate
FROM TABLE
order_item
Nested Iteration
Index:  prod_idx
TO TABLE
Worktable             (worktable created from index access of order_item)
STEP 2
The type of query is SELECT
FROM TABLE
Worktable
Nested Iteration
Table Scan            (table scan of aggregate worktable in tempdb)
```

This is an identical format of execution plan with use of the prod_no index in STEP 1. Note that the existence of the having makes no difference to the STEP 2 plan.

```
SELECT prod_no, sum(qty) FROM order_item
       GROUP BY prod_no
       HAVING prod_no LIKE 'ABC%'
```

```
STEP 1
The type of query is SELECT (into a worktable)
GROUP BY
Vector Aggregate
FROM TABLE
order_item
Nested Iteration
Table Scan
TO TABLE
Worktable
STEP 2
The type of query is SELECT
FROM TABLE
Worktable
Nested Iteration
Using Clustered index
```

Note the heavy overhead of putting the selection onto the worktable using the having, instead of onto the data table using a where. Although the worktable is treated as a clustered index because it is in sequence of the selection field, the data table is scanned instead of an index access when the where is used. In this extreme example of equality, the where will do an index access onto order_item to extract a few records and then table scan the small worktable. However, the having clause will table scan order_item, creating a large worktable that then has an indexed access.

This will always be a significant difference so restrict the records with where and use having only with aggregates.

SQL Server does allow you to write:

```
SELECT prod_no, ord_no, price FROM order_item
       HAVING prod_no LIKE 'ABC%'
```

This gives the same execution as a where.

```
STEP 1
The type of query is SELECT
FROM TABLE
order_item
Nested Iteration
Index: prod_idx
```

But when a group by is present, restrict the having to aggregates and the where to records.

10.3.9 Data Maintenance Commands

In general, these are trivial as they are the same as the select optimization with a table scan completed if there is no search argument supplied, no index available or the index is not useful. But, as with anything in optimization, it is always worth checking practice against theory. Covering is not an option here as we must access the data record.

Insert

```
INSERT INTO customer VALUES (.........)
```

No Index

```
STEP 1
The type of query is INSERT
The update mode is direct
Table Scan
TO TABLE
customer
```

Clustered/Nonclustered Index

```
STEP 1
The type of query is INSERT
The update mode is direct
Table Scan
TO TABLE
customer
```

The plan is the same regardless of whether there is no index, a clustered index or a nonclustered index on the table. If you use set statistics io on to look at the number of disk accesses it does in each case, a table scan is not done at any time to insert one record into a table.

```
INSERT INTO customer SELECT * FROM old_customer
```

No Index/Clustered or Nonclustered Index

```
STEP 1
The type of query is INSERT
The update mode is direct
FROM TABLE
old_customer
Nested Iteration
Table Scan
TO TABLE
customer
```

Again the plan indicates a table scan of the target table regardless of the indexing, but a table scan is never done to insert records. Also notice the use of direct update mode, which indicates one record at a time processing, although the command is inserting multiple records into the table.

Update/Delete

The plans for update and delete are identical.

The table customer had a clustered index on cust_no and was 51 records large enough to be two records per page (that is, 26 data pages).

```
UPDATE customer SET name = 'fred'

Table: customer
scan count 1, log reads = 26, phys reads = 26
STEP 1
The type of query is UPDATE
The update mode is deferred
FROM TABLE
customer
Nested Iteration
Table Scan
TO TABLE
customer
```

We have: no index, multiple records updated and a table scan done. Note the deferred update mode indicating multiple records processed and the two stage iteration against the table. It is worth noting the overhead of the deferred update. The trace flag 311 output indicates that all 26 data pages will be read and written as you would expect. But this is where the 311 setting is insufficient, as it is telling you the number of estimated accesses. A set statistics io on for the above command gives a very different picture and indicates the overhead of a deferred update.

```
Table: customer        scan count 0, logical reads: 354, physical reads: 1
Table: customer        scan count 1, logical reads: 26, physical reads: 26
Total writes for this command: 120
```

(I do not know where the 354 came from but it is quite an overhead.) The deferred update is reading the data pages and writing the record IDs to the log. The pages are exclusively locked so there is no chance of the record IDs changing during this. At the commit time, the log records are reread, the record IDs sort/merged to eliminate duplicates and the data pages updated. The sort/merge elimination is done because an update containing joins is done using deferred updating and the join may produce duplicate rows.

```
UPDATE customer SET name = 'fred'
       WHERE cust_no = '12'
```

Clustered Index (Unique)

```
STEP 1
The type of query is UPDATE
The update mode is deferred
FROM TABLE
customer
Nested iteration
Using clustered index
TO TABLE
customer
```

Nonclustered Index (Unique)

```
STEP 1
The type of query is UPDATE
The update mode is direct
FROM TABLE
customer
Nested iteration
Index: cust_idx1
TO TABLE
customer
```

There are no surprises here except for the deferred mode used in the clustered index and direct mode used in the nonclustered index.

```
UPDATE customer
       SET name = 'fred'
       FROM customer, orders
       WHERE cust_no = '12'
       AND customer.cust_no = orders.cust_no
```

Index

```
STEP 1
The type of query is UPDATE
The update mode is deferred
FROM TABLE
orders
Nested Iteration
Table Scan
FROM TABLE
customer
Nested Iteration
Table Scan
```

```
TO TABLE
customer

Table customer, Scan count: 0, logical reads: 2
Table customer, Scan count: 1, logical reads: 26
Table orders, Scan count: 1, logical reads: 25
Total writes for this command: 2
```

Clustered Index On Customer

```
STEP 1
The type of query is UPDATE
The update mode is deferred
FROM TABLE
customer
Nested Iteration
Using clustered index
FROM TABLE
orders
Nested Iteration
Table scan
TO TABLE
Table customer, Scan count: 1, logical reads: 3
Table orders, Scan count: 1, logical reads: 26
Total writes for this command: 2
```

So there are no surprises here. However, a word on the update/delete syntax when using the from clause.

```
UPDATE customer
       SET name = 'fred'
       FROM customer, orders
       WHERE cust = '1234'
       AND customer.cust_no = orders.cust_no
```

can be written in SQL Server as:

```
UPDATE customer
       SET name = 'fred'
       FROM orders
       WHERE cust = '1234'
       AND customer.cust_no = orders.cust_no
```

which gives the same execution plan and the same results.

This is not the case in all SQL syntaxes (for example, Ingres) as the first command, where the customer table is repeated in the FROM clause, usually gives a syntax error. However, take care with the names of the tables as the documentation states that the same table aliased in the FROM clause causes a syntax error. Even worse, I have been told that it may cause a cartesian product by treating both instances as separate tables because of the alias. In practice, I have not found any problem with aliasing the table name in the FROM clause but better safe than sorry.

So do NOT write:

```
UPDATE customer
       SET name = 'fred'
       FROM orders o, customer c
       WHERE cust = '1234'
       AND c.cust_no = o.cust_no
```

10.4 Nested Queries

In the examples of this and the following section I have used the tables:

```
CREATE TABLE jk1_tab
              (a int,
              b char(255),
              c char(255),
              d char(255),
              e int)
```

with 512 rows numbered 1–512 (two rows per page = 256 pages) and jk2_tab with the same layout but 256 rows numbered 257–512 (two rows per page = 128 pages). The indexing may vary from example to example but in general it will be obvious from the plan.

10.4.1 Classification

Subqueries are classified by the type of WHERE test that is present.

Expression

This is a simple nesting of a SELECT in a single equals test or an arithmetic expression; in other words, anywhere in a predicate or an expression where a single value is expected.

```
WHERE  x = (SELECT a FROM tab_1
              WHERE pkey = value)
SELECT @var_1 = isnull((SELECT sum(qty)
                     FROM ord_item),0)
```

Existence

This is a nesting of a SELECT in a test where a value is checked as belonging to a set of values. This is most commonly identified with the IN, ANY or EXISTS operators.

```
WHERE x IN (SELECT a FROM tab_1)
WHERE EXISTS (SELECT 1 FROM tab_1
                       WHERE pkey = value)
WHERE x = ANY (SELECT a FROM tab_1)
```

Nonexistence

This is a nesting of a SELECT where a value is checked as not belonging to a set of values. This is most commonly identified with the NOT operator but also with the ALL operator.

```
WHERE x NOT IN (SELECT a FROM tab_1)
WHERE NOT EXISTS (SELECT 1 FROM tab_1
                       WHERE pkey = value)
WHERE x > ALL (SELECT a FROM tab_1)
```

10.4.2 Nested Query Flattened to a Join

The optimizer flattens the nested query into a join whenever it can. This operates differently in System 10 from version 4.x by always taking the nested table as the inner table in the join and no longer displaying any duplicates from the join by doing an existence join instead of an equality join.

```
SELECT * FROM jk1_tab
      WHERE e IN (SELECT e from jk2_tab
                            WHERE e = 4)
```

No Indexes

```
STEP 1
The type of query is INSERT
Update mode direct
Worktable created for REFORMATTING
From Table
jk1_tab
Nested iteration
Table scan
To Table
Worktable
```

```
STEP 2
The type of query is SELECT
From Table
jk2_tab
Nested Iteration
Table scan
From Table
Worktable
EXISTS TABLE: Nested Iteration
Using clustered index
```

This is a standard reformatting strategy (because there are no useful indexes) with jk2_tab as the inner table in an existence join.

With a nonclustered index on e on jk2_tab, we avoid the reformatting strategy.

```
STEP 1
The type of query is SELECT
From table
jk1_tab
Nested iteration
Table scan
From table
jk2_tab
EXISTS TABLE: Nested iteration
Index: jk2_idx2
```

This is a standard nested iteration strategy with jk2_tab as the inner table in an existence join.

The suppression of any duplicate display rows from the join is fine, but I have a problem with this plan as the order of the nesting is fixed and there is the obvious possibility of the wrong plan. I got the same plans when I executed the above nesting as a join, but the nesting of the tables was reversed. Without doing a set statistics io on there is no way to determine which plan is better. However, which one is better is not the point, as this will vary from one situation to another. The important point is that the sequence of table nesting must now be chosen carefully when the nesting can be flattened into a join. Writing them all as joins is not the answer either because you are expecting the nesting to provide a different answer by suppressing any duplicates from the join. Be careful of performance in a simple nesting. SQL Server does no checking for best iteration sequence but forces the nested table to be the inner table in the join strategy, which may not be the optimum plan.

Note that the use of distinct in a nesting is now unnecessary. However, you do not need to change all your current code as the distinct keyword in a nesting is simply ignored and:

```
SELECT * FROM jk1_tab
       WHERE e IN (SELECT DISTINCT e FROM jk2_tab
                                     WHERE e = 4)
```

gives exactly the same plan as above.

10.4.3 Non-Join Subqueries

When the nested command cannot be flattened into a join, the command is evaluated from the inside out. The inner query is evaluated and the results joined with the outer query, which is then evaluated, and so on for each level of nesting.

Subqueries Returning a Single Value

This type of subquery is not flattened into a join as it is really just a simple expression in the nested query that returns a value to the outer query. This is achieved by the use of a two-step evaluation with a variable being used to hold the result of the inner query. So:

```
SELECT tab_1.a FROM tab_1
       WHERE tab_1.b = (SELECT sum(tab_2.b) FROM tab_2)
```

is evaluated as:

```
DECLARE @sum int
SELECT @sum = sum(tab_2.b) FROM tab_2
SELECT tab_1.a FROM tab_1
       WHERE tab_1.b = @sum
```

For example:

```
SELECT a FROM jk1_tab
       WHERE e = (SELECT avg(e) from jk2_tab)
```

```
STEP 1
The type of query is SELECT
Scalar aggregate
FROM TABLE
jk2_tab
Nested iteration
Table scan
STEP 2
The type of query is SELECT
FROM TABLE
jk1_tab
Nested iteration
Table scan
```

As mentioned previously, this gives the optimizer a problem as it is unable to determine the nested value at optimization time and will default to the fixed percentages for the where clause operator. This problem is most common with nested aggregates but will also occur with a single column value if written as a nesting.

```
SELECT * FROM jk1_tab
       WHERE e = (SELECT e from jk2_tab WHERE a = 128)
```

This will still execute as a two stage plan even though it could be evaluated as a join, which would avoid the problem of the index statistics on jk1_tab.e not being used.

Outer Query Contains an OR Clause

```
SELECT a FROM jk1_tab
       WHERE e IN (SELECT e from jk2_tab)
       OR a = 128
```

```
STEP 1
The type of query is SELECT (into a worktable)
GROUP BY
FROM TABLE
jk1_tab
Nested Iteration
Index: jk1_idxe
TO TABLE
Worktable
STEP 2
The type of query is SELECT (into a worktable)
GROUP BY
Vector aggregate
FROM TABLE
jk1_tab
Nested iteration
Index: jk1_idxe
FROM TABLE
jk2_tab
EXISTS TABLE: nested iteration
Index: jk2_idxe
TO TABLE
Worktable
STEP 3
The type of query is SELECT
FROM TABLE
jk1_tab
Nested iteration
Table Scan
FROM TABLE
Worktable
EXISTS TABLE: nested iteration
Table scan
```

This is a surprisingly poor performance plan caused by the OR with an initial pass of the outer table to create a worktable, which is then updated by a join across the nesting. The outer table and the worktable are then joined to provide the results. Note the use of the nonclustered index on "e" for the initial pass as all that the optimizer is looking for is row IDs, so any nonclustered index provides a covered index.

Outer Query Contains an AND Clause

In this situation, SQL Server takes any external search argument into the nested query to find the best plan for the inner query.

The query:

```
SELECT a FROM jk1_tab
       WHERE e IN (SELECT e FROM jk2_tab)
       AND a = 128
```

gives an execution plan of:

```
STEP 1
The type of query is SELECT
FROM TABLE
jk1_tab
Nested iteration
using clustered index
FROM TABLE
jk2_tab
EXISTS TABLE: nested iteration
Index: jk2_idxe
```

which is a simple nested evaluation in one step, as the optimizer has been able to flatten the nesting into an existence join. Fortunately, the restriction on "a" is on the outer table so the table sequence is correct. The addition of the AND has not altered the nested evaluation.

When the optimizer cannot flatten the query into a join, there is no way the optimizer knows if the outer query search arguments are true or not, so it generates the same plan by evaluating the nesting first and then the full outer query. When the inner query uses a lot of disk accesses but the and does not (for example, equality on uniqueness), it is often worthwhile to do the and portion as a separate query.

```
IF EXISTS (SELECT 1 FROM jk1_tab WHERE a = 128)
BEGIN
       SELECT a FROM jk1_tab
              WHERE e = (SELECT avg(e) FROM jk2_tab)
              AND a=128
END
```

Nested Query Contains a GROUP BY Aggregate

```
SELECT * FROM jk1_tab
       WHERE a IN (SELECT sum(a) FROM jk2_tab
                              GROUP BY e)

STEP 1
The type of query is SELECT (into a Worktable)
GROUP BY
Vector aggregate
FROM TABLE
jk2_tab
Nested iteration
Table scan
TO TABLE
Worktable
STEP 2
The type of query is SELECT
FROM TABLE
Worktable
Nested iteration
Table scan
FROM TABLE
jk1_tab
Nested iteration
Using clustered index
```

Again, there is no real complication. The nested query is evaluated to a worktable and this is joined with the outer table.

Nonexistence Checks

Not In

This is such an expensive plan that it is worth looking at with the 311 trace flag.

```
dbcc traceon(311)
go
SELECT a FROM jk1_tab
       WHERE a NOT IN (SELECT a FROM jk2_tab)
go

Table: jk1_tab,scan count 1,   logical reads: 256,   physical reads: 256
       jk1_tab,scan count 1,   logical reads: 256,   physical reads: 256
       jk2_tab,scan count 512, logical reads: 65536,physical reads: 128
       worktable,scan count 1, logical reads: 10,    physical reads: 10
       jk1_tab, scan count 10, logical reads: 30,    physical reads: 30
```

```
STEP 1
The type of query is SELECT (into a worktable)
GROUP BY
FROM TABLE
jk1_tab
Nested Iteration
Table Scan
TO TABLE
Worktable
STEP 2
The type of query is SELECT (into Worktable)
GROUP BY
Vector Aggregate
FROM TABLE
jk1_tab
Nested Iteration
Table Scan
FROM TABLE
jk2_tab
EXISTS TABLE: Nested Iteration
Table scan
TO TABLE
Worktable
STEP 3
The type of query is SELECT
FROM TABLE
Worktable
Nested Iteration
Table Scan
FROM TABLE
jk1_tab
Nested Iteration
Using Clustered index
```

This involves a read of the outer table to create a projected, restricted worktable of row IDs. The worktable is then updated to flag all rows in jk1_tab which match with jk2_tab, doing an exists as required in the ANSI standard. The final step is the join between the worktable and jk1_tab to get all rows which do not have the flag set.

This is an expensive plan and it is better to do it in two stages with an outer join to a temporary table and a selection on this.

```
SELECT jk1_tab.a a1, jk2_tab a2 INTO #jktemp
       FROM jk1_tab, jk2_tab
       WHERE jk1_tab.a *= jk2_tab.a
```

```
Table: jk1_tab,  scan count 1,  logical reads: 256,physical reads: 256
       jk2_tab,  scan count 512,logical reads: 1024,physical reads: 1
```

```
STEP 1
The type of query is CREATE TABLE
STEP 2
The type of query is INSERT
The update mode is direct
Worktable created for REFORMATTING
FROM TABLE
jk2_tab
Nested iteration
Table scan
TO TABLE
Worktable
STEP 3
The type of query is INSERT
The update mode is direct
Worktable created for SELECT_INTO
FROM TABLE
jk1_tab
Nested iteration
Table scan
FROM TABLE
Worktable
Nested iteration
Using clustered index
TO TABLE
Worktable
```

```
SELECT a1 FROM #jktemp WHERE a2 IS NULL
```

```
Table:  #jktemp,  scan count 1,      logical reads: 4,      physical reads: 4
STEP 1
The type of query is SELECT
FROM TABLE
#jktemp
Nested iteration
Table scan
```

I reran these with set statistics io on and got different I/O values.

not in

```
jk1_tab,       scan count 258,       logical reads: 1408
jk2_tab,       scan count 512,       logical reads: 49208
worktable,     scan count 1,         logical reads: 1563
```

outer join

```
select into
jk1_tab,       scan count: 1,  logical reads: 256
jk2_tab,       scan count: 1,  logical reads: 128
#jktemp,       scan count: 0,  logical reads: 522
worktable,     scan count: 512,logical reads: 1304
```

```
select
#jktemp,                scan count: 1, logical reads: 4
```

As usually happens, the actuals are different than the estimates but the saving is still significant (2,200:52,000). This does stress how important it is to check actuals even though you have the trace flags on.

Exists

```
SELECT a FROM jk1_tab
       WHERE EXISTS (SELECT 1 FROM jk2_tab
                            WHERE jk1_tab.a = jk2_tab.e)
STEP 1
The type of query is SELECT
FROM TABLE
jk1_tab
Nested Iteration
Table Scan
FROM TABLE
jk2_tab
EXISTS TABLE: Nested Iteration
Index jk2_idxe
```

There is nothing unusual here: an existence join between the two tables.

Not Exists

```
SELECT a FROM jk1_tab
       WHERE NOT EXISTS
                      (SELECT 1 FROM jk2_tab
                                   WHERE jk1_tab.a = jk2_tab.e)

STEP 1
The type of query is SELECT (into worktable)
GROUP BY
FROM TABLE
jk1_tab
Nested Iteration
Table Scan
TO TABLE
Worktable
STEP 2
The type of query is SELECT (into worktable)
GROUP BY
Vector Aggregate
FROM TABLE
jk2_tab
Nested Iteration
```

```
Index: jk2_idxe
FROM TABLE
jk1_tab
Nested Iteration
Using Clustered index
TO TABLE
Worktable
STEP 3
The type of query is SELECT
FROM TABLE
Worktable
Nested Iteration
Table Scan
FROM TABLE
jk1_tab
Nested Iteration
Using Clustered index
```

This is a similar plan to the not in with a first pass of jk1_tab to load the worktable. Then, there is a join of the two tables to update the worktable with the matching rows and finally a join of the outer table and the worktable to display the rows not updated in STEP 2.

10.5 Practice versus Theory

Let's look at some proofs of these strategies by checking the showplan against the actual scan counts of logical reads and the I/O statistics. I am using the same tables as in section 10.4 (512 rows in 256 pages and 256 rows in 128 pages).

10.5.1 Join with No Indexes

```
SELECT a.a, b.a FROM jk1_tab a, jk2_tab b
       WHERE a.a = b.a
```

As expected, we get a reformatting strategy with jk2_tab as the inner table. As the worktable row size is the same, the smaller table is chosen as inner.

```
Table   jk1_tab,        Scan count 1,  logical reads 256
Table   jk2_tab,        Scan count 1,  logical reads 128
Table   worktable,      Scan count 512,logical reads 1306
```

The theory says this is correct because, with no other criteria, the nested iteration puts the smaller table as inner on the basis that fewer accesses are required to join each value.

But this does not take into account that the smaller table has fewer rows (as there is little difference in size in the two worktables) and more weight should be given to fewer iterations by placing the table with fewer rows as the outer table. The reformatting strategy does not seem to take this into account. Look what happens when I force jk1_tab to be the inner table. How? Simply make reformatting think that it is better as the inner table by making the worktable row smaller.

```
SELECT a.a, b.b FROM jk1_tab a, jk2_tab b
       WHERE a.a = b.a

Table jk1_tab,        Scan count 1,  logical reads 256
Table jk2_tab,        Scan count 1,  logical reads 128
Table worktable,      Scan count 256,logical reads 1052
```

10.5.2 Indexed Joins

```
SELECT a.a, b.b FROM jk1_tab a, jk2_tab b
       WHERE a.a = b.a
```

jk2_tab Nonclustered

As expected, we get a nested iteration with the indexed table as the inner table.

```
Table jk1_tab,        Scan count 1,  logical reads 256
Table jk2_tab,        Scan count 512,logical reads 1026
```

Both Tables Clustered

Here, we get a nested iteration with jk2_tab as the outer table and jk1_tab as the inner table.

```
Table jk1_tab,        Scan count 256,logical reads 895
Table jk2_tab,        Scan count 1,  logical reads 128
```

Notice that this time it put the smaller table as outer and did fewer iterations of the inner table, which produces the better plan. Why does the reformatting not do this? (And no, I do not know where the 895 comes from.)

One Covered Index and One Clustered Index

With this, we get a nested iteration with the covered index table jk2_tab as outer and the clustered index table jk1_tab as inner.

```
Table jk1_tab,        Scan count 256,logical reads 895
Table jk2_tab,        Scan count 1,  logical reads 2
```

Use of the covered index has reduced the number of logical reads significantly.

Both Nonclustered (i.e. Both Covered)

This produces a nested iteration with jk2_tab as the outer table, which is consistent with the previous both clustered case.

```
Table jk1_tab,          Scan count 256,logical reads 514
Table jk2_tab,          Scan count 1,  logical reads 2
```

10.5.3 Nested Statements

Flattened to Join (Both Clustered)

```
SELECT a FROM jk1_tab
      WHERE a IN (SELECT a FROM jk2_tab)
```

This gives a nested iteration with jk2_tab as the inner table as required by the existence join, which eliminates duplicates.

```
Table jk1_tab,          Scan count 1,  logical reads 256
Table jk2_tab,          Scan count 512,logical reads 1024
```

Notice the difference in total logical reads compared to the previous both clustered join, which is done with jk1_tab as the inner table: 1,280 logical reads compared with 1,023.

Distinct in Nesting

```
SELECT a FROM jk1_tab
      WHERE a IN (SELECT DISTINCT a FROM jk2_tab)
```

```
Table jk1_tab,          Scan count 1,  logical reads 256
Table jk2_tab,          Scan count 512,logical reads 1024
```

As expected, we get the same plan and execution as the flattened nested query. The distinct keyword in a nesting is now ignored.

Scalar Aggregate in Nesting

```
SELECT a FROM jk1_tab
      WHERE e = (SELECT avg(e) FROM jk2_tab)
```

This evaluates the nested command and then the outer command, as expected.

```
Table jk1_tab,          Scan count 1,          logical reads 256
Table jk2_tab,          Scan count 1,          logical reads 128
```

10.5.4 Correlated versus Noncorrelated Nesting

Noncorrelated

```
SELECT a FROM jk1_tab
       WHERE e IN (SELECT jk2_tab.e FROM jk1_tab, jk2_tab
                               WHERE jk1_tab.a = jk2_tab.a)
```

This produced 256 result rows (as expected) but created two worktables and did two existence joins.

```
STEP 1
The type of query is INSERT
The update mode is direct
Worktable created for REFORMATTING
From table
jk2_tab
Nested iteration
Table scan
To table
Worktable
STEP 2
The type of query is SELECT
From table
jk1_tab
Nested iteration
Table scan
From table
Worktable
EXISTS TABLE: nested iteration
Using clustered index
From table
jk1_tab
EXISTS TABLE: Nested iteration
Using clustered index

Table jk1_tab,       Scan count 1,  logical reads 256
Table jk1_tab,       Scan count 256,logical reads 768
Table jk2_tab,       Scan count 1,  logical reads 128
Table worktable,     Scan count 512,logical reads 1303
```

Correlated

```
SELECT a from jk1_tab
       WHERE e IN (SELECT e FROM jk2_tab
                          WHERE jk1_tab.a = jk2_tab.a)
```

This produced the same 256 result rows, as expected.

```
STEP 1
The type of query is SELECT
FROM TABLE
jk1_tab
Nested iteration
Table Scan
FROM TABLE
jk2_tab
EXISTS TABLE: Nested Iteration
Using Clustered index
Table jk1_tab,              Scan count 256,       logical reads 896
Table jk2_tab,              Scan count 512,       logical reads 1024
```

However, this time the execution was more efficient as a simple nested join between the two tables. This floored me because I have always preached that noncorrelated was never any worse than correlated. I take it back. Of course, I checked it with more examples.

Based on a more detailed analysis that I carried out to support these figures, it appears that the simpler the nesting, the faster it is using correlated nestings. But as the command gets more complicated, it is better to write in a noncorrelated fashion. My tests indicated that those which could be flattened to a join were better when correlated and those which could not be flattened into a join were better when noncorrelated. But please check. Much more importantly, it is difficult to take a query written in one mode—say, correlated—and rewrite it in the other mode without altering the meaning of the query. All I can really say is to write the query as you feel comfortable but be aware that the correlated join can be quite expensive when the nesting is complicated.

10.6 Stored Procedure Optimization

SQL in stored procedures is optimized the same as SQL elsewhere; the difference is in the frequency and the timing. The stored procedure SQL is optimized when the stored procedure is loaded into procedure cache and is not optimized again while the procedure remains in cache. With procedures that contain parameterized statements with range based retrievals, the first parameter values may generate an execution plan which is unsuitable for subsequent executions of the statement with different parameter values.

A WHERE clause such as:

```
WHERE name LIKE @name + '%'
```

will probably use a nonclustered index if the parameter value is KIRKWOOD but may do a table scan if the parameter value is S (on a nonclustered index, of course).

Therefore, stored procedures which have:

- parameterized statements;
- range based tests such as like, between, >, <;
- a wide range of parameter values on different executions of the procedure;
- access on a nonclustered index;

should be highlighted as potential performance problems.

The simplest answer is to recompile the procedure to force a new execution plan. This may be done in three ways:

1. create proc....with recompile;
2. execute proc...with recompile;
3. sp_recompile [table_name].

10.6.1 Create Proc...with Recompile

This causes a recompile of the procedure at every execution. This defeats the CPU savings that you are trying to gain with procedures; however, all is not lost as it still reduces network traffic and modularizes the programs at the server. On the other hand, it is an extreme measure and not my first choice. Several of my colleagues disagree with me on this one, so please make up your own mind when you have a procedure which needs regular recompilation. I am not sure that it is that black and white in practice, and you may find justification for using both approaches.

10.6.2 Execute Proc...with Recompile

In a single user situation, the first execution of a procedure causes it to be read from disk, compiled and optimized. When the above parameter and range problems exist, subsequent executions of the procedure using different parameter values will use the copy in procedure cache and the execution plan may not suit the new parameter values, causing a poor response time. This may be overcome by executing the procedure with recompile to create an execution plan which suits the input parameter values.

In a multiuser environment with more than one user executing the same procedure, life gets a little bit more complicated. The procedure copies in cache may be reused but are not re-entrant, which means that only one user at a time may be executing a procedure copy in cache. If a user executes a procedure while it is not being executed by any other user, any current copy of the procedure in cache is used. This clearly leads to the same optimization problem as the single user execution. If a user executes a procedure while all cache copies are being executed by other users, the current copies in cache will be locked by the executing users and a new copy will have to be read from disk, compiled and optimized.

It is interesting when several cache copies are currently free as there is no guarantee that a user making several executions of the procedure will always get the same cache copy for every execution. The copies in cache are being allocated to users on a first come, first served basis. So, if there are several copies in cache, there is no guarantee that a user will always get the same cache copy. Clearly, this aggravates the problem of an unsuitable execution plan.

As complicated as this sounds, the problem of unsuitable execution plans applies to only the heavily-parameterized procedures that are executed with widely-varying parameter values on nonclustered indexes. The times when this occurs will be reasonably obvious and simple to correct with recompile. Do not panic; execute with recompile is usually sufficient to overcome this problem.

10.6.3 sp_recompile

SQL Server uses procedure cache very efficiently and there is a reasonable chance that a frequently-used procedure will remain in cache for long periods of time. When SQL Server is looking for space in procedure cache to load in a fresh copy of a procedure, it works on a least-used basis except that it tries to retain at least one copy of each procedure in cache. So, even if you do not use a procedure for some time, there may still be a copy of the procedure in cache. There is no guarantee that unused versions are no longer in cache and the performance problem may recur from an old version. Occasionally, you will need to flush the procedure from cache to ensure that all cache versions have gone.

There is no command to flush a named procedure from cache. The common approach is to drop and recreate the procedure. This is not as foolish as it sounds. Most SAs will have scripts to do this and even have a routine in the operational system that automatically drops any procedure before loading it into the operational system. We are really discussing simple version control in the operational system here.

```
IF EXISTS (SELECT 1 FROM sysobjects
                     WHERE type = 'P'
                     AND name = @name)
BEGIN
       DROP PROC @name
END
GO
CREATE PROC @name as...
```

SQL Server provides a system procedure **sp_recompile** which will recompile all procedures or all procedures for a named table.

sp_recompile

```
sp_recompile table_name
```

This does not recompile the procedures immediately but tags them in sysobjects and recompiles at the next execution. However, be careful as each recompilation using sp_recompile increases the size of the procedure by a small amount. Section 11.4 describes trace flag 241, which may be set for the server to automatically recover this space, but it is a resource intensive activity and not recommended in normal operation.

10.6.4 Automatic Recompilation

SQL Server requires the table option on sp_recompile because it does not automatically recompile procedures for every change to a table. If a procedure is in cache and does not need to be recompiled, SQL Server simply checks that everything it needs is available. So it is only when an object is not available (e.g., table, index, column) that the procedure will initiate a recompile. When the recompilation happens, if the dropped object is essential to the execution of the procedure (such as a column or a table), the compilation will fail. However if it is a nonessential object (such as an index) then a new execution plan is generated, the compilation is successful and the procedure executes. Adding an index, rebuilding the index statistics or adding a new column does not force a recompile. If you have added an index or updated the index statistics to make the procedure go faster, you must recompile it to take advantage of the new situation.

It is important to realize that any new object does not cause an automatic recompilation of a procedure, so writing select * in a procedure does not show all of the fields after you have changed the table unless you recompile.

If you write:

```
CREATE PROC jk_proc AS
BEGIN
        SELECT * FROM tab_1
RETURN
END
```

and add a new field to tab_1, the procedure will not show the new field until you recompile it.

10.7 Summary

The System 10 optimizer is as good as they come and subquery optimization has been improved further, as we'll discuss in Chapter 12. It does not always produce what you might expect but usually there are good reasons for it doing so. You need to be careful of the usual things: keep the statistics up-to-date, use search arguments, choose the column sequence of composite indexes carefully, watch out when the value is not known at optimization time, make optimum use of covered indexes, avoid the use of NOT and always check what you expect with a showplan.

11
What If? Problem Anticipation and Solving

This chapter is a collection of configuration, monitoring and problem-solving techniques and tools.

The System 11 changes to sp_configure are mentioned here but discussed in detail in Chapter 12, along with the new sp_configure parameters. There are a few other small changes, mainly in the output of the commands sp_spaceused, sp_who and dbcc. A new monitoring system procedure—sp_sysmon – has been added

COMMAND SYNTAX

```
reconfigure
set statistics
dbcc
```

SYSTEM PROCEDURE SYNTAX

```
sp_configure
sp_monitor
sp_indsuspect
sp_spaceused
sp_lock
sp_who
sp_recompile
sp_sysmon
```

11.1 Server Configuration

There is a set of parameters held in the master system table sysconfigures that defines the configuration of the server. These parameters are defined and displayed by the system procedure **sp_configure**. Some of the configuration parameters—recovery interval, allow updates, nested triggers, upgrade version, default language, CPU flush, I/O flush, password expiration interval—are altered dynamically. All of the others require a restart of the server. Sysconfigures contains the current setting of each variable but, as this may not yet be in effect, a temporary table—syscurconfigs—is created and displayed by sp_configure to display the current settings.

sp_configure

```
sp_configure

name                     minimum maximum    config_value  run_value
recovery interval        1       32767      0             5
allow updates            0       1          0             0
user connections         5       1024       0             25
memory                   1000    2147483647 0             3200
open databases           5       2147483647 0             10
locks                    5000    2147483647 0             5000
open objects             100     2147483647 0             500
procedure cache          1       99         0             20
fillfactor               0       100        0             0
time slice               50      1000       0             100
database size            2       10000      0             2
tape retention           0       365        0             0
recovery flags           0       1          0             0
nested triggers          0       1          1             1
devices                  4       256        15            15
remote access            0       1          0             0
remote logins            0       2147483647 0             0
remote sites             0       2147483647 0             0
remote connections       0       2147483647 0             0
pre-read packets         0       2147483647 0             0
upgrade version          0       2147483647 420           420
default sort order id    0       255        20            20
default language         0       2147483647 0             0
language in cache        3       100        3             3
max on-line engines      1       32         1             1
min on-line engines      1       32         1             1
engine adjust interval   1       32         0             0
cpu flush                1       2147483647 0             300
```

```
i/o flush                     1      2147483647   0      1000
default character set id      0      255          1      1
stack size                    20480  2147483647   0      28672
password expiration interval  0      32767        0      0
audit queue size              1      65535        100    100
additional netmem             0      2147483647   0      0
default network packet size   512    524288       0      512
maximum network packet size   512    524288       0      512
extent i/o buffers            0      2147483647   0      0
identity burning set factor   1      9999999      5000   5000
```

The settings are changed by quoting the appropriate parameter and value.

```
sp_configure 'parameter', value
```

```
sp_configure 'recovery interval', 10
```

The dynamic parameters are then reset immediately using **reconfigure**. (This is no longer required in System 11.)

reconfigure

```
reconfigure [with override]
```

The with override option is used for the option **allow updates**.

```
sp_configure 'recovery interval', 15
go
reconfigure
go
sp_configure 'allow updates', 1
go
reconfigure with override
go
```

11.2 Parameters

If you are in doubt about the units for each parameter have a look in the comments column of sysconfigures.

```
select comment from sysconfigures
```

```
Comment
Maximum recovery interval in minutes
Allow updates to system tables
Number of user connections allowed
Size of available memory in 2 K pages
Number of open databases allowed among all users
Number of locks for all users
Number of open database objects
Percentage of remaining memory used for procedure cache
Default fillfactor percentage
Average timeslice per process in milliseconds
Default database size in megabytes
Tape retention period in days
Recovery flags
Allow triggers to be invoked within triggers
Number of devices
Allow remote access
Number of remote logins
Number of remote sites
Number of remote connections
Number of pre-read packets per remote connection
Upgrade version
Default language
Language cache
Max on-line engines
Min on-line engines
CPU accounting flush interval
I/O accounting flush interval
Default character set ID
Stack size
System wide password expiration interval
Audit queue size
Additional netmem
Default network packet size
Maximum network packet size
Number of extent I/O buffers
Identity burning set factor
```

A large number of the parameter names have changed in System 11. I have indicated these in brackets after the System 10 name.

recovery interval [recovery interval in Minutes]

```
sp_configure 'recovery interval', 10
go
reconfigure
go
```

The recovery interval is set in minutes with a default value of five, which is as good as anything else.

The recovery interval determines the checkpoint frequency. The value is taken as the maximum amount of time that transaction recovery from a system failure should take. When the transaction management system determines that it has written enough images to the transaction log for recovery to take this long, it takes a checkpoint. So, although it determines when a checkpoint is taken, the figure is not the time between checkpoints but the maximum time it should take to recover from system failure. As mentioned in Chapter 5, the time is the number of log records multiplied by 10 ms.

Note that the interval specified is not an upper bound for the recovery interval. If the server goes down during the execution of a long-running transaction, the recovery interval may exceed this time by a considerable amount.

allow updates [allow updates to System Tables]

```
sp_configure 'allow updates', 1
go
reconfigure with override
go
```

Allow updates is set as 1 (true) or 0 (false) with a default of 0. Set this to 1 only under very special circumstances and have the database as **dbo use only** to make sure that no one else is allowed to use the database.

This setting allows updates to the system tables. This really is for emergency use only as users—including the SA—should not require update capability on the system tables. You need the system tables to operate the database, so be careful. Speak to Sybase first about what you intend to do and, you may not get their approval, but at least they may indicate if you are about to cause a disaster.

If you create a procedure to make the changes to the system tables, this procedure will still be able to update the system tables after the **allow updates** flag has been set to zero. So make sure that you revoke execute from public to prevent another user being able to execute the procedure.

user connections [Number of user connections]

```
sp_configure 'user connections', 30
```

This sets the total number of concurrent connections to the server.

The maximum depends on the operating system, so check your specific system: Sun: 25–1024 depending on the system; Digital VMS: 500 depending on the Decnet limit; Ultrix 256–2000; Pyramid: 1024; and so on.

Each connection requires about 50 K (64 K for open server) of memory, depending on the stack size. If you make a large increase to the number of connections, remember that you may need to increase the memory allocation. At a default of 25, this costs 1.25 MB. At 100 connections, it costs 5 MB. So be careful of the memory requirements here. The stock size and connection overhead is platform-specific, so be sure to check this. This is especially true for 64-bit platforms.

The server requires three connections by default for master device, error log and standard output. Each device which you create requires one connection and each dbopen from an application requires a connection.

Sybase software requires:

isql	one connection per user;
DWB	1–4 connections, depending on the level of screen nesting; two connections when using the data dictionary;
APT	It's up to you, but one per channel; (APT-Build uses at least two).

memory [Total memory]

```
sp_configure 'memory', 8000
```

This sets the available memory for the server in units of 2 K pages. I deal with the size calculation in Appendix F but the rules of thumb are:

system, etc.	4 MB
SQL Server kernel	4 MB
connections	3 per user @ 50 K each
databases	17 K per open database
objects	315 bytes
locks	80 bytes
procedure cache	3 procedures per connection @ 12 K per procedure
data cache	5–20% of data

Set this for all that you need—close to the maximum if you have a dedicated server, but be careful not to cause SQL Server to swap. At start-up, the server will grab all that you have allocated and not release it when another process requests memory unless the server is quiescent. If this happens, it will page fault to get back to full size again and no user processes can execute until the server is loaded back into memory. This is not a good idea. In Unix, remember to allocate enough swap space to hold the server if it is swapped out. Even if not used, this swap space must be available. Try not to have the server paging in and out. Relational databases love memory so give it what it needs all of the time.

open databases [Number of open databases]

```
sp_configure 'open databases', 20
```

This sets the total number of concurrently-open databases for the server. The default is 10, which at 17 K per database costs 170 K.

It is unlikely that you will need to set this very high but there is no point in setting it too low and having to restart the server. Quite simply, it depends on how many databases you expect to have on the server.

locks [Number of locks]

```
sp_configure  'locks', 8000
```

This sets the total number of concurrent locks for the server. The default is 5,000. At 80 bytes per lock, this costs about 400 K.

I deal with this in Appendix F but the rule of thumb is the number of connections multiplied by 20.

open objects [Number of open objects]

```
sp_configure 'open objects', 2000
```

This sets the number of objects open at the same time on the server. The default is 500. At 315 bytes per object, this costs about 160 K. You will need a lot of these—one for each entry in sysobjects for all databases.

procedure cache [procedure cache Percent]

```
sp_configure 'procedure cache', 10
```

This sets the percentage of "leftover" memory that is allocated to hold the compiled procedures. Leftover memory is the memory available in that set by "memory" after the server, connections and objects have had their share; in other words, what is left for procedures and data. The default is 20%.

Be careful to alter the percentage when you increase memory to provide more data cache. I cover this in Appendix F.

The error log after startserver shows the actual allocation of memory for data and procedures in 2 K pages.

number of buffers in buffer cache:	400	(data cache)
number of proc buffers allocated:	70	(procedure cache)
number of blocks left for proc headers:	60	

The first figure is the number of data cache pages: 400 * 2 K (0.8 MB).

The second figure is the number of procedure cache pages: 70 * 2 K (0.14 MB).

The third figure indicates how many compiled objects (procedures, triggers, views, rules, defaults) you can have in procedure cache at the one time. A proc buffer is a structure used to manage a compiled object. A 2 K page can hold 21 proc buffers, so the above 60 proc buffers require three pages, which increases the procedure cache to 73 pages.

fillfactor [Default fillfactor Percent]

```
sp_configure  'fillfactor', 75
```

This sets the percentage to which index and clustered data pages are filled during initial create. The default is 0, which means the clustered data pages are packed to 100% and the index pages have enough space to add one or two index records. The literature says this is a "comfortable amount of space" but this may be too little on a volatile table.

When a new entry is added to a full index page, it splits 50:50, into two. This is a very high overhead to the transaction and may be minimized by allocating an initial amount of free space in each index page via the fillfactor. The percentage used is application-dependent but as full pages split 50:50, the index will navigate to 75% occupancy so—unless there is a good reason like a high insert rate—you might as well start at 75%.

The server-wide fillfactor may be overridden in the individual index create.

timeslice [time slice]

```
sp_configure  'timeslice', 100
```

This sets the time in milliseconds that the server allocates to each task in turn. The server has its own scheduler that allocates processing time to each task on a "round robin" basis. Each process runs until it uses up its timeslice and then waits until it is its turn again. You should not need to adjust this but, if you feel that you must, please discuss it with Sybase. There is some merit in considering a longer timeslice than the default 100 ms for batch work. At the end of each timeslice, SQL Server has to do some work to see if another process is ready to run. In a batch situation, this is an overhead which can be reduced by setting a longer timeslice so that the batch process can run for longer each time it gets control. In a normal interactive environment, do not set this too high as it will increase the response time to users.

database size [Default database size]

```
sp_configure  'database size', 10
```

This sets the default database size in megabytes. The default is 2 MB.

If no size is specified in the create database statement, the maximum of this value and the size of model is used. If other than 2 MB is required, it is better to increase this value as increasing model takes up space on the master device. Use model as the template and this value as the default size.

tape retention [tape retention in Days]

```
sp_configure 'tape retention', 5
```

This sets the number of days before a tape written by dump database should be reused. A warning message is issued if you try to reuse a tape in dump database before its retention period.

recovery flags [Print Recovery Information]

```
sp_configure 'recovery flags', 0
```

If set to 1 (true), this displays all messages during recovery. The default is 0 (false).

Set to 1 is useful during testing to see what the recovery mechanism is doing. Once you have satisfied your curiosity—and it is useful to know what recovery does in case you have a problem—set if off. Do not set this on operational recovery as it will significantly slow down the recovery.

allow nested triggers [allow nested triggers]

```
sp_configure 'allow nested triggers', 1
```

This is set to 1 (true) to enable the firing of nested triggers so that a trigger may be invoked by action within a trigger. The default is 1. This is useful for allowing the writing of modular triggers. If there is a hierarchy of tables (as in Figure 11.1) with deletion cascaded from the order table then with no nesting, the order trigger must delete both items and deliveries. This requires duplication of the delete delivery code in the item trigger. With nesting, the delete of item from order fires the item trigger, which deletes the deliveries. So there is no duplication of code.

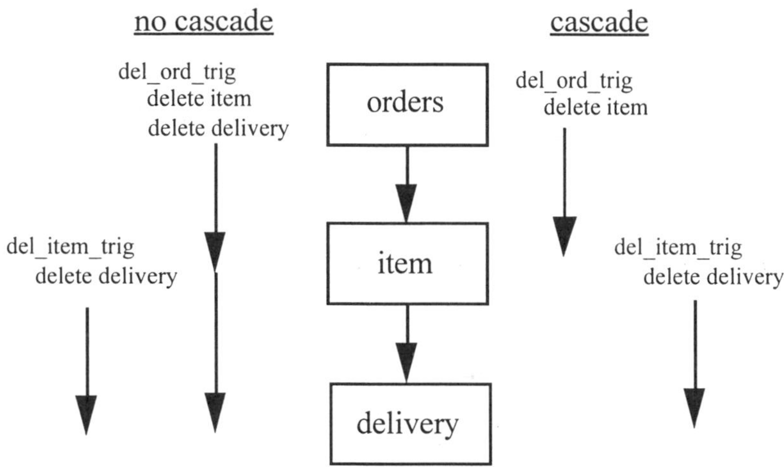

Figure 11.1 *Trigger nesting.*

This option is provided for backwards compatibility only. It should be left at one unless you intend running very old applications (consider recoding these to make use of nested triggers).

devices [Number of devices]

```
sp_configure "devices", 60
```

This sets the number of logical devices (vdevno in disk init) available to the server. The default is 10, configurable up to 256. Be careful: do not set this lower than the highest value currently in use or databases on these devices will not be recoverable.

remote access [Allow remote access]

```
sp_configure "remote access", 1
```

This is set to 1 (true) to allow other servers to function as remote servers for execution of stored procedure calls defined on other servers. Remote access must be configured to write Open Server programs. Configuring remote access allows the definition of four other parameters:

1. remote logins — the maximum number of users allowed to login remotely to another server from this server. Default is 20.
2. remote sites — the maximum number of active remote sites. Default is 10.
3. remote connects — the maximum number of user connections to remote sites. Default is 20.
4. pre-read packets — the number of packets which are pre-read for a user over a connection. Default is 3.

Remember that all of these remote access features are system configuration options. For that reason, you need to restart the server before they take effect and before the remote servers/logins are known so that you can execute remote procedure calls.

Upgrade Version [Upgrade Version]

This is simply the version you are running and not something you need to touch. This is changed automatically by the upgrade program provided with new releases.

Default Sortorder ID [Default Sortorder ID]

The default sort is binary sort order (ISO 8859-1)—numbers followed by uppercase alphabetic followed by lowercase alphabetic. Other sort orders may be defined at installation. This can be seen using sp_helpsort.

Default Language [Default Language ID]

The default is US/English. This is used for the language of the system messages and the date internationalization. New languages can be added using the system procedure sp_addlanguage. The current language may be altered using the "language" parameter of the "set" command.

Language In Cache [Number of Languages in Cache]

The maximum number of languages which can be held currently in the language cache.

Max Online Engines [Max Online Engines]

The number of engines in symmetric multi-processing (SMP) environments. The term "engine" is a process which runs a SQL Server and represents a CPU-worth of processing power but is not necessarily related directly to a particular CPU.

Min Online Engines [Min Online Engines]

This parameter is not currently used.

Engine Adjust Interval [no System 11 configuration parameter]

This parameter is not currently used.

CPU Flush [CPU Accounting Flush Interval]

I/O Flush [I/O Accounting Flush Interval]

These are used in chargeback accounting to specify how many CPU ticks or read/write I/Os to accumulate before flushing the data to syslogins.

Default Character Set ID [Default Character Set ID]

This specifies the default character set used by the server. It is set and changed using the installation routine **sybinit**. You really do not want to touch this one—or the default sort order—after you have decided what it is to be at installation. If you do change either of these, you will need to check the indexes to see if they are still valid. This requires a run of **sp_indsuspect** on each table and a **dbcc reindex** if you find any problems.

sp_indsuspect

```
    sp_indsuspect [table_name]
```

```
sp_indsuspect
```

```
Suspect indexes in database fred
Own.tab.ind (obj_id, ind_id) =
dbo.jkl_tab.idxe(460003208, 2)
```

Stack Size [Stack Size]

This defines the server's execution or argument stack size. If a query exceeds this size, it generates an error message and rolls back the query. This is not likely to occur in normal operation but may occur if the query has many where clauses,especially with in operators. If it does occur, the first approach should be to split the large query into several smaller ones. Changing the stack size has a direct effect on the memory requirements of all user connections, as each connection requires 23 K plus the stack size of memory. Stack sizes are always rounded up to multiples of 2 K.

Password Expiration Interval [Systemwide Password Expiration]

This specifies the number of days that passwords remain in effect until they must be changed. The default of 0 means that passwords do not expire.

Audit Queue Size [Audit Queue Size]

This is the number of audit records held in the audit queue. The default is 100, which equates approximately to a memory requirement of 42 K, depending on the type of auditing enabled.

Additional Netmem [Additional Network Memory]

This sets the maximum size of additional memory that can be used by network packets that are larger than the default server size of 512 bytes. Note that this memory allocation is in addition to the **memory** parameter, so make sure that there is enough memory available or you may start swapping the server.

Default Network Packet Size [Default Network Packet Size]

This configures the default network size for all users. The default is 512 bytes. You can set this up to 524,288 with the value being rounded down to multiples of 512. Each connection uses three buffers—read, overflow, write—so the memory required for network packets is:

user connections * 3 * default network packet size

If you increase this parameter, you must also increase the **maximum network packet size**.

Maximum Network Packet Size [Max Network Packet Size]

The transfer of large amounts of data across the network—bulk copy or text/image—will benefit by using a larger packet size than the default 512 bytes. Setting this maximum allows connections to request a larger packet size than the default. As for the default size, this may be set to a maximum of 524,288 bytes rounded to multiples of 512. If you wish to set this parameter, you must also set the **additional netmem** value, otherwise connections will not be able to use the increased sizes. The additional netmem value should be set to:

> number of parallel user connections * 3 (plus a 2% overhead)
> using larger sizes

Extent I/O Buffers [Number of Extent I/O Buffers]

The number of extents allocated for use by the create index command. This is discussed in section 7.7.1. This memory allocation comes from the **memory** parameter allocation and effects the amount of data and procedure cache available.

Identity Burning Set Factor [Identity Burning Set Factor]

This determines the number of identity numbers that are made available in a block. This is a percentage value times 107. To set a value of 15%, specify a value of 0.15 times 107.

```
sp_configure "identity burning set factor", 1500000
```

This will release 15% of the potential identity values (determined by the precision of the numeric datatype) at a time. Note that a rollback will lose the unused portion of the block of numbers defined by this value. The default is 5,000 (i.e. 0.05%).

Finally, be careful when you alter configuration variables. They do not take effect until you restart the server (except the dynamic ones mentioned earlier) Consequently, you can easily create a combination which the server is unable to accept and startserver will fail. This is not always checked as you change the variables, only when you start the server. If you do get into this position, you will have to rebuild the master device using “buildmaster -r” as described in Appendix B.

11.3 Monitoring System Activity

SQL Server provides a few system procedures for monitoring assistance:

1. sp_spaceused space used by databases and tables (Appendix A);
2. sp_lock locks set by a transaction (Appendix D);
3. sp_who user and process information;
4. sp_monitor system activity.

System 11.0.1 has introduced a significant new monitoring procedure—sp_sysmon.

11.3.1 Spaceused

The current space allocation of databases, individual tables and indexes in the database may be displayed using **sp_spaceused**.

sp_spaceused

```
sp_spaceused [table_name [, 1]]
```

```
sp_spaceused jkl_tab
```

name	rowtotal	reserved	data	index_size	unused
jkl_tab	512	796 KB	512 KB	202 KB	82 KB

where

reserved	amount of space currently reserved for use;
data	amount of space being used by data;
index_size	amount of space being used by indexes;
unused	amount of reserved space not currently in use.

The space is allocated in extents of eight pages. Empty pages are not released from the table allocation until the complete extent is empty, so there will usually be an amount of unused space in the reserved figure. If data+index+unused does not add up to reserved, you have a problem.

Used without a table name, it provides space information on the database.

```
sp_spaceused
```

database_name		database_size	
fred_db		10.0 MB	

reserved	data	index_size	unused
2566 KB	1112 KB	322 KB	1132 KB

Used with the "1" parameter in System 11, it provides size information on each index of the table.

```
sp_spaceused jkl_tab, 1
```

index_name	size	reserved	unused
jkl_tab	0 KB	572 KB	60 KB
jkl_idx1	202 KB	224 KB	22 KB

name	rowtotal	reserved	data	index_size	unused
jkl_tab	512	796 KB	512 KB	202 KB	82 KB

11.3.2 Transaction Locks

The locks held by a transaction are displayed using **sp_lock**.

sp_lock

```
sp_lock [spid1 [, spid2]]
```

where

spid	the optional SQL Server process ID.

```
sp_lock
```

spid	locktype	table_id	page	dbname	class
1	ex_intent	122004611	0	fred	non cursor lock
1	ex_page	122004611	509	fred	non cursor lock
1	ex_page	122004611	1419	fred	non cursor lock
1	ex_page	122004611	1420	fred	non cursor lock
1	ex_page	122004611	1440	fred	non cursor lock
1	sh_page	122004611	1440	fred	non cursor lock
1	sh_table	122004611	0	fred	non cursor lock
1	update_page	122004607	1440	fred	non cursor lock
5	sh_intent	26004256	0	master	non cursor lock
6	ex_intent	0	1128	tempdb	non cursor lock

11.3.3 User and Process Information

Information on all processes or processes for a specific login/spid is displayed using **sp_who**.

sp_who

```
sp_who [login_name|"spid"]
```

Note that the spid must be enclosed in quotes as a character parameter is expected.

```
sp_who

spid  status      loginame  hostname  blk  dbname      cmd
1     recv sleep  sa        LNW312    0    fred_db     AWAITING COMMAND
2     sleeping    NULL                0    master      NETWORK HANDLER
3     sleeping    NULL                0    master      DEADLOCK TUNE
4     sleeping    NULL                0    master      MIRROR HANDLER
5     sleeping    NULL                0    master      HOUSEKEEPER
6     sleeping    NULL                0    master      CHECKPOINT SLEEP
7     running     sa        LNW312    0    fred_db     SELECT
```

where

blk	indicates the spid which is blocking the process. An sp_lock on that spid will indicate the pages being locked to assist in resolving the problem. A dbcc page on the page number (see 11.5.2) will indicate if the page is a data or index page. You can then ask the user to close any open transaction or, more commonly, you will need to kill the blocking process.
status	indicates the current status of the process including: sleeping running runnable recv sleep (waiting on a network read) send sleep (waiting on a network send) alarm sleep (waiting on an alarm from a waitfor) lock sleep (waiting on acquiring a lock).

The DEADLOCK TUNE and HOUSEKEEPER are System 11 tasks.

11.3.4 System Activity

The activity system procedure sp_monitor shows CPU, I/O and network activity as a total since the last sp_monitor.

sp_monitor

```
sp_monitor

last_run                  current_run                  seconds
May 26 1995 18:55         May 26 1995 18:56            24985
cpu_busy                  io_busy                idle
430(427)-0%               410(410) - 0%                0(0) - 0%
packets_received          packets_sent           packet_errors
4310(4124)                9901(9719)                   5(5)
total_recd                total_write            total_errors   connections
28657(28556)              100890(100038) 0(0)          127(125)
```

The first set of figures is the cumulative values since the server was started. The second set is the values since the last issue of sp_monitor. Therefore, this activity monitoring tool has a limited use and is really only effective at peak loading times to highlight any bottlenecks.

The System 11 system procedure **sp_sysmon** provides a snapshot of the system activity.

sp_sysmon

Some sample output from sp_sysmon is as follows.

```
Task Management                      per sec   per xact  count    % of total
Connections opened                   0.3       0.0       17       n/a
Task Context Switches by Engine
Engine 0                             64.5      7.5       3962     100.0%
Task Context Switches due to
Voluntary Yields                     6.6       0.8       406      10.2%
Cache Search Misses                  5.6       0.7       347      8.8%
System Disk Writes                   1.4       0.2       87       2.2%
I/O Paging                           2.1       0.2       129      3.3%
Logical Lock Contention              1.4       0.2       89       2.2%
Address Lock Contention              2.1       0.2       131      3.3%
Log Semaphore Contention             1.2       0.1       75       1.9%
```

```
Group Commit Sleeps             4.8        0.6        331        7.4%
Last Log Page Writes            5.4        0.6        331        8.4%
Modify Conflicts                1.0        0.1        59         1.5%
I/O Device Contention           0.0        0.0        0          0.0%
Network Packet Received         10.6       1.2        649        16.4%
Network Packet Sent             10.4       1.2        640        16.2%
SYSINDEXES Lookup               0.0        0.0        0          0.0%
Other Causes                    11.8       1.4        725        18.3%
```

Another sample output:

```
Default Cache                   per sec    per xact   count      % of total
Utilization                     n/a        n/a        n/a        42.0%
Spinlock Contention             n/a        n/a        n/a        23.0%

Cache Searches
Cache Hits                      156.8      1.4        313        80%
Found in Wash                   20.5       0.3        41         10.%
Cache Misses                    23.2       0.4        49         20.0%
Total Cache Searches            180.0      1.8        362

Large I/O Summary
Large I/Os Performed            20.0       0.2        1211       87.4%
Large I/Os Denied               2.9        0.0        174        12.67%
Total Large I/O Requests        22.9       0.2        1385
```

This is an extremely useful monitoring tool with enough information to keep us quiet for some time.

Individual SQL commands may be analysed by examining the execution plan as in Chapter 10 and by examining the I/O using the statistics option of the set command. With the options on, an analysis of the I/O activity is output after the command has executed.

set statistics

```
set statistics io on

Table:  customer  scan count 1,  logical reads:  5,  physical reads:  1   Total
writes for this command:  0

set statistics time on

Execution time 0
SQL Server cpu time:  0 ms   SQL server elapsed time:  5715784 ms
Execution time 1
SQL Server cpu time:  20 ms  SQL server elapsed time:  126 ms
```

11.4 Stored Procedures

A general comment on SQL Server: use stored procedures for all of the frequently-run SQL; in practice, anything but ad hoc SQL. This global statement is far too black and white of course, and not all SQL benefits greatly from being a stored procedure. However, you will see little difference if you make all of the SQL stored procedures, but things will go much slower if you do not use stored procedures at all. So follow the general rule but, as always, know why you are doing so. (This was dealt with in detail in Chapter 10 but I have summarized it here for completeness.)

If the routine is large and run infrequently, there will be only a small saving in parse time. A procedure is parsed when it is created but then stored on the system catalog until executed. At the first execution, it is read from disk, optimized, compiled and loaded into procedure cache. It will remain in procedure cache as long as it is used and/or there is room for it. Any other user who executes the procedure while it is in cache and not currently being used gets a copy of the optimized, compiled cache version.

So if you do not use the procedure often, it will be one of the first targets to be swapped out when space is required in procedure cache. Once all versions have been swapped out, the next execution reads the disk copy and optimizes and compiles as before, negating the expected savings.

The timing of the procedure optimization (when first loaded from disk) means that subsequent executions of the cache version will use this execution plan. If the procedure is parameterized, the first execution plan may not be suitable for subsequent executions.

```
CREATE PROC jk_proc
        (@low int, @high int)
AS
BEGIN
        SELECT prod_no FROM ord_item
                WHERE price BETWEEN @low AND @high
END
RETURN
```

Depending on the values of the parameters, a nonclustered index on price could generate a table scan or an index search. The first value range will determine the execution plan for all executions. This may not be suitable, causing a table scan when the index should have been used and vice versa.

When the user complains about an unusual response time on a procedure with parameter ranges as above, don't panic. Recompile the procedure and try again. If it still runs slowly, then start to worry.

This is not as serious a problem as it first seems, as it occurs only with ranges of parameter values such as:

```
WHERE x BETWEEN @var1 AND @var2
WHERE x LIKE @var1+'%'
```

and nonclustered indexes. You can identify when these are liable to occur and keep them under control.

Control is based on recompilation to create an efficient execution plan.

```
EXECUTE jk_proc WITH RECOMPILE
CREATE jk_proc ..... WITH RECOMPILE
```

The first recompiles the copy of the procedure in cache for that execution only and lasts until the cache copy is swapped out. The second recompiles the procedure at every execution.

The create with recompile may be a bit of an overhead if most versions of the procedure execute quite happily. It is not invalid to have such procedures as it still controls the code as small modules under the server dictionary control; however, you have no performance savings (apart from a little parse time).

Execute with recompile is the normal solution but even this has its problems.

Consider two users executing proc_1 with both using the same version of the optimized procedure. If one user executes with recompile because of a performance problem, then that user creates a new compiled version and we have two different versions in cache. If that user stops using the procedure and the new version is swapped out, the next execution by that user may use the other user's version if it is not currently being used, which reinstates the performance problem.

The reverse is also true if the non-recompiled user's copy is swapped out, as the next execution by this user will get a copy of the recompiled version which may introduce performance problems for the first user.

Again this is not a serious problem (in fact, a high incidence may indicate an underlying problem with the size of procedure cache), but be aware of it. This is often a good reason for using create with recompile as it ensures that there is no problem and it is as efficient as the raw SQL.

Also be careful when you adjust the indexing of a table to improve SQL performance. You need to recompile the procedures that are using that table. Any change which does not effect the optimization plan or the compilation plan does not cause the procedure to be recompiled. If the procedure is in cache, only the presence of the required objects and the permissions on them are checked. The presence of a new index does not effect the execution of the compiled version as it does not know about the new index. You could wait until the next time the procedure is loaded from disk or execute with recompile, but the easiest way is to use the system procedure **sp_recompile**, which will recompile all procedures or all procedures that access or modify a table.

sp_recompile

```
sp_recompile  [table_name]
```

This does not recompile the procedures immediately but sets a flag on sysobjects, which the procedure checks before execution and recompiles if set. Use of sp_recompile used to add a little to the procedure size as it did not overwrite the query plan, but added the new pieces to it without deleting the old, unused pieces. This no longer occurs in System 10/11. If you do not want to use sp_recompile, you will need to drop and recreate the procedure to ensure that all copies are flushed out of cache, or shutdown and restart the server to get them all.

There is a trace flag—241—which may be set in the runserver file which automatically compresses recompiled procedures. This is very resource intensive in normal running and is not recommended. To set a trace flag in the runserver file, add -T241 to the -d line in Unix or /trace=241 to the /device line in VMS.

11.5 DBCC

SQL Server has a database consistency checker (largely undocumented, which is a great pity) that allows detailed investigation of the consistency of table and index information. This is a very powerful and dangerous piece of software with which you can easily corrupt your database so I shall describe only the read features of DBCC. There are update facilities but I am not going to explain them and would strongly advise you not to touch them. If you have a problem which you believe involves the consistency of the data and requires you to use DBCC to find out what is causing the problem, and you decide that a piece of information needs altering, talk to Sybase. Do not change it yourself using DBCC.

Having given this "government health warning," the read-only investigative facilities of DBCC are extremely useful. Even if you are not having any problems with the tables and indexes, you can learn a lot about how SQL Server structures its data layout by spending some time with DBCC. However, Sybase does not pretend to support these DBCC commands and they may change between releases. There is a help command, **dbcc help**, which displays the syntax of a specific DBCC command.

dbcc help

```
dbcc help(command)
```

However, it does not give any additional information on the parameter values.

During the examples of DBCC, I shall use the table:

```
CREATE TABLE jk_tab (
            a       int,
            b       char(200),
            c       char(200),
            d       char(200),
            e       char(200),
            f       char(200),
            g       char(200))
CREATE CLUSTERED INDEX jk1_idx ON jk_tab(a)
CREATE NONCLUSTERED INDEX jk2_idx ON jk_tab(b)
```

with five records:

```
INSERT INTO jk_tab VALUES(1,'1','2','3','4','5','6')
INSERT INTO jk_tab VALUES(2,'1','2','3','4','5','6')
INSERT INTO jk_tab VALUES(3,'1','2','3','4','5','6')
INSERT INTO jk_tab VALUES(4,'1','2','3','4','5','6')
INSERT INTO jk_tab VALUES(5,'1','2','3','4','5','6')
```

This gives a five-page table with two indexes, each of which will require only the one index node.

11.5.1 Documented Commands

checktable

This checks the consistency of the data and index pages of a table.

```
dbcc checktable (table_name [, skip_ncindex])
```

where

skip_ncindex	skips the checking of the nonclustered indexes.

```
dbcc checktable(jk_tab)
```

```
Checking jk_tab.
The total number of data pages in this table is 5.
Table has 5 data rows.
DBCC Execution completed. If DBCC printed error messages, contact a user with
System Administrator (SA) role.
```

dbcc checktable carries out four main integrity checks:

1. the page pointer chain is intact: each page points back to the page that pointed to it;
2. the row offset table is consistent: each data row has an entry in the page matching its offset in the row offset table;
3. index rows are located in the index pages in ascending key sequence;
4. the nonclustered leaf index key(s) match the column(s) in the data row pointed to.

reindex

This is a fast dbcc checktable that looks at the indexes and rebuilds them if there is a problem. This command does not operate on the data of a table or on the system tables.

```
dbcc  reindex(table_name)
```

```
dbcc reindex(jk_tab)
```

```
One or more indexes are corrupt. They will be rebuilt.
DBCC Execution completed. If DBCC printed error messages, contact a user with
System Administrator (SA) role.
```

checkdb

This is a checktable on every table in the database. Note that if syslogs is on a separate device, you get a report on used and free space during checkdb (or using checktable).

```
dbcc  checkdb(database_name [, skip_ncindex])
```

where

skip_ncindex	skips the checking of the nonclustered indexes.

```
dbcc checkdb(fred)

...
...
...
Checking 1742629251
The total number of data pages in this table is 5.
Table has 5 data rows.
Checking syslogs
The total number of data pages in this table is 2.
        Space used in the log segment is 0.40 MB, 10%
        Space free in the log segment is 3.60 MB, 90%
DBCC Execution completed. If DBCC printed error messages, contact a user with
System Administrator (SA) role.
```

This does not report the size of syslogs if the log is not on a separate device.

checkcatalog

This checks for consistency of the system tables and reports on any defined segments.

```
        dbcc  checkcatalog [(database_name)]
```

```
dbcc checkcatalog(fred)

Checking fred.
The following segments have been defined for database 20(database name fred).
virtual_start_addr      size    segments
4100                    1536    0
                        1       2
DBCC Execution completed. If DBCC printed error messages, contact a user with
System Administrator (SA) role.
```

Some of the principal checks are:

- every row in syscolumns has an entry in systypes and sysobjects;
- every row in sysobjects has an entry in syscolumns or sysprocedures;
- every row in sysindexes has an entry in sysobjects and syssegments;
- bit settings in sysusages.segmap for the database reference an entry in syssegments;
- the last checkpoint in syslogs is valid.

checkalloc

This checks the consistency of the data and index pages with the corresponding extent structure.

```
dbcc  checkalloc(database_name [,fix|nofix])]
```

where

fix	fixes allocation errors;
nofix	does not correct allocation errors (default).

```
dbcc checkalloc(fred)

Checking fred.
Database "fred" is not in single user mode - may find spurious allocation prob-
lems due to transactions in progress.
***********************************************************************
TABLE:  jk_tab OBJID:  1838629593
INDID=1 FIRST=2736     ROOT=2760      SORT=1
        Data level: 1. 5 data pages in 2 extents.
        Indid: 1.              2 index pages in 2 extents.
INDID=2 FIRST=2768     ROOT=2768      SORT=0
        Indid: 2.              2 index pages in 2 extents.
TOTAL # of extents = 6
***********************************************************************
TABLE:  jk2_tab        OBJID:  1616008788
INDID=0 FIRST=817      ROOT=821       SORT=0
        Data level: 0. 5 data pages in 1 extents.
INDID=2 FIRST=1016     ROOT=1016      SORT=1
        Indid: 0.              2 index pages in 2 extents.
TOTAL # of extents = 3
***********************************************************************
Processed 32 entries in the Sysindexes for dbid 6.
Alloc page 0          (# of extent= 32  used pages = 98  ref pages = 98)
Alloc page 256        (# of extent= 32  used pages = 119  ref pages = 111)
Alloc page 512        (# of extent= 32  used pages = 159  ref pages = 143)
Alloc page 768        (# of extent= 29  used pages = 206  ref pages = 86)
Alloc page 1024       (# of extent= 9    used pages = 17  ref pages = 17)
Alloc page 1280       (# of extent= 1    used pages = 1  ref pages = 1)
Total (# of extent = 135  used pages = 600  ref pages  = 456) in this database.
DBCC Execution completed. If DBCC printed error messages, contact a user with
System Administrator (SA) role.
```

The initial warning of "single user mode" is worth paying attention to as checkalloc can take some time. Additionally, page linkage errors, which are caused by updates taking place while checkalloc is checking the page allocations, are often displayed. So run in "single user mode." You must be in single user mode when using the **fix** mode.

The fix option replaces the dbcc fix_al command which was available in version 4.9. To put a database in single user mode, use sp_dboption.

```
use master
go
sp_dboption fred, "single user", true
go
use fred
go
checkpoint
go
```

If running a database in single user mode gives problems such as 24-hour availability, then the Troubleshooting Guide explains the DBCC 2512 trace flag. This keeps checkalloc from checking the transaction log, which is the source of the spurious allocation errors. You may then use **dbcc tablealloc** to check syslogs.

```
dbcc traceon(2512)
go
dbcc checkalloc(fred)
go
dbcc traceoff(2512)
go
dbcc tablealloc(syslogs)
go
```

The output indicates that our database has six allocations with 600 used pages (i.e., 600*2 K = 1.2 MB) and 135 extents (i.e,. 135*8*2 K = 2.16 MB).

This compares with a sp_spaceused:

```
sp_spaceused

database_name                            database_size
fred                                     3MB
reserved          data                   index_size              reserved
2118KB            658KB                  384KB                   1076KB
```

Close but not exact.

For consistency, checkalloc checks that:

- the extent is for the correct table/index by checking that the object_id and index_id in the extent is the same as the object_id and index_id in sysindexes (i.e. all pages are correctly allocated);
- an extent occurs only once in the extent chain;

- the allocation bit map settings with the pages linked into the object page chain: pages marked as USED in the extent allocation bit map match those REFERENCED in the page chain (i.e. all used pages are allocated and all allocated pages are used).

tablealloc

This does a checkalloc on the specified table.

```
dbcc tablealloc({table_name|table_id}
                [,{full|optimized|fast|null}[, {fix|nofix}]])
```

where

full	reports all allocation errors.
optimized	default mode which reports only on the allocation pages in the object allocation map (OAM). Does not check unreferenced allocation extents that are not in the OAM pages.
fast	reports only on the pages referenced but not allocated in the extent. Does not check the allocations.
null	defaults to optimized.
fix	fixes allocation errors, which is the default for user tables. To fix system tables, you need to put the database in single user mode using sp_dboption.
nofix	does not fix allocation errors, which is the default for system tables.

```
dbcc tablealloc(jk_tab)

The default report option of OPTIMIZED is used for this run.
The default fix option of FIX is used for this run.
*****************************************************
TABLE: jk_tab          OBJ_ID: 1838629593
INDID=1 FIRST=2736     ROOT=2760       SORT=1
        Data level: 1  5 data pages in 2 extents
        Indid: 1       2 index pages in 2 extents
INDID=2 FIRST=2768     ROOT=2768       SORT=1
        Indid: 2       2 index pages in 2 extents
TOTAL # of extents = 6

Alloc page 2560 (#of extents=2 used pages=3 ref pages=3)
Alloc page 2560 (#of extents=2 used pages=6 ref pages=6)
Alloc page 2560 (#of extents=2 used pages=3 ref pages=3)

Total (#of extents=6 used pages=12 ref pages=12) in this database.
```

This compares with an sp_spaceused:

```
sp_spaceused jk_tab
```

name	rowtotal	reserved	data	index_size	unused
jk_tab	5	96KB	10KB	8KB	78KB

So there is full agreement between dbcc tablealloc and sp_spaceused: 6 extents: 48 pages: 96KB.

Let's check some of the rather interesting figures:

- data object: six pages allocated, of which five are data pages;
- two index objects: three pages allocated, to each of which only one is the index page.

In some of the tests I ran, I found inconsistency in the extent allocations. What appears to happen on a create table is that an extent is allocated for the OAM, and on a create index, an extent is allocated for the OAM plus an extent for the statistics distribution page. This agrees with the above figures of two data extents with six pages used and 2 * 2 index extents, each with three pages used.

indexalloc

This does a checkalloc on the specified index.

```
dbcc indexalloc({table_name|table_id}, index_id
                [, {full|optimized|fast|null} [, {fix|nofix}]])
```

where (as for tablealloc)

full	reports all allocation errors.
optimized	default mode which reports only on the allocation pages in the object allocation map (OAM). Does not check unreferenced allocation extents that are not in the OAM pages.
fast	reports only on the pages referenced but not allocated in the extent. Does not check the allocations.
null	defaults to optimized.
fix	fixes allocation errors which is the default for user tables. To fix system tables, you need to put the database in single user mode using sp_dboption.
nofix	does not fix allocation errors which is the default for system tables.

This provides the same checks on the indexes as tablealloc does on the data. (Indid = 1 is the clustered index and therefore reports on the data allocations as well.)

```
dbcc indexalloc(jk_tab, 1)

The default report option of OPTIMIZED is used for this run.
The default fix option of FIX is used for this run.
***************************************************
TABLE: jk_tab          OBJ_ID: 1838629593
INDID=1 FIRST=2736     ROOT=2760      SORT=1
       Data level: 1   5 data pages in 2 extents
       Indid: 1        2 index pages in 2 extents

TOTAL # of extents=4

Alloc page 2560 (#of extents=2 used pages=3 ref pages=3)
Alloc page 2560 (#of extents=2 used pages=6 ref pages=6)
Total (#of extents=4 used pages=9 ref pages=9) in this database

dbcc indexalloc(jk_tab, 2)

The default report option of OPTIMIZED is used for this run.
The default fix option of FIX is used for this run.
***************************************************
TABLE: jk_tab          OBJ_ID: 1838629593
INDID=2 FIRST=2768     ROOT=2768      SORT=1
       Indid: 2        2 index pages in 2 extents

TOTAL # of extents=2
Alloc page 2560 (#of extents=2 used pages=3 ref pages=3)
Total (#of extents=2 used pages=3 ref pages=3) in this database
```

11.5.2 Much More Interesting and Largely Undocumented Commands

So much for the general consistency. Let's look in more detail at DBCC options that allow us to investigate any problems highlighted by the previous options, especially checktable and checkalloc. I repeat for emphasis: if you need to fix a table or index do NOT do it yourself, talk to Sybase.

Most of the detailed DBCC output is directed to the console where the server was booted. To redirect it, use the trace flag settings:

dbcc traceon(3604) to redirect to your terminal;
dbcc traceon(3605) to redirect to the error log.

These are turned off by:

```
dbcc traceoff(setting)
```

When you are using the following DBCC commands in System 10, you will find that most of them require you to have sybase_ts_role.

```
sp_role "grant", "sybase_ts_role", sa
go
```

Page Contents Information

page

Displays the contents of the specified page.

```
dbcc  page(dbid, page#, printopt, cache, logical)
```

where

dbid	database ID;
page#	logical or virtual number;
printopt	0: print page/buffer header only (default); 1: print header information, data in row format and row offset table; 2: print header information, unformatted data and row off set table;
cache	0: fetch disk version of page; 1: fetch cache version of page if possible (default);
logical	0: page# is virtual page number; 1: page # is logical page number (default).

```
dbcc page(6, 2736)

BUFFER
       Buffer header for buffer  0x84ee41
       page=0x8eb000  bdnew=0x7ebf9d        bdold=0x7ebf9d
       bhash=0x0      bnew=0x7ec541  bold=0x7eb0c5
       bvirtpg=5149          bdbid=20     bkeep=0      bstd=0x1000
       bwstat=0x0000         bpageno=2736

PAGE HEADER    Page header for page  0x1345000
       pageno=2736 nextpg=2737 prevpg=0 objid=1838629593
       timestamp=000100076a25  nextrno=1 level=0
       indid=0 freeoff=1238 minlen=1206
       page status bits=0x80,0x1
```

```
DBCC Execution completed. If DBCC printed error messages, contact a user with
System Administrator (SA) role.
```

This does not tell the nonvendor SA much but we know from checkalloc that page 2,736 is in jk_tab, which this confirms. We can also see the previous and next page numbers, that the record is 1206 bytes long, and free space is at 1,238 (1,026+32). From our knowledge of the table, we know that it is one fixed length record of 1,204+2 bytes. This is useful only when you need to investigate the actual contents of a page.

tab

This shows all data pages in use by the specified table.

```
dbcc tab(db_name, table_name, printopt)
```

where

printopt:	0 - all 1 - row 2 - header

ind

This shows all pages in use by indexes of the specified table.

```
dbcc ind(db_name, table_name, printopt)
```

where

printopt:	0 - all 1 - row 2 - header

prtipage

This prints the page number pointed to by each row in the index page.

```
dbcc prtipage(dbid, object_id, index_id, page#)
```

where

dbid	database ID;
object_id	object_id of object that index is on;
index_id	index_id to which page belongs
page#	logical page number.

```
dbcc prtipage(6, 1838629593, 1, 2760)

***INDEX LEVEL 0 - PAGE #  2760
Leaf row at offset 32 points to datapage 2736, row number 0
Leaf row at offset 41 points to datapage 2737, row number 0
Leaf row at offset 50 points to datapage 2738, row number 0
Leaf row at offset 59 points to datapage 2739, row number 0
Leaf row at offset 68 points to datapage 2740, row number 0
Page finished...
DBCC Execution completed. If DBCC printed error messages, contact a user with
System Administrator (SA) role.
```

We know from checkalloc that this is the nonclustered leaf index page which points to the five data pages. The index entries are 11 bytes long, which is consistent with a fixed length key on the integer column (a); that is, key (4 bytes) + record_id (6 bytes) + overhead (1 byte).

locateindexpgs

This displays all references in an index to a specified page number.

```
dbcc locateindexpgs(dbid, object_id, page#, index_id, level)
```

where

dbid	database ID;
object_id	object_id of object that index is on;
page#	logical page number which we are looking for references to: When set to -1 returns last page of level requested;
index_id	index_id to search;
level	level of index to search for references; (0 for data page references).

```
dbcc locateindexpgs(6, 1838629593, 2760, 2, 0)

INFO ON INDEX ROWS POINTING TO GIVEN PAGE
INDEX ROW ON:
Index page#:          1088
```

```
At offset:            32
Pointer to data row:  0
DBCC Execution completed. If DBCC printed error messages, contact a user with
System Administrator (SA) role.
```

As we only have one index page and one data record per page, which is fixed length, this is not very informative here. But it can be very useful if you have an index pointer problem.

pglinkage

This traverses the page chain, printing logical page numbers and checking the consistency of the page pointers.

```
dbcc pglinkage(dbid,  startpg#,      #_of_pages,
                      printopt, targetpg#, ascending)
```

where

dbid	database ID;
startpg#	logical page number to start following the page chain;
#_of_pages	number of pages to scan before stopping;
printopt	0 print count of pages only: 1: print last 16 pages in scan; 2: print each page number in scan;
targetpg#	logical page number at which to stop scan;
ascending	0: descending; 1: ascending.

```
dbcc pglinkage(6, 2736, 5, 0, 0, 1)

Object id for pages in this chain = 1838629593
End of chain reached.
5 pages scanned. Objectid=1838629593. Last page in scan=2765
DBCC Execution completed. If DBCC printed error messages, contact a user with
System Administrator (SA) role.
```

This is fully consistent with our table jk1_tab, which has five pages with logical page numbers 2736–2740.

```
dbcc pglinkage(6, 2736, 5, 2, 0, 1)

Object id for pages in this chain = 1838629593
Page:  2736
Page:  2737
Page:  2738
Page:  2739
```

```
Page:  2740
End of chain reached.
5 pages scanned. Objectid=1838629593. Last page in scan=2740
DBCC Execution completed. If DBCC printed error messages, contact a user with
System Administrator (SA) role.
```

11.5.3 Allocation and Extent Information

allocdump

This shows all of the extents on a given allocation page.

```
dbcc allocdump(dbid, page#)
```

where:

dbid	database ID;
page#	allocation page logical page number.

```
dbcc allocdump(6, 2560)

*** DISPLAY ALL EXTENTS ON ALLOCATION PAGE
EXTID: 2720  objid:  5          indid:  0  alloc:  ff  dealloc: 0  status:  2
EXTID: 2728  objid:  0          indid:  0  alloc:  0   dealloc: 0  status:  0
EXTID: 2736  objid:  1838629593 indid:  0  alloc:  1f  dealloc: 0  status:  3
EXTID: 2744  objid:  1838629593 indid:  0  alloc:  1   dealloc: 0  status:  3
EXTID: 2752  objid:  6          indid:  1  alloc:  1   dealloc: 0  status:  3
EXTID: 2760  objid:  1838629593 indid:  0  alloc:  1   dealloc: 0  status:  2
EXTID: 2768  objid:  1838629593 indid:  2  alloc:  1   dealloc: 0  status:  3
EXTID: 2776  objid:  1838629593 indid:  1  alloc:  1   dealloc: 0  status:  2
EXTID: 2784  objid:  1838629593 indid:  2  alloc:  1   dealloc: 0  status:  2
etc:
DBCC Execution completed. If DBCC printed error messages, contact a user with
System Administrator (SA) role.
```

extentcheck

This displays the extents allocated to an object by scanning all allocation pages sequentially.

```
dbcc extentcheck(dbid, object_id, index_id, sortbit)
```

where

dbid	database ID;
object_id	object ID to which extent belongs (else 0);
index_id	index ID to which extent belongs (else 0);
sortbit	set to the same status as the sort bit in the status word of sysindexes.

```
dbcc extentcheck(6, 1838629573, 0, 0)

EXTID: 2736  objid: 1838629573 indid  0  alloc  1f  dealloc 0 status  3
EXTID: 2760  objid: 1838629573 indid  0  alloc  1   dealloc 0 status  3
Total extents 2.
DBCC Execution completed. If DBCC printed error messages, contact a user with
System Administrator (SA) role.
```

Make sure that you get the sort bit correct; otherwise, you get no information on the object/index. Also the object_id and index_id columns function as a composite key to the extent entries.

```
dbcc extentcheck(6, 1838629573, 1, 1)

EXTID: 2760  objid: 1838629573 indid  1  alloc  1  dealloc 0 status  3
EXTID: 2776  objid: 1838629573 indid  1  alloc  1  dealloc 0 status  3
Total extents 2.
DBCC Execution completed. If DBCC printed error messages, contact a user with
System Administrator (SA) role.
```

extentdump

This displays the extent information for a specific logical page number.

```
dbcc extentdump(dbid, page#)
```

where

dbid	database ID;
page#	logical page number.

```
dbcc extentdump(6, 2760)

DISPLAY EXTENT FOR GIVEN PAGE REQUESTED
Logical page 2760:
Extent ID  2760  on allocation page  2560
Object ID is  1838629573
Index ID is  1
Allocation bit map:  0x1
Sort bit is on.
Reference bit is off.
```

findnotfullextents

This displays all of the extents for the specified object that have free pages in them.

```
dbcc findnotfullextents(dbid, object_id, index_id, sortbit)
```

where

dbid	database ID;
object_id	object ID to search;
index_id	index ID to search;
sortbit	set to the same status as the sort bit in the status word of sysindexes.

```
dbcc findnotfullextents(6, 1838629573, 0, 1)

** EXAMINE ALL NOT FULL EXTENTS ON ALLOC PAGES FOR SPECIFIED OBJECT
Id of extent not full:2752
Id of extent not full:2760
Total extents that are not full:  2
```

usedextents

This displays or counts the status of used/unused extents for specific databases and devices.

```
dbcc usedextents(dbid, option, display)
```

where

dbid	database ID;
option	0: both data and log; 1: log only; 2: data only;
display	0: display extents; 1: count extents.

```
dbcc usedextents(6, 2, 1)

Total used extents = 3
Total free extents = 2
```

report_al

This reports on differences between bitmaps and the page chains.

```
dbcc report_al(db_name)
```

11.5.4 Memory Information

memusage

This displays the memory allocation and the current memory usage for the top 20 users of memory.

```
dbcc  memusage

                          Meg     2K blks bytes
       configured memory  24.4141 12500   25600000

       code size          0.1860  96      195052
       kernel structures  4.9708  2546    5212273
       server structures  5.2499  2688    5504964
       page cache         10.9645 5614    11497136
       proc buffers       0.0877  45      92004
       proc headers       2.9550  1513    3098571

number of page buffers:   5324
number of proc buffers;   1320

       Buffer cache, Top 20:

       Dbid          Object id              Index id      2K buffers
       19            1042102753             0             682
       19            274100017              0             566
       etc

       Procedure cache information (top 10):

       Database id:  4
       Object id:  1424008104
       Object name; sp_help
       Version:  1
       Uid:  1
       Type:  stored procedure
       Number of trees:  0
       Size of trees:  0.000000 Mb, 0.000000 bytes, 0 pages
       Number of plans:  1
       Size of plans:  0.086540 Mb, 90744.000000 bytes, 45 pages
```

Use of dbcc memusage requires a serious warning. Do not use it on an active production server as the command locks the data and procedure cache, preventing any user activity. Even worse on SMP servers, running memusage can result in timeslice errors for other tasks, especially if the procedure cache is large.

bhash

This verifies and optionally displays the buffer hash table.

```
dbcc bhash(cache_name, print_opt, bucket_limit)
```

where

cache_name	name of the cache (a System 11 parameter);
print_opt	"no_print" displays only buffers with problems;
	"print_bufs" displays all buffers in cache;
bucket_limit	number of buffers allowed in bucket: 0 indicates no limit.

The verification carried out is:

- the bucket_limit is not exceeded;
- the page number in the buffer agrees with the page number in the page;
- the dbid and the objectid are not zero;
- the buffer status is set to hashed.

```
dbcc bhash("default data cache", "print_bufs", 0)

.
.
.
BUCKET #8106
bufptr 4def40, bpageno 163584, bdbid 10, pobjid 99, bstat 1000
bufptr 4df900, bpageno 155392, bdbid 10, pobjid 99, bstat 1000
bufptr 4e02c0, bpageno 147200, bdbid 10, pobjid 99, bstat 1010
BUCKET #8107
bufptr 4e1bbc, bpageno 32257, bdbid 10, pobjid 1920009871, bstat 1010
.
.
.
** NO ERRORS DETECTED
** BUFFER DUMP COMPLETE
```

This is a lot of output which is not very useful, so use it with care.

buffer

This displays the appropriate buffer headers and pages from buffer cache.

```
dbcc buffer(dbid, objectid, #buffers, print_opt, type [, cache_name])
```

where

#buffers	0	all buffers in MRU to LRU sequence;
	>0	the specified number of buffers in MRU to LRU sequence;
	<0	the specified number of buffers in LRU to MRU sequence
print_opt	0	headers;
	1	header and data in row format;
	2	full page output;
type	buffer status	(some values)
	hashed	hashed;
	not hashed	not hashed;
	rlock	resource locked
	kept	being used by a process
	rwait	waiting for a resource lock
	dirty	different from the disk version
	io	being read or written;
	ioerr	error occurred during write;
	trip	the buffer ages out of cache more slowly than normal
	new	new page which has not been written;
cache_name	the name of the cache (a System 11 parameter).	

```
dbcc buffer(6, 75147313, 5, 0, "hashed", "default data cache")
```

The output is lengthy and looks like a dbcc page output for data pages, with the addition of information on the buffer associated with the pages.

```
BUFFERS (in MRU to LRU order):
starting with KEPT BUFFERS (not on LRU chain)

BUFFERS IN CACHE default data cache (ID0):

BUFFERS IN POOL 0 (MASS SIZE = 2 K):

BUFFER
Buffer header for buffer 0x4c79b4
       (buffer contents as DBCC page)

PAGE HEADER
Page header for page 0x5f8000
       (page contents as DBCC page)
```

bufcount

This displays up to ten longest buffer chains, the minimum buffer length and the average buffer chain length.

```
dbcc bufcount(#chains [, cache_name])
```

where

cache_name	the name of the cache (a System 11 parameter.) If the cache name is not input, all caches are reported on.

```
dbcc bufcount(6, "ind_cache")

Looking for the 3 longest chains in the hash table for cache ind_cache
Cluster mask for ind_cache: -8
**** THE 6 LONGEST BUFFER CHAINS ****

bucket number = 1706  chain size = 6
bucket number = 938   chain size = 5
bucket number = 426   chain size = 5
bucket number = 1450  chain size = 5
bucket number = 682   chain size = 5
bucket number = 1194  chain size = 5
The smallest chain size is 0.
The average chain size is: 0.154785
```

This is a bit more interesting and may indicate cache size problems if the average gets too high.

show_bucket

This displays the buffer number for the specified logical page number.

```
dbcc show_bucket(dbid, page#, look_up [, cache_name])
```

where

look_up	1	use hash algorithm;
	2	scan entire buffer cache;
cache_name	the name of the cache (a System 11 parameter).	

```
dbcc show_bucket(6, 272, 1, "pubs_cache")

Hash bucket for dbid 6, pageid 272 in cache pubs_cache is 4470
Looking for buffer in cache pubs_cache...
*** cache pubs_cache buffer 4c79b4, page 272, dbid 6, object 75147313, bstat
1000, bsize 16
```

procbuf

This displays the procedure buffer headers and proc headers from procedure cache.

```
dbcc procbuf(dbid, objectid, #bufs, print_opt)
```

where

#bufs	0	displays all proc buffers;
	>0	displays the number of proc buffers in MRU to LUR sequence;
	<0	displays the number of proc buffers in LRU to MRU sequence;
print_opt	0	displays proc buffer and header only;
	1	displays proc buffer, header and contents of buffer (this can be a very large output, be careful).

```
dbcc procbuf(6, 107147427, 1, 0)

PROCEDURES (in MRU to LRU order):
PROCBUF:
address=0x44ef44 id=107147427 pbdbid=6
pbuid=1 pbihash=0x0 pbnhash=0x0 pbold=0x44eee8
pbnew=0x44ee30 pbprochdr=0x46a000 pbspid=0
pbname=jkl_prc pbprocnum=1

PROC_HDR:
address=0x46a000 p_hdrstep=0x46a3fa p_hdrseq=0x0 p_hdrcrt=0x0
p_hdrpbuf=0x44ef44 p_hdrtmps=0x0
p_hdrcaller=0x46000 p_hdrelease=0 p_hdrtabid=107147427
p_hdrstatus=0x1
p_lastpg=0 p_lastoff=13 p_procnum=0
mempgptr=0x46a000      byte_count=2048        byte_save=2048
mempgptr=0x46a800      byte_count=2048        byte_save=2048
mempgptr=0x46b000      byte_count=2048        byte_save=2048
.
.
.
mempgptr=0x472000      byte_count=878 byte_save=878
```

bytes

This dumps the bytes from the specified address.

```
dbcc bytes(start_address, length)
```

where

start_address	decimal start address;
length	number of bytes to dump.

I've never used this one but if you like reading byte dumps, this is the one for you.

11.5.5 Sundry Commands

lock

This command displays the lock chains for table locks, page locks and extent locks.

```
dbcc lock

LOCKS:
TABLE LOCK TABLE
locks at slot 26:
EX_INT lockid=176003658 spid=3 dbid=4

PAGE LOCK TABLE
locks at slot 22:
UP_PAGE lockid=40 spid=3 dbid=4
EX_PAGE lockid=40 spid=3 dbid=4
locks at slot 231
UP_PAGE lockid=458 spid=3 dbid=4
EX_PAGE lockid=458 spid=3 dbid=4

EXTENT LOCK TABLE

DBCC Execution completed. If DBCC printed error messages, contact a user with
System Administrator (SA) role.
```

The dbcc lock output has changed significantly in System 11. As sample of the output follows.

```
dbcc lock

LOCKS:
TABLE LOCKS
00b78050        objid 208003772, dbid 5, (bucket 26)
00b781b0        swstatus=(), swskipped=0, swsemaphore=0xb378050
00b78350        lrsprd=8, lrtype=ex_int, lrsemwait=0xb781b0
                lrstatus=(granted0, lrsuffclass=0
```

log

Log displays the contents of the transaction log.

```
dbcc log(dbid, object_id, page#, row#, #of_records,
                                record_type, data_flag)
```

where

page#, row#	together these specify a transaction ID or row ID to begin the scan from;
#of_records	number of records to print: 0 all; <0 number to print;
data_flag	0 displays data for insert, update, delete; 1 header only;
record_type	the op number in syslogs. The most common are: 0 begin transaction 4 insert 5 delete 6 location and rowid for insert of deferred update 7 index insert 8 index delete 9 modify 11 data record for insert of deferred update 12 row id for delete of deferred update 13 allocation of page 15 extent allocation 16 page split 17 checkpoint 20 extent deallocation 21 page deallocation 24 new page allocation for page split 30 end transaction: commit or rollback.

dbcc log (dbid) displays all log records: header and data.
dbcc log(dbid, object_id) displays all log records for object.

```
dbcc log(6, 107147427)
```

```
LOG RECORDS
        INSERT (2083, 3)
        attcnt=1 rno=3 op=4 padlen=2 xactid=(2083, 2) len=60
        status=0x0000 oampg=424 pageno=425 offset=32
        status=0x00 oldts=0x0001 0x0001360b
        newts=0x0001 0x00013610
        xrow:
0075f918: 00000100 00007d88 0000d82c 9100 ......}.....,../
```

dbcc log(6, 107147427, 2083, 2) displays all log records and data for transaction(2083, 2).
dbcc log(6, 0, 425, 0, 0, 4, 0) displays all log records and data for inserts to page 425.

Have fun with this one but be very careful of the volume of output. Do not mess around in production systems; the log is too important.

pss

```
dbcc pss(suid, spid, print_opt)
```

where

print_opt	0	all process status structures;
	1	process status structures and current sequence tree;
	2	all locks held by the process on the error log.

This displays the contents of the specified process status structure (the output varies depending on the SQL Server release).

```
dbcc pss(1, 1, 0)

PSS:
pstat=0x0 pcurdb=6 psuid=1 puid=1
puname=    ploginflags=3 prowcnt=0 pstatlist=0x0
pnumplan=0 pcurcpktdb=0x0
plasterror=0 prowcount=0 plastprocid=0 pprocnest=0
pgid=0 phid=0 pspid=1 pkspid=44
poptions=0x400000 poffsets=0 plockdeny=0 pcurcmd=253
pcputot=212 pcpucur=0 pmemusage=1 pbufread=0
pbufwrite=0 pcmderrs=0 pntext=36 ptext=0x0
donestat=0x0 donespare=0 donecount=0
.
.
.
```

dbrecover

This runs recovery on a suspect database without rebooting the server.

```
dbcc dbrecover(db_name)
```

fix_text

This updates text values after a character set change.

```
dbcc fix_text(table_name)
```

showtext

This shows the text or image data contained on the specified page.

```
dbcc showtext(cache_name, db_name, logical_page_num)
```

Cache_name is a System 11 parameter.

11.5.6 dbinfo Area

This is an area in each database which contains information about the database. This is located in the syslogs entry in sysindexes, using the keys fields, as the log never has any indexes set on it. As the log row in sysindexes is always in the same location, it gives a fixed reference to certain values. These values are of interest to some of the system routines but not a lot of use for general SA use.

If you do not believe me (and for completeness):

```
dbcc dbinfo(fred)

DBINFO STRUCTURE:

dbi_lastrid:          page 136, rownum 0
dbi_dpbegxact:        page 1032, rownum 132
dbi_oldseqnum:        Jan 1 1900 12:00:00:00:000 AM
dbi_curseqnum:        Oct 29 1992 4:40:22:320 PM
dbi_nextseqnum:       Jan 1 1900 12:00:00:00:000 AM
dbi_deallocpgs:       0
dbi_drprowcnt:        0
dbi_pgcnt:            0
dbi_nextcheckpt:      page 0, rownum 0
dbi_dbid:             20
dbi_suid:             1
dbi_version:          2
dbi_status:           0x8
dbi_checkpt:          page 1032, rownum 1032
dbi_nextid:           1516532436
dbi_complete:         1207959552
dbi_crdate:           Sep 3 1992 10:30:13:340 AM
dbi_dbname:           exercisedb
dbi_ldstate:          0
dbi_rambots:          0x0000  0x00000000
```

```
dbi_dmplastckpt:        page 0, rownum 0
dbi_dmplastrid:         page 0, rownum 0
dbi_pretruncpg:         0
dbi_posttruncpg:        0
dbi_ltmtruncpg:         0
dbi_rep_stat:           0
dbi_rep_gen_id:         0
```

The output varies depending on the SQL Server release.

11.6 Summary

SQL Server is not the most helpful piece of software in assisting the SA to anticipate and solve problems. The system tables do contain a lot of necessary information but the system procedures are not extensive and a lot of homegrown routines have to be created.

Prior to version 11.0.1, the monitoring tools did not supply much useful information. Space and object placement was best retrieved yourself and activity monitoring was best done at the operating system level. The introduction of the System 11 procedure sp_sysmon has changed this, with enough monitoring information now available to keep us busy for quite some time. The new procedure is discussed in Chapter 12.

12

New System 11 Features

This chapter describes some of the new features in System 11. The new features covered include data cache and buffer pool management, partitioning heap tables, optimizer improvements, in-place update rules, the housekeeper task, the max_rows_per_page facility and the lock promotion thresholds. Configuration parameters are described in Chapter 13.

COMMAND SYNTAX

```
alter table
```

SYSTEM PROCEDURE SYNTAX

```
sp_bindcache
sp_cacheconfig
sp_chgattribute
sp_dropglockpromote
sp_helpartition
sp_helpcache
sp_helpindex
sp_logiosize
sp_poolconfig
sp_setpglockpromote
sp_unbindcache
sp_cachestrategy
```

12.1 Data Cache Management

12.1.1 Introduction

SQL Server has a default data cache of 2 K pages, the size of which depends on the amount of memory allocated to the server and the overhead of other server objects, such as user connections and procedure cache. The calculation of available data cache is described in detail in Appendix A, section A.6.

System 11 now allows the data cache to be segmented into multiple named caches of specified sizes each of which—including the default cache—may be configured to have multiple pools of varying I/O sizes.

Objects (databases, tables, indexes, text/image and the transaction log) may be bound to one of the named caches so that the object uses only that specific allocation of memory. If multiple I/O pools are configured in that cache, the I/O for the object may be made in the cache multiples of 2 K–16 K, i.e. from one page to one extent. Objects not explicitly bound to a named cache use the default cache.

12.1.2 Named Caches

Creation

Named caches are defined using **sp_cacheconfig** or by editing the configuration file. I deal with the configuration file later in section 12.1.4.

sp_cacheconfig

```
sp_cacheconfig          [cache_name
                        [, "cache_size[size_unit]"]
                        [, logonly | mixed]]
```

where

size_unit	K	kilobytes (the default);
	P	pages;
	M	megabytes
	G	gigabytes;
logonly	reserves the cache for the transaction log.	

```
sp_cacheconfig temp_cache, '20M'
```

This creates a named cache of 20 MB. If we started with 60 MB, we now have a cache segmentation as in Figure 12.1.

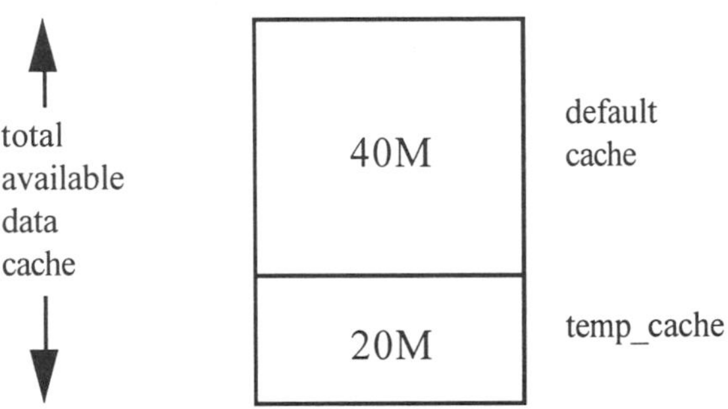

Figure 12.1 *Named data cache.*

You need to restart the server for the sp_cacheconfig to take effect. You can see the current cache segmentation using sp_cacheconfig with no size parameter. The above cache displays as below.

Before defining the temp_cache:

```
sp_cacheconfig 'default data cache'

Cache name          Status Type         Config value   Run value
Default data cache  Active Default      0.00 Mb        60.00 Mb
                                        -------        -------
                         Total          0.00 Mb        60.00 Mb
                                        -------        -------
==============================================================
Cache: default data cache,  Status: active,  Type: Default
          Config Size: 0.00Mb,  Run Size: 60.00Mb

IO Size Wash Size     Config Size   Run Size
2 Kb    512 Kb        0.00 Mb       60.00 Mb
```

where

status	active	the cache is currently active;
	pend/act	the cache has just been defined and will be active after a server restart;
	pend/del	the cache is currently active but will be deleted after a server restart;

type	default	the default cache;
	mixed	may store data and log pages;
	logonly	may store log pages only;
io sz	the size of I/O buffers in the cache pool;	
wash sz	the wash size for the buffer pool (see 12.1.3);	
config value	the size of the cache after the next server restart. The above output shows 0 for the default because it has not been explicitly configured. The default cannot be reduced below 512 K.	
run value	the current size of the cache.	

This shows one line for the total cache and one line for each pool in the cache. For the moment we have only the default pool of 2 K in each cache. Configuring multiple pools in a cache is described in section 12.1.3.

Issuing the "temp_cache" configuration command:

```
sp_cacheconfig temp_cache, '20M'
```

displays the message:

```
The change is completed. The SQL Server must be rebooted for the change to take
effect."
```

Before restarting the server we have:

```
sp_cacheconfig

Cache name          Status       Type        Config value   Run value
Default data cache  Active       Default     0.00 Mb        60.00 Mb
temp_cache          Pend/Act     Mixed       20.00 Mb       0.00 Mb
                                             -------        -------
                                 Total       20.00 Mb       60.00 Mb
                                             -------        -------
================================================================
Cache: default data cache,  Status: active,  Type: Default
        Config Size: 0.00Mb,  Run Size: 60.00Mb

IO Size Wash Size       Config Size  Run Size
2 Kb    512 Kb          0.00 Mb      60.00 Mb
```

After a restart of the server we have:

```
sp_cacheconfig

Cache name          Status Type          Config value   Run value
Default data cache  Active Default       0.00 Mb        38.94 Mb
temp_cache          Active Mixed         20.00 Mb       20.00 Mb
```

```
                                  Total              20.00 Mb      58.94 Mb
=============================================================
Cache: default data cache,  Status: active,  Type: Default
          Config Size: 0.00Mb,  Run Size: 58.94Mb

IO Size Wash Size      Config Size    Run Size
2 Kb          512 Kb        0.00 Mb 38.94 Mb
=============================================================
Cache: temp_cache,  Status: active,  Type: Default
          Config Size: 20.00Mb,  Run Size: 20.00Mb

IO Size Wash Size      Config Size    Run Size
2 Kb    512 Kb         0.00 Mb        20.00 Mb
```

We now have "lost"some cache from our default 60 MB in addition to the 20 MB of temp_cache. This is the cache overhead required to manage the segmented caches. As a rule of thumb, there is a 5% overhead associated with a named cache. The actual amount can be displayed using sp_helpcache.

```
sp_helpcache "size [size_unit]"
```

```
sp_helpcache "40M"

2.13M of overhead memory will be needed to manage a cache of size 40M

sp_helpcache "20M"

1.06M of overhead memory will be needed to manage a cache of size 20M
```

So our 60 MB of data cache is split as:

temp_cache	20.00 MB
temp_cache overhead	1.06 MB
total	21.06 MB
available for default cache	38.94 MB

If you want the default cache to have a minimum allocation, you explicitly define a size for the default.

```
sp_cacheconfig "default data cache", "25M"
```

In our configuration above, a restart of the server will show:

```
sp_cacheconfig

Cache name            Status Type          Config value   Run value
Default data cache    Active Default       25.00 Mb       38.94 Mb
temp_cache            Active  Mixed        20.00 Mb       20.00 Mb
```

```
                              Total                 -------      -------
                                                    45.00 Mb     58.94 Mb
                                                    -------      -------
==============================================================
Cache: default data cache,  Status: active,  Type: Default
          Config Size: 0.00Mb,  Run Size: 58.94Mb

IO Size Wash Size     Config Size    Run Size
2 Kb          512 Kb         25.00 Mb        38.94 Mb
==============================================================
Cache: temp_cache,  Status: active,  Type: Default
          Config Size: 20.00Mb,  Run Size: 20.00Mb

IO Size Wash Size     Config Size    Run Size
2 Kb    512 Kb        0.00 Mb        20.00 Mb
```

Binding Objects To Cache

Objects (databases, tables, indexes, logs, text/image) are bound to a specific cache using sp_bindcache.

sp_bindcache

```
sp_bindcache   cache_name, db_name
               [, object_name][, text]
```

```
sp_bindcache temp_cache, tempdb
```

binds all objects which use tempdb to temp_cache.

```
sp_bindcache tab_scan_cache, sales_hist_db, order_hist
```

binds the order_hist table of sales_hist_db to the tab_scan_cache.

```
sp_bindcache log_cache, prod_db, syslogs
```

binds the transaction log of prod_db to log_cache.

There are rules for binding to caches:

- you must be in master to bind a database;
- you must be in the database to bind a database object;
- the type of cache must be mixed, which means that you cannot bind to the default cache;

- to bind the database, syslogs, or any other system tables, the database must be in single user mode.

You can bind to a mixed cache when binding syslogs, which means that you can also bind data objects to that cache. You may find it advisable and easier to remember what you have done if you reserve a specific named cache for log use only, using the "logonly" option of sp_cacheconfig.

```
sp_cacheconfig psales_log, "10M", "logonly"
```

This creates a named cache psales_log of 10 MB for log use only.

```
sp_cacheconfig pmktg_log, "logonly"
```

This changes the type of an existing cache from mixed to logonly. You can do this only if there are no non-log objects currently bound to the cache.

Sybase recommends that the log be bound to a 4 K buffer pool cache for optimum performance. In fact, the default log I/O size is 4 K, but this value is used only if a 4 K buffer pool exists. The size of the log I/O is configured using **sp_logiosize**.

sp_logiosize

```
    sp_logiosize  ["default"|"size"]
```

```
sp_logiosize "8"
```

This changes the I/O size for the log to an 8 K buffer pool. Use of "default" sets the log I/O size to the default size of 4 K.

Unbinding Objects from Cache

As all objects are bound to the default cache by default on initial object creation, the sp_bindcache is actually changing the object binding. This means that you can dynamically change an object's cache binding using sp_bindcache without having to unbind it from its current cache binding.

However, because you cannot bind anything to the default cache, you still need an explicit unbinding to return the object to the default cache. This is done using **sp_unbindcache** or **sp_unbindcache_all**.

sp_unbindcache

```
sp_unbindcache db_name [, object_name][, text]
sp_unbindcache_all cache_name
```

```
sp_unbindcache sales_hist_db, order_hist
```

unbinds the order_hist table from its current named cache (tab_scan_cache) and returns it to using the default cache.

```
sp_unbindcache_all psales_cache
```

unbinds all objects in psales_cache and returns them to using the default cache.

Dropping a cache binding clears all the pages currently in the cache. This, combined with a system lock on the object while binding or unbinding, means that this is not a high performance operation and you must time it very carefully. Also the binding or unbinding will fail if there is currently a "dirty read" or an open cursor active on the object.

Displaying Cache Binding Information

You can get information about the cache binding using **sp_helpcache**.

sp_helpcache

```
sp_helpcache [cache_name]
```

```
sp_helpcache tab_scan_cache

Cache name          Config size    Run size       Overhead
tab_scan_cache      10M            10M            0.53M
──────────cache binding information──────────
Cache name          Entity_name                         Type    Index name
tab_scan_cache      sales_hist_db.dbo.order_hist        table
tab_scan_cache      mktg_db.dbo.all_orders              table
tab_scan_cache      mktg_db.dbo.all_sales               index   INC1_all_sales
```

You can use the wildcard characters on the cache name in sp_helpcache.

```
sp_helpcache "log%"
```

This will display cache information on all caches whose name contains the string "log."

And, as mentioned earlier, you can get cache overhead sizes using sp_helpcache.

```
sp_helpcache "size[size_unit]"
```

```
sp_helpcache "20000P"

2.08M of overhead memory will be needed to manage a cache of 20000P.
```

Resizing Caches

You can change the size of a cache using sp_cacheconfig with a new total cache size.

```
sp_cacheconfig cache_name, new_size
```

This can increase or decrease the size of the cache with the restriction that the default cache cannot go below 512 K or the limit imposed by specifying a default cache size. As all new named cache comes from the default cache, this limits you based on the total allocation of cache. Also, all new allocations are of the default 2 K buffer pool size, so the practical limit is that you cannot decrease the size of the default 2 K buffer pool below 512 K.

```
sp_cacheconfig tab_scan_cache, "20M"
```

alters the size of tab_scan_cache to 20 MB, moving it up or down depending on the current value. This new size does not take effect until a server restart.

Let me emphasize that, by default, all cache resizing is done using 2 K buffer pool pages. So if the above resizing reduced tab_scan_cache from 30 MB to 20 MB, this reduces the 2 K buffer pool of tab_scan_cache. Therefore, you always need the required amount of cache in the 2 K pool to reduce a cache size. This is particularly relevant in a logonly cache that you may have configured to use 4 K. If you want to reduce the size of a 4 K log cache, you will first have to make the appropriate amount of 2 K buffer pool available.

To completely remove a data cache, reset the size to zero.

```
sp_cacheconfig tab_scan_cache, “0”
```

This takes effect at the next server restart. If you do not unbind all objects before this restart, the bindings are marked invalid and you get warning messages in the error log. You will also have to be careful with dump and load as the bindings are stored in sysattributes and may have changed since the last dump.

12.1.3 Buffer Pools in a Cache

Creating Buffer Pools

All data caches are created with the standard I/O page size of 2 K. Additional buffer pools of pages in mulitples of two, up to eight pages, may be configured in a data cache to allow large I/O with multiple pages read from disk at a time. When this occurs, the group of pages is treated as one unit in cache so that they are aged and written to disk at if all the pages were one page.

Configuring additional buffer pools in a cache is done using **sp_poolconfig**.

sp_poolconfig

```
sp_poolconfig  cache_name,
               "size[size_unit]",
               "config_poolK"
               [, "effected_poolK"]
```

where

size	the size of the buffer pool;
size_unit	P pages;
	K kilobytes;
	M megabytes;
	G gigabytes;
config_pool	the page size of the buffer pool;
	2 K, 4 K, 8 K, 16 K (i.e. a maximum of one extent);
effected_pool	the existing buffer pool size from which the config_pool allocation is taken; defaults to the 2 K pool.

```
sp_poolconfig log_cache, "10M", "4K"
```

This command allocates a 10 MB pool of 4 K buffers in log_cache, taking the 10 MB from the current 2 K buffer pool in log_cache.

Each buffer pool allocation shows as a separate line on sp_helpcache output.

```
sp_poolconfig "default data cache", "5M", "4K"
sp_poolconfig "default data cache", "5M", "16K", "2K"
```

gives a default data cache of:

```
sp_cacheconfig "default data cache"
```

```
Cache name               Status Type              Config value   Run value
Default data cache       Active Default           25.00 Mb       37.64 Mb
                                                  ------         ------
                               Total              25.00 Mb       37.64 Mb
                                                  ------         ------
==============================================================
Cache: default data cache,   Status: active,   Type: Default
         Config Size: 0.00Mb,   Run Size: 60.00Mb

IO Size Wash Size        Config Size    Run Size
  2 Kb   512 Kb           25.00 Mb      27.64 Mb
  4 Kb   512 Kb            5.00 Mb       5.00 Mb
 16 Kb   512 Kb            5.00 Mb       5.00 Mb
```

Note that the buffer pool configuration takes effect immediately, so make sure that the cache is active before you start assigning parts of it to buffer pools.

Changing The Buffer Pool Size

Altering the memory allocated to a buffer pool is done simply by issuing sp_poolconfig with the new total pool size. The new size can increase or decrease the memory allocated to the buffer pool. You cannot allocate more memory than is available in the named cache and you cannot reduce the default cache below 512 K.

```
sp_poolconfig large_io_cache, "20M", "8K", "4K"
```

This sets the 8 K pool in large_io_cache to 20 MB. If increasing in size, the original memory must be available in the 4 K pool of large_io_cache. If decreasing in size, the available memory will be returned to the 4 K pool.

As with caches, you remove a buffer pool by setting the size to zero.

```
sp_poolconfig "default data cache", "0", "4K"
```

All pages will be returned to the 2 K pool in the named cache. You cannot delete the 2 K pool from any cache. If some of the pages are in use or in the dirty page chain waiting to be flushed to disk, as many pages as possible are transferred and you get a message indicating how much has been left in the specified buffer pool. The remaining pages are not transferred automatically when they become free and you need to reissue the zero size sp_poolconfig for the buffer pool.

Wash Size

When a disk page needs to be read into cache, an unused cache page—a clean page—has to be found for the disk page to use. Pages in cache that have been altered by a maintenance command are considered "dirty" and have to be written to disk (cleaned) before they are available for further use. This cleaning is done when a page passes a wash marker and enters the wash area. Therefore, all clean pages are available once they have passed the cache wash marker. If there are no current clean pages, a physical disk read will have to wait until the required number of pages have been cleaned. The setting of the wash marker is therefore quite important to SQL Server performance. Setting it too small means that physical disk accesses will have to wait for clean pages. Setting it too high means that the server is writing cache pages to disk more often than it needs to. Consider cache as a string of pages, as in Figure 12.2, with the most recently used (MRU) on the left and the least recently used (LRU) on the right.

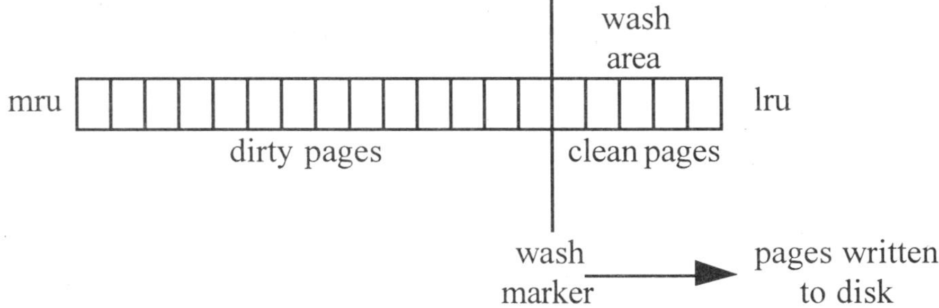

Figure 12.2 *Buffer chain and wash marker.*

This means that pages migrate along the string from left to right (MRU to LRU) and as they age they pass the wash marker. At this point, they are written to disk and are now available for further use.

When a cache page is requested, it is taken from the LRU end of the chain and placed on the MRU end of the chain, when it repeats its migration from MRU to LRU.

Sybase set the wash marker to the smaller of 512 K or 20% of the buffer pool size. This is a highly recommended figure and you should think carefully about changing it. If you have a large cache with a high update rate, try 1–2%. But it is probably better to try other changes first before moving the wash marker. Getting it wrong will have a significant effect on physical I/O, which can seriously degrade the overall performance.

If you set it too low, the number of clean pages is lower and some disk I/O may have to wait for a clean page to become available. If you set it too high, pages will be cleaned much earlier than they need to and the server will be doing unnecessary disk I/O cleaning pages.

Some Guidelines for Named Caches and Buffer Pools

Do not starve any of the caches of 2 K I/O buffers, as commands which do not retrieve more than one page of information will be slower with large I/O buffers. The optimizer defaults to choosing the optimum buffer pool for a command so make sure that you always have 2 K I/O available. The exemption is log activity which defaults to 4 K I/O, so configure log cache accordingly. Some commands always use 2 K I/O: disk init, drop table and some DBCC.

If tempdb is heavily used, bind it to its own cache. You will need to experiment with the size, depending on your application profiles. Start with 5% and see how it goes. If you use **select into** frequently when creating temporary tables, you should configure a large 16 K buffer pool. And remember that tempdb still has a log that defaults to 4 K I/O.

Match application activity to pool sizes: on-line transaction processing to 2 K and decision support to large I/O; e.g. 16 K.

Start at the database level and then manage a few large objects which benefit from large I/O. Do not get too detailed with allocating cache. Be very sensitive to the point of diminishing return. Sybase states that they have not found it advantageous to create more than two buffer pools in a named cache.

Sysindexes is in constant use by SQL Server and will benefit from being bound to its own cache.

Consider a separate cache for small active tables and/or indexes. In a high concurrency OLTP application on SMP systems, it may be advantageous to separate the index and date pages to reduce spinlock contention.

Binding and unbinding objects to cache flushes the object from cache and recompiles all procedures and triggers which use the object. So do not adjust production without testing it completely in development.

However, be careful of not getting the maximum benefit of large buffer pools if the data chains are fragmented. A high deletion activity, or out-of-place update, can cause pages in existing extents to be emptied and returned to the free page chain. These pages are reused when more space is required, causing nonlinear page chains. Each of these "misplaced" pages in the chain can cause an additional I/O when using greater than 2 K I/O buffers. If you find that you are doing logical I/O more than 85% of the time, then leave well alone. It is unlikely that you will get much benefit from tuning named caches with this logical I/O hit rate.

12.1.4 Using the Configuration File

Each data cache has an entry in the configuration file that is maintained automatically by the server. This has the format:

```
[Normal cache: cache_name]

        cache size = {size|DEFAULT}
        cache status = {mixed cache|log only|default data cache}
```

For example:

```
[Named cache: default data cache]
        cache size = 38.94M
        cache statistics = default data cache
[Named cache = log_cache]
        cache size = 20M
        cache statistics = logonly
```

If you configure buffer pools in a cache, the named cache entry is followed by the buffer pool entries in the format:

```
[Buffer Pool I/O Size]
        pool size = size
        wash size = size
```

For example:

```
[8K I/O buffer pool]
        pool size = 10M
        wash size = 2M
```

12.2 Partitioned Tables

12.2.1 Creating Partitions

System 11 has introduced the ability to partition a heap table into two or more partitions to which SQL Server randomly assigns inserts. This alleviates the hot spot on the end of the table and allows concurrent insert activity to a heap table. A heap table has no clustered index so every insert is made to the last page of the table. The last page is exclusively locked by every insert and can quickly become a single thread bottleneck to concurrent insert activity.

Splitting the table into multiple partitions, each looking and acting like a separate heap table, reduces this bottleneck by spreading the insert activity across the several partitions, as in Figure 12.3.

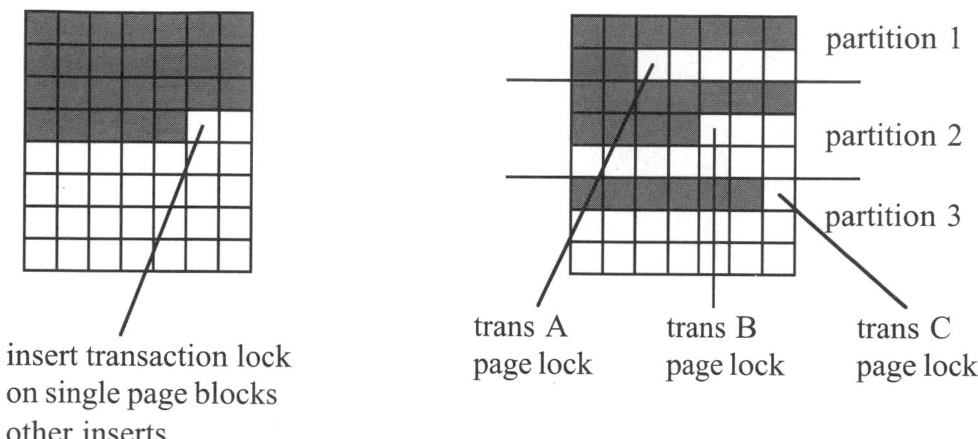

***Figure 12.3** Reducing blocking by table partitioning.*

Splitting to three partitions, as in Figure 12.3, has improved the concurrency to the table by a factor of three by reducing page contention. This will give a related I/O throughput increase. However, I/O throughput may not increase by the same reduction in locking contention if the table partitions are located on the same physical disk. Maximum increase in I/O throughput will be achieved by placing the partitions on separate segments on separate physical disks.

A table is partitioned using the **alter table** command.

alter table

```
ALTER TABLE table_name PARTITION no_of_partitions
```

```
ALTER TABLE orders_tab PARTITION 2
```

This splits orders_tab into two partitions. This results in two separate page chains, one for each partition, with two "last pages" allowing concurrent insert activity to each partition. Each partition has a control page and an entry in **syspartitions**. The control page keeps track of the last page of the partition, similar to sysindexes.last, and syspartitions contains the object ID, partition ID and the page numbers of the first page and control page of each partition.

Partition information is displayed using **sp_helpartition**.

sp_helpartition

```
sp_helpartition table_name
```

```
sp_helpartition orders_tab
```

partition_id	first_page	control_page
1	2056	2057
2	312	313

The same partition information is also displayed at the end of the **sp_help tab_name** output. The physical location of the partitions depends on the segment that the table is created on. If the segment is on the same disk, all partitions will be created on the same disk. If the segment spans multiple disks, the partitions will be placed on separate disks. For orders_tab above, if defined on a segment which spans two disks, each partition would be created on a separate disk.

As concurrent I/O is one of the important performance aspects of partitioning, the optimum sequence of events to define partitions is:

- create the appropriate segment covering several physical disks;
- create the table on the segment;
- partition the table into the required number of partitions.

```
sp_addsegment big_seg, prod_db, dev_1
sp_extendsegment big_seg, prod_db, dev_2
sp_extendsegment big_seg, prod_db, dev_3
sp_extendsegment big_seg, prod_db, dev_4

CREATE TABLE prod_tab ( ......) on big_seg

ALTER TABLE prod_tab PARTITION 4
```

This creates four partitions distributed as evenly as possible across the disks used by the segment big_seg.

You do not need to match the number of partitions to the number of disks. SQL Server will distribute as evenly as possible across the available disks. A heap table split into four partitions is distributed across numbers of devices as:

partition	2 devices	4 devices	8 devices
1	dev1	dev1	dev1, dev5
2	dev2	dev2	dev2, dev6
3	dev1	dev3	dev3, dev7
4	dev2	dev4	dev4, dev8

SQL Server then randomly assigns insert transactions to a partition; you cannot control the partition used by an individual insert. If the transaction is a multiple insert, all of the inserts for that transaction are made to the same partition. You cannot spread one transaction across several partitions. If you create partitions on existing data, all of the existing data is allocated to the first partition. If you run out of space on one device, SQL Server will continue to allocate space to the partition from another device available to the segment. If you partition a table that has text/image columns, the storage for these is not partitioned but is retained on the existing separate page chains.

bcp is also treated as one transaction and inserts to one partition. To improve the speed of a data load and to get an even spread of data across the partitions, you need to run multiple bcp processes for the separate partitions.

Nonclustered indexes on partitioned tables are not themselves partitioned but look like normal indexes on a single table.

12.2.2 Unpartitioning

You unpartition a table using alter table.

```
    ALTER TABLE table_name UNPARTITION
ALTER TABLE orders_tab UNPARTITION
```

This simply concatenates the page chains of the existing partitions into one page chain. All control pages and entries in syspartitions are deleted and sysindexes.last is updated with the last page of the table. None of the existing data is moved. You need to unpartition a table before you can create a clustered index on it.

12.2.3 Changing the Number of Partitions

This is done in two steps: unpartition the existing table and then respecify with the new number of partitions.

```
ALTER TABLE orders_tab UNPARTITION
ALTER TABLE orders_tab PARTITION 6
```

Again, this does not move any existing data but it will result in all of the data being in the first partition of the new partitioning, as a consequence of the unpartitioning.

12.3 Optimizer

12.3.1 Introduction

In general, the System 11 changes to the optimizer are in the presentation of the showplan output and the handling of subqueries. The use of large I/O buffer bools has also altered the cost figures and table scans may now be preferred more often. This may make some of your existing indexes redundant. You will need to check this.

The general showplan changes are:

- a line identifying the start of each statement;
- indentation of the table name;
- a number on each worktable;
- information on the direction of the scan (all scans are ascending at present but it is a useful indication of future descending scans);
- information on how scans are being carried out:
  - at start of table (table scan);
  - by row identifier;
  - by key;
  - at index start;
- the name of the clustered index;
- the index keys used;
- information on when the index covers the query;

- information on the I/O size strategy;
- information on the caching strategy (see section 12.3.11 for a description of how this works).

But there is still no indication of the estimated number of I/Os per nested iteration. You still need **dbcc traceon(311)** to provide this essential piece of information.

The general subquery changes are as follows.

- More subqueries are flattened into an existence join (some of the Sybase literature now calls this unnesting). Most subqueries containing IN, ANY, EXISTS are now flattened to an existence join. The exceptions are correlated subqueries containing aggregates and subqueries under an OR clause.
- When the subquery is independent of the outer query, it is elevated separately and the results passed to the outer query. Sybase calls this materializing the subquery.
- In all other cases, the subquery processing is now outside-in instead of the current inside-out approach. In this situation, the outer query is checked first to eliminate unnecessary executions of the subquery.
- A subquery can now contain both DISTINCT and GROUP BY. These used to cause error 152.

An interesting change in both System 10 and 11 is that the default fixed percentages are no longer used when statistics are available but cannot be used. In this case, the optimizer uses the density figures for the index column. This provides a more realistic data distribution figure and makes it more likely that the index will be used. Now the only time the fixed percentages are used is when there are no statistics for the index.

Let's look at these new showplans in detail.

12.3.2 Table Scan

```
SELECT * FROM customer
```

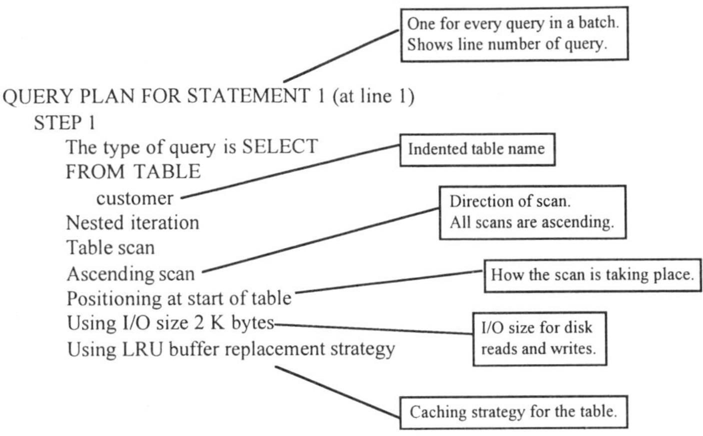
QUERY PLAN FOR STATEMENT 1 (at line 1)
STEP 1
The type of query is SELECT
FROM TABLE
customer
Nested iteration
Table scan
Ascending scan
Positioning at start of table
Using I/O size 2 K bytes
Using LRU buffer replacement strategy
One for every query in a batch. Shows line number of query.
Indented table name
Direction of scan. All scans are ascending.
How the scan is taking place.
I/O size for disk reads and writes.
Caching strategy for the table.

12.3.3 Clustered Index

```
SELECT * FROM customer
       WHERE name LIKE 'KIRK%'
```

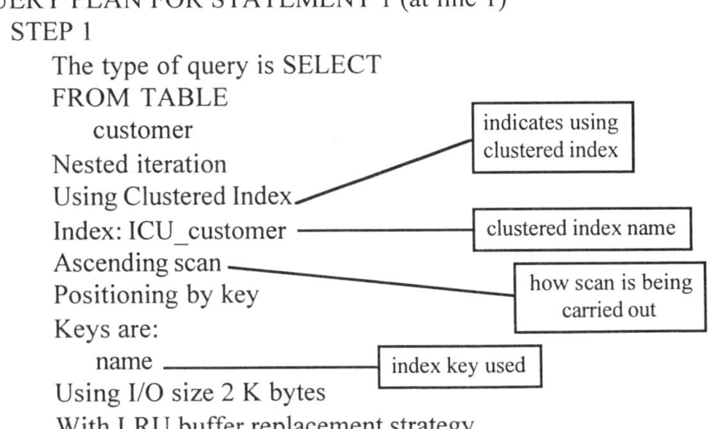
QUERY PLAN FOR STATEMENT 1 (at line 1)
STEP 1
The type of query is SELECT
FROM TABLE
customer
Nested iteration
Using Clustered Index
Index: ICU_customer
Ascending scan
Positioning by key
Keys are:
name
Using I/O size 2 K bytes
With LRU buffer replacement strategy
indicates using clustered index
clustered index name
how scan is being carried out
index key used

12.3.4 Nonclustered Index

```
SELECT * FROM customer
       WHERE cust_no = 12345
```

```
QUERY PLAN FOR STATEMENT 1 (at line 1)
    STEP 1
        The type of query is SELECT
        FROM TABLE
            customer
        Nested iteration
        Index: INCU_customer                 nonclustered index name
        Ascending scan
        Positioning by key
        Keys are:
            cust_no                          index key used
        Using I/O size 2 K bytes
        With LRU buffer replacement strategy
```

12.3.5 Covered Index

```
SELECT cust_no, discount FROM customer
       WHERE discount = 0
```

```
QUERY PLAN FOR STATEMENT 1 (at line 1)
    STEP 1
        The type of query is SELECT
        FROM TABLE
            customer                         indicates index
        Nested iteration                     covers query
        Index: INCU_customer
        Ascending scan
        Positioning at index start
        Index contains all needed columns. Base table will not be read.
        Using I/O size 2 K bytes
        Using LRU buffer replacement strategy
```

12.3.6 Distinct

This is a two-step query plan: the creation of a worktable and then the sorting of this to remove duplicate values.

```
SELECT DISTINCT post_code
       FROM customer
```

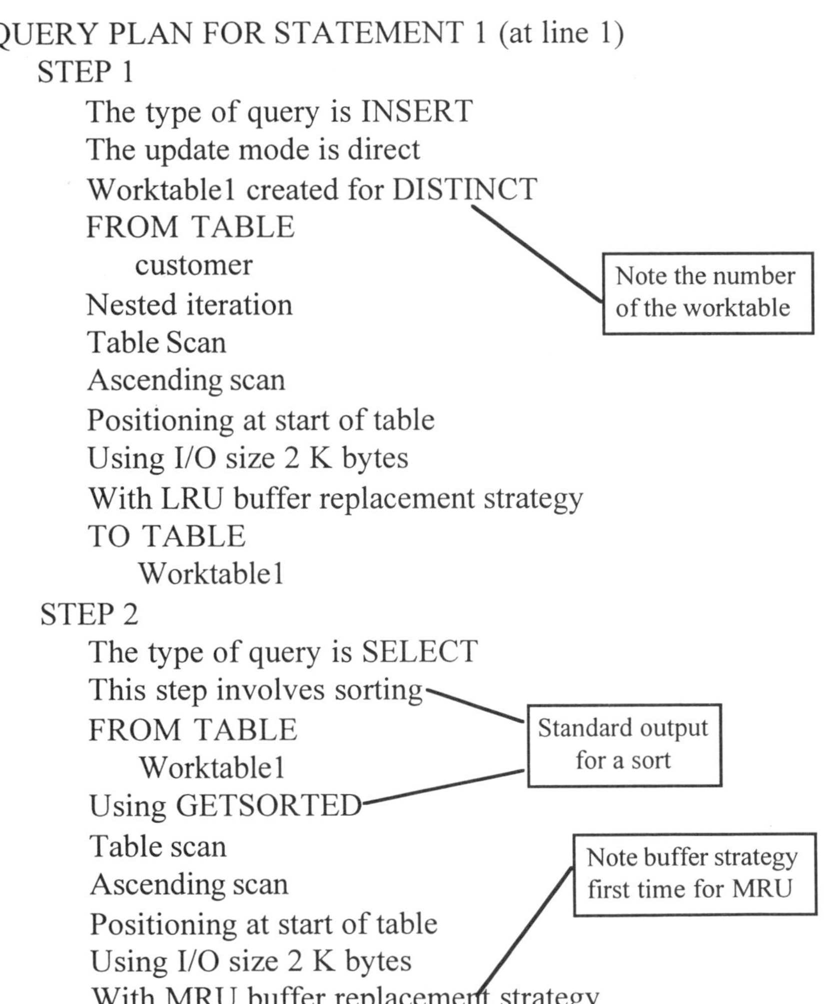

QUERY PLAN FOR STATEMENT 1 (at line 1)
STEP 1
The type of query is INSERT
The update mode is direct
Worktable1 created for DISTINCT
FROM TABLE
customer
Nested iteration
Table Scan
Ascending scan
Positioning at start of table
Using I/O size 2 K bytes
With LRU buffer replacement strategy
TO TABLE
Worktable1
STEP 2
The type of query is SELECT
This step involves sorting
FROM TABLE
Worktable1
Using GETSORTED
Table scan
Ascending scan
Positioning at start of table
Using I/O size 2 K bytes
With MRU buffer replacement strategy
Note the number of the worktable
Standard output for a sort
Note buffer strategy first time for MRU

An ORDER BY that requires a sort has an identical plan to the DISTINCT.

12.3.7 Aggregates

The **scalar aggregate** is now called a **grouped aggregate** and has the same two-step plan as before, where step 1 calculates the results of the aggregate function into an internal variable and step 2 simply selects this variable value.

```
SELECT COUNT(*) FROM customer
      WHERE name LIKE 'S%'
```

```
QUERY PLAN FOR STATEMENT 1 (at line 1)
   STEP 1
      The type of query is SELECT
      Evaluate ungrouped COUNT aggregate
      FROM TABLE
         customer
      Nested iteration
      Using clustered index
      Index: ICU_customer
      Ascending scan
      Positioning by key
      Keys are:
         name
      Using I/O size 2 K bytes
      Using LRU buffer replacement strategy
   STEP 2
      The type of query is SELECT
```


The **vector aggregates** are now called **grouped aggregates** with a two-step plan: step 1 calculates the results into a worktable and step 2 reads the worktable.

```
SELECT town, sum(std_price) FROM customer
GROUP BY town
```

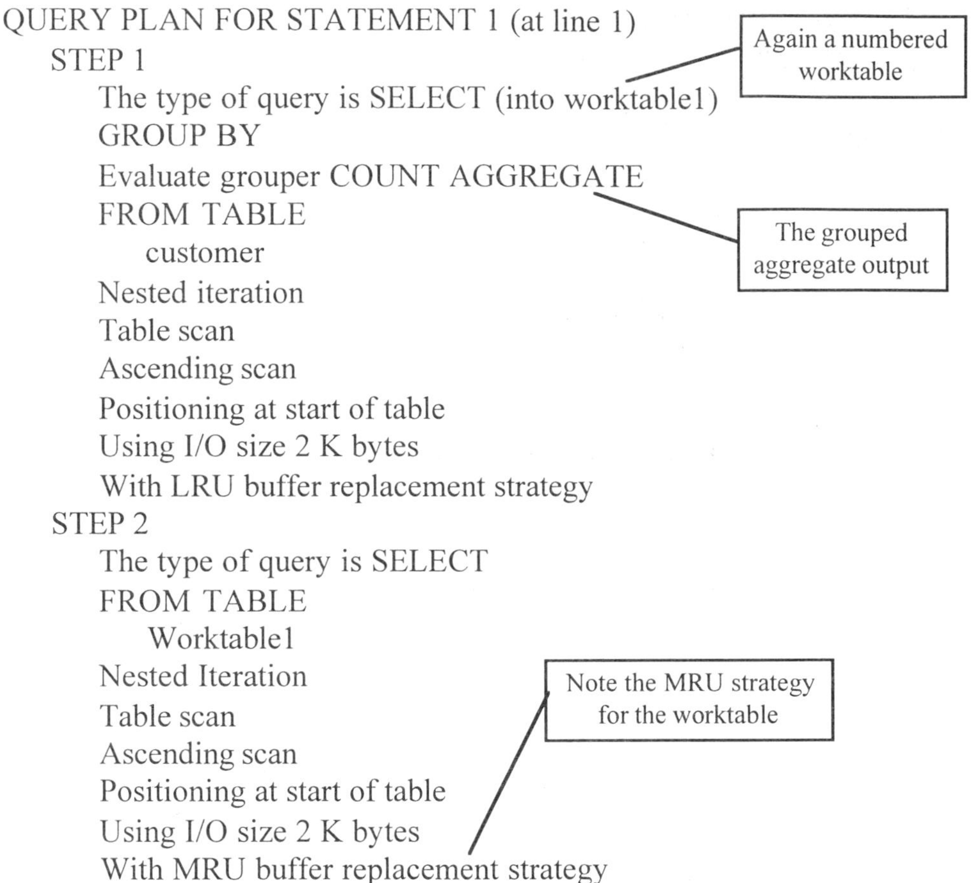

QUERY PLAN FOR STATEMENT 1 (at line 1)
STEP 1
The type of query is SELECT (into worktable1)
GROUP BY
Evaluate grouper COUNT AGGREGATE
FROM TABLE
customer
Nested iteration
Table scan
Ascending scan
Positioning at start of table
Using I/O size 2 K bytes
With LRU buffer replacement strategy
STEP 2
The type of query is SELECT
FROM TABLE
Worktable1
Nested Iteration
Table scan
Ascending scan
Positioning at start of table
Using I/O size 2 K bytes
With MRU buffer replacement strategy
Again a numbered worktable
The grouped aggregate output
Note the MRU strategy for the worktable

12.3.8 OR Strategies

This has the same **dynamic index** style strategy with one pass to generate the row IDs of qualifying records and a final pass to read the records using the internal row IDs.

```
SELECT name, town, post_code
       FROM customer
       WHERE name LIKE 'KIR%'
       OR town like 'WOK%'
```

```
QUERY PLAN FOR STATEMENT 1 (at line 1)
    STEP 1
        The type of query is SELECT
        FROM TABLE
            customer
        Nested iteration
        Using clustered index
        Index: ICU_customer
        Ascending scan
        Positioning by key
        Keys are:
            name
        Using I/O size 2 K bytes
        With LRU buffer replacement strategy
        FROM TABLE
            Customer
        Nested Iteration
        Index: INC2_customer
        Ascending scan
        Positioning by key
        Keys are:
            town
        Using I/O size 2 K bytes
        With LRU buffer replacement strategy
        FROM TABLE
            customer
        Nested Iteration
        Using Dynamic Index
        Ascending scan
        Positioning by Row Identifier (RID)
        Using I/O size 2 K bytes
        With LRU buffer replacement strategy
```

The dynamic index (OR) output

Note the use of the LRU replacement cache strategy all of the time in the dynamic index plan.

12.3.9 Reformatting

No difference here. The only benefit is that if you do a multitable join, the worktables are numbered. You can easily see how the final nested iteration is being carried out.

```
SELECT c.name, c.std_price, o.ord_no, i.act_price, i.del_date
       FROM customer c, orders o, ord_item i
       WHERE c.std_price = i.act_price
       AND i.del_date = o.reqd_date
```

```
QUERY PLAN FOR STATEMENT 1 (at line 1)
    STEP 1
        The type of query is INSERT
        The update mode is direct
        Worktable1 created for REFORMATTING
        FROM TABLE
            ord_item
        Nested iteration
        Table scan
        Ascending scan
        Positioning at start of table
        Using I/O size 2 K bytes
        With LRU buffer replacement strategy
        TO TABLE
            Worktable1
    STEP 2
        The type of query is INSERT
        The update mode is direct
        Worktable2 created for REFORMATTING
        FROM TABLE
            orders
        Nested Iteration
        Table scan
        Ascending scan
        Positioning at start of table
        Using I/O size 2 K bytes
        With LRU buffer replacement strategy
        TO TABLE
            Worktable2
```

Reformatting of two of the tables

```
STEP 3
    The type of query is SELECT
    FROM TABLE
        customer
    Nested iteration
    Table scan
    Ascending scan
    Positioning at start of table
    Using I/O size 2 K bytes
    With LRU buffer replacement strategy
    FROM TABLE
        Worktable 1
    Nested Iteration
    Table scan
    Ascending scan
    Positioning at start of table
    Using I/O size 2 K bytes
    With LRU buffer replacement strategy
    FROM TABLE
        Worktable 2
    Nested Iteration
    Table scan
    Ascending scan
    Positioning at start of table
    Using I/O size 2 K bytes
    With LRU buffer replacement strategy
```

Nested iteration join indicating the worktable sequence

12.3.10 Subquery Optimization

As mentioned earlier, there are some significant differences to the subquery optimization.

Whenever possible, the nesting will be flattened into a join and an existence join will be carried out to limit the access required to the nested table (see Chapter 10). When the subquery is noncorrelated and it can be evaluated independently of the outer query, it is evaluated first and the result set passed to the outer query. In all other cases, any additional AND/OR clauses in the outer query are evaluated first to reduce the number of times the subquery has to be executed.

Fortunately System 11 has significantly improved the presentation of the subquery showplan—to the extent that it is now readable. Improvements include:

- a begin ... end delimiting the subquery showplan;
- a statement of where the subquery executes in the overall showplan;
- the type of subquery being executed:
  - correlated;
  - noncorrelated;
  - subquery under an IN predicate;
  - subquery under an ANY predicate;
  - subquery under an ALL predicate;
  - subquery under an EXISTS predicate;
  - subquery under an EXPRESSION predicate;
- an indication that the subquery is using an internal aggregate value (the ONCE and ANY internal aggregates used to evaluate some subqueries).

Subquery Flattened to a Join

```
SELECT * FROM customer
      WHERE cust_no IN (SELECT cust_no from orders
                              WHERE cust_no = '12345')
```

```
QUERY PLAN FOR STATEMENT 1 (at line 1)
   STEP 1
      The type of query is SELECT
      FROM TABLE
         customers
      Nested iteration
      Index: INCU1_customer
      Ascending scan
      Positioning by key
      Keys are:
         cust_no
      Using I/O size 2 K bytes
      With LRU buffer replacement strategy
      FROM TABLE
         orders
      EXISTS TABLE: Nested Iteration
      Index: INCU2_orders
      Ascending scan
      Positioning by key
      Keys are:
         cust_no
      Using I/O size 2 K bytes
      With LRU buffer replacement strategy
```

Subquery Evaluated and Results Passed to Outer Query

System 11 has removed the fixed nesting sequences of the tables when flattening to a join. Before System 11, the inner table was always nested after all of the tables in the outer query. In System 11, all table iteration sequencing is an optimizer decision.

Sybase calls this **materializing** the query.

```
SELECT name, post_code
       FROM customer
       WHERE tot_orders in
              (SELECT max(units_sold) FROM orders_summary
                     GROUP BY area)
```

```
QUERY PLAN FOR STATEMENT 1 (at line 1)
   STEP 1
      The type of query is SELECT (into Worktable1)
      GROUP by
      Evaluate grouped MAXIMUM AGGREGATE
      FROM TABLE
         orders_summary
      Nested iteration
      Table scan
      Ascending scan
      Positioning at start of table
      Using I/O size 2 K bytes
      With LRU buffer replacement strategy
      TO TABLE
         Worktable1
   STEP 2
      The type of query is SELECT
      FROM TABLE
         customer
      Nested iteration
      Table scan
      Ascending scan
      Positioning at start of table
      Using I/O size 2 K bytes
      With LRU buffer replacement strategy
      FROM TABLE
         Worktable1
      EXISTS TABLE: Nested Iteration
      Table scan
      Ascending scan
      Positioning at start of table
      Using I/O size 2 K bytes
      With MRU buffer replacement strategy
```

Evaluation of sub-query with results in worktable

An existence join of customer and the worktable from step 1

Subqueries Which Cannot Be Flattened or Materialized

Before System 11, the subquery result was formed first and then joined with the outer query. This could result in a larger work set than was needed and it was often necessary to repeat any outer AND predicates inside the subquery to reduce the work set. The inner query evaluation was also done as a GROUP BY ALL, which returned all possible groupings and required an extra pass over the worktable. This has been changed in System 11 to an outside-in evaluation as a nested iteration. This allows any external predicates to be evaluated first, which may eliminate the need to evaluate the subquery.

```
SELECT name FROM customer
       WHERE tot_orders > ALL
             (SELECT tot_orders FROM customer
                    WHERE area = 'SE')
```

```
QUERY PLAN FOR STATEMENT 1 (at line 1)
   STEP 1
      The type of query is SELECT
      FROM TABLE
         customer
      Nested iteration
      Table scan
      Ascending scan
      Positioning at start of table
      Run subquery 1 (at nesting level 1)
      Using I/O size 2 K bytes
      With LRU buffer replacement strategy
NESTING LEVEL 1 SUBQUERIES FOR STATEMENT 1
QUERY PLAN FOR SUBQUERY 1 (at nesting level 1 and at line 3)
   Correlated subquery
   Subquery under the ALL predicate
   STEP 1
      The type of query is SELECT
      Evaluate ungrouped ANY AGGREGATE
      FROM TABLE
         customer
      EXISTS TABLE: Nested iteration
      Index: INC3_customer
      Ascending scan
      Positioning by key
      Keys are:
         area
      Using I/O size 2 K bytes
      With LRU buffer replacement strategy
END OF QUERY PLAN FOR SUBQUERY 1
```

Subquery runs here

Outer query plan

Type of subquery

Internal any aggregate

subquery plan

End of subquery plan

12.3.11 Optimizer Assists

System 11 provides some times when you can override the optimizer choice and force a different execution plan. These come under the headings of:

- forcing the table order in a join;
- altering the number of tables considered together in a multitable join;
- forcing use of an index;
- specifying the I/O buffer size;
- specifying the cache replacement strategy.

Table Join Order

This is now official support for an existing unsupported feature.

```
set forceplan {on|off}
```

This forces the join order of tables from left to right in the FROM clause. This has already been dealt with in section 7.9.

Number of Tables Grouped Together in Join Nested Iteration

As discussed in section 10.3.7, the tables in a multitable join are considered in groups of four to determine the best outer table, in further groups of four for the next best table in the iteration sequence, and so on. This can miss some useful table combinations and you can now force the optimizer to increase the number of tables grouped in join evaluation using:

```
set table count number
```

Clearly, increasing this number will increase the time and CPU it takes to optimize the query. SQL Server does not have any limit on this time and it will always check all permitted permutations. So, in my opinion, the approach is to check the optimization to see if you can get a better plan by increasing the number of tables. You can then rewrite the command so that the tables are in this join sequence in the FROM clause and **set forceplan on** for this query to force the optimizer to use this table sequence. You should not have many of these statements, making the maintenance overhead quite small. (Sybase has informed me of small overheads when setting this to eight for all application sessions. You might wish to check this.)

Forcing Use of an Index

This was always available by using the indid after the table name in the FROM clause.

```
SELECT * FROM ord_item(2)
        WHERE ord_price > 50
        AND ord_qty < 100
        AND ord_date BETWEEN '1/1/90' AND '1/1/95'
```

This was very dangerous as the indid could change without warning during an index rebuild, which could result in some very interesting response times.

System 11 has improved on this by allowing you to use the index name after the table name in the FROM clause.

```
SELECT * FROM ord_item (index INC2_ord_item)
        WHERE ord_price > 50
        AND ord_qty < 100
        AND ord_date BETWEEN '1/1/90' AND '1/1/95'
```

You can force a table scan by using the table name in place of the index name or by using indid 0 as pre-System 11. Using indid 0 is not a problem as this number never changes; indid 0 is always the table itself.

Specifying I/O Size (Prefetch)

The available caches, both default caches and normal cache, may be split up into buffer pools of 2 K–16 K in size (see section 12.1.3). Although SQL Server chooses the optimum buffer pool size by default, you can specify any of the available sizes using the prefetch clause after the index clause described above.

```
SELECT * FROM ord_item (index INC2_ord_item prefetch 8)
        WHERE ord_price > 50
        AND ord_qty < 100
        AND ord_date BETWEEN '1/1/90' AND '1/1/95'
```

If you do not have the appropriate buffer pool size configured or the required pool has no free pages, the best available size is chosen.

The object that uses the specified buffer pool size is determined by the index name used in the index clause.

Index name	**object using prefetch size**
nonclustered index	index leaf pages
table	data pages
clustered index	data pages

The effectiveness of prefetch is reduced by the complication of existing object pages in cache when the query executes. Consider 2 K and 16 K buffer pools available and prefetch 8 specified. The query will attempt to use the 16 K buffer pool for all I/O. However, if one of the pages in the extent is already in the 2 K pool, then 2 K I/O will be used for all pages in that extent.

Specifying the Cache Strategy

SQL Server has two cache strategies: MRU and LRU replacement strategies (most recently used and least recently used). MRU is also called fetch and discard.

Be careful of the terminology here. There is an MRU and LRU end to the buffer chain in cache. These indicate the most recently—and least recently—used cache pages; in other words, the ones which have just been used (MRU) and the ones which have not been used for the longest time (LRU). We are not discussing this aspect of MRU and LRU here. We are discussing the replacement strategy where MRU replacement strategy reuses the pages that have just been used and LRU replacement strategy tries to use a new page every time.

Figure 12.4 illustrates the difference in usage of these terms.

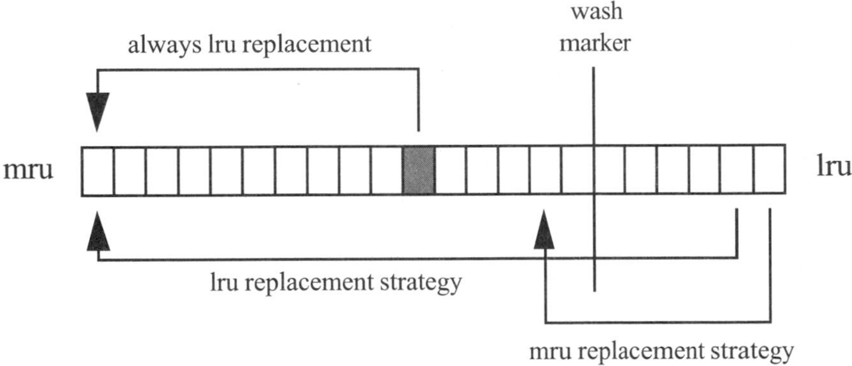

Figure 12.4 *Updating.*

When a page is read from disk, it needs to be allocated a cache page. These are always taken from the LRU end of the buffer chain, after the wash marker, as only these pages have been flushed to disk. If using MRU replacement strategy, the page is placed just before the wash marker which ensures that it is cleaned as soon as possible and becomes available for reuse immediately. If using LRU replacement strategy, the page is placed at the MRU end of the buffer chain, which means that it remains in the cache for the longest possible time until it migrates down past the wash marker.

If a page is found in cache and does not have to be read from disk, it is always placed at the MRU end of the buffer chain, regardless of the replacement strategy.

The optimizer will normally choose MRU for:

- table scans;
- clustered index for a range query;
- index scans;
- inner table in a join when the table is larger than cache;
- outer table of a join;
- when the estimated pages to be accessed for a table in a non-named data cache exceeds 50% of the cache.

The rationale is that MRU replacement strategy is used when the data pages are being read only once so will not be required again. In this case, the most recently used pages are reused for the next read from disk. This destroys as little of the contents of cache as possible with reuse of pages that are not expected to be needed again in the short term.

In effect, a table scan using MRU replacement strategy will use the same portion of data cache repetitively as it scans through the table, leaving the most active cache pages untouched. You can alter the cache replacement strategy chosen by specifying MRU or LRU with the index and prefetch clauses after the table name in the FROM clause.

```
SELECT * FROM ord_item (index ord_item prefetch 16 LRU)
```

If you do not want a particular application to use large I/O, you can disable this for the session using:

```
set prefetch {on|off}
```

If you wish to override prefetch or the cache strategy for a specific table and/or index, you can use the system procedure **sp_cachestrategy**.

sp_cachestrategy

```
sp_cachestrategy db_name
                 [, tab_name
                 [, index_name | 'text only' | 'table only'
                 [, {prefetch | mru}, { 'on' | 'off' }]]]
```

Once disabled with sp_cachestrategy, the specific strategy cannot be overridden at the query level.

12.4 Updating

System 11 has simplified the update processing by decreasing the occasions when a deferred update is done. In general, the danger times have been reduced to updates which involve joins or updates to primary key columns used for Referential Integrity. In these cases, SQL Server does a deferred update. In most other cases, SQL Server does a direct update, the overhead depending on whether the size of the row changes or an index column is updated. For single table updates, the most common situation now is that the row is not moved out of its current page and a direct update is performed as often as possible.

Let's look at this in more detail.

12.4.1 Deferred Update

A deferred update is carried out when:

- the update involves a join;
- the update is to a primary key column used in Referential Integrity;

and is actioned as:

1. the required data rows are located and transaction log entries written for the delete and insert of the data rows;
2. having located all rows, the log records are reread, the rows deleted and any related index entries deleted;
3. the log is reread and the updated rows and index entries are inserted.

This is clearly a high overhead as it requires extra reads of the transaction log and repetitive traversals of the index trees.

Although the join and Referential Integrity occasions are the most common, there are other times when a deferred update is done:

- the update moves the row to a new page when the access is via a table scan or a clustered index;
- duplicate rows are not allowed but there is no unique index to enforce this;
- the update moves the rows to a new page and the index used to locate the row is not unique.

It is worth trying to avoid deferred updates. You can eliminate two of the above by ensuring a unique index on the primary key. It is well worth the small design effort.

12.4.2 Direct Updates

A direct update is effectively the opposite of a deferred update. It is actioned as:

1. locate the required rows;
2. write the log records for data and index updates;
3. make the changes to the data and index rows.

All direct updates require the opposite of a deferred update:

- the update must not involve a join;
- the update must not be to a column involved in Referential Integrity.

There are then three categories of direct update (depending on what is updated), each with their specific criteria.

In-Place Direct Update

An **in-place direct update** has the least overhead as it changes the data row in its current page without moving the row or any other data. The in-place update requires that:

- the length of the row must not change;
- an updated column must not be part of a clustered index;

- there must not be a trigger on the table;
- the table must not be replicated.

The in-place update updates the row in its current position in the page. This means that there are no changes to page locations or row offset entries in the page, which leaves the record IDs unchanged. This is important as, with no change to the record ID, there is no need to update any index entries. The only proviso on this is if an index column is updated.

Cheap Direct Update

The trigger and replication restrictions on in-place update are necessary because the trigger and Replication Server require the deleted and inserted tables to be available. These virtual tables require the appropriate transaction log information, which can be formed only if the log entries are a deletion followed by an insertion.

However, if the row can still be written back to the same page, it is done as a **cheap direct update**. The length of the row may now change, which will alter other row offset entries and may cause the row offset number of the record being updated to change. However, this is still an efficient update with the record IDs generally remaining unchanged with no requirement to change the index entries. Figure 12.5 shows a cheap direct update increasing the length of a row and updating the offset entry values. None of the offset numbers have changed; offset 0 is still record 1, offset 1 is record 2 and so on. No updating is required to index entries.

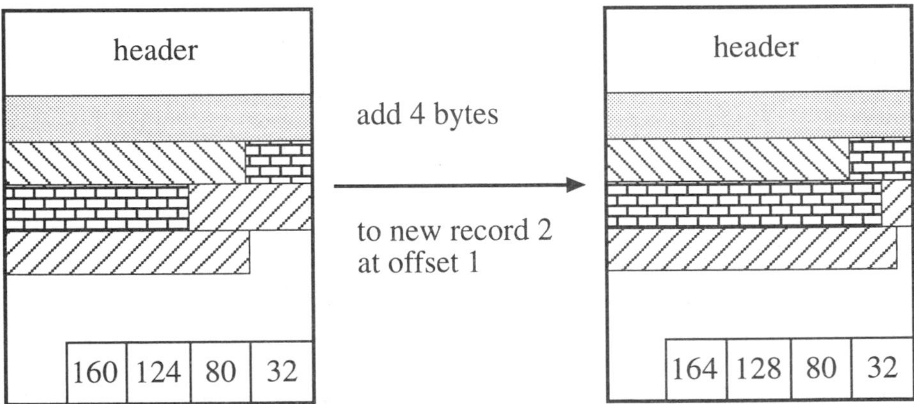

Figure 12.5 *Cheap direct update.*

Although the rows are now at different offsets from the start of the page, the record IDs have not changed as long as an index value has not been update, so no index entries need to be updated. Because the updated row is deleted and inserted, the insert stage may reuse a different offset entry, which will change the record ID of the row being updated. This will require any nonclustered index entries to be updated. Appendix E section E.4.2 discusses this situation in detail.

Expensive Direct Update

For a single row update, if the row no longer fits on the page or a clustered index column is updated that necessitates the row to move, the update is done as an **expensive direct update**.

In this situation, the row is deleted from its current page and inserted in its new location. If the table has a clustered index, this will be used to insert the row; otherwise, it will be inserted into the last page of the table. Clearly, this is quite an overhead as all indexes are also updated as a deletion followed by an insertion. Also, if the index is clustered and the row does not fit into its current page because of the update, the page must split to accommodate the increase in size This will alter several record IDs with consequent additional index update overhead.

12.4.3 Index Update

The indexes may be updated in deferred mode even though the data is updated in direct mode. This occurs when you update a unique index column or update a column in an index used to locate the record. In this case, the update is actioned as:

1. the index rows are deleted;
2. the data rows are updated directly;
3. index insert entries are written to the log;
4. the log is reread to insert the index entries.

This deferred index update eliminates any duplicate index updates when the log records are reread so that there is only one index update per qualifying index row. As the index values are being changed by the update command, even though the index row may be updated only once, we do not know if it violated any uniqueness constraint, so a deferred approach of waiting until all updating has completed has to be adopted. This is identical reasoning to using a deferred update for a join.

12.4.4 Update Summary

To summarize the types of update in System 11, I borrow directly from a presentation made by Brijesh Agarwal of the Sybase Product Performance Group.

In the following cases, the update is a deferred update.

- Update involves a join.
- Update has subqueries in an OR clause.
- Clustered index is unsafe and unique.
- Clustered index is unsafe and nonunique.
- Update variable length column and row no longer fits on the current page.

The remaining cases are all direct updates.
In the following cases, the update is an expensive direct update.

- New data row does not fit on the current page.
- Clustered index is unsafe and nonunique.

The remaining cases are all cheap direct updates, as follows.

- There are triggers.
- The table is replicated.
- The new row length is different from the current length.

The remaining cases are all in-place direct updates.

The term **safe index** refers to an index that does not need to be modified as a result of a data update. This occurs when the updated row does not change.

The scan index is the index chosen to do the scan on the table being updated.

12.5 Housekeeper Task

This is a system task which writes dirty buffers to disk during idle server times. This reduces the amount of effort expended at a checkpoint and decreases the need for buffer washing during transaction processing. If the housekeeper task flushes all dirty pages to disk, it wakes up the checkpoint process to take a checkpoint. In general, the housekeeper task will reduce the overhead of checkpoints but, if the system is disk-bound already, it may simply exacerbate the situation.

The increase in write activity caused by the housekeeper task can be configured using sp_configure, as described in Chapter 13.

```
sp_configure "housekeeper free write percent", value
```

This specifies the maximum increase in disk activity that the housekeeper task may cause. The default is 20. A value of 0 disables the housekeeper task and a value of 100 allows it to work continuously.

12.6 Maximum Rows Per Page

You may specify a maximum rows per page for data and/or index pages to limit the occupancy of each page. This is useful for reducing the contention for records, as discussed in Appendix D. It can also increase the incidence of updates in "cheap direct" mode by leaving free space on every page.

The max_rows_per_page may be set when you create the table or index.

```
CREATE TABLE orders_tab (
       ord_no          int,
       .
       .
       ord_date        datetime)
       WITH MAX_ROWS_PER_PAGE = 5
```

This limits the number of rows in a data page to five for the life of the table. If you subsequently create a clustered index on the table, it inherits the max_rows_per_page value and retains the data page occupancy limit. However, select into does not inherit the value. The default is zero, which is normal full occupancy (depending on the fillfactor). The maximum value is 256.

Specifying a max_rows_per_page on a nonclustered index effects the leaf level of the index only and leaves the data pages unchanged.

```
CREATE INDEX jk_idx1 ON orders_tab(ord_no)
       WITH MAX_ROWS_PER_PAGE = 20
```

This is less obviously useful than a max_rows_per_page on the data pages. However, maintenance commands do update and lock the index pages and reducing contention on any locked resource is important. Index page locks are often a source of deadlocks. If you are getting a high incidence of deadlock and one of the tables has a large number of indexes (more than five), it may be worth trying a lower max_rows_per_page to see if you can reduce the contention on the index pages.

You may alter an existing table or index max_rows_per_page using sp_chgattribute.

sp_chgattribute

```
sp_chgattribute object_name, "max_rows_per_page", value
```

This does not affect any existing data but limits the page occupancy for further maintenance commands. The simplest way to alter existing data is to create or recreate a clustered index with the required max_rows_per_page value.

The current max_rows_per_page is displayed using **sp_helpindex**.

sp_helpindex

```
sp_helpindex object_name
```

```
sp_helpindex orders_tab

index_name    index_description    index keys    index_max_rows_per_page
ICU_ord_no    clustered, unique    ord_no 4
              located on default
```

12.7 Lock Promotion Thresholds

System 11 allows lock promotion thresholds to be set, which determine when multiple page locks are escalated into a table lock. When the number of page locks set while the query is executing exceeds a lock promotion threshold, the page locks are escalated to table locks. Note that the decision is taken on one scan of the table, so a command which does multiple scans of the table may request more locks in total than the lock promotion threshold.

The server-wide number of available locks is set using sp_configure:

```
sp_configure "number of locks", 20000
```

If this is exceeded, the command fails with an error message.

There are three lock promotion thresholds.

1. lock promotion HWM — This sets the maximum number of locks on a table. The default is 200, the pre-System 11 fixed value. If a command attempts to acquire more than this number of locks on a table, it is escalated to a table lock.

2. lock promotion LWM — This sets the minimum number of locks that must be set on a table before SQL Server will attempt to obtain a table lock for a command. The default is 200, the pre-System 11 fixed value. Setting this high will override the lock promotion HWM and cause transactions to hold many page locks. This means that you could quickly run out of available server locks if you set this too high.

3. lock promotion PCT — This is the percentage of locks above which SQL Server attempts to acquire a table lock. The percentage is based on the number of rows in the table as:

   (pct * number of rows) ÷ 100

   This percentage is relevant only when the number of locks is between the LWM and the HWM.

So setting HWM=1,000, LWM=100, PCT=50 means:

- a table lock will never occur until the number of locks exceeds 100;
- a table lock will always occur if a scan of the table acquires more than 1,000 locks;
- between these figures, a table lock will occur if the number of locks exceeds half the number of rows.

Got it? It's actually quite useful: No escalation below the minimum (LWM), guaranteed escalation above the maximum (HWM) and controlled escalation between these values based on the percentage of rows locked.

The lock promotion values are set using **sp_setpglockpromote**.

sp_setpglockpromote

```
sp_setpglockpromote    {"server"|"database"|"table"},
                       {table_name|null},
                            lwm, hwm, pct
```

```
sp_setpglockpromote "server", null, 500, 2000, 20
```

```
sp_setpglockpromote "table", orders_tab, 200, 500, 50
```

The smaller object setting takes precedence. So the table setting overrides the database setting, which overrides the server setting. The default server HWM is 200, the pre-System 11 value, and I see no reason to alter this. Individual table settings may be set based on application knowledge to override this.

You may change a database or table setting using sp_setpglockpromote with null values for the values you do not want to change.

```
sp_setpglockpromote "table", orders_tab, null, null, 40
```

You can drop table and database settings using sp_dropglockpromote.

sp_dropglockpromote

```
sp_dropglockpromote  {"database"|"table"}, object_name
```

You cannot drop the server values.

12.8 Summary

System 11 adds a number of very useful performance features, especially the ability to segment data cache and bind objects to specific portions of cache. And finally we have the ability to stop a large table scan trashing the cache. Another useful change is the removal of the "hot spot" at the end of heap tables, although this one is going to make us use segments more carefully.

It is is also nice to get optimizer plans which are readable and more understandable.

13
System 11 Configuration Parameters

This chapter describes the new configuration parameters that may be set in System 11 using sp_configure.

COMMAND SYNTAX

none

SYSTEM PROCEDURE SYNTAX

sp_configure
sp_displaylevel

13.1 Introduction

System 11 has expanded the parameters that you can configure with sp_configure to include all of those that we used to set in buildmaster and some of the documented DBCC trace flags. As there are now a large number of configurable parameters, they are grouped according to the aspect of the server that they configure. These groups are:

- Backup/Recovery
- Cache Manager
- Disk I/O
- General Information
- Languages
- Lock Manager
- Memory Use
- Network Communication
- O/S Resources
- Physical Memory
- Physical Resources
- Processes
- SQL Server Administration
- User Environment.

Make sure that you get these exactly correct, including the uppercase letters. Physical Resources has no parameters at present. The grouping is for display purposes to make it easier to use related parameters and to reduce the amount of output that is displayed. You do not have to use the group names but I would advise it as the full output is rather lengthy.

The format to display a group is:

sp_configure

```
sp_configure "group_name"
```

```
sp_configure "Languages"

Group: Languages
```

Parameter Name	Default	Memory used	Config value	Run value
default character set id	1	0	1	1
default language id	0	0	3	3
default sortorder id	50	0	50	50
number of languages in cache	3	4	3	3

In addition to the parameter groups, each parameter is now defined with a display level of **basic**, **intermediate** or **comprehensive**.

The display level is set using **sp_displaylevel**.

sp_displaylevel

```
sp_displaylevel        [user_name
                       [, "basic"|"intermediate"|"comprehensive"]]
```

```
sp_displaylevel fred, "comprehensive"
```

Your current display level is shown by:

```
sp_displaylevel
```

Finally, before we discuss the system configuration parameters, Sybase has changed a number of parameter names. If you have any of these in scripts you will have to change them. The sp_configure does display based on wildcarding and any conflict of name is resolved by displaying all parameter names which include the input value.

```
sp_configure "lock"
```

Parameter Name	Default	Memory used	Config value	Run value
lock shared memory	0	0	0	0
number of locks	5000	469	500	500
lock promotion hwm	200	0	200	200
lock promotion lwm	200	0	200	200
lock promotion pct	100	0	100	100
print deadlock information	0	0	0	0

.
.
.

To set a value, enter:

```
sp_configure "recovery interval", 10
```

To reset a value to its default value, enter:

```
sp_configure "recovery interval", 0, "default"
```

If you try to set a parameter value with a nonunique input name, you get all possible names displayed with the current parameter setting.

13.2 Parameters

The tables below give parameter name, old name, restart required and display level by group. The following section (13.3) describes the new System 11 parameters in detail. Any parameters which have not changed from System 10 are referenced back to the section they are described in. Note that none of the parameters now require the reconfigure command and you should remove this from any scripts. In System 11.0, reconfigure has no effect but it will not be supported in later releases. Some of the parameters still require a server restart and these are indicated in the table as static parameters. The oldname format indicates the original source of the parameter:

- cxxxx are pre-System 11 buildmaster parameters (e.g, calignment);
- Tnnnn are pre-System 11 trace flags (e.g., T1603);
- the others are pre-System 11 sp_configure parameters.

Backup/Recovery

name	oldname	restart	level
allow remote access	remote access	static	intermediate
print recovery information	recovery flags	static	intermediate
recovery interval in minutes	recovery interval	dynamic	basic
tape retention in days	tape retention	static	intermediate

Cache Manager

name	oldname	restart	level
memory alignment boundary	calignment	static	comprehensive
number of index trips	cindextrips	static	basic

number of oam trips	coamtrips	dynamic	basic
procedure cache percent	procedure cache	static	basic
total data cache size	n/a	calculated	basic
total memory	memory	static	intermediate

Disk I/O

name	oldname	restart	level
allow sql server async i/o	T1603	static	comprehensive
disk i/o structures	cnblkio	static	comprehensive
number of devices	devices	static	basic
page utilization percent	n/a	dynamic	comprehensive

General Information

name	oldname	restart	level
configuration file	n/a	dynamic	comprehensive

Languages

name	oldname	restart	level
default character set id	default character set id	static	intermediate
default language id	default language	dynamic	intermediate
default sortorder id	default sortorder id	static	comprehensive
number of languages in cache	cnlanginfo	static	intermediate

Lock Manager

name	oldname	restart	level
address lock spinlock ratio	n/a	static	comprehensive
deadlock checking period	n/a	dynamic	comprehensive
freelock transfer block size	n/a	dynamic	comprehensive
max engine freelocks	n/a	dynamic	comprehensive
number of locks	locks	static	basic
page lock spinlock ratio	n/a	static	comprehensive
table lock spinlock ratio	n/a	static	comprehensive

Memory Use

name	oldname	restart	level
additional network memory	additional network memory	static	intermediate
audit queue size	audit queue size	static	intermediate
default network packet size	default network packet size	static	intermediate
disk i/o structures	cnblkio	static	comprehensive
event buffers per engine	n/a	static	comprehensive
executable code size + overhead	sql server code size	calculated	basic
max number network listeners	cmaxnetworks	static	comprehensive
max online engines	max online engines	static	intermediate
number of alarms	cnalarm	static	comprehensive
number of devices	devices	static	basic
number of extent i/o buffers	extent i/o buffers	static	comprehensive
number of languages in cache	cnlanginfo	static	intermediate
number of locks	locks	static	basic
number of mailboxes	cnmbox	static	comprehensive
number of messages	cnmsg	static	comprehensive
number of open databases	open databases	static	basic
number of open objects	open objects	static	basic
number of remote connections	remote connections	static	intermediate
number of remote logins	remote logins	static	intermediate
number of remote sites	remote sites	static	intermediate
number of user connections	user connections	static	basic
partition groups	n/a	static	comprehensive
permission cache entries	cfgcprot	dynamic	comprehensive
procedure cache percent	procedure cache	static	basic
remote server pre-read packets	pre-read packets	static	intermediate
stack guard size	cguardsz	static	comprehensive
stack size	stack size	static	basic
total data cache size	n/a	calculated	basic
total memory	memory	static	intermediate

Network Communication

name	oldname	restart	level
additional network memory	additional network memory	static	intermediate
allow remote access	remote access	static	intermediate
default network packet size	default network packet size	static	intermediate
max network packet size	maximum network packet size	static	intermediate
max number network listeners	cmaxnetworks	static	comprehensive
number of remote connections	remote connections	static	intermediate
number of remote logins	remote logins	static	intermediate
number of remote sites	remote sites	static	intermediate
remote server pre-read packets	pre-read packets	static	intermediate
tcp no delay	T1610	static	comprehensive

O/S Resources

name	oldname	restart	level
max async i/os per engine	cnmaxaio_engine	static	comprehensive
max async i/os per server	cnmaxaio_server	static	comprehensive
o/s asynch i/o enabled	n/a	read-only	comprehensive
o/s file descriptors	n/a	read-only	comprehensive
tcp no delay	T1610	static	comprehensive

Physical Memory

name	oldname	restart	level
additional network memory	additional network memory	static	intermediate
lock shared memory	T1611	static	comprehensive
shared memory starting address	mrstart	calculated	comprehensive
total memory	memory	static	intermediate

Processors

name	oldname	restart	level
max online engines	max online engines	static	intermediate
min online engines	min online engines	static	intermediate

SQL Server Administration

name	oldname	restart	level
allow nested triggers	nested trigger	static	intermediate
allow updates to system tables	allow updates	dynamic	comprehensive
audit queue size	audit queue size	static	intermediate
cpu accounting flush interval	cpu flush	dynamic	comprehensive
cpu grace time	ctimemax	static	comprehensive
deadlock retries	n/a	static	intermediate
default database size	database size	static	intermediate
default fill factor percent	fillfactor	static	intermediate
event buffers per engine	n/a	static	comprehensive
housekeeper free write percent	n/a	dynamic	intermediate
i/o accounting flush interval	i/o flush	dynamic	comprehensive
i/o polling process count	cmaxscheds	dynamic	comprehensive
identity burning set factor	identity burning set factor	static	intermediate
identity grab size	n/a	dynamic	intermediate
lock promotion HWM	n/a	dynamic	intermediate
lock promotion LWM	n/a	dynamic	intermediate
lock promotion PCT	n/a	dynamic	intermediate
number of alarms	cnalarm	static	comprehensive
number of extent i/o buffers	extent i/o buffers	static	comprehensive

name	oldname	restart	level
number of mailboxes	cnmbox	static	comprehensive
number of messages	cnmsg	static	comprehensive
number of open databases	open databases	static	basic
number of open objects	open objects	static	basic
number of pre-allocated extents	cpreallocext	static	comprehensive
number of sort buffers	csortbufsize	dynamic	comprehensive
partition groups	n/a	static	comprehensive
partition spinlock ratio	n/a	static	comprehensive
print deadlock information	T1204	dynamic	intermediate
runnable process search count	cschedspins	dynamic	comprehensive
size of auto identity	n/a	dynamic	intermediate
sort page count	csortpgcount	dynamic	comprehensive
sql server clock tick length	cclkrate	static	comprehensive
time slice	time slice	static	comprehensive
upgrade version	upgrade version	calculated	comprehensive

User Environment

name	oldname	restart	level
default network packet size	default network packet size	static	intermediate
number of pre-allocated extent	cpreallocext	static	comprehensive
number of user connections	user connections	static	basic
permission cache entries	cfgcprot	dynamic	comprehensive
stack guard size	cguardsz	static	comprehensive
stack size	stack size	static	basic

name	oldname	restart	level
systemwide password expiration	password expiration	interval	dynamic intermediate
user log cache size	n/a	static	comprehensive
user log cache spinlock ratio	n/a	static	comprehensive

There are a total of 81 parameters, most of which you are well-advised to leave alone. In my opinion, the ones which you should pay most attention to are:

parameter	default	recommended setting
procedure cache percent	20	as required
number of devices	20	as required
allow sql server async i/o	on	on
page utilisation percent	95	lower for large inserts
number of locks	5000	20 per concurrent transaction
total memory	8M	as required
lock promotion hwm	200	consider individual object settings using sp_setpglockpromote
lock promotion lwm	200	consider individual object settings using sp_setpglockpromote
lock promotion pct	100	consider individual object settings using sp_setpglockpromote

The multiple engine server requires care with what used to be the buildmaster settings. I have removed some configuration problems on multi-engine servers on System 10 with the following settings:

configuration parameter	buildmaster parameter	default setting	recommended setting
runnable process search count	cschedspins	2000	32 1 for single CPUs
disk i/o structures	cnblkio	256	1000
max async i/o per server	cnmaxaio_server	200	500
cpu grace time	ctimemax	200	800
no equivalent	cnblkmax	n/a	800
i/o polling process count	cmaxscheds	10	decrease for I/O-bound tasks increase for CPU-bound tasks

13.3 Configuration Parameter Detail

This section gives a detailed description of each parameter. The parameters are listed in alphabetical sequence, not in groups. If a parameter already existed prior to System 11, there is a reference to section 11.2, where it is described.

Additional Network Memory

See **additional network memory** in section 11.2.

Address Lock Spinlock Ratio

This specifies the number of rows in the address locks hash table that is protected by a single spinlock. The default value is 100.

A spinlock is an internal locking mechanism which controls access to a resource so that two processes cannot use a resource at the same time. If the resource is currently being used, all other processes trying to access the resource must wait or **spin** until the lock is released.

SQL Server controls address locks using an internal hash table containing 1,031 rows or **hash buckets**. In a single engine configuration, there is only one spinlock as there is only one engine trying to access the address lock hash table. In a multiengine configuration, you can tune this parameter to determine how many hash buckets a spinlock will control. With the default value of 100, there are (1,031÷100)+1; that is, 11 spinlocks. If you specify a value of 1,031 or greater for this parameter, one spinlock is taken for the entire hash table.

The memory used by a spinlock is platform-dependent and will be about 256 bytes, so the maximum memory required is in the area of 256 K. However, Sybase does not recommend altering this value and quote contention of less than 3% for address spinlocks using the default of 100.

Allow Nested Triggers

See **allow nested triggers** in section 11.2.

Allow Remote Access

See **remote access** in section 11.2.

Allow SQL Server Async I/O

The allows SQL Server to operate with asynchronous disk I/O which means that SQL Server does not have to wait for a response to one I/O before it can initiate another I/O. The default is on (1) but you must have asynchronous I/O enabled at both SQL Server and the operating system level for it to work.

Allow Updates to System Tables

See **allow updates** in section 11.2.

Audit Queue Size

See **audit queue** size in section 11.2.

Configuration File

This specifies the location of any configuration file currently in use. The default directory is $SYBASE.

CPU Accounting Flush Interval

See **CPU flush** in section 11.2.

CPU Grace Time

This specifies the amount of time in milliseconds that a user process can run without yielding the CPU before it is terminated with a timeslice error. The default is 200, which is twice the default timeslice.

SQL Server operates a "round robin" scheduler where each process is allowed a finite CPU time—the timeslice—before it must yield and allow another waiting process to use the CPU. If there are no ready processes, the process which has just yielded may reacquire the CPU immediately.

If the process does not yield voluntarily (e.g. at an I/O event), it is allowed to run for the CPU grace time after it has used the timeslice. It is then infected by being removed from the internal queues so that it does not get run again, as illustrated in Figure 13.1.

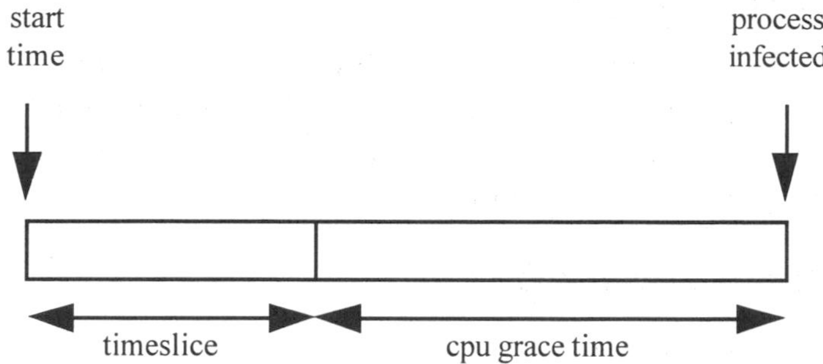

Figure 13.1 *Infected process after CPU grace time.*

This prevents a single process monopolizing the CPU as it will be preempted by the SQL Server and removed from the run queues after it has used its timeslice plus the CPU grace time. Note that the process may run slightly longer than the timeslice plus the grace time as the clock does not start ticking until the next server tick occurs after the process has started. If the process starts just after a clock tick, the process will run for almost two timeslices plus the grace time before it is infected. Figure 13.2 illustrates this.

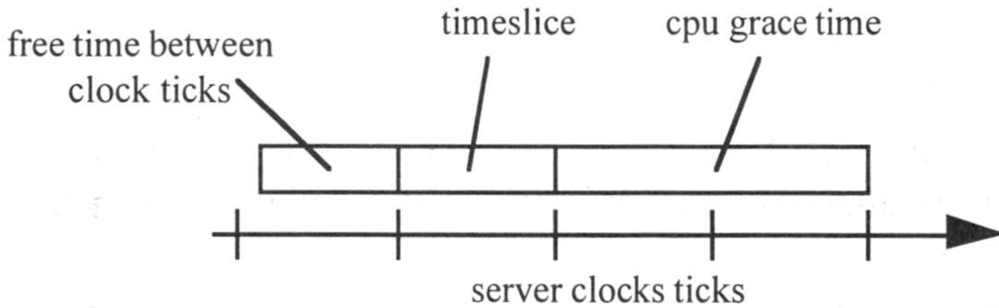

Figure 13.2 *Process elapsed time before being infected.*

Deadlock Checking Period

This parameter determines the number of milliseconds before a deadlock check is initiated on a process waiting for a lock to be released. The default is 500.

If you set this to zero, the check for deadlock is done immediately. A process has to wait for a lock to be released; this is the pre-System 11 behavior. Deadlock checking is essential but the overhead can be reduced by increasing this value. If you know that deadlock is infrequent in the application, you can increase this so that most processes that wait for a lock to be released will be granted the lock before being checked for deadlock. This clearly reduces the amount of deadlock checking but will increase the length of time before a deadlock situation is resolved. Delaying this resolution has a follow on effect on other processes, as they may be delayed waiting on some locks held by the deadlocked process.

Again, the default of 500 looks good enough unless you know that the average time waiting for a lock is greater than this, which is extremely unlikely. If this is the case, you should increase this value to be greater than the average wait time for a lock to be released.

Deadlock Retries

This specifies the number of times a transaction retries to acquire a lock after it has become a deadlock victim. The default is five.

Default Character Set ID

See **default character set id** in section 11.2.

Default Database Size

See **database size** in section 11.2.

Default Fill Factor Percent

See **fillfactor** in section 11.2.

Default Language ID

See **default language** in section 11.2.

Default Network Packet Size

See **default network packet size** in section 11.2.

Default Sortorder ID

See **default sortorder id** in section 11.2.

Disk I/O Structures

This determines the number of disk I/O control blocks allocated on start-up. The default is 256.

Each user process requires a disk I/O control block so that SQL Server can initiate I/O for the process. The memory for the control blocks is fully allocated at start-up so do not set this value too high, although you may need to consider a higher value for multiengine servers.

Event Buffers Per Engine

This determines the maximum number of events that Monitor Server can simultaneously monitor on a SQL Server engine. The default is 100.

If you are not using Monitor Server, set this to one as each event buffer uses about 100 bytes. If you are using Monitor Server, the default should be increased to about 2,000 per engine.

Executable Code Size + Overhead

See **SQL Server code size** in section 11.2.

Freelock Transfer Block Size

This parameter determines the number of locks moved between the global freelock list and the engine freelock list in a multiengine configuration. The default is 30.

When a process requests a lock, the request is serviced from the engine's freelock list. If there are no free locks on this list, a number of locks are moved from the global freelock list to the engine's freelock list. The number moved at any one time is determined by this parameter. When the engine releases a lock, it is returned to the engine's freelock list. When the number of locks in the engine freelock list reaches the maximum as determined by the parameter **max engine freelocks**, this number of locks is returned to the global freelock list. Increasing the freelock transfer block size increases the number of locks available on the engine freelock list. This subsequently reduces the activity on the global freelock list, which reduces the contention on the global list.

This parameter has a maximum value of half the maximum number of locks available to an engine's freelock list. This is determined by the parameters **max engine freelocks** and **number of locks** as:

(max engine freelocks * (number of locks÷max on-line engines))÷2

For example:

number of locks 20,000
max engine freelocks 10
max on-line engines 5
giving a freelock transfer block size of (0.1*20,000÷5)÷2 = 200

Setting a higher value than the allowed maximum generates an error. An error is also generated if you alter any of the other parameters in the calculation to a value that causes the freelock transfer block size to exceed the maximum.

Housekeeper Free Write Percent

This determines the maximum percentage by which the housekeeper task can increase the database writes. The default is 20.

The housekeeper task reduces the work done at a checkpoint by writing dirty cache pages to disk when there is no user process activity. So when the server is not active, the housekeeper task will start to flush cache pages to disk. This optimizes the CPU usage and decreases the work required by buffer washing and the checkpoint. However, the housekeeper task is making physical disk writes that will add to the overall disk activity. If this is already high, the housekeeper task may overload the disk system. This parameter value ensures that there is a limit to the amount of disk activity that the housekeeper task can add to the system disk activity.

The default of 20 limits the housekeeper task to increasing disk I/O by 20%. A value of zero disables housekeeping and a value of 100 means that it operates continuously. Be careful of setting this too high as it may increase disk activity significantly and cause I/O bottleneck.

I/O Accounting Flush Interval

See **I/O flush** in section 11.2.

I/O Polling Process Count

This determines the maximum number of processes that will be run before SQL Server checks for disk and/or network I/O completions. The default is ten.

SQL Server checks for I/O completions at every SQL Server clock tick or after running this parameter number of tasks. As the default clock tick is 100 ms, the I/O polling process count is the principal parameter in determining how often I/O is checked for. Increasing this value will increase the time between checking for I/O and will favor CPU bound tasks but reduce the response time to I/O-bound tasks. Reducing this value will favor I/O-bound tasks since they will wait for less time on I/O completion, as it will be checked more often.

If you do decide to change this parameter value, you must also consider the settings of the other timing parameters:

- SQL Server clock tick length;
- time slice;
- CPU grace time.

Identity Burning Set Factor

See **identity burning set factor** in section 11.2.

Identity Grab Size

This allows each process to reserve a block of identity column values for inserts. The default is one.

Reserving blocks of identity values for processes means that no other process can use the reserved block of numbers. If a process does not use some of the allocation, the unused numbers are lost. Using this facility can result in an increase in the frequency of gaps in the identity values. It is described in more detail in Chapter 12.

Lock Promotion HWM

This determines the maximum number of page locks permitted during a table or index scan before the page locks are escalated to a table lock. The default is 200, the pre-System 11 fixed escalation value.

Note that this is a maximum for one scan. An execution which makes several scans of a table could exceed this value in total locks without escalating to a table lock. Reducing this value will increase the incidence of table locking, which is seldom good for concurrency. Increasing this value will reduce the incidence of table locking, which may be beneficial if you have many small tables with a high level of contention. However, it will increase the total number of concurrent locks and you should think very carefully before increasing this value. Try other solutions to reduce contention before changing this parameter. Be careful not to increase this value above the number of locks available to the server.

This high water mark is server-wide. Individual object levels may be set using sp_setpglockpromote. This is discussed in Chapter 12.

Lock Promotion LWM

The lock promotion low water mark specifies the minimum number of locks which must be held by a process on a table/index before escalation can occur. The default is 200.

Increasing this value will reduce the incidence of table locking but will increase the total number of concurrent locks. Reducing this value will increase the likelihood of table locks. As with the high water mark, think very carefully before changing this value.

This low water mark is server-wide. Individual object levels may be set using sp_setpglockpromote. This is discussed in Chapter 12.

Lock Promotion PCT

This specifies the percentage of page locks—based on number of records in the table—that is permitted before escalation occurs. This value operates between the lock promotion LWM and the lock promotion HWM. The default value is 100.

SQL Server will escalate to a table lock when the number of page locks exceeds

lock promotion pct*number of rows in table÷100

This lock promotion percent is server-wide. Individual object levels may be set using sp_setpglockpromote. This is discussed in Chapter 12.

Lock Shared Memory

This stops the swapping of SQL Server pages to disk. The default is zero (off). Again, this is not one to play around with.

If you find that the server is swapping, you will have serious performance problems since nothing can run until the swapped pages are restored. However, this swapping is being caused by a conflict for the available memory. Forcing the server to remain memory-resident is not normally the answer as other processes may not be able to run. If these are your client processes, you will have gained nothing. It is much better to reduce the memory conflict, say by reducing the memory available to the server or by running the client processes on another machine.

Max Async I/Os Per Engine

This specifies the maximum number of asynchronous disk I/O requests which may be outstanding for one server engine. The default is 2,147,483,647.

There is often an operating system limit to asynchronous I/O requests which will cause an error if it is exceeded. To reduce making operating system calls which are not serviced, SQL Server maintains a count of outstanding asynchronous I/Os for the engine. When this count exceeds the parameter value, SQL Server delays the I/O request until the value falls below the limit. This delay is more efficient than making operating system calls that cannot be serviced. You should set the engine limit as high as the operating system will allow.

The limiting factor is often the available disk I/O structures. The total amount of disk I/O is limited by the number of disk I/O structures. You should not set the max async I/O limit above the number of disk I/O structures. Otherwise, you run the risk of the disk I/O failing because there are no free disk structures to service the request.

Max Async I/Os Per Server

This limits the maximum asynchronous disk I/O requests outstanding for the server. This is not effected by the engine maximum described above. The default is 200. You should normally set it as high as allowed by the operating system.

This gives two occasions when I/O may be delayed: exceeding the engine limit and exceeding the server limit. If the engine limit is 50 and the server limit is 200, then a four-engine scenario of:

engine #	# pending I/Os
0	30
1	50
2	50
3	20

means that engines 1 and 2 will have I/Os delayed until the number pending falls below 50. As the server limit is four times the engine limit, none of the I/Os will be delayed because of the server limit. However, a server limit of 150 in the above situation means that all engine I/O will be delayed. Engines 0 and 3 will recommence when any pending I/O is cleared but engines 1 and 2 must wait for their own I/O to fall below the engine limit.

Again, the practical limit is the number of disk I/O structures. Configure the max async I/Os per server below the number of disk I/O structures. See the recommended settings for these parameters at the end of section 13.2.

Max Engine Freelocks

This parameter determines the maximum number of locks available to all the engines' freelock lists as a percentage of the total number of locks available to the server. The default value is ten with a maximum of 50.

This server maximum is then shared between the number of engines currently running to determine the maximum locks available to each engine's freelock list.

For example:

total number of locks 20,000
max on-line engines 5
max engine freelocks 20

gives 4,000 locks available to all of the engines and a maximum of 800 to each engine.

Note that this means that the actual maximum freelocks per engine will vary as the number of locks and number of engines varies, even though this parameter remains unchanged.

Max Network Packet Size

See **maximum network packet size** in section 11.2.

Max Number Network Listeners

This parameter specifies the maximum number of network listeners for the server. The default is 15.

You should not need to adjust this figure. A network listener is required for each master port. You may need to consider configuring this only if you have a mixed network protocol. In a mixed protocol network, a network listener is required for each different protocol the master has to support.

Max On-Line Engines

See **max on-line engines** in section 11.2.

Memory Alignment Boundary

This determines the memory alignment for data caches. The default is 2,048.

This really is a low-level technical parameter and not to be adjusted without prior consultation with Sybase or your hardware vendor. Some hardware platforms will process I/O better when the cache is aligned on a particular memory address boundary. As SQL Server uses 2 K pages, the value should always be a multiple of 2 K. Leave this alone.

Min On-Line Engines

See **min on-line engines** in section 11.2.

Number of Alarms

This specifies the number of alarm structures allocated by SQL Server. The default is 40.

An alarm structure is required for the **waitfor** command. You should configure this based on the expected number of concurrent waitfor executions. Exceeding this figure causes a **uasetalarm** message to be written to the error log.

Number of Devices

See **devices** in section 11.2.

Number of Extent I/O Buffers

See **extent I/O buffers** in section 11.2.

Number of Index Trips

This determines the number of times an index page cycles the used buffer chain before it passes the wash marker and is written to disk. The default is zero.

As an index page contains pointers to multiple data pages, it is likely that the index pages will be accessed more often than the data pages. In general, the increased I/O activity is sufficient to keep the index pages in cache. However, the data pages will always be the most recently used pages and it is possible for the index pages to be written to disk more often than you would like. To prevent this, you may set the number of trips the index pages make down the buffer chain before they are allowed to pass the wash marker and be written to disk.

Be careful with this one. Setting it high will retain index pages in cache, effectively reducing the available cache and possibly delaying the acquisition of a clean page by a data disk read.

Number of Languages in Cache

This determines the maximum number of languages that can be held in language cache. The default is three.

Number of Locks

See **locks** in section 11.2.

Number of Mailboxes

This specifies the number of mailbox structures allocated by SQL Server. The default is 20.

Mailboxes are used internally by SQL Server for communication and synchronization between kernel service processes. Do not change this parameter.

Number of Messages

This specifies the number of message structures allocated by SQL Server. The default is 64.

Messages are used internally by SQL Server for communication and synchronization between kernel service processes. Do not change this parameter.

Number of OAM Trips

This is the same as the number of index trips but for the object allocation map pages. The default is zero.

It determines the number of times an OAM page cycles the used buffer chain before it passes the wash marker and is written to disk. Again, setting this too high can overload cache with pages, which may not be aged out, and delay the acquisition of a clean page.

Number of Open Databases

See **open databases** in section 11.2.

Number of Open Objects

See **open objects** in section 11.2.

Number of Preallocated Extents

This specifies the number of extents allocated in a single access to the page manager. The default is two.

This is used only by **bcp** (bulk copy). Each time bcp allocates, an extent a record is written to the log. Increasing this value causes multiple extents to be allocated at a time, with only one log record written for each multiple allocation. This is a useful parameter to increase if you are loading large amounts of data with bcp. Unfortunately, it is a static parameter which requires a server restart so you cannot adjust it frequently based on the amount of data being loaded.

Number of Remote Connections

See **remote connections** in section 11.2.

Number of Remote Logins

See **remote logins** in section 11.2.

Number of Remote Sites

See **remote sites** in section 11.2.

Number of Sort Buffers

This specifies the number of buffers used to hold pages read from input tables. The default is zero.

This is described in detail in section 7.7.2. If tuning this and the **number of extent I/O buffers**, the Sybase recommendation is to set the number of sort buffers to eight times the number of extent I/O buffers. Be careful with this one as setting it too high can reduce performance. It is best to leave this one alone unless you are doing many large sorts.

Number of User Connections

See **user connections** in section 11.2.

O/S Asynch I/O Enabled

This indicates if asynchronous I/O has been enabled at the operating system level. The default is zero (off). This is a read-only parameter that simply reports on the operating system setting.

O/S File Descriptors

This indicates the maximum number of file descriptors allowed for a process by the operating system. The default is zero. This is a read-only parameter that simply reports on the operating system setting.

Page Lock Spinlock Ratio

This parameter determines the number of rows in the page locks hash table which is protected by a single spinlock. The default is 100.

As for address spinlocks, the page locks are held in a hash table of 1,031 rows. Concurrent access to these is protected by spinlocks. This parameter determines how many rows are controlled by each spinlock. The default of 100 gives 11 spinlocks. A single engine server has one spinlock and multiengine servers may have up to 1,031; that is, one spinlock per hash bucket.

Page Utilization Percent

This determines how much of the OAM is scanned to locate an unused page. The default is 95.

Set to 100, the complete OAM will be scanned. For a large table, this is proportional to the number of extents and you may want to reduce the time spent doing this. If you set the percent less than 100, then a request for a new page compares the page utilization percent with the value:

(used pages ÷ (used pages + unused pages)) * 100

If the page utilization percent is higher than this percentage, SQL Server allocates a new extent without scanning the OAM. You need to have a good feel for the amount of data fragmentation that you have and that you can afford. The higher the data fragmentation, the more disk I/O will be done to retrieve sets of records. This seems a good one to leave as the default.

A low page utilization percent will result in a high number of unused pages. A high page utilization percent will increase the time to allocate a new page. The most obvious time when page allocation is a significant overhead is for a large number of inserts to an already large table. In this scenario, you may speed up the insert processing by reducing the page utilization percent. But be careful as it is easy to significantly increase page fragmentation by reducing the page utilization percent. The above ratio ensures that you eventually scan the OAM but a low page utilization percent can be wasteful of pages. If you do set it for a large insert, it is advisable to reset it when the insert has finished. Bulk copying with bcp ignores the page utilization percent and always allocates new extents.

Partition Groups

This parameter specifies the number of partition groups. The default value is 64.

Partition groups are internal structures used to control access to table partitions. Each partition group controls one table and has up to 16 partition caches that each control one partition of the table. If a table has more than 16 partitions, multiple partition groups are required for the table. The default should be sufficient. It allows up to 64 partitioned tables with each table having up to 16 partitions; that is, a maximum of 1,024 partition caches. The partition group is allocated after you have partitioned the table or on the first access after a server restart. If there are insufficient partition groups available, the partitioning or access fails.

Partition Spinlock Ratio

This determines the number of partition caches that each spinlock protects. The default is 32.

A partition spinlock is an internal lock which prevents a process accessing a partition cache currently used by another process. Sybase recommends a partition spinlock setting of 10% of the total number of partitions in use at one time. Based on the default values, each partition spinlock controls access to 32 partition caches. However, you should not need to alter this value. Each partition spinlock uses 256 bytes of memory.

Permission Cache Entries

This determines the number of cache protectors per task. The default is 15. This is effectively the size of cache allocated to user permission settings.

Permission checking is done by first checking the permission cache for the required permission. If this is not found in cache, the sysprotects table is accessed for the required permission. So the size of permission cache determines the amount of disk I/O required to check permissions. The obvious comment is that you should allocate enough to contain all of sysprotects but the practical amount depends on how often permissions are checked and how often the **grant** and **revoke** commands are issued. An important consideration is that the permission cache is flushed completely when a **grant** or **revoke** command is issued. This is because the permissions are timestamped and every permission needs to be refreshed when one is changed.

If processes need to check permissions frequently, you may find a small improvement by increasing this parameter but unlikely that it will be sufficient. This is not really one to worry about.

Print Deadlock Information

This enables printing of deadlock information to the log. The default is zero (off). This is useful when troubleshooting a deadlocking problem as it indicates which processes were deadlocked and which ones were rolled back.

Print Recovery Information

See **recovery flags** in section 11.2.

Procedure Cache Percent

See **procedure cache** in section 11.2.

Recovery Interval in Minutes

See **recovery interval** in section 11.2.

Remote Server Pre-read Packets

See **pre-read packets** in section 11.2.

Runnable Process Search Count

This determines the number of times a SQL Server engine will loop looking for a runnable task. The default is 2,000 but this is one parameter that should be considered for change.

If there are currently no runnable tasks, SQL Server can either continue to look for runnable tasks or relinquish the CPU. Increasing this value causes SQL Server to hold the CPU for longer while it continues to look for a runnable task. Reducing this value causes SQL Server to relinquish the CPU sooner.

For single CPU machines, this parameter should be set to a low value (such as one) so that the CPU is released as often as possible.

For multi-CPU machines, the manuals recommend 50–200 for I/O-intensive applications and 750–1,250 for CPU-intensive applications. The Sybase suggestion is to combine these settings with a SQL Server clock tick length of 50,000. My own default setting for multiengine servers is 32.

Shared Memory Starting Address

This determines the virtual address at which SQL Server starts its shared memory. The default is zero. This is not one to adjust.

Size of Auto Identity

This sets the precision of identity columns automatically created with the **sp_dboption** "**auto identity**" option. The default is ten.

Sort Page Count

This specifies the maximum amount of memory that can be used by a sort. The default is zero. The optimum value for this parameter may be calculated as:

(number of sort buffers * rows per data page) ÷ 50

This is described in more detail in section 7.7.3. Be careful with this parameter as the sort memory is taken from data cache.

SQL Server Clock Tick Length

This specifies the server clock tick duration in microseconds. The default is 100,000; that is, the same as the default timeslice.

SQL Server runs its internal service tasks every clock tick. Shortening the tick length will fire these more frequently and will favor tasks which require server tasks to continue. Therefore, shortening the tick length will favour I/O-intensive tasks and lengthening the tick length will favour CPU-intensive tasks.

A value of 20,000 may be tried to assist I/O-bound processes and a value of 1,000,000 should be considered as an upper limit to assist CPU-bound tasks. However, adjust this parameter with extreme caution as it can have severe effects on the server performance. Consult with Sybase before you touch this one.

Stack Guard Size

This sets the size of the stack guard area. The default is 4,096.

SQL Server allocates one command stack for each user connection. These stacks are allocated contiguously in cache and a task which exceeds its stack will overwrite and corrupt the next stack. The stack guard area is added to the end of each stack to provide an indication if stack overflow is close to occurring. In addition, each stack guard area has a guard word at the end to indicate if stack overflow has occurred.

SQL Server checks the location of the stack pointer to see if it has entered the stack guard area. If it has, the task is aborted with error 3626. SQL Server also checks the pattern of the stack guard word. If this is not as expected, then it means that stack overflow has occurred and the server shuts down with the error message:

```
kernel: *** Stack overflow detected: limit: nnnnn sp: nnnnn
kernel: *** Stack Guardword corrupted
kernel: *** Stack corrupted, server aborting
```

Limit is the address of the end of the stack guard area and sp is the current value of the stack pointer.

Even if the stack guard word is not corrupted, SQL Server checks the current stack pointer position. If it is outside the stack area and stack guard area, the server shuts down with error message:

```
kernel: *** Stack overflow detected: limit nnnnn sp: nnnnn
kernel: *** Stack corrupted, server aborting
```

Stack overflow problems are better dealt with by increasing the stack size, although you may wish to retain the stack to stack guard size ratio and proportionally increase the stack guard size. Keep increments to multiples of a page. I have found a need to increase the stack size in System 10 upgrades but have not increased the stack guard size and have experienced no problems.

Stack Size

See **stack size** in section 11.2.

System-wide Password Expiration

See **password expiration interval** in section 11.2.

Table Lock Spinlock Ratio

This determines the number of spinlocks protecting the table locks hash table in an identical fashion to the address and page spinlock ratios. The default is 20.

There are only 101 rows in the table lock hash table, as the incidence of table locking is considered to be much less than page locking. The default of 20 is subsequently lower based on the lower number of hash buckets.

Tape Retention in Days

See **tape retention** in section 11.2.

TCP No Delay

This parameter disables transmission control protocol (TCP) packet batching. The default is off, which is normal TCP operation with batching of small logical packets into larger physical network frames. This causes an average delay to the logical packets as they have to wait to be batched together.

Disabling this batching will result in the packet being sent immediately but will increase the network traffic by sending more packets. Although not normally advantageous to increase network traffic, disabling this delay could be beneficial if you know the packets are few and infrequent,.

Time Slice

See **timeslice** in section 11.2.

Total Data Cache Size

This is a display-only parameter which shows the amount of memory currently available for data cache after all the other overheads have been subtracted from the available memory.

Total Memory

See **memory** in section 11.2.

Upgrade Version

See **upgrade version** in section 11.2.

User Log Cache Size

This specifies the size of each user's log cache in bytes. The default is 2,048.

SQL Server configures one user log cache for each connection to buffer the user transaction log records before they are written to syslogs. Each connection uses this area for the log records until the user log cache is full when it is flushed to the database log. This reduces the write contention to the end of the transaction log by buffering each log record write in the user log cache area.

Set this to the maximum amount of log information written by a transaction. The amount of log information written by a transaction depends on the amount of update activity and the size of the records updated. A deletion or insertion will require a copy of the record to be written to the log. An in-place update will record only the changed bytes. An update actioned as a deletion followed by an insertion will require twice the record space. Configuring the user log cache too high increases the user log cache spinlock contention. Configuring this parameter too low will increase the number of times it is flushed to syslogs, consequently increasing the contention on the transaction log.

User Log Cache Spinlock Ratio

This specifies the ratio of user log caches per user log cache spinlock. The default is 20, which allows one spinlock for every 20 user log caches.

A user log cache spinlock prevents a process accessing a user log cache when it is currently being accessed by another processes. This is a multiengine parameter. For single CPU machines, the server allocates one spinlock regardless of the number of user log caches. As with all spinlock ratios, this is best left alone.

13.4 Summary

This is a database administrator's worst nightmare: more configurations parameters than pager calls at the weekend. However, it is nice to see so many of the "undocumented" buildmaster parameters finally seeing the light of day. But please be careful. Apart from those that you already set, such as memory, user connections, etc., and the better known SMP buildmaster ones, such as cschedspins, cnblkio, etc., you really should leave the majority of these at the defaults.

If you do decide to see what happens, please do it to the development system and test it thoroughly before trying it in production. I know that production is the only place that you can really see the proper effect, but be careful.

APPENDIX A

Allocating Space and Creating Databases

This appendix describes the initialization of disk space and its allocation to databases and logs, including disk mirroring and use of the default device. Creation and expansion of databases and logs is covered with a treatment of how to estimate the necessary sizes. The logical segmentation of the space to allow object placement and space management using the threshold manager is described in Chapter 4.

System 11 has introduced two new options to sp_dboption: auto identity and identity in nonunique index.

COMMAND SYNTAX

```
disk init
disk mirror
disk unmirror
disk remirror
create database
alter database
drop database
```

SYSTEM PROCEDURE SYNTAX

```
sp_diskdefault
sp_estspace
sp_helpdevice
sp_spaceused
sp_extendsegment
sp_logdevice
sp_dboption
sp_helpdb
sp_helpsegment
```

A.1 Introduction

SQL Server allocates space in several steps:

- physical allocation;
- logical segmentation;
- database creation.

The physical initialization reserves areas of the actual disk drives for the server. SQL Server calls these devices. These devices are then logically divided into segments to allow object placement. The databases are created on the preallocated devices and the objects of the databases are created on the logical segments belonging to these devices. This placement of objects into segments of a database that occupies specific disk areas allows complete control at the object level over disk usage, both for space and disk access utilization. The creation and use of segments is described in Chapter 4.

A.2 Disk Initialization

SQL Server allocates disk space to a server. The physical disk drives of your installation are initialized as SQL Server devices and are available for the server that you are logged on at the time you issue the initialize command. SQL Server has no practical limit to the amount of space that you may allocate to a server. However, there are limits to the number of devices per server and segments per database, and in practice, you will tend to be hardware restricted. In general, however, you will plan your disk allocation according to your database requirements and, therefore, may I recommend a simple disk initialization of one or a few devices per physical disk drive. If your databases are large enough or you can share several into one device, then one device per physical disk drive is good enough. However, there are excellent reasons for smaller devices for logs, the master device, the system procedure device and for small, secure databases.

Sybase unfortunately interchanges the words device and disk in all of its literature. Wherever you see the term disk in Sybase literature, it means a SQL Server device; that is, a physical allocation of disk space that belongs to a server and resides on a physical disk drive as an operating system file or a raw partition. I shall always use the word device, except in the command syntax where disk is used.

Note that the SQL Server allocation of disk space is a physical allocation that takes up disk space as an operating system file or a raw partition. (Unix actually creates a sparse file and does not grab the space until you request it in a create database command. So you may not have what you think you have if other systems are contending for the physical space. Be careful. And although I keep referring to it as a physical device, you can use VMS logical names.)

It is essential in Unix that you make the operational logs and master devices as raw partitions. Give careful consideration to making the operational databases raw partitions as well. As raw partitions, SQL Server has complete control over cache management and when the SQL Server cache manager writes a page to disk, it is physically output to the disk. If you use Unix files, then, when the SQL Server cache manager writes a page to disk, the Unix file manager intercepts this request. If Unix has room in its cache, the write does not go to disk at that time but waits until the Unix cache manager needs space or until the periodic flush exercise. So when a system failure occurs, SQL Server cannot guarantee 100% that it can recover a Unix file because of the Unix operating system intervention in the cache management. The server cannot always recover because the Unix cache may not write the pages in the order that they were written by the server. If a data page is written before a corresponding log page, and there is a failure between the writes, recovery is impossible. This is probably not a serious problem for test and development databases, but is not recommended for logs, master and production databases.

To initialize device space, issue the **disk init** command:

disk init

```
DISK INIT       NAME = "logical_name",
                PHYSNAME = "physical_name",
                VDEVNO = device_number,
                SIZE = number_of_pages
                [, VSTART = virtual_address,
                CNTRLTYPE = controller_number]
                [, CONTIGUOUS]
```

where:

name	the name of the device in all references within SQL Server.
physname	the name of the operating system file or raw partition. In Unix, the operating system file must not already exist. The Sybase account must have read/write access to the directory containing the raw partition and file creation privilege to the directory which will contain the operating system file. In OpenVMS, use of a logical name for the path will allow you to change the device location without altering the SQL Server definition.
vdevno	a unique device number from one up to a configurable maximum. sp_helpdevice shows the device numbers already used and sp_configure shows the maximum. Device number 0 is reserved for the master device and the maximum is 255 devices per server. If you simply want to see the next device number: `SELECT max(low/power(2, 24)) FROM sysindexes` will display the maximum used device number.
size	the size of the device in SQL Server pages (generally a page is 2 K).
vstart	the virtual address of the start of the device. Do NOT touch this parameter; SQL Server will allocate it automatically.
cntrltype	a type number which identifies the device type: disk or tape. Do NOT set this for disks. The server sets it automatically.
contiguous	used with VMS disk files only to ensure contiguous space on the disk. The device will not be created if enough contiguous space is not available.

```
DISK INIT NAME = 'test_dev', PHYSNAME = '/dev/rsd3d',
          VDEVNO = 10, SIZE = 204800
```

This creates a disk device called test_dev as a raw partition with a size of 400 MB. The easiest way to calculate is Meg * 512. If you make a mistake in this command, such as specifying an already existing disk file, the error log contains the error message. If disk init fails while setting up the disk space, it can leave you with problems. In Unix, there is a reasonable chance that the file will remain in existence and you will need to delete the file to reissue the same command. Also under Unix, the server may have registered the virtual device number and you may not be able to reuse this number until you have rebooted the server. Under VMS, the logical_name may be still in use and not reusable until you have restarted the server.

Before we talk any more about devices, let's take a slight digression to paint the overall physical picture of a server environment.

Figure A.1 illustrates the basic relationships between the objects that define the server space allocation.

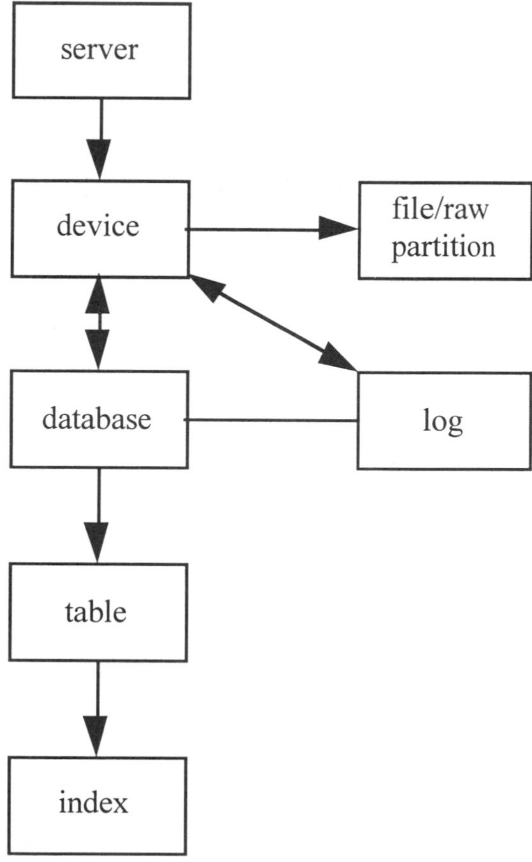

Figure A.1 *Physical relationships.*

There is an additional logical segmentation of devices which I deal with in Chapter 4.

The server has many devices and a device belongs to one and only one server. This is true of database devices only, as dump devices may be shared by several servers.

A device may have many databases and a database may be spread across many devices.

Each database has one log and the log belongs to one database but may be on one or more devices, which may also be data devices. However, a data device is always a data device that may contain a log. A log device is reserved solely for logs. You may redesignate a data device as a log device; however, you will be unable to write data pages to the device and reads will cause warning messages to be written to the error log. There is no system procedure to reverse this accidental designation and you need to update the system tables by resetting the segmap in sysusages. This requires "allow update" access to the system tables and is not a good idea. Try not to make this mistake. (Recovering the data without updating sysusages is discussed in section C.12.)

Each database may have many tables and each table may have many indexes, with an index being defined on one table and a table being defined on one database. I have diagrammed this rather simply as it is a logical relationship where a given table or index name may be present in several databases, although they are separate objects that are fully qualified by the database name. In other words, the primary key to an index is database_name.table_name.index_name. Allocation of tables and indexes is further defined by the logical segments.

A.3 Device Mirroring

The mapping of devices to operating system files or raw partitions is shown as one to many but this is not a true one to many relationship as a device is mapped to a file or partition on a one to one basis. The many aspect is caused by the ability to mirror a device to maintain a physical up-to-date copy of the device's contents. Thus a device is mapped to one partition or file, which may be mirrored, and each file or partition can contain only one device or the mirror of the device.

Devices are mirrored with the **disk mirror** command.

disk mirror

```
DISK MIRROR
        NAME = "logical_name",
        MIRROR = "physical_name"
        [, WRITES = {serial  |  noserial}]
        [, CONTIGUOUS]
```

where

name	logical name of the device to be mirrored, as defined in the "disk init" command;
mirror	physical file or raw partition name of the mirror device;
writes	specifies whether the writes to the devices are serial in that the primary finishes before the secondary device starts or parallel, which permits the writes to take place at the same time; default is serial;
contiguous	allocates contiguous disk space for VMS as with disk init.

```
DISK MIRROR NAME = "disk_mirr1", MIRROR = "/mirr/rsd4m"
```

Note that SQL Server mirroring is on a device basis and that device to database mapping is many-to-many. So to retain a physical mirror of a database, you must mirror every device that the database is allocated to. This may cause portions of other databases to be mirrored if a device is being shared. Ideal candidates for mirroring are the master device and the log device(s). If you lose the master device, the server crashes and no work can take place. So mirror it to ensure that a single failure does not bring the system down. Have a **waitfor mirrorexit** to ensure early warning when one of the mirrors fails. The failure is recorded in the error log. Similarly, the log device(s) should be mirrored. Each database has a log that should be on a separate device from the database for recovery reasons (see Chapter 9). The logs may share one log device although this may create a bottleneck on disk activity. No matter the configuration, mirror the log device(s). A log device failure means that the database is unusable. So again, to protect from a single failure bringing the system down, mirror the log device(s).

In an ideal world, every device would be mirrored for redundancy purposes. This is applied by some fault-tolerant systems. If data fault tolerance is essential, then you must mirror the data devices. This has no effect on retrieval as the read is always made to the primary device when both primary and mirror are active, but will degrade updates.

Updates, of course, are degraded as the write has to take place to two devices. The choices are in series or in parallel. Serial writes take place to the primary device and, once that has been committed, to the mirrored device. Parallel writes take place at the same time to both devices. Note that only the transaction commits take place to disk during the database transaction; all of the data page updates take place in cache and the cache manager or checkpoint decides when the page will be written to disk. So the majority of the update is logical and does not take place during the transaction lifetime. It has no effect on the individual transaction response time (unless the system is disk bound, when any increase in disk activity will have a detrimental effect). But do not ignore the overhead; it is twice as many writes, which must be absorbed by the overall disk capacity. And remember that it is the device which is mirrored, so any page updates—including indexes—are mirrored.

My personal preference is to mirror the master device(s) and the log devices, but consider data mirroring very carefully. When the master device is mirrored, it may be a good idea to reduce the mirroring load by reducing the size of tempdb on the mirrored master and placing the main portion of tempdb on another nonmirrored device using the alter database command. If you do this for performance reasons, it is worth remembering that the piece of tempdb on master will be used first when temporary space is required. So, you are unlikely to see much improvement for small space requests to tempdb. In this case, you may consider removing tempdb from master or preallocating the space with a table as one of the commands in the system start up in order to force all temporary space requests to the low activity disk. Failure of a nonmirrored tempdb is not as a serious problem as it may seem, since not all transactions will fail when tempdb is not available.

Removing tempdb completely from master is not straightforward and requires updates to the system tables to alter sysdatabases and sysusages.

```
/* do a sp_helpdb on tempdb and write down the database options just in case they
do not recreate properly  */
/* print out sysdatabases and sysusages JUST IN CASE  */

/* create a new_tempdb which you place on the new device and subsequently redefine
as tempdb  */

use master
go
create database new_tempdb on tempdb_dev = 100
go
sp_configure "allow updates", 1
go
```

```
reconfigure with override
go

/* in a transaction delete the tempdb entries and update the new_tempdb entries to
be the new tempdb  */
/*  you should be in single user mode for this  */

begin tran
delete sysusages where dbid = 2
delete sysdatabases where dbid = 2
go
/* check if number of deletes is OK */
update sysusages set dbid = 2
       where dbid = db_id("new_tempdb")
update sysdatabases set dbid = 2, name = "tempdb"
       where dbid = db_id("new_tempdb")
go
/*  check if number of updates is OK  */
commit tran  /* or rollback tran if ANY doubt  */
go

sp_configure "allow updates", 0
go
reconfigure with override
go

/* reset any database options with sp_dboption  */

/*  !!!!!!   AND  !!!!!!!  */

dump database master to master_dumpdev
go
```

SQL Server data mirroring is an overhead and there are alternatives which you should consider, such as mirroring at the hardware level; for example, Digital's disk shadowing, RAID or processing the transaction log dumps against a database dump to maintain an up-to-date database dump as stand by. System 10 replication server is also a viable option to maintain a secondary site database standby.

A.3.1 Mirroring the Master Device

Mirroring the master device is an excellent idea but requires both a mirror device and a new entry in RUNSERVER. The entry of the master device mirror must be present in RUNSERVER to start the server when the mirrored master is being used.

The disk mirror of the master device is not a special execution of the command—an option would be nice—so it does not update the RUNSERVER file. You have to do this yourself using an editor. This requires you to add the -r entry to indicate the physical name of the mirror device.

```
#!      /bin/csh -f
#       Server name:production
#       dslisten port: 1025
#       master name:/dev/rc1d0
setenv DSLISTEN production
exec  /$SYBASE/bin/dataserver
               -d/usr/master.dat -r/usr/master.mir
               -e/$SYBASE/install/error log_production
```

(The -d, -r, -e options must be entered on the same line.)

A.3.2 Unmirroring and Remirroring

Devices may be temporarily or permanently unmirrored using the **disk unmirror** command.

disk unmirror

```
DISK UNMIRROR
        NAME = "logical_name"
        [, SIDE = {"primary" | secondary}]
        [, MODE = {retain | remove}]
```

where

name	the logical name of the device as defined in disk mirror.
side	specifies which one of the pair—primary or secondary—to unmirror. The default is secondary. Note that "primary" requires the quotes because it is a reserved word.
mode	specifies if the unmirroring is permanent (remove) or temporary (retain). The default is temporary (retain).

```
DISK UNMIRROR NAME = "disk1", SIDE = "primary"
```

If unmirrored temporarily, the device may be remirrored using the **disk remirror** command.

disk remirror

```
DISK REMIRROR NAME = "logical_name"
```

where

name	the logical name of the device as defined in disk mirror.

```
DISK REMIRROR NAME = "disk1"
```

When the "disk mirror" command is issued, SQL Server writes a copy of the primary device contents onto the mirror device. Thereafter, updates take place identically to both devices to maintain a hot standby copy of the device. When one of the devices is not available (either planned unmirroring or unplanned crash—there is no difference to the mirrored device), SQL Server recognizes that one device is unavailable and continues in degraded mode making the updates to the single device. No log or "catch-up" file is maintained by SQL Server while one device is down. When the failed device is reintroduced by the "disk remirror" command, SQL Server takes a fresh copy of the current device contents onto the device just reintroduced.

So be careful when you reintroduce a mirrored device after a failure or planned unmirroring. SQL Server will copy the device contents, which will significantly impact on disk throughput. So do not reintroduce mirror devices during the busiest period of the day. You may have to, of course, to reestablish fault tolerance, but it is a significant overhead in SQL Server which, as an administrator, you may defer by taking a deliberate decision to wait a little until the system is quieter. You'll be able to tell if an administrator has done this. (S)he will be sitting with fingers, arms, legs and anything else crossed hoping that the unmirrored device does not fail. If this is too much of a risk to you, do not take it. Suffer the performance overhead to let you relax.

A.4 Default Device

When no specific placement is made in the create database command, the database must be placed somewhere and a default device is defined to be used when no device is specified. Default devices are specified, by the administrator only, using the system procedure **sp_diskdefault**:

sp_diskdefault

```
sp_diskdefault logical_name, option
```

where

option	defaulton or defaultoff.

Once a device has been created, it may be defined as a default device.

```
DISK INIT       NAME = 'disk_1', PHYSNAME = '/usr/disk.dat',
                VDEVNO = 6, SIZE = 102400
sp_diskdefault disk_1, defaulton
```

Any number of devices may be defined as default devices. In this case, the space is allocated device by device in sequence of the device number. The server fills the devices up one by one, moving to the next available default device.

Even if a device has been used as a default, it may be removed from the defaults at any time.

```
sp_diskdefault master, defaultoff
```

Existing allocations are not effected by removing a device from the defaults; the device is simply not reused for default allocation.

The initialization makes the master device a default device. It is highly recommended that you change this to avoid user objects accidentally being allocated to the master device.

A.5 Database Creation

Now that we have the devices, we can create our databases using the **create database** command. This is the command that reserves the disk space exclusively for the database.

create database

```
CREATE DATABASE db_name
       [ON device_name [= size]
              [, device_name [= size]]...]
       [LOG ON device_name [= size]
              [, device_name [= size]]...]
       [WITH OVERRIDE]
       [FOR LOAD]
```

where

db_name	server-unique database name.
device_name	a device as created by "disk init."
size	the database size in MB.
with override	you need to quote this clause if you specify the same device for log and data; otherwise, the create command fails. Even if you use this clause, you still get a warning. If you simply default the log to the data device, i.e. no log on clause, this override clause is not necessary.
for load	a fast option that must be used only when creating a data base for loading a dump. This option does not initialize the database space as initialization is done by the load database. When a database fails, it often has be dropped and recreated before the load. The for load option ensures that the page initialization is not duplicated. Do not use this option without load database.

```
CREATE DATABASE test_db

CREATE DATABASE systest_db ON diska = 5,
                              diskb = 4, diskc = 2

CREATE DATABASE prod_db ON diska = 20
                              LOG ON log_dev = 6
```

The create database command obtains and initializes the required amount of disk space from the device. If not all of the requested space is available, the result depends on how much space can be obtained. If the minimum database size cannot be allocated, the command fails. If the minimum is available, as much as possible is allocated and a warning message output. Minimum database size defaults to a configuration variable (set with sp_configure) or to the size of the model database in the master device, whichever is the greater. Model defaults to 2 MB. This is about the minimum database size that you need to do any useful work, as the system catalog information loaded in at create time takes up about 1 MB.

The create database command uses model as a template in the creation. In doing this, it locks model until the create is complete. Therefore, create database is a single thread command; that is, only one at a time. Create database creates two distinct portions to the database, one for the data and one for the log. There are three combinations to placement of each portion.

Both Data and Log on the Same Device by Default

```
CREATE DATABASE fred
```

or

```
CREATE DATABASE fred ON dev1 = 6
```

or

```
CREATE DATABASE fred ON default = 5
```

This creates both the data and log of the database on the same device. The first is created on the default device with default size, the second on the device dev1 with 6 MB and the third on the default device with 5 MB. With the log on the same device as the data, we have no control over how big the log can grow; it may use up the complete device.

Both Data and Log on the Same Device Explicitly

```
CREATE DATABASE fred ON dev1 = 4
                     LOG ON dev1 = 2
                     WITH OVERRIDE
```

or

```
CREATE DATABASE fred ON default = 3
                     LOG ON default = 1
                     WITH OVERRIDE
```

There is no difference from the first one as for placement and space usage. However, because we have a separate log (even though it is on the same device), we have more control over it as it cannot now grow beyond the size we specified.

Data and Log on Separate Devices

```
CREATE DATABASE ON default = 60 LOG ON dev2 = 12
```

or

```
CREATE DATABASE fred ON dev3 = 40 LOG ON dev4 = 12
```

This option of data and log on separate devices is the recommended option for all production systems as it gives you maximum control over size, placement and recovery. The separate log on options are important because you need to have the log segment on its own device to use the no_truncate option of the dump tran command and to use the threshold manager to set a last chance threshold.

You do, of course, need a reasonable number of disks before data and log separation gives you much disk performance improvement. If you have a simple one disk system, there is little advantage in separate devices for log and data for performance reasons. In a one disk system, I would suggest three devices with a choice of placement as shown in Figure A.2.

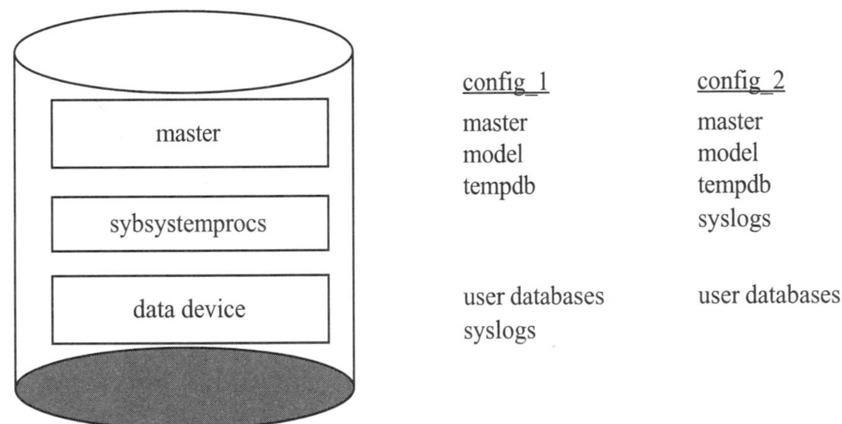

Figure A.2 *Single disk configuration.*

The first configuration has one device for the master, one for sybsystemprocs and the other device for data and log. This suffers a little as the allocation of pages in the data device will be mixed between the data and the log, which can effect the log read/write times as the log pages are not sequential. Also—and possibly more importantlyif you lose a single device, you have lost both data and log with no chance of complete roll forward from a dump. The second configuration has the master and log on the same device. This allows full recovery from a device failure and increases the sequential nature of the page allocation to the log. However, it may create a disk access bottleneck as tempdb and the log are sharing the same device. But if this is significant, it will be significant on a one disk system no matter where tempdb and the log are located. (On a multiple disk system, it is not normally a good idea to put a user database log on the master device.)

My recommendation in a one disk system is one device for master and log, sybsystemprocs on its own device and one device for the data.

Even in a shared data/log device, it is advisable to explicitly state the size of the data and log as:

```
CREATE DATABASE fred ON default = 20
                     LOG ON default = 4
                     WITH OVERRIDE
```

This means that the log cannot grow beyond 4 MB. And if you get a device full problem, you know whether the data or log has caused the problem and can take the appropriate corrective action. If you have not explicitly created a size for the log, it will grow to the maximum available in the device. When a device full message occurs, you will not be sure whether the data or log is too big.

Why be concerned with which one is too big? Well, if the data has expanded to use up all of the device allocation, you need to decide whether some application-specific action such as archiving is necessary or whether extra space is required. If the log has is too big, then you need to consider if it needs to be cleared out more often or whether extra space is needed. Having no knowledge of what has caused the problem gives you less control, which is a bad idea for the administrator.

More importantly, the separate declaration of the log space places the log on a separate segment on the device, which allows much more control on dumping and recovery by permitting the use of the "no truncate" option of "dump transaction." The separate size declaration, even on the same device, allows the recovery system to treat the log as a separate object. Also, the separate definition of the log allows the log segment free space to be monitored by the threshold manager. I would always advise this. You can increase your control in a larger disk configuration by placing the log on a separate device. You can construct any combination from one log device per database to one shared log device for all databases. The latter is still one log per database but all logs are placed on the same physical device. Each database has its own syslogs table; there is no global log table, although they may all share the same device. This sharing of the log device may create a disk access bottleneck, so be wary of putting all of the logs on the same log device.

```
CREATE DATABASE fred1 ON dev1 = 20 LOG ON dev8 = 4

CREATE DATABASE fred2 ON dev2 = 10 LOG ON dev8 = 1

CREATE DATABASE fred3 ON dev1 = 15 LOG ON dev8 = 2
```

We now have additional control in that we can place the log on a separate disk from the data to optimize disk head movement; we can mirror the log device(s) for fault tolerance and we have total monitoring of size and dumping of the log.

Do not go overboard on this. As much as it is the ideal and, in my opinion, essential for production databases, it does not need to be applied to everything. Test, training, development databases often do not need this level of sophistication and a simple data and log on the same device will be sufficient.

```
CREATE DATABASE prog_test ON test_dev = 100
```

A database configuration setting of "truncate log on checkpoint" (see section A.14 on sp_dboption later in this appendix) will ignore the log by clearing it out regularly without dumping it. This leaves the test database "unrecoverable" except to the previous dump so, if you adopt this scenario, make sure that you dump the database regularly and that everyone using the database is aware of the amount of work that they may need to reinput. Note that the "unrecoverable" nature applies only to a media failure; that is, loss of the database that requires a roll forward from the previous dump. Any rollback situation or restart after a system failure should still work.

Small, slowly changing production databases also lend themselves to this approach. If you only do a handful of updates to a database between dumps, then there is little reason to dump the log. Simply dump the database, in which case the log does not need to be on a separate device. In this case, truncate the transaction log to clear it out before dumping the database as it will save time in the database dump. (See Chapter 9 for the "dump tran" options.)

So use a separate log device for most production databases, but decide each case on its merit. As a rule of thumb on size, Sybase recommends that it is advisable to have a separate log to issue dump transaction if the database is greater than 4 MB. I find this figure strange as it's not the database size that is crucial but the combination of size and update activity between dumps. It all depends on how long you can afford the on-line system to be down. You need to allow for the load of the dumped database and then the roll forward from the transaction logs. So structure your dump scenario based on how long you have to recover.

The size that you request for the data and log is initialized by the create database command and is reserved totally for that database. No one else can use that disk space and you cannot release unused space once it has been reserved by the initial create command. You can expand the space allocation, but you cannot reduce it. So it is reasonable to determine your space requirements as accurately as possible before you issue the create command. This really is crucial in space allocation for the administrator. You cannot reduce the space allocated to a database except by bcp out, drop database, recreate to reduced size and bcp in. This is NOT a good idea.

A.6 Data Size Calculation

You can do this at various levels of sophistication, depending on how detailed you want the calculation to be. No matter how detailed you calculate sizes, the approach is to estimate the size of each table. Add these together and make an allowance for indexes and free space.

At the simplest level, I calculate:
size of table = number of records * average record size
size of database = sum of table sizes
data space allocation = size of database * 3

(If you think that a "fudge" factor of 3 is high, remember that we have not allowed for indexes and free space in the actual calculation.)

By comparison the detailed calculation is:

average record size = sum of average field sizes
+ 2 byte fixed overhead
+ 3 byte variable overhead
+ 1 byte overhead for each variable field

(See Appendix C for an explanation of the record layout.)

records per page = page size * 0.75 ÷ average record size
(assuming an initial packing density of 75% and rounding up to the nearest integer)

table size = number of records ÷ records per page

size of database = sum of table sizes
data space allocation = size of database * 2
(We have allowed for free space but not indexes.)

Of course you will put the detailed calculation into a stored procedure and simply enter the appropriate parameter values. But I normally consider that the margin of error in such basic figures as number of records is so large that the simple rough calculation is sufficient. A comparison of the calculations using a 150 byte record with 1,000,000 records in the table is:

Rough calculation:

size of table	= 150 * 1,000,000 bytes
	= 75,000 pages (2 K pages)
data space allocation	= 75,000 * 3 = 225,000 pages

Detailed calculation:

records per page	= 2000 * 0.75 ÷ 150
	= 10
table size	= 1,000,000 ÷ 10
	= 100,000 pages
data space allocation	= 100,000 * 2 = 200,000 pages

Regardless of how you do the calculation, you must do it. I know that you can expand the allocated space later, but getting it as close as you can is important to the initial choices in object placement.

I have left the index sizes out of the initial calculations as the final index choices will not be known until you are finalizing the physical design and the initial allocation is often earlier than that. If you are able to delay your choice on disk space until you have finalized the physical design, then you can make more accurate index calculations.

SQL Server has provided the **sp_estspace** system procedure to estimate space requirements when you already have the tables defined.

sp_estspace

```
sp_estspace table_name, no_of_rows,
                fill_factor, cols_to_max, textbin_len, iosec
```

where

table_name	name of the table;
no_of_rows	the number of rows to calculate with;
fill_factor	the page fillfactor (default of 0 uses sp_configure value);
cols_to_max	a list of variable length columns for which the maximum length should be used instead of the average (default is null);
textbin_len	the length of all text and image fields per row (default is 0);
iosec	the number of I/Os per second for the disk (default is 30).

```
sp_estspace tab_1, 100000, 50

name   type          level    pages    Kbytes
tab_1  data          0        1923     3846
ind_1  clustered     0        23       46
ind_1  clustered     1        1        2
ind_2  nonclustered  0        529      1059
ind_2  nonclustered  1        31       62
ind_2  nonclustered  2        2        4
ind_2  nonclustered  3        1        2

Total_Mbytes
5
```

This is a very useful system procedure that gives you important information on the number of index levels. You do need to have an existing table definition but usually you will have this in the development/test database. A slight word of warning: the version that I was using had a minor rounding problem that sometimes displayed two root levels for an index.

A.7 Index Size Calculation

The number of pages taken up by an index is so dependent on the size of the index key that the large ones are always worth calculating during the physical design stage.

Let's take the 1,000,000 record, 100,000 page table and a 10 byte fixed length field that is to be indexed. The various index overheads are explained in Appendix C.

Clustered

index entries per page = page size * 0.75 ÷ index entry size
= 2,000 * 0.75 ÷ 15
= 100

first level number of pages	= 100,000 ÷ 100
	= 1,000
second level number of pages	= 1,000 ÷ 100
	= 10
root level	= 10 ÷ 100
	= 1
number of pages for the clustered index	= 1,011

(The clustered index has index entries for each page in the table, i.e. 100,000 pages)

Nonclustered

leaf level entries per page	= 2,000 * 0.75 ÷ 17
	= 88
intermediate level entries per page	= 2,000 * 0.75 ÷ 21
	= 71
leaf level pages	= 1,000,000 ÷ 88
	= 11,363
first intermediate level pages	= 11,363 ÷ 71
	= 160
second intermediate level pages	= 160 ÷ 71
	= 3
root level	= 3 ÷ 71
	= 1
nonclustered index number of pages	= 11,427

So the space requirements for indexes are not insignificant. Once you know which fields will be in the indexes, you must calculate the sizes.

These figures are reasonably typical for indexes and a rough rule of thumb is:

clustered index:	1% of data size
nonclustered index:	15% of data size

A.8 Free Space

The database obviously needs free space for data expansion and a growth factor should be made in the initial calculations. However, there is always a need for an amount of free space in the database for such aspects as index creation. Although index creation uses work space, there is also a need for free space in the database itself.

When creating a clustered index, the data records are sorted into sequence of the key values. This means that the data records move into new pages to achieve the new sequence. The new data table is written before the old table is deleted so at least enough free space to take the full new version of the table is required to create a clustered index. Most of the Sybase literature requests that you make allowance of 120% of the table size as free space to create a clustered index on a table. However, I would suggest that you allow more in the order of 150–200% of the table as free space.

This is significant as it must be available all of the time and can be considerable. A 600 MB database with a 200 MB table will need an extra 300–400 MB simply to cater for the creation of a clustered index on the large table. You may think that you could temporarily expand the database just to create enough space to do the index creation and then release it, but this is not possible. Any expansion of the database space remains a permanent assignment as with the initial assignment of space. So it is a good idea but not possible.

You need enough free space to take two times the size of the largest table in your database. It must always be free or you must make it free immediately before the creation and then it remains allocated to the database. If this is a real problem, an alternative is to bcp out to a disk on another system and reload with the clustered index in place. Drop any nonclustered indexes for the reload and rebuild them once the data is reloaded. I'm not recommending this; it's only if you have a serious space problem.

A.9 Log Size Calculation

How long is a piece of string? (Twice the length from the beginning to the center.) The initial rule of thumb used by most administrators is 20% of the data size. But it depends on the activity and the frequency with which you dump and clear out the log. SQL Server operates a changes log, which usually means that inserts and deletes use up most room in the log as they are effectively copies of the record. So a high activity insert rate may require a larger log than an update intensive system. If you have a large table in the database, then a major update to that table will require a log of 2–3 times the size of the table.

However, be careful here as SQL Server updates are often actioned as a delete followed by an insert.

- update which includes a join;

- when the table has a trigger defined;
- when the table is replicated.

System 10 and 11 has continuously refined the update in-place and deferred updating rules. These are detailed in Appendix E.

A.10 Monitoring Space Usage

With the exception of the threshold manager SQL Server does not provide much in the way of space monitoring tools. The system procedure sp_spaceused is all that is on offer to display used and free space and this provides:

sp_spaceused

```
db_name db_size reserved      data        index_size    unused

fred    40 M    16320   K     12480 K     3680 K        160 K
```

where

database_size	amount of space requested in the create and alter commands;
reserved	amount of space currently reserved for use;
data	amount of space being used by data;
index_size	amount of space being used by indexes;
unused	amount of reserved space not currently in use.

This uses sysusages to determine the amount of used space in the database and sysindexes to determine the space used by each object—table and index.

When an object requests more space, SQL Server allocates an extent of eight pages (16 K). So an object will have space reserved for it but not currently contain information. The allocated extent is reserved exclusively for the object and not available to any other object. The object will use the extent pages until there is no more room in the extent, when it will request another extent. (This is a reasonably efficient use of space as the pages in the extent are always allocated to the object if there is any data in them. Pages that become empty remain allocated as part of the extent and are used first by the object before it requests another extent from the free space.)

So, in the extreme, a one record table with three nonclustered indexes will have space allocated to four objects—data plus three indexes—and will be reserving 4 * 8 pages, i.e. 64 K.

Figure A.3 illustrates the unused and free space situation.

The unused space is reserved for each object that requested it. The free space is available for new objects or more space for existing objects. Free space is database size—reserved.

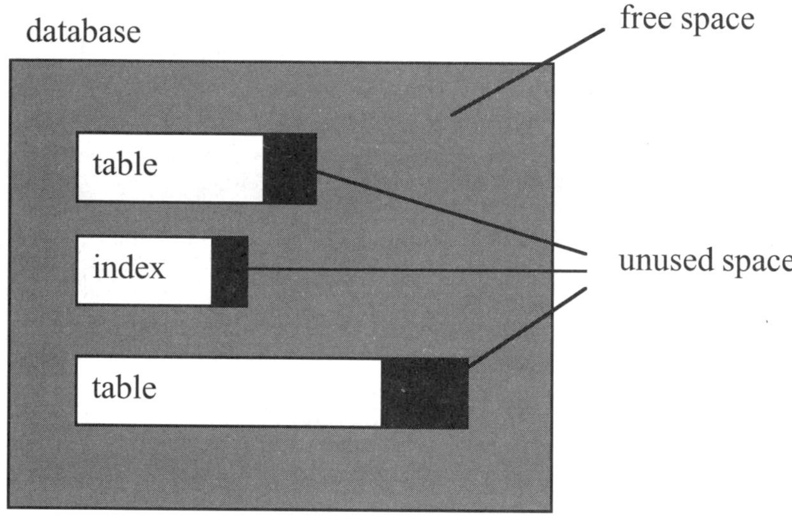

Figure A.3 Space allocation.

sp_spaceused can also be used on a table.

```
sp_spaceused fred_tab
```

name	rows	reserved	data	index_size	unused
fred_tab	20	32 K	10 K	2 K	20 K

A couple of quick calculations will save you some time and some headaches when a create fails. Each new object requires an extent of free space, i.e. 16 K. Execute sp_spaceused on the database to make sure that there is at least this amount of free space before running a create table. (Of course, if you are this close to full, you are in trouble anyway.)

More importantly, if you are building a clustered index on a table, do a sp_spaceused on the table to check the table size and on the database to check the free space. If there is not twice the table size as free space, think carefully about increasing the database size before building the clustered index. And if you do not have the table size free, then the clustered index build will fail.

A.11 Expanding Databases

As already mentioned, you cannot reduce the space allocated to a database. So planning is important. But even the best of plans will need to be adjusted as data volumes grow beyond even your most generous estimates. And remember that as the data tables grow, the free space required for clustered index creation must grow. The space allocated may be increased using the **alter database** command.

alter database

```
ALTER DATABASE db_name
               [ON device_name [= size]
               [,ON device_name [= size]]...]
               [WITH OVERRIDE]
               [FOR LOAD]
```

The size and device allocation are similar to the create database command. The for load option is used after create database for load when recreating a database for loading from a dump. (Both create and alter are necessary to redefine the database allocation exactly as at the dump. This is explained in detail in Chapter 9.) Again the with override is required to accept data and log on the same device.

```
ALTER DATABASE fred
```

allocates the default expansion size (1 MB) on the default device.

```
ALTER DATABASE fred ON default = 20
```

allocates an additional 20 MB on the default device.

```
ALTER DATABASE fred ON dev1 = 15
```

allocates an additional 15 MB on the device dev1.

```
ALTER DATABASE fred ON dev1 = 5
ALTER DATABASE fred ON dev2 = 10
ALTER DATABASE fred ON default = 5
```

expands the database fred by 20 MB into three devices.

A worrying problem is for tempdb to fill up during a large query. Do not panic when this happens. It may just be an unfortunate combination of tempdb requirements that will not happen again. Such occurrences are often infrequent and may be avoided once known. If you are sure that you need extra space then simply expand tempdb:

```
ALTER DATABASE tempdb ON dev5 = 40
```

But once you have done this you cannot get it back. If disk space is reasonably scarce, do not be panicked into expanding tempdb. Consider it carefully and take your time.

A more important reason for expanding tempdb is for disk placement. You want tempdb to be by itself on a device which does not share the disk with any other disk intensive device, like the log device. (Note my previous exception in a one disk system. There are always exceptions.) You can expand tempdb into a larger device located on a low activity disk. As mentioned earlier, you may want to fill up the 2 MB on the master device to force all tempdb usage to your named device or remove tempdb completely from the master device.

Using a separate device for tempdb can also increase the performance of the system. I have seen the throughput of tempdb improve when it is defined on a Unix file and not a raw partition. This often depends on the type of activity with more reads favoring a Unix file and more writes favoring a raw partition. Because of the extra possibility of the record being in cache, the Unix file may favour a high read activity. The logical extension to this is to use a RAM device for tempdb—if you can afford the cost. If you get into really serious temporary space problems, such as a large **order by**, you will need to increase tempdb. If you really need to get this space back, you can remove the entries from sysusages and restart the server. You will need to enable **allow updates** and remove all device fragments. And be careful.

Note that a database cannot consist of more than 32 device fragments and that a single request for space may be satisfied by multiple device fragments. This will only occur when the use of create/drop database has been excessive. Sysusages shows you the device fragmentation.

A.12 Expanding the Log

Expanding the log is as for any other segment expansion; you use **sp_extendsegment** to extend the log segment to another device.

sp_extendsegment

```
sp_extendsegment logsegment, prod_db, dev_8
```

If you wish to move the log to a larger (smaller) device then use **sp_logdevice** which repositions syslogs.

sp_logdevice

```
        sp_logdevice db_name, device_name

ALTER DATABASE fred ON log_dev2 = 15
sp_logdevice fred, log_dev2
```

This increases the log of the database fred by 15 MB on the device log_dev2. The new device is used for future space allocation to the log so there will be a small, but finite, time when the old device is still being used. This is a potentially dangerous time for a failure to occur so try to do log size increases to new devices at noncrucial times.

If there is free space on the device containing the log, an alter database by itself will increase the log on the current device. Interestingly, the alter database on a separate device creates an allocation which is available for use by both data and log. The sp_logdevice then exclusively reserves the device for the log. Be careful here as sp_logdevice takes no notice of any existing use of the device and will change a device previously used for data into a log only device. This can be a nuisance as there is no command to change a log device into a data (or shared) device. This means that the device is no longer used for new data and all reads to data pages on this device will cause warnings to be written to the error log. To recover the data pages from the log device, recreate the clustered index containing the pages on the log device (you can get the indid from the warning messages).

A.13 Database Deletion

A database is deleted using the **drop database** command:

drop database

```
DROP DATABASE db_name [, db_name...]
```

```
DROP DATABASE fred_db
```

This deletes the database and all of its objects, deallocates and frees the storage allocation and removes all references to the database from the system tables. This is an administrator/DBO command and must be run from master. The database being dropped must not be in use by a user (including the administrator) or the command will fail.

Sometimes the database is in a damaged state and this command does not have sufficient power to delete the damaged database. In this case the consistency checker (DBCC) must be used to delete the damaged database:

```
dbcc dbrepair (fred_db, dropdb)
```

A.14 Database Environment

There is a set of database environment options for a database that allows customizing of what may be done in each database. These options are set using **sp_dboption**.

sp_dboption

```
sp_dboption db_name, "option", {true | false}
```

where **option**:

abort tran on log full	determines whether transactions are suspended or aborted when the last chance threshold fires. Default is false, which suspends transactions.
allow nulls by default	sets the default column null|not null status to ANSI null (true) or SQL Server not null (default false).

auto identity	a System 11 option that automatically creates a ten-digit identity column in every table created. The precision of this automatic identity column may be set with the sp_configure parameter "size of auto identity column."

```
sp_configure "size of auto identity column", 8
```

dbo use only	makes the database single user for use by the DBO (administrator) only. This is useful for the administrator after a restore to allow him/her to check a few things before letting the rest of the users into the database.
ddl in tran	allows the use of DDL commands such as create, alter, drop, grant, revoke in transactions. The default of false, normal SQL Server operation, forces DDL commands to be in their own transaction, which is why you cannot put several creates in a batch. Allowing DDL statements in transactions which have several other statements is not a good idea as the DDL commands often take table locks on the system tables.
identity in nonunique index	a System 11 option that automatically includes an existing identity column on a table in the table's indexes so that all indexes are internally unique. Unique indexes are required for cursors and isolation level 0 reads.
no chkpt on recovery	is used when a secondary copy of the database is being kept up-to-date by recovering the primary transaction log against the secondary database. Normally (false) a load tran against a database will write a checkpoint to the log and update the sequence number to ensure that it is not accidentally rerun against the database. However, when the one log has to be used against both secondary and primary databases, the first load tran against the secondary must not write this checkpoint or update the sequence number. Setting this option to true on the secondary ensures that the log may be reused against the primary if necessary.
no free space acctg	suppresses free space accounting and the associated firing of threshold procedures for non-log segments. This speeds recovery but will leave you with inaccurate free space figures.

read only	makes the database read only.
select into/bulk copy	if this is not set, then neither of these commands may be carried out in the database. This is not a particularly good setting to have on a production database but often worth having on a test/development database to allow ad hoc creation of tables. Any use of select into or bulk copy invalidates the transaction log based recovery and any dump transaction command will fail. So use with caution on production databases which must be recovered from transaction dumps and transaction logs.
single user	as for "dbo use only" but this time the user may be anyone. From your viewpoint as administrator this is not a relevant option as you will use "dbo use only" but be careful even of this if there are multiple users aliased as the DBO in a test environment.
trunc log on chkpt	clears out the transaction log at each checkpoint by deleting completed transactions from the log. Use of this means that the database cannot be recovered from the transaction log as the log is not dumped by this option. So use this only when you are confident that lost input is not a problem (e.g. in a training database).

sp_dboption is an administrator- or DBO-only command and must be executed from master. Once issued, the settings do not take effect until you have issued a checkpoint in the database.

```
use master
go
sp_dboption fred, "select into/bulk copy", true
go
sp_dboption fred, "truncate log on chkpt", true
go
use fred
go
checkpoint
go
```

It is not possible to use this command on master but if you want system-wide settings (such as all databases as read only), then you could make the settings on model and they will be copied in the create database command.

A.15 System Tables

There are five system tables which contain information on space allocation:

- sysdevices
- sysdatabases
- sysusages
- syssegments
- sysindexes.

The Table A.1 is a summary of the commands which update them and the system procedures which extract information from them for reference purposes.

Table A.1 *Summary of system tables and their commands and system procedures*

Table	system procedure	commands
sysdevices	sp_helpdevice	disk init
	sp_addumpdevice	disk mirror
		disk unmirror
		disk remirror
sysdatabases	sp_helpdb	create database
	sp_changedbowner	drop database
	sp_dboption	
sysusages	sp_helpdb	create database
	sp_logdevice	alter database
	sp_addsegment	drop database
	sp_extendsegment	
syssegments	sp_helpsegment	
	sp_addsegment	
	sp_dropsegment	
sysindexes	sp_spaceused	create table
		create index

Let's have a detailed look at each table.

A.15.1 sysdevices

There is one row for each device with the information:

```
select * from sysdevices

low       high      status  type  name       phyname            mirrorname
16777216  16875022  3       0     data       /dev/rsd3e         null
0         20000     16      2     diskdump   /dev/null          null
33554432  33603638  2       0     logs       /dev/rsd3f         null
0         10239     3       0     master     the_master_device  null
0         610       16      0     tapedump1  /dev/rmt4          null
0         20000     16      2     tapedump2  /dev/rst           null
```

where

name	the logical name and primary key;	
phyname	file/raw partition name of the device;	
mirrorname	file/raw partition name of the mirror device;	
status	2	database disk
	3	default database disk
	16	dump device (tape or disk)
	24	tape dump with noskip (no label checking)
	32	serial writes
	64	device mirrored
	128	mirroring temporarily disabled
	512	mirroring active
cntrltype	0	database disk
	2	disk or tape streaming dump device
	3–8	tape dump device.

This is created by disk init, updated by the disk mirroring commands and displayed by **sp_helpdevice**.

sp_helpdevice

```
sp_helpdevice

device name    physical name
description
status         cntrltype          device        low          high
log            /log.dir/log.dat
special, physical disk, 4 MB
2              0                  5             83886080     83888127
```

```
master          /sybase/master.dat
special, default disk, physical disk, 30 MB
3               0                   0               0               15359
tapedump1       /dev/rmt4
tape, 19 MB, dump device
16              3                   0               0               610
tapedump2       /dev/rst0
disk, dump device
16              2                   0               0               20000
proddisk        /prod.dir/prod.dat
special, MIRROR ENABLED, default disk, mirrored on  /mirr.dir/mirr.dat, serial
writes, reads mirrored, physical disk, 12 MB
738             0                   10              167772160       167772671
sysprocsdev     /dev/SYS1/SYSPROCS
special, MIRROR ENABLED, mirrored on  /dev/SYS1/SYSPROCS_MIRROR, serial writes,
physical disk, 20 MB
738             0                   10              33554432        33580072
```

The installation creates the devices: master, sybsystemprocs, tapedump1 and tapedump2.

Information on a specific device is shown with:

```
sp_helpdevice [device_name]
```

The system procedure sp_helpdevice is quite sufficient to show what is in sysdevices. This is usually true of the system procedures but there is often some useful information missing.

In the case of sysdevices, there is little extra that can be displayed outside of sp_helpdevice except for which disk devices are database devices and which are dump devices. This separation is sometimes useful to the administrator and is easily achieved by:

```
SELECT name, phyname, mirrorname,
       status, size = high - low + 1
       FROM sysdevices
       WHERE cntrltype = 0
```

name	phyname	mirrorname	status	size
data	/dev/rsd3e	null	3	97807
logs	/dev/rsd3f	null	2	49207
master	the_master_device	null	3	10240

which shows the database devices (and similarly for dump devices with cntrltype = 2 or 3).

Note that mirroring a device alters the status so use the cntrltype to check for database/dump devices, not the status.

Another useful output from sysdevices is the total database space:

```
SELECT total_disk_usage = SUM(high - low + 1)
       FROM sysdevices
       WHERE cntrltype = 0

total_disk_usage
157254
```

Note that the output is in pages (i.e. 2 K).

A.15.2 sysdatabases

There is one row for each database containing the information.

```
select * from sysdatabases

dbname  dbid    suid     status  version logptr        crdate
dumptrdate               status2  audflags        deftabaud       defvwaud defpraud
master  1       1        0       1                1289            Jan 1 1990 12:00 am
Apr 2 1992 8:00 pm       0  null          null            null            null
model   3       1        0       1                46              Jan 1 1990 12:00 am
Mar 30 1992 9:00 pm      0  null          null            null            null
pubs    5       1        0       1                47              Mar 30 1992 9:30 pm
Apr 4 1992 11:00 pm      0  null          null            null            null
tempdb  2       1        0       1                45              Jan 1 1990 12:00 am
Mar 30 1992 8:30 pm      0  null          null            null            null
fred    4       1        0       1                1030            Mar 30 1992 9:00 pm
Apr 4 1992 10:00 pm 0      null          null            null            null
```

where

dbid	the unique database ID allocated by the create database command;
suid	the unique server ID of the database owner;
mode	an internal lock set during database create;
status	indicates the settings of sp_dboption and also if the database needs to be recovered. The binary control bit settings are: 0x04 4 select into/bulk copy 0x08 8 truncate log on checkpoint 0x10 16 no checkpoint on recovery 0x20 32 crashed while loading database 0x40 64 database still being recovered 0x100 250 database is suspect: will need to drop

with dbcc dbrepair			
	0x400	1,024	read only
	0x800	2,048	dbo use only
	0x1000	4,096	single user only
	0x4000	16,384	database name has changed
version	the version of SQL server running when the database was created;		
logptr	a pointer to the transaction log;		
status2	additional control bits:		
	0x01	1	abort tran when log full
	0x02	2	disable free space acctg
audflags	audit settings for the database;		
deftabaud	audit settings for the tables;		
defvwaud	audit settings for the views;		
defpraud	audit settings for the procedures.		

The system procedure **sp_helpdb** interprets this data and picks up the database size from sysusages.

sp_helpdb

```
        sp_helpdb

dbname  db_size owner   dbid    created                 status
master  2       sa      1       Jan 1 1990 12:00 am     no options set
model   2       sa      3       Jan 1 1990 12:00 am     no options set
tempdb  20      sa      2       Jan 1 1990 12:00 am     select into/bulk copy
pubs    2       sa      5       Mar 30 1992 1:00 pm     no options set
fred    40      sa      4       Mar 30 1992 2:00 pm     no options set
```

A.15.3 sysusages

There is one row for each distinct space allocation to a database containing the information:

```
select * from sysusages

dbid    segmap     lstart     size       vstart      unreservedpgs
1       7          0          1024       4           104
2       7          0          1024       2564        80
3       7          0          10240      1540        2048
4       7          0          1024       3588        96
5       7          0          10240      50331648    4096
5       7          10240      10240      10266314    4096
```

where

segmap	a bit for each segment which includes this device allocation;
lstart	the first logical database page number;
size	the size in pages of this allocation;
vstart	a virtual disk address which points to the physical disk that the allocation is on. Vstart lies in one of the high/low pairs on sysdevices indicating which device the allocation is on.
pad	unused;
unreservedpgs	free space not part of an allocated extent.

This is rather useless and you need to make the join to sysdevices to pick up the device name. **sp_helpdb** with the database name does this quite adequately.

```
sp_helpdb  fred

name    db_size owner  dbid   created               status
fred    40         sa  4      Mar 30 1992 11:00 pm  no options set
device_fragments       size         usage
dev_1                  20 MB        data and log
dev_2                  20 MB        data and log
```

So sp_helpdb can assist in answering nonspecific questions such as:

- which devices are for data sp_helpdb on each database and note device names;
- allocated space per device sp_helpdb on each database and sum the figures;
- free space per device take the above sum away from the total device allocation.

But none of these are particularly friendly and there is no help in the simple requests, such as what databases are on a specific device.

A.15.4 sysindexes

There is one row for each object in the database containing, among other data, the actual space used by the object. For the moment, I shall ignore all but the space allocation data and the segment number field. If the table has a clustered index then this indicates the size of the table; otherwise, the table has an entry in sysindexes.

```
SELECT name,  data_pages = data_pgs(id, doampg),
              index_pages = data_pgs(id, ioampg),
              rows = rowcount(doampg), segment
              FROM sysindexes
```

name	data_pages	index_pages	rows	segment
tab_1	20	24	360	12
ind_1	5	8	0	25

where

data_pages	the number of pages used by the object;
index_pages	the number of pages used by the index.;
rows	the number of rows in the table;
segment	the number of the segment in which the object resides and which is used for current space allocation.

A.15.5 syssegments

There is one row for each segment mapping the segment name to the segment number.

```
select * from syssegments
```

segment	name	status
0	system	0
1	default	1
2	log segment	0
3	myseg_1	0

where

status	1 indicates a default segment.

The system procedure **sp_helpsegment** displays the **syssegments** information with no difference from a **select * from syssegments**.

sp_helpsegment

```
sp_helpsegment
```

segment	name	status
0	system	0
1	default	1
2	log segment	0
3	myseg_1	0

However, sp_helpsegment is more useful with a specific segment name as input, when it displays the devices and objects related to the segment.

```
sp_helpsegment  system

segment name          status
0       system        0

table_name            name                    indid
sysalternates         sysalternates           1
syscolumns            syscolumns              1
syscomments           syscomments             1
etc                   etc                     etc
```

where

indid	0	table
	1	clustered
	2–254	nonclustered
	255	text.

Further information on segments is available using **sp_helpdb** with the database name when it displays the device fragments and the associated segments.

```
sp_helpdb  fred

name  db_size owner  dbid  created              status
fred  5 MB    sa     4     Mar 30 1992 1:00 pm  no options set

device_fragments           size        usage
dev_1                      1 MB        data only
dev_2                      2 MB        data only
dev_3                      2 MB        data only

device                segment
dev_1                 myseg_1
dev_1                 myseg_2
dev_2                 system
dev_2                 default
dev_3                 myseg_3
```

This is useful but note again that there is nothing that goes the other way around to give segments on a device.

That's the standard output, now let's look at some extra commands on these system tables to extract the missing information.

A.16 Some Useful Extracts from the System Tables

A.16.1 Which Databases and Who is the DBO

```
SELECT d.dbid, d.name, l.name
       FROM sysdatabases d, syslogins l
       WHERE d.suid = l.suid
       ORDER BY d.name
```

This information is available from sp_help but this does not give the dbid, which is often useful to the administrator.

A.16.2 Which Databases and How Big

```
SELECT d.name, d.dbid,
       "size MB" = sum(u.size) * 2048 / 1048576
       FROM sysdatabases d, sysusages u
       WHERE d.dbid = u.dbid
       GROUP BY d.name, d.dbid
```

If you want to be more precise, the page size can be obtained from spt_values.

A.16.3 Which Databases Are on a Device and How Much Is Allocated to Them

```
SELECT u.dbid, db.name, u.size
       FROM sysusages u, sysdevices d, sysdatabases db
       WHERE d.cntrltype = 0
       AND u.vstart between d.low and d.high
       AND d.name = 'device_name'
       AND db.dbid = u.dbid
       ORDER BY u.dbid
       COMPUTE sum(u.size) by u.dbid
       COMPUTE sum(u.size)
```

or a simple sum(size) group by u.dbid, db.name.

A.16.4 List of Tables and Sizes

```
SELECT  o.name, dpgs=data_pgs(i.id, doampg),
               rows=rowcnt(doampg)
       FROM sysindexes i, sysobjects o
       WHERE indid IN (0, 1)
       AND o.id = i.id
```

```
AND o.type = "U"
ORDER BY o.name
COMPUTE sum(data_pgs(i.id, doampg)),
        sum(rowcnt(doampg))
```

A.17 Summary

The disk init command allocates physical space on the disk storage for the server. The create database command then reserves space on these devices for exclusive use by the named database. Create database reserves space for both data and log, with these being allocated on the same device or on separate devices. Separate allocation of the log to its own device is recommended.

Tables and indexes created in a database then use the devices to which the database is allocated in device number sequence. This default object placement may be overridden by defining named segments on the devices. These segments have no physical space allocated within the device and are limited only by the device size.

APPENDIX B

Master Database and Logical System Rebuild

This appendix describes the requirements for rebuilding the master database and for conducting a complete system rebuild.

System 11 has added two options to buildmaster.

COMMAND SYNTAX

```
buildmaster
disk reinit
disk refit
isql
defncopy
bcp
```

SYSTEM PROCEDURE SYNTAX

None

B.1 Rebuilding the Master Database

There are many problems in an administrator's life, not least the appearance of not seeming to do anything. As an ex-administrator, I believe that the best administrator never appears to be doing anything because that means that the system is running OK. Just keep the terminal facing away from the center of the office and have a function key that displays what looks like a stack dump.

However, the real problem is when the system goes down because one of your required resources has failed. Obvious candidates are the log and the master database. At the very least, have both of these mirrored so that a single failure does not stop the system. If a log fails, then the database is unusable. Everybody writes to the log so if it is not available, nobody can use that database. Don't panic. Fix the problem, create a log device, dump the database and get back to normal. When you let the users back into the system is up to you, but you must dump the database as you do not have a recoverable situation until you have an up-to-date dump. The log has failed so you cannot recover completely from the previous dump. If you have been dumping the transaction log regularly, you will be able to roll forward to the end of the last dump of the log. But you will be unable to recover up to the last completed transaction.

At least in this situation, the failure effects only one database and other users may still be working. But a failure of the master database stops everybody on the server, so make sure that you can recover the master database quickly. This is one area where you should be as prepared as possible. Keep users out of the master database so that it contains system tables only. This keeps it as tidy with no user tables, which keeps it as small as possible with faster dump and load times.

Keep an up-to-date dump of master. The most important times are after updates to sysdatabases, sysdevices and syslogins.

So dump master after:

create/alter/drop database	sysdatabases
add/drop devices	sysdevices
add/drop logins	syslogins

If you do not do this, the restored dump will not reflect the actual disk configuration and you will need to run rebuilding commands to update the system tables in master to reflect the current disk configuration. These take time and the whole system is down. Keep an up-to-date dump of master.

Even if you have an up-to-date dump, the master database holds the system tables that define the complete configuration and therefore require a little special attention to recover. This is given by the special command **buildmaster**.

buildmaster

```
buildmaster -m
```

The buildmaster command is part of a regular install; the -m option simply reinitializes the master database leaving model and tempdb intact. The full syntax of buildmaster is:

```
                 Unix               VMS
buildmaster      -d  disk           /disk=name
                 -c cntrltype       /cntrltype=value
                 -s size            /size=value
                 -r                 /reconfigure
                 -m                 /master
                 -v                 /contiguous
                 -q
                 -x
```

All parameters are optional.

where

disk	the physical name of the device for the location of the master database.
cntrltype	controller type for the master device as for a disk init command. Defaults to 0. Leave it alone.
size	the master database size in 2 K pages.
-r	rebuilds the master database with the default configuration parameters. When you are changing the configuration variables using sp_configure, there is no check that you have not specified garbage until you reboot the server, at which point it will not reboot. This option gets you out of trouble.
-m	simply recreates the master database as described above. Does not change the configuration parameters.
-v	displays the version number.

-q	a System 11 option which does not clear unallocated pages in the master and model databases.
-x	a System 11 option which rebuilds the model database only without altering any configuration parameters or initialising the master database. Overrides the -q option.

You will be asked for device and size information:

```
buildmaster -m
device: /dev/rst1d
controller:    0        ALWAYS ENTER 0. Do not get clever.
size:   in pages (be careful as the original install may have requested sectors)
```

Once the master database is initialized, the buildmaster command shuts down the server. Start it up in single user mode to make sure that no other users can get near the system yet and reload your dump of master.

Make sure you alter your "SA" password as the rebuild will have reset it to null. If your disk dump is on a named device, you will have to add the disk dump device before you load master. The load of master will again shutdown the server so you can now start it for all of the users.

If you have an up-to-date dump:

```
DUMP DATABASE master TO dump_dev
```

then the recovery of master is:

```
buildmaster -m
device: /dev/rst1d
controller:    0
size:          10000

cd /usr/sybase/install
startserver -m

isql -Usa

sp_password sa, special
go
sp_addumpdevice "disk", "dump_dev", "dump.dat1", 2
go
LOAD DATABASE master FROM dump_dev
go
startserver
```

If you have not been keeping an up-to-date dump of master, the dump that you have just restored will not reflect the devices, databases or logins that you have added since the last dump. You need to issue further commands to make master reflect the existing configuration. To update the system tables in master we need to run:

disk reinit for devices

disk refit for databases

scripts for logins.

You cannot do disk init or create database as these initialize the disk areas as well as updating the system tables, so the above commands are required simply to update the system tables. Also, there is no relogin command so you will need to rerun the isql script to re-add any logins and users. (Of course you do not have any users in master because you do not allow named users into master.) All rebuilding from an out-of-date dump assumes that you know what you have to rebuild.

When you have this rebuilding work to do, start the server in single user mode after the load database. Again, you do not want users in the system when you are rebuilding the system tables.

B.1.1 Devices

disk reinit

```
DISK REINIT
        NAME = logical_name,
        PHYSNAME = physical_name,
        VDEVNO = virtual_device_no,
        SIZE = number_of_pages
        [, VSTART = virtual_address]
        [, CNTRLTYPE = controller_number]
```

The parameters are the same as for the disk init and the values must be the same as the original disk init. You must be in master to issue disk reinit.

```
DISK REINIT
        NAME = "sales",
        PHYSNAME = "/usr/sales.dir/sales.dat"
        VDEVNO = 5,
        SIZE = 8192
```

This recreates the entry in sysdevices without initializing the disk space.

B.1.2 Databases

disk refit

```
DISK REFIT
```

This is run from master and uses the rebuilt information in sysdevices and the current disk allocations to rebuild sysusages and sysdatabases.

Even running this on each database, Sybase still recommends that you run the database consistency checker (DBCC):

```
dbcc checkalloc(fred_db)
```

to check the allocations and have a look at the relevant tables (sysdevices, sysdatabases, sysusages), as mentioned above. Updating a reinitialized, refitted system that is not quite right can have disastrous results which are unrecoverable.

B.1.3 Logins

I must confess that even I would not always dump the database after adding a login to master. But do record the new login in a script so that you can rerun the script after recovering master. Of course, if you take this approach, the user's password will revert to what it was originally. Make sure that you tell them this.

The latter comment of keeping scripts up-to-date applies to everything you do as administrator. You are adjusting the system configuration with almost everything that you do so make sure that you can repeat it by recording it in a script. I know that this is extra work but do it; you do not want to have to think too much when the system has crashed. All you want to do is to press the button and watch an automatic recovery.

Keep a master script of your system configuration so that you can rebuild it at any time. Every change that you make—new login, new device, new database, increase to a database, new segment, everything—must be kept up-to-date in this script. This is not a substitute for regular dumps of master but an essential tool to allow you to rebuild the system configuration.

B.2 Rebuild of Sybsystemprocs

Sybsystemprocs contains all of the system stored procedures. So it is not a disaster if you lose it but still a single point of failure that you should have mirrored and should be able to recover as quickly as possible.

Although it is a system database, its recovery is no different from a normal database except that you must be careful to ensure that any system procedures you may need during the restore are available to you. This is particularly relevant to **sp_volchanged**, **sp_configure**, **sp_addumpdevice** and possibly **sp_dboption**, copies of which should be placed on master. If you need to change dump volumes during the restore of sybsystemprocs, you will not be able to do so if sp_volchanged is on the database you are trying to recover. Even more importantly, if you run startserver and fail before you have recovered sybsystemprocs, you will probably want to "allow updates" on master to reset the database status. But you will not be able to do so as sp_configure has not been recovered.

B.3 Logical System Rebuild

Let's look at a full system rebuild in a little more detail.

Database dump and load are not always possible; for example, when moving from one machine type to another or when recreating only part of the database (although there are some third-party products that can help). In such cases, we need to go back to the beginning and reissue the appropriate create commands. It would be incredibly tedious, as well as drastically error-prone, to manually reenter every command, so it is advisable to keep an isql script that contains the create commands for everything in the current database.

Being practical, it is much better to keep one script for each object set (devices, segments, databases, logins, users, tables, indexes, rules, defaults, permissions, procedures, triggers and views) as it is much easier to control and maintain. And remember to keep the scripts up-to-date.

So what is a script file?

B.3.1 isql

A script file is an operating system file of the commands that you would execute in **isql** to create the various objects. It is included when entering isql from the operating system.

isql

Unix

```
isql -Usa -Psa < db_create.sql
```

VMS

```
isql /user="sa" /pass="sa" /input=proc_create.sql
```

Get into the habit of using scripts for all of your administrator creation commands and incorporate them into the overall system scripts as soon as possible. The full syntax of isql is:

```
        Unix                                VMS
isql    [-e]  [-p]  [-F]  [-n] /echo       /statistics   /noprompt
        [-g[  [-v]  [-X]  [-Y]
        [-a display_charset]
        [ -c  cmdend]                       /terminator = string
        [ -h  headers]
        [-E editor]
        [ -w  col_width]                    /colwidth = integer
        [ -s  col_sep]                      /colseparator = character
        [ -t  timeout]                      /timeout = integer
        [ -m  error_level]                  /errorlevel = integer
        [ -H  host_name]                    /hostname = host_name
        [ -U  user_name]                    /username = user_name
        [ -P  pwd]                          /password = password
        [ -I  interface]                    /interfaces = file_name
        [ -S  server]                       /server_name = server_name
        [-i  input_file_name]               /input = file_name
        [-o  out_file_name]                 /output = file_name
        [-J client_charset]                 /rowsinpage = integer
        [-l login_timeout]
        [-y Sybase_directory]
        [-z language]
        [-A size]
```

where

-e	echoes input;
-p	prints statistics;
-n	removes the numbering and > prompt from input lines;
-c cmdend	resets the command terminator. Default is "go";
-h headers	specifies number of rows between column headings;
-w col_width	sets the screen output width;

-s col_sep	resets column separator. Default is space;
-t timeout	specifies number of seconds before a command times out; default is no timeout;
-m error_level	specifies level below which no error message is displayed;
-H host_name	specifies different host computer name;
-U user_name	user name;
-P pwd	password;
-I interfaces	specifies name and location of interfaces file to be used for connection;
-S server	specifies name of server to connect to;
-a display_charset	specifies the display character set;
-E editor	specifies the editor to be invoked from the isql command line;
-J client_charset	specifies the client character set;
-l login_timeout	specifies the login timeout period; default is 60 seconds;
-y Sybase_dir	specifies the location of the Sybase directory;
-z language	specifies the server language;
-A size	specifies the network packet size;
-X	specifies client password encryption.

In Unix, you may also use the redirection symbols for input and output files <input_file and >output_file.

The following points in isql are worth remembering.

- Use small batches, especially each create command in a batch by itself. I know that some of them do not need a separate batch but it saves some thinking if you put each create command in its own batch.
- **Quit** or **exit** to exit.
- **Reset** to discard incorrect batches of commands without running them.
- **Execute** in front of stored procedures. Only the first procedure in a batch executes without the key word, so make it a habit to always use the keyword especially in front of system procedures.
- Do a **use database** as often as possible. There is no point in being in the wrong database and no harm in too many use databases. Remember to put it in its own batch.

- Always check to see if an object exists before using the create. The create will fail if the object already exists so check the appropriate system table before creating it (or do not create it if it exists already).

```
IF EXISTS (SELECT 1 FROM sysobjects
       WHERE name = 'upd_proc'
       AND type = 'P')
DROP PROC upd_proc
go
CREATE PROC upd_proc AS
etc
```

Sybase has some installation scripts in $SYBASE/scripts which are reasonable examples, so have a look at them; for example, installmaster, installmodel and installpubs.

B.3.2 defncopy

Scripts are essential for devices, segments, databases, tables, logins, users and permissions but there is an operating system command—**defncopy**—that copies the definitions of views, rules, defaults, procedures and triggers.

defncopy

	Unix	VMS
defncopy	[-U name	/username = user_name
	[-P pwd	/password = password
	[-S server]	/server_name = server_name
	[-I interfaces]	/interfaces = file_name
	[-v] [-X]	
	[-a display_charset]	
	[-J client_charset]	
	[-z language]	
	{in file_name db_name |	
	out file_name db_name}	
	object_name	
	[object_name]...}	

where

out/in	specifies the direction of the copy, out from database to operating system;
file_name	the operating system file_name;
db_name	the SQL Server database name which contains or will contain the objects.

As with any create, the objects created belong to the person executing the command, so use defncopy as administrator or DBO.

Copy out:

```
defncopy -Usa -Psa out tabs_proc fred_db tab_1.proc
```

Copy in:

```
defncopy -Usa -Psa in tabs.proc fred_db
```

B.3.3 Bulk Copy

Finally, we need to load the data to the tables we have just recreated. When we cannot use load database, the best method is to use bulk copy: **bcp**.

bcp

```
bcp      table_name     {in|out} data_file
```

Unix	VMS
`[-m  max_errors]`	`/max_errors = integer`
`[-f  format_file]`	`/format_file = file_name`
`[-e  err_file]`	`/errorfile = file_name`
`[-F  first_row]`	`/first_row = integer`
`[-L  last_row]`	`/last_row = integer`
`[-b  batch_size]`	`/batch_size = integer`
`[-n]`	`/native_default`
`[-c [-N]]`	`/character_default`
`[-t  field_terminator]`	`/column_terminator = string`
`[-r  row_terminator]`	`/row_terminator = string`
`[-i  input_file]`	`/input = file_name`
`[-o  output_file]`	`/output = file_name`
`[-U  user_name]`	`/username = user_name`
`[-P pwd]`	`/password = password`

```
[-I interfaces]              /interfaces = file_name
[-S server]                  /server_name = server_name
[-v]                         /version
[-T text/image size]
[-a display_charset]
[-q datafile_charset]
[-J client_charset]
[-z language]
[-A size]
[-E]
[-X]
[-Y sybase_dir]
```

where

in/out	the direction of the copy: in is from the data_file to the table;
data_file	the full path name of the input data;
-m max_errors	the maximum number of errors before the copy is aborted. T he default is 10;
-f format_file	the path name of a stored set of responses to a previous run of bcp;
-e err_file	the file_name for any rows which were unable to be copied;
-F first_row	the number of the first row to copy. Default is 1;
-L last_row	the number of the last row to copy. Default is end of the file;
-b batch_size	the number of rows per batch for copy in. A checkpoint is taken after the batch_size;
-n	performs the copy using the datatypes of the database columns;
-c	performs the copy using character type as default with \t as field_terminator and \n as row_terminator;
-N	skips an identity column;
-t field_terminator	specifies the field_terminator;
-r row_terminator	specifies the row_terminator;
-v	reports the current version of bcp;
-T text/image size	specifies the text/image size;
-a display_charset	specifies the display character set;
-q datafile_charset	specifies the datafile character set;
-J client_charset	specifies the client character set;
-z language	specifies the server language;
-A size	specifies the network packet size;

-E	specifies the identity column value;
-X	specifies client password encryption;
-Y	specifies the Sybase directory.

Bulk copy may be run from the operating system, data workbench or db_library. Data workbench is the easiest as you are protected from the parameters but not all of the options are available to you so I would recommend running bcp from the operating system.

Bulk copy runs in two modes: fast and slow. Fast copy runs when there are no indexes or triggers on the table and select into/bulk copy is set using sp_dboption. In this mode, no rules fire, no triggers fire and the inserts are not logged. Defaults are assigned. As awkward as this can be with a separate integrity program needed to check domain and referential integrity and uniqueness of primary key, I would strongly recommend this method from a performance aspect. Slow bulk copy is exactly that—slow. You will have time to code the additional integrity program, test it extensively and run fast bulk copy in the time it takes slow bulk copy to run.

An exception to this is when the records are loaded in clustered index sequence to an existing clustered index. This can be fast. However, you need to consider any effort to presort the records, which may negate any savings. Try it. Also you will have no clustered index statistics if you create the clustered index prior to loading in the data. This is not a disaster for a clustered index but you may get some unusual plans especially for joins as there are no density figures. So you will still have to run **update statistics** on the clustered index after the bulk copy.

To load a table:

1. create table (using script);
2. bcp data into table;
3. run uniqueness check;
4. create indexes;
5. run integrity checks.

Specifying a batch size is highly recommended when loading data with bcp. Because fast mode bcp is not logged, it is not recoverable. However, specifying a batch size forces a checkpoint after the specified number of records have been loaded. This gives an intermediate point to which the system can recover. More importantly, the checkpoint clears out the log. Even though fast bcp does not log the inserts, the page allocations are logged and a large bulk copy can cause more use of the log than you may expect. So always specify a batch size for this reason.

Remember that, even with checkpoints, bcp inserts are not logged in fast mode and therefore the full bulk copy is not recoverable. Do a dump database after a fast bulk copy. Be careful when you have the “select into/bulk copy” option enabled. This allows the “select into” command to be executed in the database. This is a non-logged command; that is, the record updates are not written to the log. Therefore, the database is not recoverable after a “select into.” So it is extremely dangerous to leave this option enabled on a database.

The execution of a bulk copy is, of course, much more interesting than talking about it. Copy out is really not a problem but copy in from a file created from another system, such as Oracle or Ingres, can be a trial.

Let me use an example of an ASCII file containing two records in the format:

1, john kirkwood, 01734 771776, 1 Wren Close, 22/09/48, 300.45, 15e+07
2, jill kirkwood, 01734 731513, 18 Fistead Road, 18/7/82, 895.71, 5000000

and copying this into a table:

```
tab_1 (pkey_col     int,
       name         varchar(30),
       tel_no       char(15),
       address      varchar(40),
       trn_date     datetime,
       salary       numeric(6, 2),
       value        float)
```

The field terminator is *comma* and the row terminator is *newline*. The first attempt is to let bcp use its defaults with the exception of the terminators.

In Unix:

```
bcp "fred_db.dbo.tab_1" in data_file.in
        -Usa -Pwhatever -Stest
        -t, -r\\n -c
```

(Note the double backslash for the newline so that the second one is recognized as a backslash.)

In VMS:

```
bcp “fred_db.dbo.tab_1” in data_file.in
        /username = “sa” /password = “whatever”
        /server_name = “test” /column_terminator = “,”
        /row_terminator = “n” /character_default
```

This does not work and fails with a conversion overflow error message. Interestingly, if you run it in interactive mode (without /character_default), you are prompted for the column definitions and it executes with no conversion errors. But it loads in rubbish. Be careful, the interactive mode can seriously damage your data—and waste your time.

The first reaction is that the float field is causing an overflow problem but closer investigation establishes that it is the date field. The simple date format of dd/mm/yy is not always the best with bcp and I usually find it better to have the dates in default format dd mm yy.

B.4 Summary

I believe that the important point is to keep the master database clear of any user information and to have an up-to-date dump of master. Then the recovery is straightforward. Also, it is extremely important to keep copies of some of the system procedures in master to ensure that you can recover sybsystemprocs.

Finally, it is advisable to practice all of this recovery as you have a server failure when master fails and you do not want to have to think about anything while getting back to a working situation. And practice is also useful with defncopy and bcp, which are not the most intuitive syntaxes in the world. Especially with bcp, get a working syntax and stick with it.

APPENDIX C

Storage Structures and Indexing

This appendix takes a detailed look a the SQL Server B-tree index structures—clustered and nonclustered. The appendix covers the data storage structures, the index structure and the processing involved in insert/update/delete against each combination of index. The other types of page structure—allocation, distribution and text/imaging—are also discussed.

System 11 has made significant changes to the update in place rules.

COMMAND SYNTAX

None

SYSTEM PROCEDURE SYNTAX

None

C.1 Indexes

It is impossible to separate the index method of a SQL Server table and the underlying storage structure. SQL Server uses B-tree to index the tables and has two types: clustered and nonclustered. The clustered B-tree is a sparse index where the records are held in sequence of the index values and only the first record in each data page has an index entry. The nonclustered B-tree is a dense index where there is no imposed sequence on the data records and each record in the table has an index entry.

Therefore, a SQL Server table with a clustered index has the data records maintained in sequence of the index field values. So records are placed in specific pages depending on the value of the index field. A SQL Server table that has only nonclustered indexes has the data records added to the last page of the table with no notice taken of the index field value. So only the index entries of the nonclustered index are maintained in sequence; any sequencing of the data in a nonclustered table is coincidental.

Consequently, a SQL Server table may have one clustered index but may have up to 250 nonclustered indexes. Clustering one index on a table is not mandatory as all indexes may be nonclustered, but the storage and processing of the data records is significantly different if a table has a clustered index defined on it.

C.1.1 Clustered Index

I believe the easiest way to understand any index method it to go through how it is built. But if you are happy with the layout of sparse B-trees, then you may skip the initial discussion.

The likelihood is that the data table already has records in it when we create the index so we shall start with a set of records as in Figure C.1. As previously discussed in Chapter 10, creating an index on existing data is the recommended approach as it ensures that the index statistics are initialized.

1	22	19	18	26
16	8	6	11	12
3	2	28	4	27
17	20	7	24	14

Figure C.1 *Initial record population.*

The first thing that the clustered index requires is the records in sequence of the key, as in Figure C.2.

1	6	12	18	24
2	7	14	19	26
3	8	16	20	27
4	11	17	22	28

***Figure C.2** Data sequenced for clustering.*

To index these records, we now have a traditional sequenced storage—ISAM is the most typical—where not every record needs to be indexed. We need only to index the first record in each data page as we know that the sequence is being maintained. Therefore, all records from 1 up to (but not including) 6 must always be in the first page, all records from 6 up to 12 must always be in the next page and so on. So we can build a first level of index entries that simply point to the first record in each data page, as in Figure C.3.

(I have put four index entries per index page to illustrate the index build. In reality, there will be many more index entries in an index page, depending on the size of the index field. We shall look at sizing shortly.)

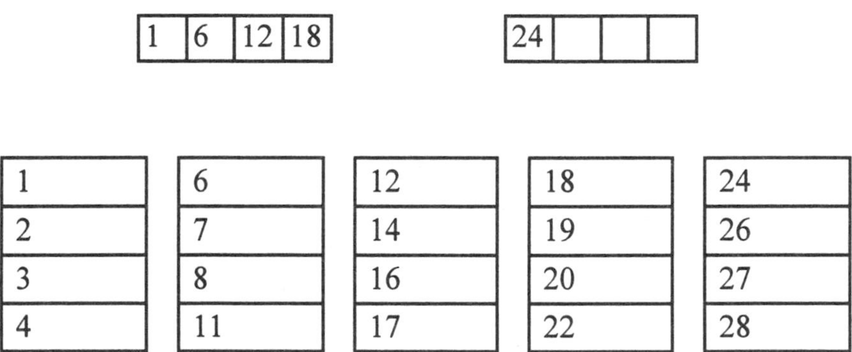

***Figure C.3** First level clustered index.*

To locate a record (say 19) we can now browse along the index level until we find the index entry for the page that the record is in (18–24) and read that page to locate the record. Note that we do not know if the record exists until we have read the data page. This is not uncommon in sparse indexes. This is clearly more efficient than reading all of the data pages but still not as efficient as we can make it, because we are usually talking of a reduction of one order of magnitude only between the number of data pages and the number of first level index pages.

The B-tree solves this by continuing to index each level until it reaches a level with a single index page. In our small example, this is reached at the second index level, as shown in Figure C.4.

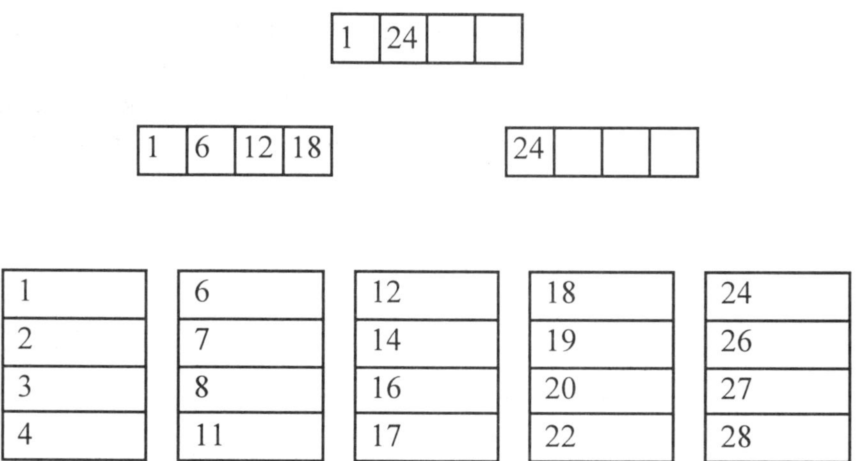

Figure C.4 *Clustered B-tree index.*

Now to locate record 19, we read in at the top level and find that 19 is in the left hand branch of the tree (between 1 and 24). We read the index page at the next level and find that 19 is in the page beginning with 18 and we read that data page to locate the record.

The SQL Server clustered index is one of the best examples of a sparse index that I have seen.

The index is called **sparse** because not every data record has an index entry. The single index page entry point is called the **root node**. The page number of this is held in the field "root" in sysindexes.

The level at which the entries (data or index) are first in sequence is called the **leaf level** or **sequence set**; that is, the data for the clustered index. Any other levels between the leaf level and the root node are called **intermediate levels**.

Each index page is called an **index node**.

Each level in the index is linked horizontally by page pointers. So if a range of records (10–20) is required once the first record is located vertically via the index levels, the leaf level may be browsed horizontally to locate the subsequent records without retraversing the index.

This is a very significant benefit of the clustered index. Because the data records themselves are in sequence of the key, once the first record is located only the data pages need to be read for a range enquiry. (I'll come back to this later when comparing the two indexing methods.)

Let's take a closer look at the pointers of the clustered index. Every index entry of the clustered index is a page pointer. A page pointer in SQL Server is 4 bytes plus a 1 byte overhead, so every index entry in the clustered index is the key value plus a 5-byte pointer. Introducing page pointers, our index now looks like Figure C.5.

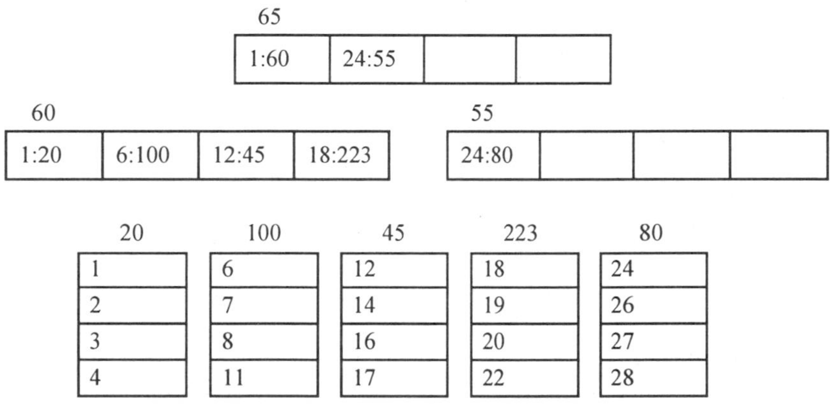

Figure C.5 *Clustered index pointer structure.*

The root node is page 65, the intermediate level pages 60 and 55 and the data pages 20, 100, 45, 223 and 80.

Now to locate record 27 we read the root node page 65—from sysindexes—which tells us that record 27 is in the right hand branch, which starts at page 55. This page tells us that record 27 is in page 80, which we need to scan to locate record 27.

Similarly, to read all records greater than 6 takes us via page 65 and page 60 to page 100 and then to pages 45, 223 and 80 via the page pointer chain which links each level in the index; in this case, the data records.

C.1.2 Nonclustered Index

The start point is the data table of Figure C.1. For the nonclustered index, we do not move the data but create a leaf index level containing an index entry for every record in the table, as in Figure C.6.

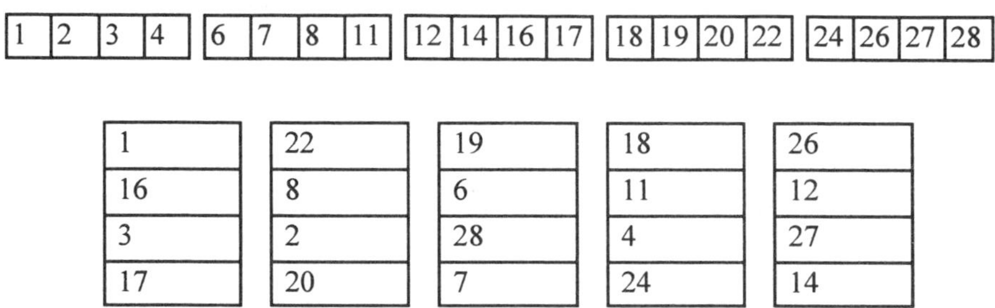

***Figure C.6** Nonclustered index leaf level.*

This is the level of the nonclustered index that is maintained in index value sequence. This is a dense index as every record in the table has an index entry. The data records do not need to be maintained in key value sequence so new records are simply inserted at the end of the table. The location of the last page in the table is held in the column "last" of sysindexes.

Now the B-tree is completed by creating further index levels on top of the leaf level until a single root node is reached, as shown in Figure C.7.

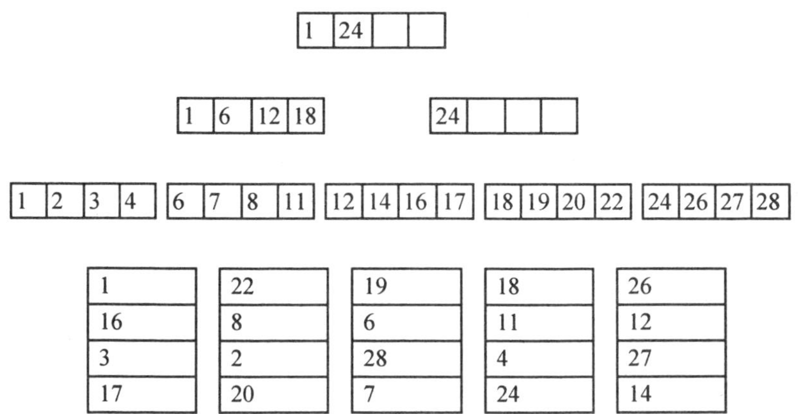

***Figure C.7** Nonclustered index.*

Because the leaf level entries are always in sequence, we can use the first record in each index page to create the intermediate and root levels, as we did before in the clustered index.

To locate record 14, we read the root node, which tells us record 14 is in the left hand branch. The intermediate level index page tells us that record 14 is in the leaf level starting with 12. This leaf level index page tells us the data page that record 14 is in. Note that we need only read as far as the leaf level of the nonclustered index to determine if the record exists. Every record has an index entry in the leaf level so if there is no entry in the leaf level, the record does not exist.

Again, each level is linked horizontally via a pointer chain, so browsing for a range of values is readily supported. However, there is a considerable difference in the amount of logical accesses between the two types of index when a range of values is required.

To read records 10–20 from the nonclustered index we need to:

- read root node;
- read intermediate index page;
- read three leaf level index pages;
- read eight data pages.

Using the clustered index of Figure C.4, we need to:

- read root node;
- read intermediate level index page;
- read three data pages.

This is already an advantage of eight logical accesses in such a small table, which was emphasized in the optimizer discussion in Chapter 10.

An SQL command that retrieves many records from a table need never do more than read every page in the table; that is, scan the complete table. However, the nonclustered index generates a data page read for every record retrieved and clearly has the potential to try to make more page accesses than there are pages in the table. The SQL Server optimizer does not allow this mistake and will do a table scan. Clearly this effects how indexes are used and which indexes should be clustered.

Let's look in detail at the nonclustered index pointers, as shown in Figure C.8.

The leaf level pointers are record pointers which are 6 bytes + 1 byte overhead.

This is composed of a page pointer plus a row number within the page (see index record discussion in section C.2.2); that is, 4+2 bytes.

The intermediate level and root node pointers need only be page pointers as before for the clustered index but SQL Server adds the record pointer of the first record in the leaf level page pointed to by the intermediate page. So the non-leaf level pointer is 4(page) + 6(record) + 1(overhead) = 11 bytes.

To locate records 10–20, we read page 150—the root node from sysindexes—which tells us that record 10 is in the branch page 200, which tells us that the leaf entry is page 70, which tells us the first record is record 11 at page 30 record 2. We then browse the leaf level reading record 12 at page 100 record 2, record 14 at page 100 record 4, and so on until we get a key value greater than 20 when we stop.

The SQL Server optimizer will not allow us to do this as the total number of data page reads is seven but there are only five pages in the table, so the optimizer would force a table scan. But that's how it locates records via the nonclustered index.

SQL Server allows up to 16 fields in an index, to a maximum of 256 bytes. These fields may be nonconsecutive, noncontiguous in the record; they may come from anywhere in the record, in any sequence. The only thing you cannot do is to put a portion of a field or a calculation into the index.. The index must contain complete, unaltered fields.

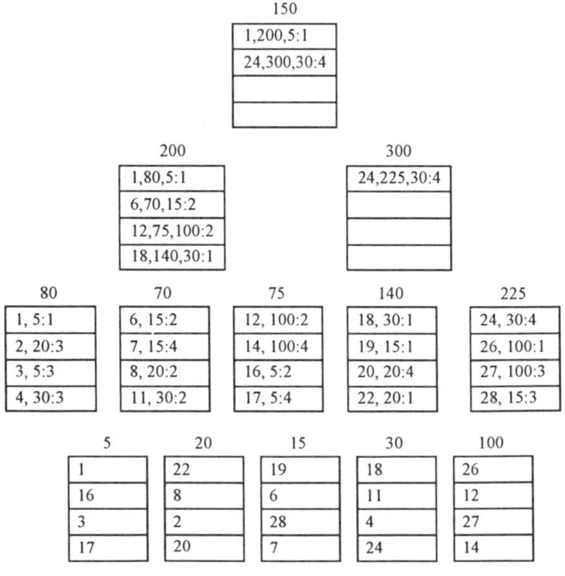

Figure C.8 *Nonclustered index pointer structure.*

C.2 Page and Record Layout

Before we continue with the indexes, it is worth looking at the data and index record layouts and the associated page structures.

The page size is 2 K, with the exception of Stratus which is 4 K, so I shall use 2 K all of the time. SQL Server holds the page value for the installation in spt_values.

There are several types of pages:

1. data page	contains data rows or log rows. Log rows are laid out differently from data rows but the construction of the page is the same.
2. index page	contains index rows.
3. text/image page	contains text/image data.
4. allocation page	contains a set of extent structures used to manage page allocation.
5. statistics page	contains distribution and sensitivity statistics for an index.
6. global allocation map	contains bit settings indicating if there is free space in allocation pages.
7. object allocation map	contains extent information indicating if there is free space in an extent.

C.2.1 Data Page

A data page is composed of three elements, as shown in Figure C.9.

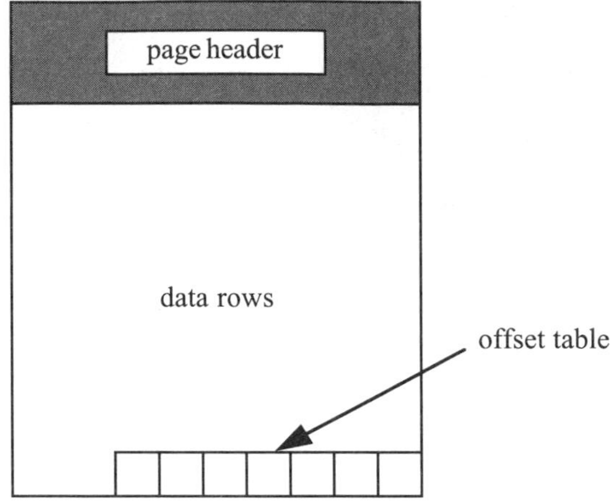

***Figure C.9** Data page layout.*

page header	32 bytes containing (among other information): logical page number; next logical page number; previous logical page number; object_id that page belongs to; next available row number in page; offset of free space; minimum row length;
data rows	an integral number of rows: a data row is not allowed to cross a page boundary;
offset table	a set of offsets from the start of the page giving the location of each row. This set grows backwards from the end of the page.

The data record is laid out as shown in Figure C.10.

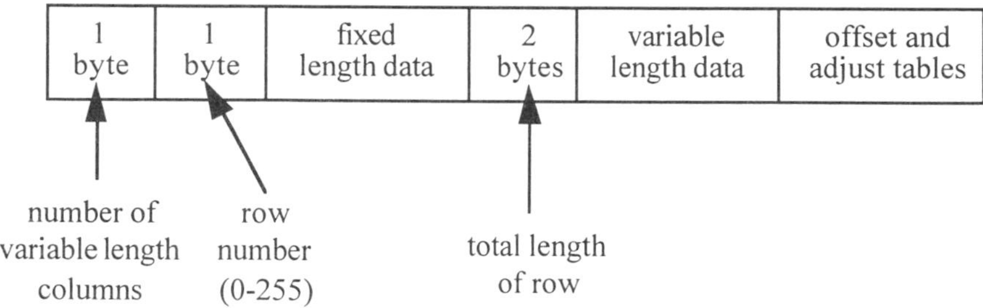

Figure C.10 Data record layout.

Each record in the page is allocated a row number. This is a 1-byte field and has a maximum value of 255, which restricts the number of records in a page to 256. The record_id used in the nonclustered index is a combination of the page number and the row number in the page.

record_id = page_number : row_number

The 2-byte row length allows the record to occupy the full page. Removing the header gives 2,016 bytes, but SQL Server further restricts this on a single record and has a maximum record size of 1,960 bytes. This additional restriction is because the syslogs entry must be contained in a 2 K page and the overhead of the syslogs record restricts the data record to a maximum of 1,960 bytes.

If the records are fixed length, then the first byte is set to zero and the record stops after the data. The table:

```
CREATE TABLE tab_1  ( a  int,  b  char(20))
```

has a record layout as shown in Figure C.11.

There are no variable length fields, a row number of 32 and no record length as it is in the header (minimum record length—they are all the same). The fields are arranged in the record in the same order as they are defined.

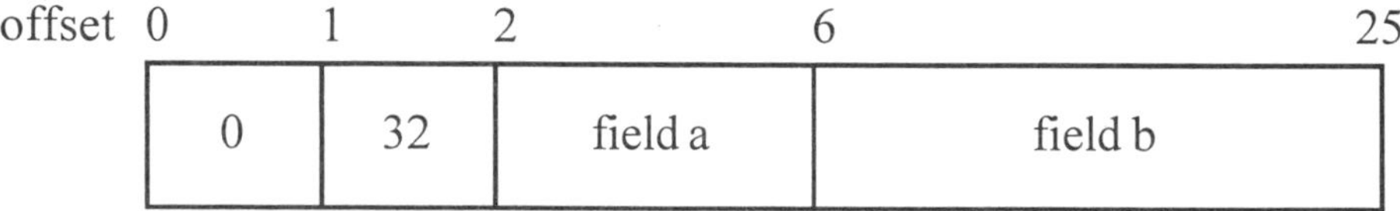

Figure C.11 Fixed length record layout.

If the record is variable length, the fixed and variable fields are separated, regardless of how you have defined them in the table. The table:

```
CREATE TABLE tab_2  (  a int,
                       b varchar(20),
                       c char(30),
                       d varchar(10))
```

has a record layout as shown in Figure C.12.

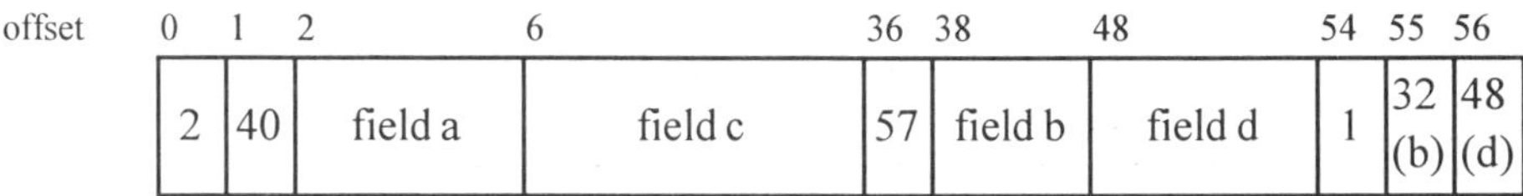

Figure C.12 *Variable length record layout.*

---

two variable fields;
a row number of 40;
fixed length fields in sequence of definition;
record length of 57 bytes;
variable length fields in sequence of definition;
offset table adjust byte;
offset table of variable field locations from start of record.

Each offset in the offset table at the end of the record is the displacement of the start of the field from the start of the record. As the offset is a 1-byte field, the maximum offset value is 255. So a 1-byte adjust field points to additional sets of offsets for each 256 bytes.

Searching for a record based on the record_id is done by a binary search on the offset table at the end of the page that contains the displacement of the record from the start of the page.

Locating record 9 in a page of records is done by searching on the offset table, as shown in Figure C.13. The record number is then the entry in the offset table that contains the location of the record.

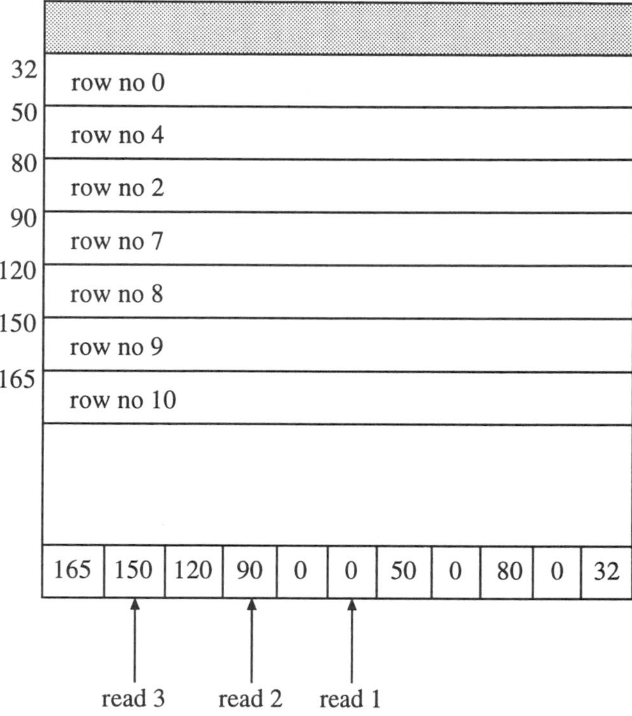

Figure C.13 *Offset table binary search.*

The zero offset for row 1 means that the record has been deleted. The next insertion to this page will reuse row number 1, although the record itself is added to the end of the data in the page.

When records are deleted, the records in the page are moved up to keep the free space at the end of the page. New records are added to the end of the records in the page, ensuring no space fragmentation within a page.

If the record update is done in place as a deletion followed by an insertion, there is the chance that the record ID will change as the deletion sets the offset entry to zero and then the insert reuses the first zero offset entry in the offset table, which may not be the original one.

Deletion of row 1 in Figure C.14 moves row 2 up to take up the free space, changing the offset value of row 2 and setting row 1 offset to zero.

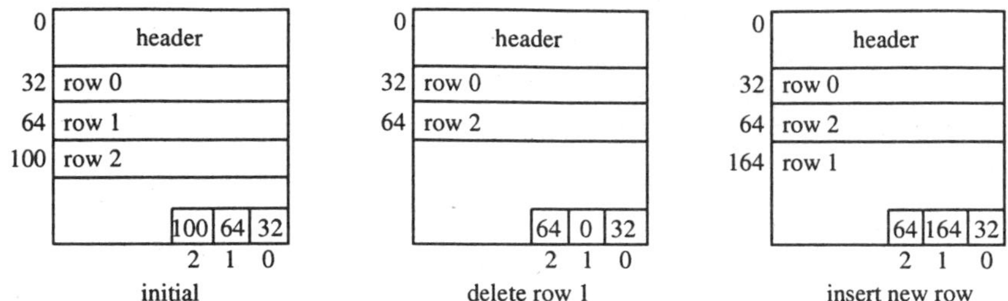

Figure C.14 *Variable row deletion and insertion.*

Addition of a new record to the page uses row 1, so in an active table it is more than likely that the rows will not be in sequence of the row number in the page. This is the internal row number of the record in the page, not the real key to the record. If our example were keyed on name, the actual records could be as in Figure C.15.

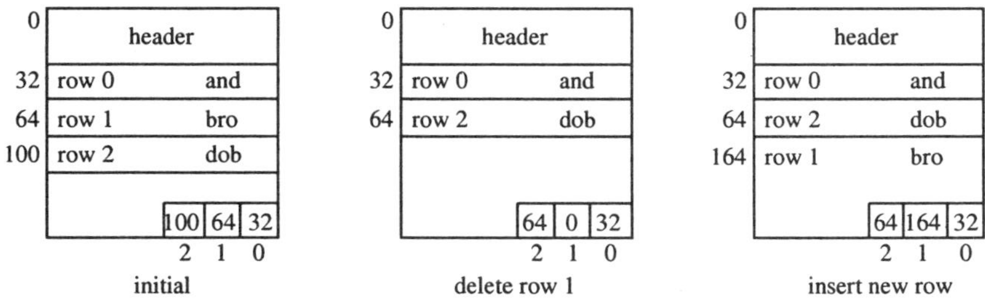

Figure C.15 *Key values versus row number.*

SQL Server updates are often done as deletion followed by insertion, which means that an update can quite easily result in a change to the row number of the record. We were lucky in this example, but take Figure C.16 and update row 2.

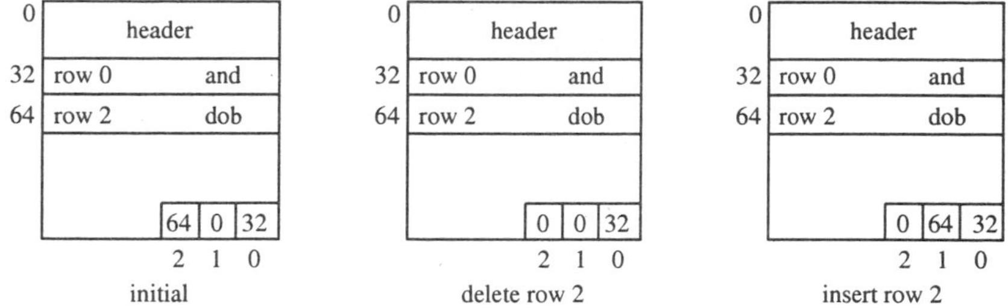

Figure C.16 *Reassigning record ID.*

After deletion, the first available row number for the insertion will be row 1. Nobody else can use row 1 as the update has the page locked. This is extremely important as the row number is part of the record_id. Therefore, any update to a record that changes the record ID has to delete and reinsert all nonclustered index entries for the record. The only exception to this is when the update is done in place in the page, as the row number does not change and the index entries are not updated. The rules for this are rather restrictive and are covered in detail in section C.4.2 later.

Any field that allows null is considered to be variable length and therefore the record is considered to be variable length. Consequently, only tables that have all fixed length, non-null fields are held as fixed length records. There are not many of these around and they usually tend to be static look-up tables that are not subject to any significant update anyway.

C.2.2 Index Page

Index pages have two components, as shown in Figure C.17.

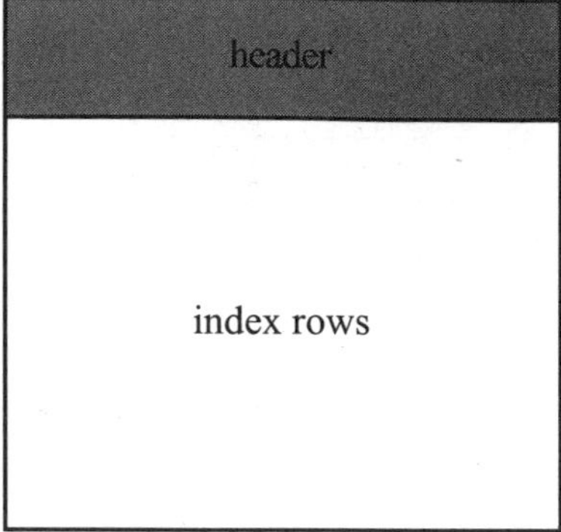

Figure C.17 *Index page.*

header	32 bytes containing (among other information): logical page number; next logical page number; previous logical page number; object_id that the page belongs to; index_id that the page belongs to; offset of free space; minimum row length on page; offset of last row in page; index level;
index rows	key value and pointer combinations.

Index rows have no row number in the page so there is no offset table at the end of the page. Because there is no row number, the index rows are located by different search algorithms than the data rows.

The index row layout is basically the same as the data row layout except that it does not have a row number and contains a page pointer to the next level of index and/or a record pointer to the record in the page. The actual structure depends on the type of index page.

Clustered Index Row

This contains a page pointer of 4 bytes, as in Figure C.18.

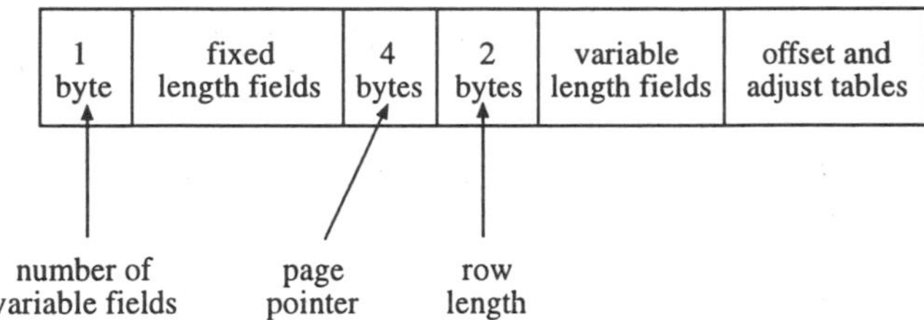

Figure C.18 *Clustered index row structure.*

Again, if the index field(s) are fixed length, the index row has less overhead and is easier to process than variable length index rows.

The table and indexes:

```
CREATE TABLE tab_1
            ( a int,
              b int,
              c varchar(20),
              d char(10),
              e varchar(20))
CREATE CLUSTERED INDEX ind_1 on tab_1(a, d)
CREATE CLUSTERED INDEX ind_2 on tab_1(e, b)
```

have index rows as in figures C.19 and C.20. (Remember that you cannot have two clustered indexes on a table—this is only for illustration of the row layout.)

0	1	5	15 18
0	field a	field d	400

Figure C.19 *Fixed length clustered index row.*

0	1	5	9	11	26	27
1	field b	1240	28	field c	1	11 (c)

Figure C.20 *Variable length clustered index row.*

The overhead of the clustered index when the fields are fixed length is 5 bytes.

The overhead of the clustered index row when a field is variable length is 8 bytes + 1 byte per variable field. There is only the one adjust field as you cannot create index entries greater than 256 bytes.

Nonclustered Leaf Row

The nonclustered leaf row contains a record_id instead of the logical page number as it points to the individual record.

Using the previous table and defining the same fields as nonclustered indexes, we now have the two row layouts shown in figures C.21 and C.22.

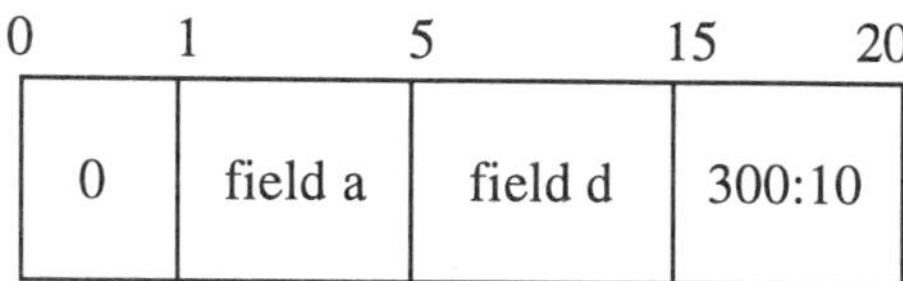

Figure C.21 *Fixed length nonclustered leaf row.*

0 1 5 11 15 28 29

1	field b	350:9	30	field e	1	13 (e)

Figure C.22 *Variable length nonclustered leaf row.*

The overhead of the nonclustered leaf row when the fields are fixed length is 7 bytes. The overhead of the nonclustered leaf row when a field is variable length is 10 bytes + 1 byte per variable field.

Nonclustered Non-Leaf Row

The nonclustered non-leaf row contains both a logical page number and a record_id. The record_id is for the first record of the node that the index page is pointing to. So the nonclustered non-leaf rows look like figures C.23 and C.24.

0 1 5 15 21 24

0	field a	field d	100:12	401

Figure C.23 *Fixed length nonclustered non-leaf row.*

0	1	5	11	15	17	32	33
1	field b	1234525	658	34	field e	1	13 (e)

Figure C.24 *Variable length nonclustered non-leaf row.*

The overhead of the nonclustered non-leaf row when the fields are fixed length is 11 bytes.

The overhead of the nonclustered non-leaf row when a field is variable length is 14 bytes + 1 byte per variable field.

In summary, the index entry overheads on the key length are:

	fixed	variable
clustered	5	$8 + n$
nonclustered leaf	7	$10 + n$
nonclustered non-leaf	11	$14 + n$

where n is the number of variable length fields in the index.

(I normally ignore most of this detail and use 10 bytes overhead for any index entry. The percentage error on variable length fields or number of records usually swamps any error on index size by using 10 bytes overhead all of the time.)

C.2.3 Allocation Page

Allocation pages contain four components, as shown in Figure C.25.

header
reserved 1
extents
unused
reserved 2

Figure C.25 *Allocation page.*

header	32-byte page header for compatibility but little of it used; logical page number; database_id of allocation;
reserved_1	a 16-byte reserved area;
extents	32 extent structures, each of 16 bytes, that control page allocation. Each extent controls eight pages so an allocation page controls 256 pages;
reserved_2	a 32-byte reserved area.

The allocation page is at the start of a 256-block of pages called an allocation unit. The allocation page controls the following 255 pages in the allocation unit, as shown in Figure C.26.

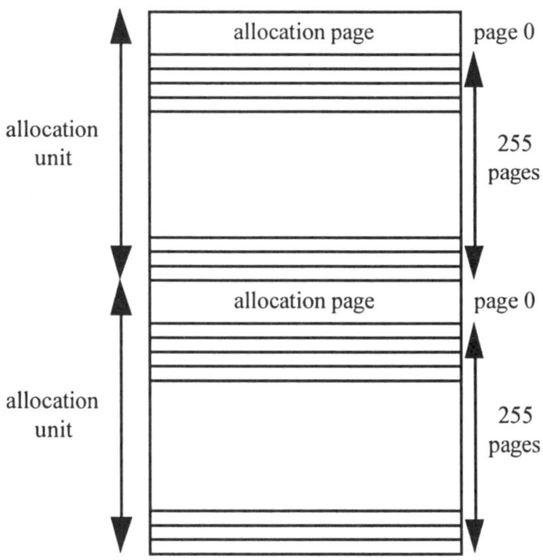

Figure C.26 *Allocation unit.*

The page numbers are logical numbers starting at zero, so allocation units are multiples of 256 pages. The physical pages are not necessarily contiguous. They may be contiguous at the start with an empty disk but once you start using the disk and adding extra space to the database, you should never assume that free space is allocated contiguously (unless you ask for it in VMS).

The logical database pages start at 0 and are in units of 256 pages, the first being the controlling page. Allocation pages control physical pages, which are mapped to user databases in a possibly noncontiguous manner. Therefore, the logical page numbers in a user database will probably not map to physically contiguous pages.

The pages in the database are controlled by the extent structures in the allocation page. Each extent structure is a 16-byte structure containing:

```
extent
            next extent_id in chain;
            previous extent_id in chain;
            object_id;
            allocation bit map;
            deallocation bit map;
            index_id;
            status.
```

The allocation bit map is 1 byte with each bit setting representing the allocation status of one of eight pages, as shown in Figure C.27.

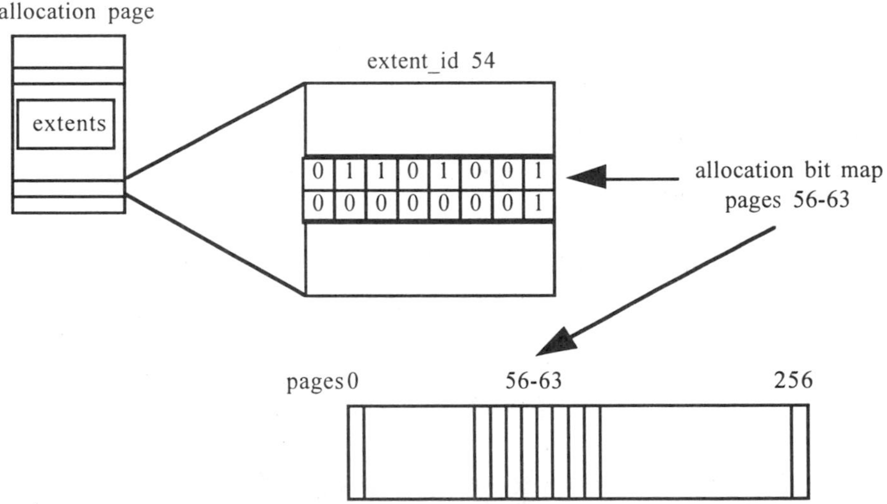

Figure C.27 *Extent structure.*

If the bit is on in the allocation bit map, the page is allocated to an object. If the bit is off, the page is reserved for the object but not currently in use.

The deallocation bit map indicates those pages that have been identified for deallocation during a transaction; that is, they have become empty and are no longer currently needed. As with any update, the deallocation is not carried out until the commit at the end of the transaction. The deallocation bit map registers which pages have to be deallocated at the end of the transaction to prevent them being allocated by another transaction before the original transaction is complete (i.e. an allocation lock).

So database space is allocated as an allocation unit of 256 pages (i.e. 512 K) and the database object space is allocated in extents of eight pages (i.e. 16 K).

Allocating space to records goes through the algorithm:

- use current page if sufficient space;
- use free page in current extent;
- get new extent from current allocation page;
- search allocation pages for object by following extent chain;
- allocate new extent from next allocation page.

The speed of the allocation pages search is increased by the Global Allocation Map (GAM), which has a bit setting for each allocation page of 0: free space, 1: no free space.

Extent allocation is assisted by the Object Allocation Map (OAM), which contains the page_id of each allocation page used by an object and an indication of any free extent space. When a new allocation page is required for an extent allocation, the OAM is checked for free space in the last entry. The OAM entries are held in sysindexes.

C.2.4 Index Statistics Page

The statistics of an index that are used by the optimizer are stored in a single page called the statistics page, which has a 32-byte header for compatibility and the rest available to store index field values. Each entry in the page is an index key value so the number of entries is:

number of distribution entries (n) = page size ÷ key size

The table is sampled *n* times and the value of the index key at each *n*th position is then recorded in the statistics page. This sampling and the use of the statistics by the optimizer is covered in detail in Chapter 10.

The index statistics page also contains a sensitivity figure, called the density, which is the percentage of duplicate values in the index. This is used in joins to estimate the number of records per join value, as explained in Chapter 10.

C.2.5 Text/Image Page

SQL Server has two datatypes—text and image—that permit the data record to hold a field larger than the page size record limit. Normal character-based datatypes are limited to 255 characters but text allows any size of variable length character string up to 2 GB. (Image is simply a binary equivalent of text.)

This is achieved in a standard fashion by holding the text/image data in a separate chain of pages linked to the data record. So the data record contains a 16-byte pointer to a set of 2 K pages containing the text or image, as in Figure C.28.

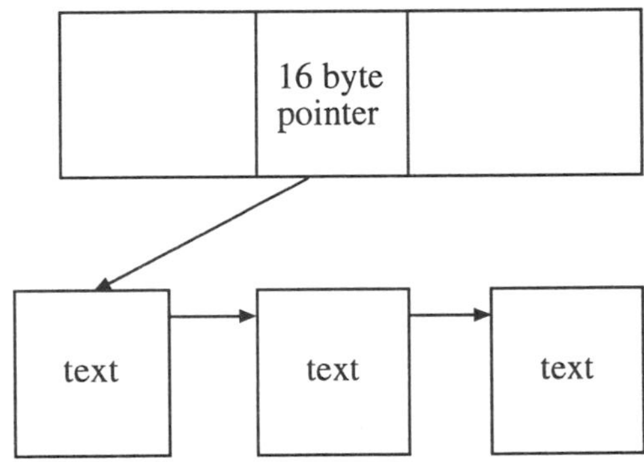

Figure C.28 *Text/image pages.*

The text/image page is a standard data page with a 32-byte header and no offset table at the end. So the minimum size of a text/image field is one page (2 K or 2,016 bytes to be more precise).

Select from such a field is quite efficient as the pages are linked together, so once the data record is located, there are embedded pointers to follow to retrieve the text (i.e. no further index accesses). However, update is horrendous as it is a SQL Server update of delete followed by insert. So to update 4 bytes of a 12 K text field, the six pages must be deleted and the new six pages inserted.

Try not to update text/image fields.

C.3 Buffer Cache Management

When a disk page is cached, it shares cache with all pages from all databases in the server. Each disk page in cache is identified via a hash key based on the database_id and the logical page number. As the logical page number is unique within a database, this uniquely identifies each page in cache. As with any hashing access method, collisions will occur mainly because the available cache will be smaller than the total number of database pages that need to be cached. So there will be an overflow situation where each hash result has several disk pages linked to it. When a disk page is requested, the hash table is checked to see if it is in cache. The number of hash buckets is calculated based on the size of cache so that a hash bucket has no more than two cache pages linked to it.

Each page in cache has a corresponding buffer controlling its stay in cache. The buffers are part of a doubly linked chain: a least recently used (LRU) chain and a most recently used (MRU) chain. When a new page needs to use cache, a free buffer is obtained from the LRU chain to manage it. The buffer is linked into the MRU chain so that pages which are referenced frequently tend to remain in cache.

Clearly, index pages are likely to be accessed more often than the data pages (there are more index rows in an index page than data rows in a data page) so it is useful if the index pages stay longer in cache than the data pages. One would expect the higher access rate of the index pages to automatically keep them in cache longer than the data pages. However, this is balanced by the fact that the data page will be the last page accessed and so the MRU chain is more likely to contain data pages. SQL Server caters for this by ageing the index pages more slowly than the data pages to try to keep them in cache longer than the data pages. (Chapter 12 has a detailed description of pages aging past the wash marker.)

Finally, when a page is modified, the buffer is linked to a "dirty" buffer chain. There is one dirty buffer chain for each object and they are used by the checkpoint routine to assist it in finding all the used pages quickly.

So, under control of the buffer, each page is in:

- a least-used chain and a most-used chain; the page is always in these chains;
- a hash table if the cache page is being used by a disk page;
- a dirty page chain for the object if the page has been updated but not written to disk.

C.4 Index Processing

Now that we know how everything is stored in the pages, let's have a detailed look at what happens when we maintain records in tables—insert/update/delete—and the processing required by the various index combinations. We shall look at no index, non-clustered and clustered combinations.

C.4.1 No Index

This is standard heap storage where there are no indexes to impose a layout on the data and the data records are simply heaped onto the end of the table. The last logical page number of the table is held in sysindexes and all new records are placed in this page until there is no room left, when a new page is obtained from the existing allocation or a new extent is requested from free space. Figure C.29 illustrates this.

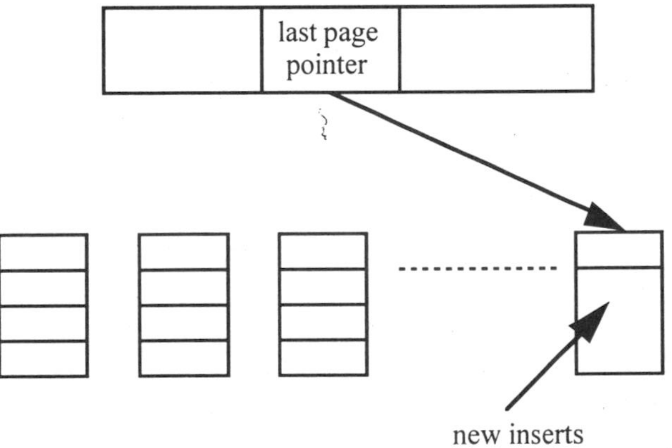

Figure C.29 *Heap storage.*

This is the fastest method of adding new records to a table as there is no index overhead. However, in a multiuser environment there will be considerable contention for the last page, so if you have an audit style table and decide not to index it, be careful of the locking (page level) contention on the last page. You can reduce last page contention in System 11 by partitioning the heap table so that the table has one "last page" per partition. This splits the heap table into multiple partitions, as demonstrated in Figure C.30.

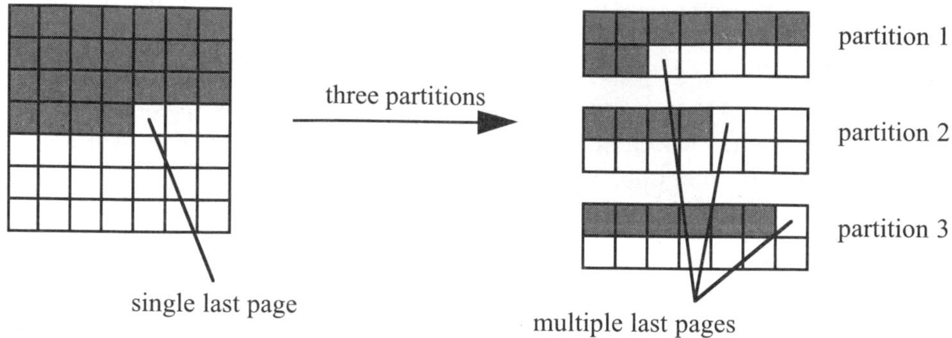

Figure C.30 *Partitioning a heap table.*

This now looks like several heap tables each with a last page, which reduces insert contention. Partitioning is explained in detail in Chapter 12.

If all you are doing is bulk loading records into a table, heap is the optimum method of storage for the load and you should use fast bulk copy (bcp) to load the records. Do not have the indexes or triggers on when building a table. If you don't believe me, try it. It will take several seconds per record; that is, in the order of one hour per thousand records. Yes, it is a long time. Create the table as heap, load the table with bcp and then build the indexes and check integrity. (There is a case for presorting the data into the clustered index sequence and loading it with the clustered index already created. You will have to balance the cost of the record sort against the clustered index build on this one. However, it is only valid when the table has no other indexes. The clustered index will require an update statistics to be run, so make sure you compare like with like.)

So use the no index heap structure for fast insertion—checking the overhead of last page contention. But what about update and delete? There isn't a thing to do without an index unless the table is small—three pages or fewer. With three or fewer pages, the disk activity with an index and the disk activity to read the whole table are about the same, so an index is not essential for such small tables. (This is a disk access argument only. If you need to enforce uniqueness—primary key or unique clause in the create table—then an index is automatically established by SQL Server. Be careful.)

However, for large tables without an index, a full table scan is required to read one record. Because there is no sequence to the data and/or no index with entries in sequence, the server does not know when to stop. Even if you are looking for record 1 and it is the first record in the table, there is nothing to tell you that it is the only record

1 in the table or that, even if the next record is record 2, that there is not another record 1 in the table. In the absence of data or index sequence, the server has to read the complete table to locate the required record. This is unacceptable for almost every application and therefore an index is created on a suitable key field or fields.

C.4.2 Nonclustered Only

The first logical step from the no index heap structure is to leave the data untouched in the heap structure and create an index onto the data records. This applies only when there is no clustered index on the table; that is, when all indexes are nonclustered.

This gives the dense B-tree structure of Figure C.7, with the data still as heap storage and a dense B-tree index built on this with every data record having an index record_id pointer in the leaf level. If the heap storage is partitioned, the index is still a separate object and is not effected by the partitioning.

To insert a record (say 5) as in Figure C.31, it is placed on the end of the table or appropriate partition (in this case, a new page) and a record_id pointer is added to the leaf level node.

In this example, there has not been enough room in the leaf node so it has split into two to accommodate the new index entry and still maintain the sequence. As there is now a new leaf node, it requires a new entry at the intermediate level, where again there is no room so the node splitting continues until the new index entries can be accommodated in an existing index page—in this case, at the root node.

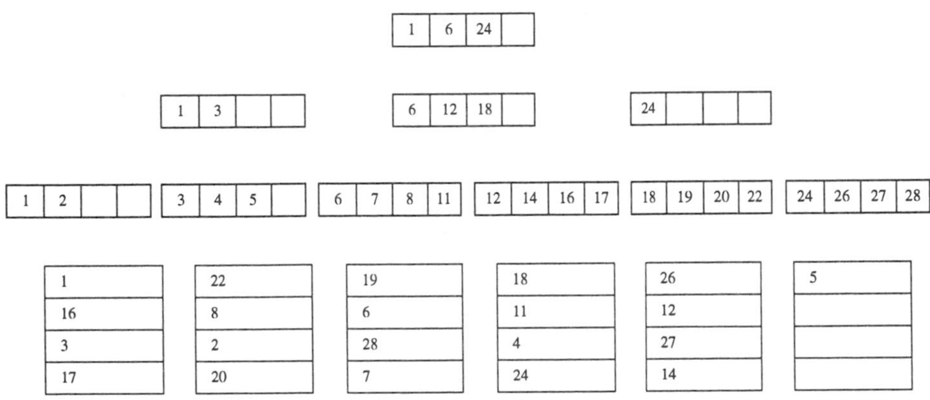

Figure C.31 *Insert record 5 to nonclustered index.*

This node splitting is clearly a significant overhead if it occurs frequently. Therefore, it should be minimized by not filling the initial index pages to capacity but leaving some free space for index growth. This is done by applying a fillfactor to the index pages. This is the percentage full that the pages will be created to. The fillfactor is set as a system-wide value by sp_configure or for an individual index in the create index command.

```
CREATE INDEX ind_1 ON tab_1(col_1)
            WITH FILLFACTOR = 75
```

When the index is created, this fillfactor is adhered to, as shown in Figure C.30. The data pages are not disturbed and they remain 100% packed as in any heap structure.

This now gives us space in the index pages for table growth and an insert of record 5 no longer causes node splitting. If we had a 10-byte key, the leaf level overhead is 7 bytes, which gives 110 index records per page. So a 75% fillfactor will give room for 28 records per page, which simply allows us 25% growth (reasonably distributed throughout the key range) before we hit any significant node splitting. Of course, it is dependent on the allocation of key values but not an unreasonable assumption.

If your nonclustered table has a large insert rate, always use a reasonable fill-factor to minimize node splitting. Deletion from a nonclustered table is simple. The record is located via the index, deleted from the page and the corresponding index entry is deleted. Because the non-leaf index entries also contain record pointers to the first record in each lower level of the index, if you delete the record pointed to by non-leaf index entries, you can propagate the delete all the way to the top of the B-tree structure as updates of the record pointer in the non-leaf index entries.

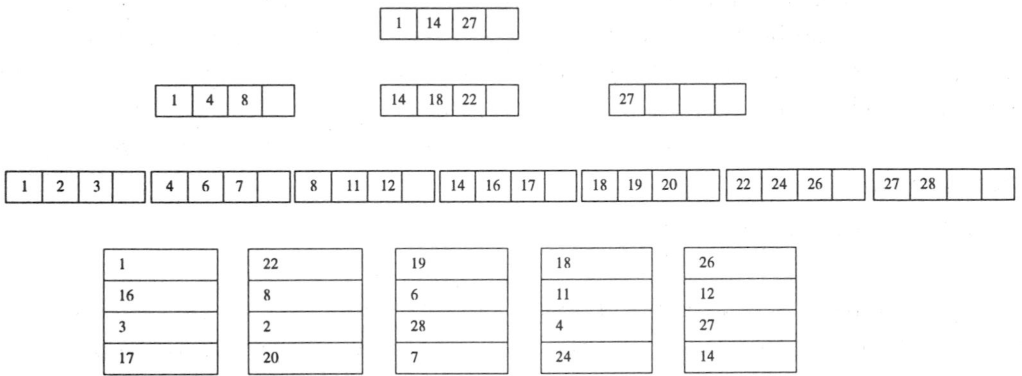

***Figure C.32** Nonclustered with fillfactor.*

However, the update in SQL Server nonclustering is a totally different matter.

When considering the overhead of updates, you should also consider whether the update is direct or deferred. A direct update is when the data is changed when the update command is issued. A deferred update is when the data is not changed until the end of the transaction at the commit. The deferred update is an additional overhead as it is actioned in the steps:

1. read the records for update and write the row IDs to the log when the update command is issued;
2. at the commit, reread the log and sort/merge the row IDs to eliminate any duplicates;
3. use the row IDs to access and update the records.

The sort/merge step is necessary as deferred updating is used for update statements that contain joins and the join stage may generate duplicate row IDs.

The update processing in SQL Server has been continuously improved over the major releases. To emphasize these changes, I have listed the conditions for System 10 and 11 together. Chapter 12 gives a more detailed of the System 11 update processing.

Direct Update In Place

This is actioned when the update command is issued and alters the data in the page directly. This requires the following conditions to be met.

In both System 10 and System 11:

- the table must not have an update trigger;
- the update statement must not contain a join;
- the table must not be replicated.

Specific to System 11:

- the length of the row must not change;
- the column being updated must not be part of a clustered index;
- the column being updated must not be involved in referential integrity.

Specific to System 10:

- the field being updated must be fixed length;
- the field being updated must be non null;
- the field being updated must not be part of an index used to locate the record;
- less than half of the record is updated;
- less than three noncontiguous columns are updated and the columns are not separated by more than 8 bytes;
- the optimizer is able to determine the number of rows effected at compilation time.

Direct Update Not In Place

This is actioned when the update command is issued but actioned as a deletion followed by an insertion. It may cause all of the nonclustered index entries to be changed —as a deletion followed by an insertion—if the row ID changes.

This requires the previous conditions with the exception that triggers and replication are allowed. These two require the deleted and inserted tables to be formed and therefore the update must be done as a delete followed by an insert.

The important difference in System 11 is that the row is put back into the current page as long as there is room for it. This is called a **cheap direct update**. If there is no room, the update actions as the System 10 update by inserting the record as if it was a new record. This is called an **expensive direct update** in System 11. Of course, if the table has a clustered index, the record will be inserted back into the same page, although it may now cause a page split.

Deferred Update

This is actioned at the commit as a deletion followed by an insertion and may cause all of the nonclustered index entries to be changed if the row ID changes.

This will occur under the following conditions:

- the update statement contains a join;
- when the optimizer cannot determine the number of rows effected at compilation time;

with the additional restrictions in System 10 of:

- the field being updated is variable length;
- the field being updated allows nulls.

In System 10, one or more of the conditions for update in place is difficult to achieve, so you should always assume that the record will not be updated in place (unless you have gone to great lengths to ensure that it is). This is less of a problem in System 11 and it is reasonable to consider occasions when update in place will occur. When update in place does not happen in the nonclustered table, the record is deleted from its current page and inserted at the end of the table. This means that the record_id of the record changes—it is made up of the logical page number and the row number in the page—which means that all nonclustered index entries for that record must be updated.

This is a significant overhead, so take great care of update overhead when a table has several indexes. It can be very high.

C.4.3 Clustered

If the table has only the one index, the index overhead is less if we have a clustered index. In this case, the data is in sequence of the index key field, as in Figure C.4. Now when we insert record 5, it must go into the first page because, according to the existing index structure, this page must contain all records from 1 up to, but not including, 6. However, there is no room for record 5 so we have to split the data page into two pages, as shown in Figure C.33.

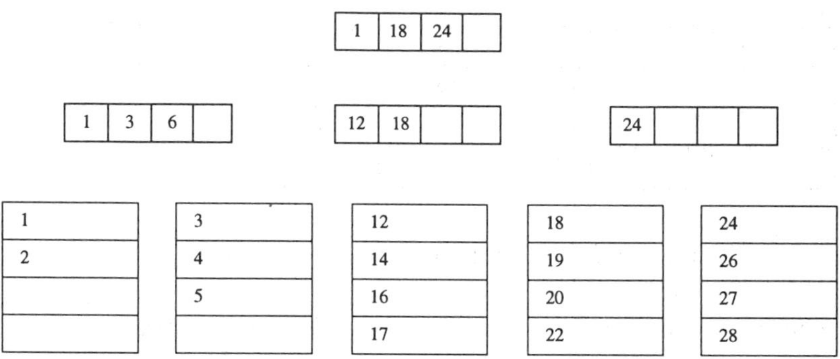

***Figure C.33** Clustered B-tree page split.*

We now have a new data page that has to be indexed at the first intermediate level. But since there is no room, the node splitting continues until enough space is available to accept the new index pointer—the root node in this case. (If there was no room in the root node this would split, creating a new level.)

Again, this node splitting can be minimized by a fillfactor that allows free space for expansion in each page. However, as the data is the leaf level of the clustered index, the fillfactor is applied to the data pages as well as the index pages. This will increase the size of the table, which causes all multirecord retrievals to be slower. A 75% fillfactor increases the clustered data by 25%, which increases all range enquiries by 25%. This is not to be ignored but normally the processing savings on insert/update are sufficient to justify it.

The clustered index with 75% fillfactor looks like Figure C.34.

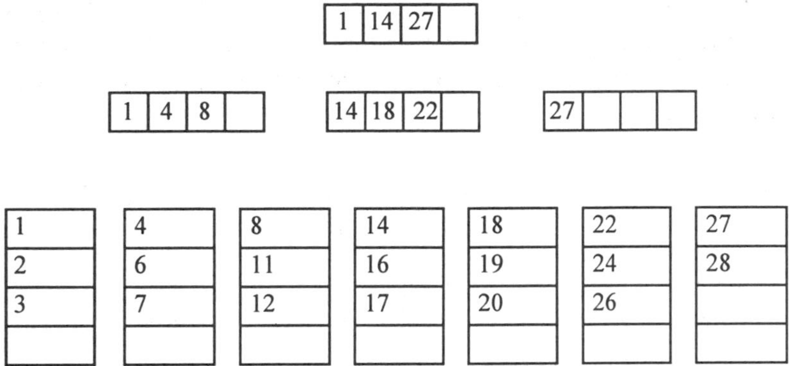

Figure C.34 *Clustered B-tree with fillfactor.*

We can now insert another 25% of the table before we need to update any index. Even then the intermediate index node will not split until we have generated enough data page splits to fill the index page. This takes a high activity rate and clustered with a fillfactor is strongly advisable. But be careful of the increase in range retrieval.

Record deletions have little effect on the clustered index. There is no need to delete the index entries unless you delete the first record in a page.

Update to the clustered index is again actioned by delete followed by insert. As long as the data page does not split, any activity is contained in the data page level with no clustered index activity. However, again you need to be very careful with SQL Server updates when the table has both clustered and nonclustered indexes. An update in place is no problem as the record ID does not change, so no index updates are necessary. However, an update out of place, although it places the record back in the same page, can still alter the record ID by assigning a new offset entry to the insert phase of the update. When this happens, the nonclustered indexes will have to be updated. It requires a reasonable deletion and insertion activity for this to happen frequently but it can.

C.5 Page Splitting

Having emphasized that it should be avoided with a reasonable choice of fillfactor, let's look at how the page splits.

Index pages always split 50:50 and data pages normally split 50:50.

The split is based on number of records. If this gives an uneven space split so that one page is almost full, the split may continue to a third page, as shown in Figure E.35. Notice that the 50:50 split is migrating the table/index towards a 75% full page on average; 100:0 when full, 50:50 when split, with an equal probability of every percentage in between. So it is worth starting at 75% with the system-wide fillfactor set by sp_configure. If sufficiently active, the table/index will migrate to 75% full pages, so why not start there so that range-based enquiries do not vary as the fillfactor settles down. Of course, if you have a very low activity table or a very high insert rate, override the system setting with an individual setting in create index.

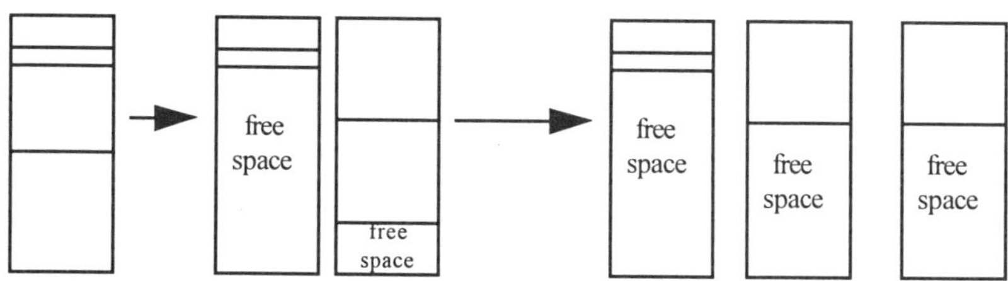

Figure C.35 *Three-way split.*

There are two exceptions to the data page usually split 50:50, index pages always split 50:50 rule:

1. monotonic data;
2. duplicate data.

In these cases, the page splits 100:0 to give an empty page for the new record. This is only on inserts of course. An update that causes a data page split will always split 50:50.

C.5.1 Monotonic Data

Monotonic data is defined as data with a regularly increasing key such as 1, 2, 3, 4.... The increase does not need to be serial and a date/time key also qualifies, as does 1, 3, 6, 7..... Such a key will be filling pages from top to bottom as if the structure was a heap structure with the next key being greater than the previous one, so going into the last page of the table. The server tries to recognize this and doesn't split 50:50. If it did split 50:50, the empty space would never be used except by updates. Instead, it splits 100:0 by allocating a new, empty page for the monotonic growth.

SQL Server does this if the new record is being added to the foot of the page and the last addition was also to the foot of the page. I have no details on how SQL Server determines this.

Of course, SQL Server will get it wrong sometimes. But getting it wrong is not going to increase the incidence of page splitting, just delay it to the next record which hits the page left 100% full. In fact, it may reduce the incidence slightly as almost-empty pages will appear occasionally instead of being half-full after a 50:50 split.

C.5.2 Duplicate Keys

The other occasion of a 100:0 split is when a duplicate key is added. Again, SQL Server detects this if the new record is being added at the end of the page and the last record was added at the end of the page and was for the same key value. In this case, SQL Server again splits 100:0 but it is different from the monotonic split as the new page is reserved for the duplicate key value.

In the monotonic case, the table continued to grow into the new page, making maximum use of the free space in the new page regardless of the key values. In the duplicate case, the new page is reserved for the one key value which caused the split.

In the duplicate case, it is not really a page split but a page overflow with the new page being linked to the original page as in Figure C.36.

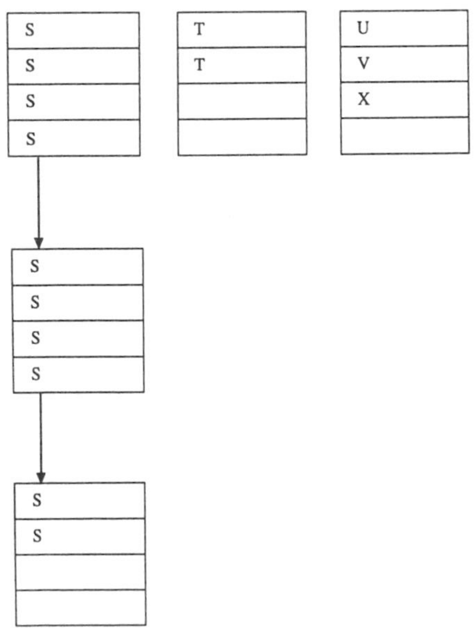

Figure C.36 *Duplicate overflow.*

To add a new record of key "S" the index points to the original page and then the two overflow pages are scanned to locate the free space for the new record.

This suffers all of the problems of overflow chains when being processed, the principal one being that to locate a specific record, the average scan time is half the number of pages in the overflow chain. So be careful if you cluster on a key field that contains replicates. It is fast for retrieval but you may see the updates hesitate occasionally when they happen to hit a long chain of duplicate values.

C.6 Fragmentation

Deletes from a table always leave holes of free space throughout the table. SQL Server shuffles the records in a page to ensure that the free space is at the end of each page, but if the key does not cause random insert hits on the pages, this free space per page will be largely unused.

In a heap table, free space in a page is never reused. All inserts to a heap structure are always at the end of the table, so any deletes throughout the table leave free space that is unused.

In a clustered table, the free space is reused as long as the key is chosen so that new records are inserted throughout the table and not concentrated on a group of pages or at the end of the table, as in monotonic data.

However, you must always be aware that there will be an element of free space throughout the table, especially within the pages.

When a data page is completely emptied, it is not returned to free space but is still part of the allocation to the table as it is still part of an eight-page extent. It is simply marked as deallocated by the extent structure bit map but still reserved for the table. SQL Server does not return pages to free space until a complete extent of eight pages is deallocated. Therefore, when a request is made for a new data page, SQL Server will allocate one of the deallocated extent pages that it has currently reserved for the table. Not until there are no deallocated extent pages will SQL Server request another extent from free space.

Index page maintenance is as for data page maintenance with one exception. When a transaction is traversing the index and it comes across an index page containing one index entry, it will merge that index entry with an adjacent index page on the same level and delete the now empty page.

Note that SQL Server does not initialize pages when they are returned to free space; they are initialized when retrieved from free space. So an insert/update that requires a new extent will need to wait while SQL Server initializes the eight pages.

C.7 Summary

Most of the Unix relational databases are on par when it comes to facilities and performance. Sybase addressed themselves to a performance-based, client/server architecture to provide a tangible difference to the other products. Such features as stored procedures and sparse B-tree indexing were new features aimed at performance, the former only now being achieved by Sybase's rivals and the latter still being unique.

APPENDIX D

Multiuser Considerations:

Concurrency and Memory Size

This Appendix describes the SQL Server approach to the important aspects of a multiuser environment, such as concurrency and locking and the allocation of memory.

System 11 has made several changes to the locking strategies, such as isolation level 0, and configurable lock escalation settings. These are included here but are also dealt with individually in Chapter 12.

COMMAND SYNTAX

None.

SYSTEM PROCEDURE SYNTAX

```
sp_lock
sp_configure
sp_setpglockpromote
```

D.1 Locking

SQL Server's strategy on locking and concurrency is probably its weakest, and is, paradoxically, potentially its strongest feature. SQL Server locks at the page level and waits for contention on resources to go away. There are two resolutions to contention: the requesting transaction rolls back when it is encountered or the requesting transaction waits for the contention to be released. The waiting strategy adopted by SQL Server causes several processing overheads in dealing with the queues that can build up and in resolving deadlocked transactions because transactions waiting for a locked resource may also have other resources locked.

SQL Server default locking does not support the ANSI standard locking strategy of the SLOCK being retained until escalated to an XLOCK or until the transaction completes at the commit or rollback. SQL Server retains the SLOCK on the page only for as long as the page is being read and then the SLOCK is released. System 10 also supports ANSI standard locking, which is discussed in section 8.2. System 11 has introduced isolation level 0 or "dirty read" locking, which is discussed in section 2.6.

In my opinion, the SQL Server type of optimistic locking strategy is essential in the client/server environment and gives SQL Server a significant advantage over its rivals. Fortunately, I believe that the client/server advantages far outweigh the page level disadvantage. However, a move towards record level locking would remove a performance bottleneck from the architecture.

D.2 Server Locking Strategy

There are two standard types of lock:

1. shared lock (SLOCK)	a multiuser lock that allows any number of concurrent read accesses to a page;
2. exclusive lock(XLOCK)	a single-user lock that allows only one maintenance access to a page.

Shared and exclusive locks are not allowed on a page at the same time and block each other.

SQL Server has a third lock, an update lock (ULOCK), which is issued at the start of a maintenance command to see if there is any contention. The ULOCK is escalated into an XLOCK when the changes are applied to the affected changes. If there is contention, the ULOCK remains but it allows readers issuing SLOCKs to access the data.

D.2.1 Isolation Level 1

Locking isolation level 1 prevents dirty reads so that one transaction may not read a row that is being changed until the change is complete; that is, committed or rolled back. This is the SQL Server default locking strategy and is illustrated in Figure D.1.

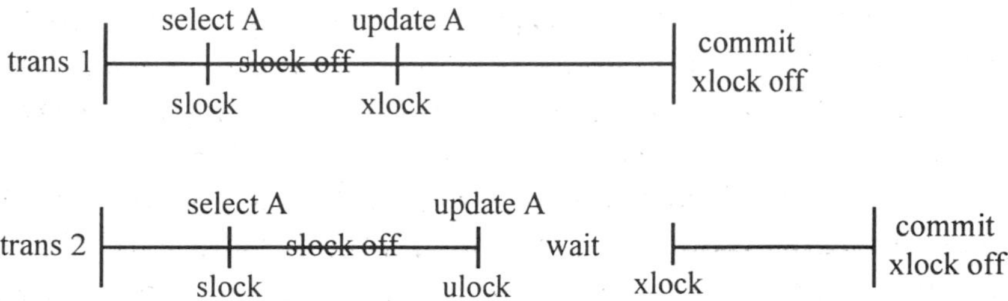

Figure D.1 *SQL Server locking strategy.*

The multireader SLOCK is set when the record is read. This prevents a read of an XLOCKed page. The SLOCK is set off as soon as the page has been read. When the transaction issues an update, a single- user XLOCK is set and retained until the end of the transaction to ensure that no other transaction can access the data until the end of the transaction. The update lock (ULOCK) has not been shown. It is issued as the first stage of the XLOCK to check if there is any contention before taking the XLOCK. If contention does exist and the transaction has to wait, it is the ULOCK that waits until the resource is free and is then escalated to an XLOCK.

Isolation level 1 may be set explicitly using the set command:

```
set transaction isolation level 1
```

This is necessary only to reset it back from another explicit setting such as isolation level 3.

D.2.2 Isolation Level 2

The above locking strategy solves the standard isolation level 1 concurrency problems. There are no lost updates by XLOCKing pages, which ensures that data cannot be corrupted by multiple, concurrent updates. Also, there is no uncommitted dependency by retaining the XLOCK until the transaction commits, which ensures that reads are not allowed while data is in a state of change during the update.

With isolation level 1, each record is guaranteed to be in a consistent state while it is being read. However, a transaction which reads many records may have to guarantee that all of the records read remain at the same state throughout the transaction. This means that the content of a record does not change until the transaction is complete. This is locking isolation level 2, which prevents nonrepeatable reads so that, if the read transaction rereads the records, the data values have not been changed by another transaction.

Figure D.2 illustrates an example of this problem.

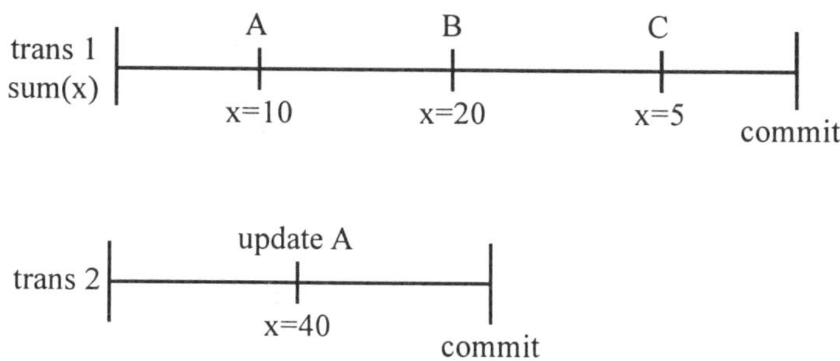

Figure D.2 *Isolation level 2 problems.*

If transaction 1 had to repeat a read of record A in the same transaction, at some time after the update of transaction 2 it should still see the value x=10 and not the updated value of x=40 from transaction 2.

SQL Server does not support this automatically. It has to be made to happen by requesting a holdlock on the select command, which retains the SLOCK until the end of the transaction; that is, commit or rollback.

```
SELECT sum(x) FROM tab_1 HOLDLOCK
       WHERE y > 50
```

This places an SLOCK on the table at the beginning of the transaction or on each page as it is read, which prevents update transactions changing any values until the SLOCK is released at the end of the transaction.

Note that the choice of table lock over multiple page locks is determined by the optimizer. If you must enforce full read consistency at isolation level 2, make sure that you take a table lock. This is taken only when the optimizer decides to do a table scan to execute the command. The above command may use an index on column y and take individual page SLOCKs instead of a single table lock. As the number of page locks held increases, escalation may occur to a table lock. This escalation point is configurable in System 11, as described in section 2.6.

This is a real sledgehammer to crack a nut and I would never recommend the use of holdlock in any performance-based system with a regular level of multiuser access. Locking a complete table is never a good idea. So although the facility is available, use it sparingly, with care, if at all. If you need read consistency, think about an application softlock on the table, which allows other readers and updates to the unimportant field(s) but bars updates to the field(s) on which read consistency is required. There is still significant contention but it is minimized by this approach.

D.2.3 Isolation Level 3

This is the ANSI standard locking isolation level. Isolation level 3 prevents a transaction from reading a different set of rows if it has to reread the data. If a second transaction inserts or deletes rows, isolation level 3 locking must still allow the first transaction to see the original set of rows.

The ANSI locking solution is shown in Figure F.3, where a multireader shared lock (SLOCK) is set when objects are read and a single-user exclusive lock (XLOCK) is set when objects are updated (insert/update/delete).

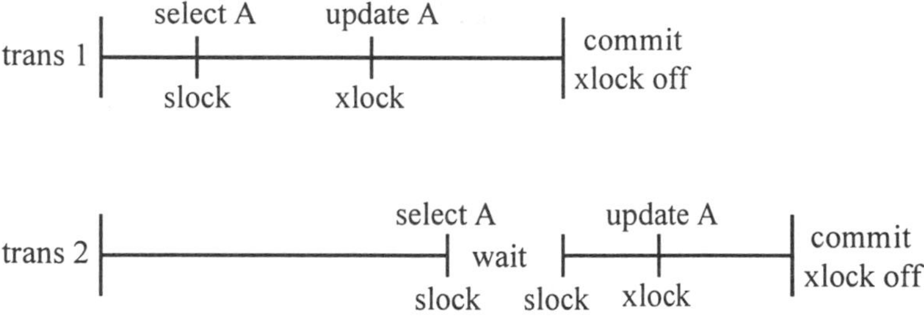

***Figure D.3** ANSI standard locking.*

If a read is made on an exclusively locked resource, the read waits until the resource is free and continues with the released resource. All locks are retained until the end of the transaction (commit or rollback) to ensure a partially updated record is not released prematurely. The SLOCK is retained until it is escalated to an XLOCK in both of the transactions. If no XLOCK occurred, the SLOCK is still retained until the end of the transaction. Retaining the XLOCK until the commit or rollback ensures 100%

integrity of the updated data in that no transaction can obtain a partially-updated record until the updating transaction has completed.

This level of concurrency control is achieved in SQL Server identically to isolation level 2 by holdlock forcing the SLOCK to remain set until the end of the transaction or until escalated to an XLOCK.

Isolation level 3 may also be set explicitly using the set command:

```
set transaction isolation level 3
```

D.2.4 Isolation Level 0

System 11 allows isolation level 0 locking, which does not try to set any locks and therefore is not blocked from reading any data, even an XLOCKed page. This is a dirty read situation that cannot guarantee the consistency or accuracy of the data read. It is set using the set command:

```
set transaction isolation level 0
```

D.2.5 Isolation Level Summary

SQL Server operates at isolation level 1 by default. Isolation level 2 is incorporated in isolation level 3 and cannot be set in SQL Server. All maintenance operations—insert/update/delete—lock in the same fashion by setting an XLOCK on the page or table and retaining this until the end of the transaction. An XLOCK cannot be granted if any other lock is outstanding on the page or table. This ensures 100% consistency of the data maintenance operations.

The use and retention of SLOCKs is governed by the isolation level. This may be controlled in the select command using holdlock or may be set explicitly using the set transaction isolation level command. The effect of the read isolation levels is summarized in Table D.1.

Table D.1 Read isolation levels

isolation level	set by	locks taken	blocked by
0	set command	none	none
1	set command default level	SLOCK on page released after page read	XLOCK
2	holdlock	SLOCK on page retained until end of transaction	XLOCK
3	set command holdlock	SLOCK on page retained until end of transaction	XLOCK

D.2.6 Deadlock

Unfortunately, isolation level 3 concurrency control can cause deadlock contention between two transactions that are trying to update the same record, as in Figure D.4.

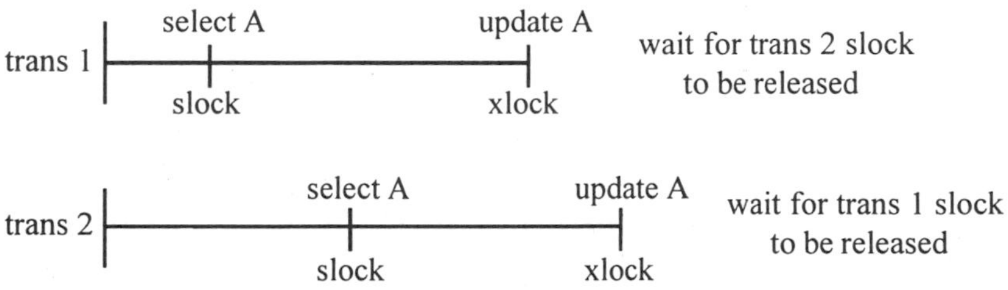

Figure D.4 *Update deadlock.*

Most software will identify this deadlock and rollback one of the transactions to allow the other to complete.

SQL Server eliminates this type of deadlock by not holding the SLOCK any longer than is necessary to read the page. Now there is no SLOCK contention to deadlock the transactions and both can proceed to a correct conclusion.

We still have the possibility of deadlock between transactions but only when they are contending for more than one resource, as shown in Figure D.5.

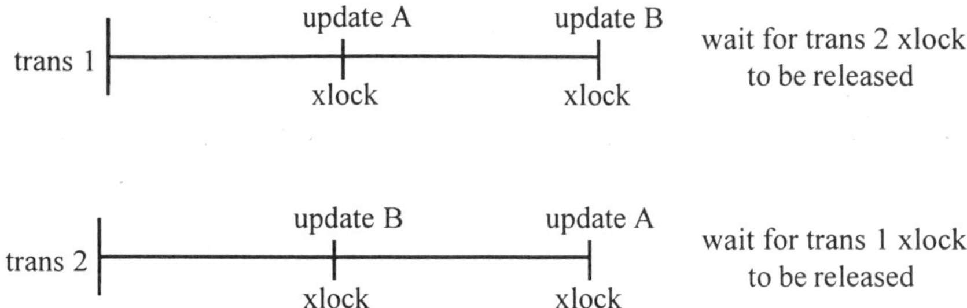

Figure D.5 *SQL Server deadlock*

SQL Server detects this automatically and rolls back one of the transactions to allow the other to proceed. You have no control over which transaction is rolled back. SQL Server decides on the basis of amount of work done and rolls back the one which has accumulated the least amount of CPU. Note that this is not necessarily the one with the shorter elapsed time, which can be a little bit annoying sometimes.

System 11 allows you to configure the time a process waits for a lock before it is checked for deadlock. Prior to System 11, each process that had to wait for a lock was checked for potential deadlock as soon as it had to wait. This can obviously be an unnecessary overhead if you have made some effort to minimize deadlocking in your application (see section 5.1.3). In System 11, you can specify the minimum amount of time (in milliseconds) that a process waits for a lock before a deadlock check is carried out.

```
sp_configure "deadlock checking period", 600
```

The System 11 default for this is 500. Setting the time to zero reverts to pre-System 11 checking as soon as the process waits for a locked resource.

D.2.7 Table Locks

The above discussion introduced the concept of locking at the table level. There are two types of table locks: intent locks and real locks.

Shared and Exclusive Table Locks

The real locks are quite simple: SLOCK, XLOCK at the table level, as opposed to the page level. The choice of page or table lock is determined by the optimizer. If the optimizer determines that a table scan is required, it will request a table lock instead of a page level lock on every page in the table. The only command that this does not apply to is the insert, which never takes an initial table lock.

Table locks may also be set when a transaction takes more than 200 page locks on a single table. If a transaction is processing a table and takes more than 200 individual page locks (such as an insert or an SLOCK with holdlock), then it will be escalated to a table lock and the page locks released. Prior to System 11, this 200 escalation limit was not configurable. System 11 now allows lock promotion levels to be configured, as explained in section 2.6.

Intent Table Locks

This escalation is facilitated by the other type of table lock: **intent locks**.

When a transaction requests a page lock, it also takes an intent lock at the table level. So an SLOCK on a page sets a shared intent (IS) lock on the table and an XLOCK on a page sets an exclusive intent (IX) lock at the table level. ULOCKs are not reflected at the table level as they are contention situations at the page level. The intent locks are not real locks and are simply used as semaphore settings by the contention system to facilitate table lock checking. As they are not real locks, any number and mixture of intent locks can coexist.

If a transaction wishes to take an exclusive table lock, it would need to check if any page in the table has a current SLOCK or XLOCK. If a page has a current lock set, the table XLOCK would have to wait. To make the checking easier, the table lock only checks against the intent locks at the table level as this contains the lock status of the pages of the table without knowing which pages are the subject of locks. The table lock cannot be set until the intent lock queue is clear on the table.

The lock settings for the various commands are:

	table	**page**
insert	IX	X
update with index	IX	U, X
delete with index	IX	X
update without index	X	——
delete without index	X	——
select with index	IS	S
select with index and holdlock	IS	S
select without index	IS	S
select without index and holdlock	S	——
create clustered index	X	——
create nonclustered index	S	——

D.2.8 Lock Promotion Thresholds

System 11 allows lock promotion thresholds to be set that determine when multiple page locks are escalated into a table lock. When the optimizer estimates that the number of locks set during a table scan will exceed a lock promotion threshold, it takes a table lock instead of multiple page locks. Note that the decision is taken on one scan of the table, so a command that does multiple scans of the table may request more locks in total than the lock promotion threshold. The lock promotion thresholds are discussed in more detail in Chapter 12.

System 11 has three lock promotion thresholds:

1. lock promotion HWM — sets the maximum number of locks on a table. The default is 200, the pre-System 11 fixed value. A command is escalated to a table lock if it attempts to acquire more than this number of locks on a table it.
2. lock promotion LWM — sets the minimum number of locks that must be set on a table before SQL Server will attempt to obtain a table lock for a command. The default is 200, the pre-System 11 fixed value. Setting this high will override the lock promotion HWM and cause transactions to hold many page locks. This means that you could quickly run out of available server locks if you set this too high.
3. lock promotion PCT — is the percentage of locks above which SQL Server attempts to acquire a table lock. The percentage is based on the number of rows in the table as:

   $$(\text{pct} * \text{number of rows}) \div 100$$

   This percentage is relevant only when the number of locks is between the LWM and the HWM.

The lock promotion values are set using **sp_setpglockpromote**.

sp_setpglockpromote

```
sp_setpglockpromote    {"server"|"database"|"table"},
                       {table_name|null},
                       hwm, lwm, pct
```

```
sp_setpglockpromote "server", null, 2000, 500, 20

sp_setpglockpromote "table", orders_tab, 500, 200, 50
```

The smaller object setting takes precedence. The table setting overrides the database setting, which overrides the server setting. The default server HWM is 200, the pre-System 11 value, and I see no reason to alter this. Individual table settings may be set based on application knowledge to override this.

D.2.9 Demand Locking

A problem with waiting for lock contention to go away before locking a page/table is that other transactions may set new locks while you are waiting and, in theory, you never obtain the required lock. This is particularly true when an XLOCK is waiting for SLOCKs to be released or a transaction is trying to set a table lock. While the XLOCK is waiting, there is a finite—albeit small—chance that other SLOCKs could be taken on the resource. Thus, although the original locks are released, subsequent new locks prevent the waiting XLOCK from obtaining the page/table.

Once a lock request has been denied, later requests for an SLOCK may be granted but that would not happen more than four times.

Because of the limited lifespan of the SLOCK, this will not occur often. Unfortunately it will tend to occur with the most-used records, so it has to be catered for and the XLOCK given preferential treatment over SLOCKs once the ULOCK request has been registered. This is called **demand locking** and effectively puts a bar on SLOCKs once an XLOCK has been denied four times on a resource.

When there is lock contention, the task that is requesting the locked resource is put to sleep until the resource is available. Any further requests are queued for the resource. When the resource becomes free the queue of waiting tasks is processed on a first in first out basis. The longest waiting task is awakened plus any other tasks sleeping on later locks requests if their locks are compatible with the lock requested by the longest waiting task.

D.3 Client/Server Considerations

The client/server environment that SQL Server works in is one where the actions at the client and the server are independent of each other between message pairs. A request for data by a client is responded to by the server sending the data. The server then has no knowledge of what the client has or what the client is doing, until another request—

possibly to update the data—is received and responded to. The traditional sequence of display some data and update some or all of the data is two separate, independent transactions to the server. The most important aspect of the independence is that there are no locks held on the records between the select and the update, even if they are in the same transaction block. SQL Server does not retain the SLOCK after the page has been read. Therefore, all records selected and displayed at the client are not locked by the server.

There is one exception to this: when the client leaves results pending at the server. Records read at the server are put into a server buffer. If more records are read than the buffer can hold, a buffer full condition is sent to the client to initiate transfer of the buffer records. Unfortunately, the page that was read when the buffer full condition occurred remains in a "read state." Therefore, the SLOCK remains on the page until the client has processed the records in the buffer and requested the next record from the database. When the records in the buffer are the result of a multitable join, this can be a serious condition as many pages may be left with SLOCKs on. Never leave results pending from a SQL Server client.

This means that when a record is returned to the server from a client for update, there is no guarantee that the record has not been updated by another transaction between the select and the update. We now have the original lost update possibility of corrupt data. Figure D.6 illustrates the problem.

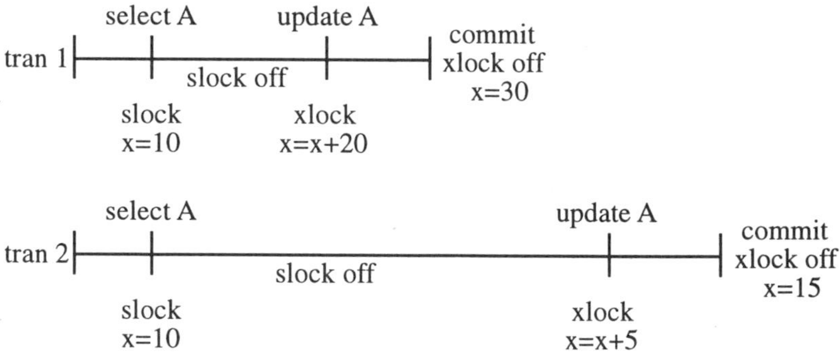

Figure D.6 Client/server lost update.

Simply because transaction 2 retained the record at the client long enough, all lock conflictions of transaction 1 are released and the update of transaction 2 may corrupt that of transaction 1.

This is not a new problem but it is exacerbated by the client/server environment where the client may be a workstation with processing power, storage capacity and a multitasking capability. In the dumb terminal environment, you need to finish what you are doing before you can start another task. This minimizes the time between events at the server and fixes the sequence of them. However in a multitasking workstation environment, you simply move the cursor to another window and carry out the new task...then answer the email message...then send your own message...then update your diary...then remember what you were doing in the first place. All of this time, the records have been sitting in your window minding their own business, happy for the rest, but potentially having the database version updated by another client. So when you finally decide to return the update, your version no longer reflects the current state of the database version.

Update in the SQL Server client/server environment requires some type of version control to check to see if the version of the record being returned for update is the same as the version of the database record. SQL Server implements this by a timestamp field on the record, which is checked by including a special clause in the update command and updated by each insert/update command. This is shown simplified in Figure D.7.

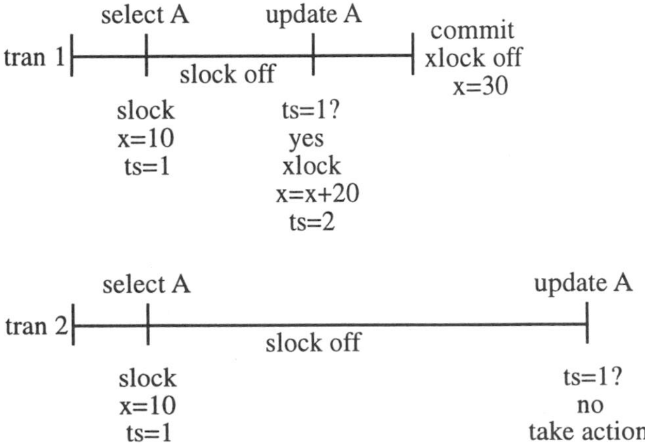

Figure D.7 *Timestamp checking.*

The action that you take is application dependent, such as rollback or reread, but at least you do not corrupt the data.

There are some conditions that need to be met to allow this type of timestamp checking to be made in SQL Server:

- the table must have a unique primary key;
- the select must be issued with the FOR BROWSE clause if using db-library;
- the table must have a "timestamp" field defined;
- the update must include a dbqual clause for db_library or a tsequal clause for T-SQL;
- the select and update should be made on separate connections from db_library.

These are not trivial, but not impossible or even out of the ordinary, and are essential to ensure data integrity in SQL Server. You can, of course, set up your own field and processing to achieve this version control but SQL Server's solution is quite adequate, the only real imposition being the requirement for FOR BROWSE in the SELECT. (Well, it used to be but unfortunately in System 10, Sybase has discontinued the support for the **for browse** mode in ct-library as it is not ANSI standard, claiming that cursors supply the necessary control. I think that they have misapplied the use of cursors and I would recommend that you do not use cursors to support optimistic locking but use your own column value setting and checking.)

D.4 Administration Considerations

Contention in any database system is always one of the biggest problems and SQL Server is no exception. If you suspect that there is a contention problem then the system procedure **sp_lock** will show the current locks and help you to unravel the problem.

sp_lock

```
sp_lock [spid1 [, spid2]]
```

where

spid	the server process number.

Consider the transaction:

```
BEGIN TRAN
        INSERT INTO tab_1 VALUES (1,2,'aaaaa')
        SELECT * FROM tab_1 HOLDLOCK
                WHERE fkey_col = 2
        SELECT sum(balance) FROM tab_1 HOLDLOCK
        UPDATE tab_1 SET name = 'bbbb'
                        WHERE fkey_col = 2
```

(where tab_1 has a clustered index on fkey_col)

An sp_lock at this stage will show the locks:

spid	locktype	table_id	page	dbname	class
1	ex_intent	122004611	0	fred	Non cursor lock
1	ex_page	122004611	509	fred	Non cursor lock
1	ex_page	122004611	1419	fred	Non cursor lock
1	ex_page	122004611	1420	fred	Non cursor lock
1	ex_page	122004611	1440	fred	Non cursor lock
1	sh_page	122004611	1440	fred	Non cursor lock
1	sh_table	122004611	0	fred	Non cursor lock
1	update_page	122004607	1440	fred	Non cursor lock
5	sh_intent	26004256	0	master	Non cursor lock
6	ex_intent	0	1128	tempdb	Non cursor lock

The **insert** is the heavy transaction here as it has locked an extent and four pages – 509, 1419, 1420, 1440. It is impossible to tell from this which each of these is, but we know that 1440 is the data page because it is locked by the **select *** and the **update**. The other pages are probably the index pages that are locked by the insert. The tempdb page lock is required by the **sum(balance)**, which uses tempdb for the aggregate value.

The number of locks available to the server is configurable and set by the system procedure **sp_configure**.

sp_configure

```
sp_configure 'number of locks', 8000
```

This is the total number of available locks, including all SLOCKs/XLOCKs at page and table level. If it is exceeded, the offending transaction is rolled back with an appropriate system error. Do not panic when this happens until you know why. Exceeding the maximum number of locks will happen but often it is because of an unusual configuration of events which may not happen again or happens so infrequently that it does not justify increasing the maximum.

Make sure that you know why it occurred so that you are forewarned and can prevent it happening again. If it occurs regularly or is caused by normal activity, then you need to consider increasing the number of locks using sp_configure. And remember that the new value does not take effect until you have restarted the server.

A rule of thumb from Sybase—and I have no better—is to allow for 20 locks per connection. A SQL Server user may have several connections—one to select and one to update—and the server views each connection as an independent transaction. So a 100 user system should be assumed to be 200–300 connections (let's overestimate and assume 300) and will require a maximum lock setting of 6,000. You will know your own system better than this average and will be able to judge the number of connections per user with more accuracy but, at initial system configuration, this is as good as it gets. Note that as the server views each connection as a separate transaction, you can lock yourself out of a resource!

Above all, do not panic when the maximum is exceeded. Reassure the user, watch them resubmit the command, take the applause when it works, find out what was happening when the maximum was exceeded and work at preventing it happening again or minimizing it. If the resubmission of the command is also rolled back, mumble something intelligent and have an immediate look at what is happening with sp_lock. Usually it is one transaction retaining a large number of locks or one transaction locking the others out of a common resource.

What can you do about it? Nothing. All you can try is to minimize the effects of the SQL Server locking strategy and get the number of locks as accurate as possible. Each lock requires 72 bytes of memory, which is 72 K per 1,000 locks. So, although it is not a drastic problem, do not increase this without some thought.

D.5 Design Considerations

D.5.1 Minimum Records Per Page

Because SQL Server locks at the page level, a single lock will lock all the records in the page. The fewer records per page, the fewer unnecessary records are locked. At the extreme, a high update activity table with a high degree of concurrent usage will benefit by having one record per page to simulate record locking. Prior to System 11, this was really only possible by artificially padding the record with large char fields to make it greater than half a page. System 11 has introduced a max_rows_per_page clause in the create table, alter table and create index commands. This defines the maximum rows allowed in a page and this page occupancy is retained for the life of the table. The max_rows_per_page is explained in detail in Chapter 12.

A parameter-style record, that is, a small table with several very small records that are frequently updated, is the type of record to consider for this. Having one parameter record with a large number of updatable parameter values in it is simply creating a contention bottleneck because almost every transaction in the system will be trying to lock and update this record. Splitting this single record into several with one parameter value per record will still leave all the records in one page which SQL Server locks for each single record update. The small records must be padded to one record per page to simulate record locking in SQL Server or define a max_rows_per_page of one.

General usage may benefit from a lower fillfactor than normal on a clustered index to reduce the number of records per page. A large insert rate will negate much of the savings but if concurrent access is a problem, this is worth trying.

D.5.2 Short Transactions

Reduce the length of time that a page is locked by keeping the transactions short. As SQL Server does not retain the SLOCK, this effectively means to keep the time between the insert/update/delete and the end of the transaction as short as possible. Delay the XLOCK commands to as close as possible to the commit/rollback. And remember that XLOCK commands lock the page even if the command produces an error. If a delete is issued and the record does not exist, the page is still locked and remains locked until the end of the transaction.

Be very careful with a nested transaction in this situation as SQL Server does not commit until the outer commit transaction.

```
BEGIN TRAN
        ....
        ....
        BEGIN TRAN
                ...
                ...
                UPDATE ctrl_tab SET ctrl = ctrl + 1
                SELECT @var_1 = ctrl FROM ctrl_tab
                ...
                ...
        COMMIT TRAN
...
...
COMMIT TRAN
```

The problem with this in SQL Server is that the nested transaction is not committed until the outer transaction commit. Nested begin/commit does no more than keep track of the nesting level. The outer transaction controls the commit of the complete transaction.

Note that this means that any rollback is to the start of the outer transaction. This is particularly relevant in triggers and procedures which contain rollback commands. Consider the sequence:

```
BEGIN TRAN
...
...
EXEC jk_proc——jk_proc
                                ...
                                ...
                                IF...ROLLBACK TRAN
                                ELSE COMMIT TRAN
...
...
IF...ROLLBACK TRAN
ELSE COMMIT TRAN
```

Both rollback tran commands will roll back to the beginning of the outer transaction, the second rollback reversing the effect of the procedure, as well as any statements in the outer transaction.

Commands executed via remote procedure calls are not rolled back from a rollback tran in an outer transaction. Remote procedure execution is independent of the calling transaction and therefore does not depend on either the commit or rollback of the outer transaction.

Commands that take or escalate to table locks will always cause contention, so avoid them as much as possible. Although indexes can be built while the system is operational, the create index takes table locks: SLOCK for nonclustered and XLOCK for clustered. Avoid doing this at the peak activity time of the day. Or at least take your phone off the hook.

D.5.3 Table Access Sequence

Although SQL Server resolves deadlock, it has to roll back one of the transactions to do so. The more traffic on the system, the more this is likely to be of concern. You may wish to minimize it during the design of your update transactions.

Always do the selects before the updates (I include insert/update/delete when I say update) as this means that there cannot be any deadlock caused by SLOCKs. In other words, read every record you need data from before you update anything. With the SLOCK always being requested first, the requesting transaction has no other locks set, so deadlock is not possible. The SLOCK request may have to wait for the page but it cannot deadlock as the transaction has no other resource locked. This alters if you use holdlock because the SLOCKs will be retained and deadlock is now a finite possibility. Try to avoid the use holdlock.

And watch the next sequential key processing.

```
BEGIN TRAN
        ....
        ....
        ....
        SELECT next_key FROM ctrl_tab HOLDLOCK
        UPDATE ctrl_tab
                SET next_key = next_key + 1
        ....
        ....
        ....
COMMIT TRAN
```

is a terrible sequence.

There is every possibility of deadlock here as we have a select with holdlock. All it needs is two transactions to select with holdlock and neither will be able to update. Simply do it as:

```
BEGIN TRAN
        ....
        ....
        UPDATE ctrl_tab
                SET next_key = next_key + 1
        SELECT next_key FROM ctrl_tab
        ....
        ....
COMMIT TRAN
```

You have the record XLOCKed until the commit so no one else can change or access the value. You will have considerable contention for this type of control record so do not keep it XLOCKed for too long.

At a higher level, you can minimize deadlock by updating the tables in the same sequence as often as possible. Most databases exhibit a hierarchical structure, as shown in Figure D.8.

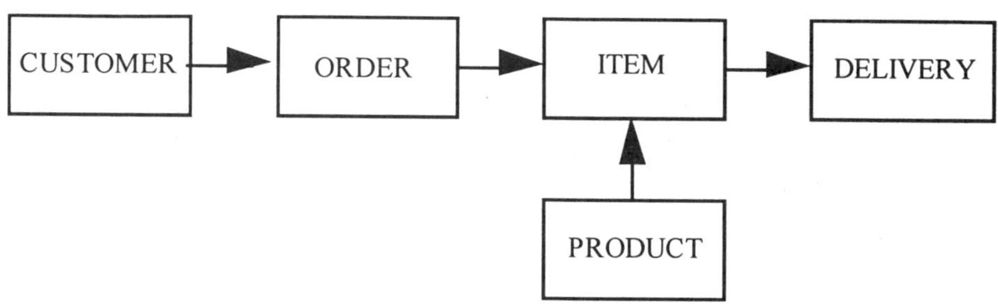

Figure D.8 *Table hierarchy.*

By always updating these tables from the top of the hierarchy to the bottom (that is, CUST to ORDER to ITEM to DELY or PRODUCT to ITEM to DELY), we eliminate intertable deadlock. As most deadlock is caused between tables, this is a significant gain. Intratable deadlock will still occur between records in the same table and unless you can limit the transactions to one update, you will never avoid this in SQL Server.

Of course, there will still be some transactions that you cannot write from top to bottom. But at least you know which ones and could introduce a programming soft-lock to prevent potential deadlock transactions getting into the application at the same time.

D.6 Memory Allocation

The other significant aspect of multiuser processing is the amount of memory that is needed to support the configuration. You cannot increase the number of concurrent users without considering how much memory is needed to support them. The available memory is being contended for by programs, data and other system components, so it is not a simple equation.

The general comment is to throw as much memory as you can at a relational database. However, although cheap, memory still costs money, so it is worth calculating how much, if only to justify what your boss will view as outrageous.

All of these will require memory allocation:

- operating system and network software;
- SQL Server kernel;
- connections;
- open objects;
- procedures;
- data.

D.6.1 Operating System and Network Software

Ask the vendors how much real memory should be allocated for the operating system and the network—not disk or swap space, but real memory. In general, you will get away with 2–3 MB for most Unix systems and about the same for the network.

D.6.2 SQL Server

Sybase normally quotes 4 MB for the server kernel. This may increase a little with new releases packed with long awaited new features but 4 MB is reasonable. You can still run a few users in a 4 MB SQL Server allocation as the kernel is not quite that big, but do not expect to get that much in the way of response time as it is very tight. So 4 MB for the SQL Server kernel.

The default memory size is 2,400 pages (i.e. 4.69 MB) of which the system component is:

executable code	1.2–2.0 MB
static server overhead	0.5–1.0 MB

which leaves about 2–3 MB for user connections, procedure and data cache.

D.6.3 Connections

Each connection to the server requires 51 K bytes of real memory—actually the SQL command stack size plus 23 K. (The stack size is configurable with sp_configure but you should not need to alter this unless you are in the habit of writing large complicated SQL commands with many tables and columns in them. However, I have found that on some upgrades to System 10 you need to increase the stack size to allow the larger commands to execute.) This is connections and not concurrent users. In general, I estimate three connections per user. For standard frontends, isql takes one connection and DWB takes two connections. The more overlaid screens you use in DWB, the more connections you use, up to a maximum of four. Program interfaces and 3GL programs obviously depend on how you write the programs but a simple update will usually require two connections to enforce browse mode and timestamping.

D.6.4 Objects

The amount of memory for objects depends on the object type:

open databases	17 K
devices	512 bytes
open objects	315 bytes
locks	72 bytes.

It is clearly worth keeping the number of open databases on the low side but these are not very large figures and should not cause you any real problem. It is unlikely that you will exceed more than 1 MB in an operational situation and, unless memory is really tight, I normally ignore these figures in any calculations.

D.6.5 Procedures

SQL Server reserves an amount of memory for the compiled procedures. This defaults to 20% of available memory and may be altered using the system procedure sp_configure.

```
sp_configure "procedure cache", 10
```

This setting is very much an estimate and will depend on how much you use procedures and how big they are.

4 M kern

50K - comd

DB = 17K

DRV 512

OUT 315

Loch 72

Let me recommend that you always use stored procedures except for ad hoc SQL. Because they are precompiled, they significantly reduce the load on the CPU; relational database software is surprisingly heavy on CPU. I know that there are potential optimisation problems with stored procedures but the decrease in CPU load gives an overall increase in throughput, which far outweighs the small disadvantage of an occasional wrong execution plan. Size is up to you but try to keep them on the small side. I normally aim for 12 K per procedure on average. The number of procedures also depends on how you have written them but I normally estimate three per connection. Of course, if you have the luxury of knowing how many concurrent procedures you have with their sizes, then use these figures but usually you will need to guess prior to the procedures being written.

So estimate 12 K per procedure with three procedures per connection.

Once the system is operational you can do a rough calculation of procedure size:

procedure size (K) = number of records in sysprocedures * 255

D.6.6 Data

I like to have 20% of the data as data cache and never like to go below 5% of the data. I make no allowances for indexes when I quote these figures, so they may be higher than you are used to. Do not neglect the size of the indexes but I like an easy life as an administrator. If I can persuade the boss to 20% of the data, I do not calculate index sizes, but if 5% is all that I can manage then I calculate index sizes to help my case for more data cache.

The more data cache the better, but do not waste it. I base my figures on the 80:20 rule of thumb that says 80% of the processing takes place on 20% of the data. If I have this 20% cached, the system performs better. If I allocate more than 20%, the extra is being used for low activity data. As it is low activity, it will not be requested often, so it will be the first to be swapped out when cache is required. Therefore, it will seldom be there when you need it again which means that you are wasting cache and money.

If you know that memory is going to be tight, then you need to be a little pragmatic and have a careful look at the use of cache by the indexes. At the least, we want the principal index levels to be cache-resident; that is, all levels except the leaf levels of the nonclustered indexes. The index pages are aged slower than data pages, so they get some priority in cache.

With enough cache for these index pages, we then need some space for the data. How much depends on your knowledge of the activity but strive to get as close as you can to the 5% figure. sp_estspace, explained in Appendix A, section A.6, can be very useful in estimating these figures when you have defined the table layout.

In System 11, you can divide data cache into multiple named caches to allow object binding to these caches. This can be extremely useful but do not get carried away as you lose a small amount of cache in overhead for each named cache. This is explained in detail in Chapter 12.

D.6.7 Memory Size Example

How much memory do we need for a 100 user system with 2 GB of data?

system overheads (OS, network, SQL Server)	10 MB
user connections	15 MB
procedure cache	10 MB
data cache	400 MB
	435 MB

where

user connections			
	100 users:	300 connections @ 51 K:	15 MB
procedure cache	300 connections:	900 procedures @ 12 K:	10 MB
data cache			
	2 GB @ 20%:	400 MB	
	2 GB @ 5 %:	100 MB	

If you consider this to be large, let's look at it in more detail.

This is a reasonably large database and is probably made up of about 100 tables. Of these, 20 or so will be quite small, taking up about 100 MB. The other 80 will take up the rest of the space, giving an average of 24 MB. If we assume that each table has one clustered index with an average size of 1% of the data, this adds 20 MB to the data size.

If we assume that each table has one nonclustered index with an average size of 15% of the data, this adds 300 MB to the data size. The majority of this is leaf level pages and a more realistic caching figure is probably 8% (160 MB).

I'm sure that most designers would like to get most of the indexes (180 MB) plus 5% of the data (100 MB) into cache. So I normally use the rough guide of 20% of the data (400 MB) as a first pass as it caters for all of the nonclustered index pages. I know it is large but relational database software loves memory.

Note that the lowest limit of 5% of data (100 MB) does not even get our estimated index sizes (180 MB) into cache. Our minimum cache is about 180 plus 100 to accommodate the indexes and about 5% of the data (about 10% of the database).

D.7 Summary

SQL Server uses an optimistic locking strategy of not retaining the SLOCK any longer than is necessary to read the data page and providing timestamp version control on the records being updated. The version control on update is no longer supported via ct-library. I would recommend that you implement it yourself as SQL Server is not ANSI standard in its default locking. Use of this timestamp version control ensures 100% integrity of data.

SQL Server has the page as the lowest level of locking granularity. Therefore, high performance systems need to consider this in their designs to minimize the amount of secondary record locking and update contention.

Memory allocation for a SQL Server system is quite standard with consideration being required for system software, user connections, procedure and data. The only special from SQL Server is that a single-user transaction may have several connections to the server. Default values and bytes required are as follows.

	default	bytes required
user connections	25	1275K
open databases	10	170K
locks	5000	360K
open objects	500	157K
devices	10	5120
memory	2400	2048

Index

A

B

C

D

E

F

G

H

I

J

K

L

M

N

O

P

T

U

V

W

X

SyBooks
Installation Guide

Document ID: 90002-01-0220

This publication pertains to SyBooks Release 2.2 software and to any subsequent release until otherwise indicated in new editions or technical notes. Information in this document is subject to change without notice. The software described herein is furnished under a license agreement, and it may be used or copied only in accordance with the terms of the agreement.

Sybase Trademarks

APT-FORMS, Data Workbench, DBA Companion, Deft, GainExposure, Gain Momentum, Navigation Server, PowerBuilder, Powersoft, Replication Server, SQL Advantage, SQL Debug, SQL Monitor, SQL SMART, SQL Solutions, SQR, SYBASE and the Sybase logo, Transact-SQL, and VQL are registered trademarks of Sybase, Inc. Adaptable Windowing Environment, ADA Workbench, AnswerBase, Application Manager, APT-Build, APT-Edit, APT-Execute, APT-Library, APT-Translator, APT Workbench, Backup Server, Bit-Wise, Configurator, Connection Manager, Database Analyzer, DBA Companion Application Manager, DBA Companion Resource Manager, DB-Library, Deft Analyst, Deft Designer, Deft Educational, Deft Professional, Deft Trial, Developers Workbench, DirectCONNECT, Easy SQR, Embedded SQL, EMS, Enterprise Builder, Enterprise Client/Server, Enterprise CONNECT, Enterprise Manager, Enterprise SQL Server Manager, Enterprise Work Architecture, Enterprise Work Designer, Enterprise Work Modeler, EWA, Gain Interplay, Gateway Manager, InfoMaker, Interactive Quality Accelerator, Intermedia Server, IQ Accelerator, Maintenance Express, MAP, MDI, MDI Access Server, MDI Database Gateway, MethodSet, Movedb, Navigation Server Manager, Net-Gateway, Net-Library, New Media Studio, OmniCONNECT, OmniSQL Access Module, OmniSQL Gateway, OmniSQL Server, OmniSQL Toolkit, Open Client, Open Client/Server, Open Client/Server Interfaces, Open Gateway, Open Server, Open Solutions, PC APT-Execute, PC DB-Net, PC Net Library, Powersoft Portfolio, Replication Agent, Replication Driver, Replication Server Manager, Report-Execute, Report Workbench, Resource Manager, RW-DisplayLib, RW-Library, SAFE, SDF, Secure SQL Server, Secure SQL Toolset, SKILS, SQL Anywhere, SQL Code Checker, SQL Edit, SQL Edit/TPU, SQL Server, SQL Server/CFT, SQL Server/DBM, SQL Server Manager, SQL Server Monitor, SQL Station, SQL Toolset, SQR Developers Kit, SQR Execute, SQR Toolkit, SQR Workbench, Sybase Client/Server Interfaces, Sybase Gateways, Sybase Intermedia, Sybase Interplay, Sybase IQ, Sybase MPP, Sybase SQL Desktop, Sybase SQL Lifecycle, Sybase SQL Workgroup, Sybase Synergy Program, Sybase Virtual Server Architecture, Sybase User Workbench, SyBooks, System 10, System 11, the System XI logo, Tabular Data Stream, Warehouse WORKS, Watcom SQL, WebSights, WorkGroup SQL Server, XA-Library, and XA-Server are trademarks of Sybase, Inc.

All other company and product names used herein may be trademarks or registered trademarks of their respective companies.

Restricted Rights

Use, duplication, or disclosure by the government is subject to the restrictions set forth in subparagraph (c)(1)(ii) of DFARS 52.227-7013 for the DOD and as set forth in FAR 52.227-19(a)-(d) for civilian agencies.

Sybase, Inc., 6475 Christie Avenue, Emeryville, CA 94608

Document ID: 90002-01-0220-01
Last Revised: January 31, 1996

This CD-ROM includes the following collections:

Sybase SQL Server™
Release 11.0.x

Replication Server®
Release 11.0.x

System Management
Release 11.0.x

Open Client/Server™
Release 10.0.3

Open Client/Server Supplements (for UNIX, PC, Macintosh)
Release 10.0.3

1. Introduction

Welcome to SyBooks™, the Sybase® online documentation facility. Online viewing is now the standard means of presenting Sybase documentation. SyBooks' advantages include:

- Distributed access to documentation. Once SyBooks is installed in a network environment, Sybase users can access any book, and no longer have to depend on a single set of documentation.
- Instant access to information. Links within and between individual books and comprehensive search capabilities enable instant access to related information.
- Decreased reliance upon paper products. Online documentation does not use paper and, therefore, helps preserve the earth's resources.

SyBooks uses the Electronic Book Technologies, Inc. (EBT) *Dyna*Text Browser to display documentation online. The *Dyna*Text Browser provides a flexible graphical environment, including search, annotation, and print capabilities throughout the SyBooks online documentation.

Using This Guide

This guide:

- Details the procedures associated with installing SyBooks on UNIX, Windows 3.1, and Macintosh systems
- Introduces both SyBooks and EBT's *Dyna*Text Browser to new users

This booklet is neither a comprehensive guide nor a tutorial for the SyBooks environment. For a thorough guide to the Browser's functionality, it is recommended that you access the *Dyna*Text online help, *Reader Guide*, available through the *Dyna*Text Browser's Help facility. The online book *SyBooks Frequently Asked Questions* is also available.

SyBooks Features

With the help of *Dyna*Text's flexible environment, SyBooks users can locate information anywhere in the Sybase documentation quickly and efficiently. SyBooks features include:

- **Search capabilities.** Users can search through individual or multiple books for occurrences of words or phrases. Search query instances are highlighted in the current book's text, and the number of query instances in each of the book's sections is displayed in the table of contents view. Boolean, proximity, and wildcard character search capabilities are supported.
- **Annotation capabilities.** Users can create publicly or privately accessible annotations within books, including margin notes, bookmarks (place holders accessible via hypertext links), and hypertext links (links between specified locations in the book).
- **Printing capabilities.** Users can print an entire book or selected sections of a book, including the table of contents, using a PostScript printer.
- **SKILS integration.** SyBooks is integrated within the SKILS™ (Sybase Knowledge Through Interactive Learning Systems) environment, providing users with instant access to Sybase documentation from the Sybase online education facility.

Supported Platforms

For platform requirements and dependencies, refer to the SyBooks *Release Bulletin*.

For More Information

Other documents that you may find useful include:

- The SyBooks *Release Bulletin*, which includes special installation instructions and other platform-specific information
- *SyBooks Frequently Asked Questions*, an online document that includes useful information about SyBooks
- The *DynaText Reader Guide*, an online guide to the *Dyna*Text browser

2. Installing SyBooks on the Macintosh

Preparing to Install SyBooks

Before installing SyBooks, be aware of the following:

- You can run SyBooks from the CD-ROM drive, but you will not be able to use annotations or modify the collections on the CD. If performance is a concern, install SyBooks on a hard disk.
- During the installation process, you can:
  - Install new collections
  - Install new books in existing collections, if the book and the collection have the same release number

- Delete an entire installation
- Update the *Dyna*Text Browser version and environment

- The SyBooks installation program must be copied to and run from a hard disk. If you are running System 7.0 or 7.1, you must run the installation program from the hard disk onto which SyBooks will be installed.
- You must have **both** AppleScript1.1 and the Scripting Additions folder installed to run the installation program. If you do not have AppleScript and the Scripting Additions folder installed, you may install the versions provided on the SyBooks CD (see the next section, "Installing AppleScript and the Scripting Additions Folder").
- The system requirements are:
  - a CD-ROM drive.
  - 4MB of RAM.
  - Free space on your hard disk. The amount varies with each installation configuration. The installation program will state how much space is needed.
- The supported operating system is: MacOS System 7.x running Applescript1.1 and Applescript Scripting Additions.

Installing AppleScript and the Scripting Additions Folder

To install AppleScript and the Scripting Additions folder:

1. Insert the SyBooks CD into the CD-ROM drive.
2. Open the SYBOOKS CD.
3. Open the sybooks folder.
4. Open the mac folder.
5. If AppleScript 1.1 is not installed on your system, copy *AppleScript* to the Extensions folder, located in the Systems Folder.
6. Copy the Scripting Additions folder to the Extensions folder, located in the Systems Folder.
7. Restart the computer.

Installing SyBooks

You may choose from three installation configurations:

- Compact installs only the *Dyna*Text browser and allows you to read books from the CD.
- Custom allows you to specify the books and collections that you would like to install onto your hard disk.
- Full installs the *Dyna*Text browser and all collections and books contained on the CD.
- The Deinstall option deinstalls any installation, whether partially or completely installed.

To install SyBooks:

1. If you do not have a previously installed version of SyBooks, create a folder by choosing New Folder from the File menu. You may choose any name for the folder; "SyBooks" is the default. Later, you will specify this folder as the "Destination Folder" when running the installation program.
2. Insert the SyBooks CD into the CD-ROM drive.
3. Open the SYBOOKS CD.
4. Open the Sybooks folder.
5. Open the mac folder.
6. Copy the *install.me* file to a hard disk. If you are running System 7.0 or 7.1, you must run the installation program from the same hard disk onto which SyBooks will be installed.
7. Double-click on the *install.me* file that you copied to the hard disk. If you receive the message:

   ```
   Where is HyperCard?
   ```

   Highlight install.me and click Open.
8. Follow the instructions on the screen.
9. The installation program is finished when the screen displays the following message:

   ```
   SyBooks 2.2 Installation has completed successfully.
   ```

Post-Installation Procedures

Making SyBooks an Apple Menu Item

1. Open the SyBooks folder.
2. Open the bin folder.
3. Click on the *sybooks* file.
4. From the File menu, choose the Make Alias command.
5. Drag the *sybooks alias* file to the Apple Menu Items folder located in the Systems folder.
6. Rename the *sybooks alias* file *SyBooks*.

SyBooks is now accessible from the Apple menu.

Starting SyBooks

To start SyBooks select SyBooks from the Apple menu. Or:

1. Open the SyBooks folder.
2. Open the bin folder.
3. Double-click on the *sybooks* file.

When starting SyBooks, you may receive one or more of the following messages at the bottom of your screen:

```
Warning: '<book folder name>' is not a valid book
```

This indicates that the named book was not selected by the user for installation. To install a specific book, run **install.me** and select the Custom installation option.

For help with using *Dyna*Text, go to the *Reader Guide* located under the Help menu.

Running SyBooks from the CD-ROM Drive

To run SyBooks from the CD-ROM drive:

1. Insert the SyBooks CD into the CD-ROM drive.
2. Open the SYBOOKS CD.
3. Open the sybooks folder.
4. Open the mac folder.
5. Open the bin folder.
6. Double-click on the *sybooks* file.

Installation Notes and Troubleshooting

Additional Installation Information in *readme.mac*

For up-to-date information, see the *readme.mac* file in the *<cd_drive>:\sybooks* directory on the CD. The *readme.mac* file contains a directory tree of a valid SyBooks installation.

Memory Errors

If you receive the error message:

```
Can't understand "createconfig".
```

or, by extrapolation:

```
Can't understand "<module_name>".
```

the installer is out of memory. It will be necessary to restart the computer, or power down and restart, before rerunning *install.me*.

3. Installing SyBooks on UNIX

Preparing to Install SyBooks

Before SyBooks can be installed, you must mount the CD-ROM drive to the system on which the installation will occur. Superuser privileges are often required to mount the CD-ROM drive.

➤ *Note*

Mounting commands and mount points vary among different UNIX platforms. For mounting instructions, see your System Administrator or the documentation associated with the UNIX platform on which SyBooks will be installed.

In addition, be aware of the following:

- SyBooks requires running the X Window System. Refer to the SyBooks *Release Bulletin* to ensure that your system is running the correct version of the X Window System and operating system software before continuing with the installation.
- The installation program does not overwrite any previously installed books. During the installation process, you can:
  - Install new collections
  - Install new books in existing collections, if the book and the collection have the same release number
  - Delete previously installed collections from your installation
  - Update the *Dyna*Text Browser version and environment
- SyBooks books must be installed on your UNIX system to be available to users. They cannot be read directly from the CD-ROM.
- For a new installation, SyBooks is installed in a directory of your choosing or in a default directory, *$HOME/sybooks*. The requirements for this directory are:
  - You must have write permissions on the parent directory (for example, *$HOME*).
  - The child directory (for example, *sybooks* or the last directory in the alternative path name) cannot already exist. It is created by the SyBooks installation program, which installs SyBooks within it.
- For previously existing SyBooks installations, the installation program uses the value of the SYBROOT environment variable and makes changes in that directory. The SYBROOT and EBTRC environment variables must already be defined in your environment.
- The SyBooks directory path, including the sybooks directory (for example, *$HOME/sybooks*), is referred to in this guide as *<SyBooks_root>*. For example, if you choose to install SyBooks at the default location, *<SyBooks_root>* would represent *$HOME/sybooks*.

Calculating Disk Space Requirements

When you are preparing to install SyBooks, it is important to calculate how much hard disk space is required for the SyBooks configuration you want to install. This section describes how to calculate these space requirements.

➤ *Note*

To ensure sufficient disk space, all size values are rounded to the nearest 1/100 megabyte.

To calculate the disk space requirements for your proposed SyBooks installation, add the values obtained for each of the following steps:

1. **Common files**. Auxiliary files required by the *Dyna*Text Browser and common to all supported UNIX platforms are gathered together in the UNIX tar file, *common.tar*. Therefore, the size of *common.tar* is a constant value for all UNIX platforms.

✔ **Common files (*common.tar*):** 2.32MB

2. ***Dyna*Text Browser executables**. Table 3-1 lists the size of each supported UNIX platform's *Dyna*Text Browser executable. If you plan to install the executable for more than one platform, total the sizes of all the executables to be installed to obtain a final value for this step.

Table 3-1: *Dyna*Text Browser Executable Size

UNIX Platform	*Dyna*Text Browser Executable Size (MB)
SunOS 4.x OpenWindows	4.32
SunOS 4.x Motif	5.63
Sun Solaris 2.x (SPARC) OpenWindows	5.71
Sun Solaris 2.x (SPARC) Motif	7.02
Solaris 2.x (Intel) OpenWindows	2.46
Solaris 2.x (Intel) Motif	3.77
IBM AIX 3.2	3.31
SGI IRIX 5.2	3.42
HP HP-UX 9.0	3.08
Novell UnixWare 1.1	3.91
AT&T System 3000	3.91
Digital UNIX	2.72

✔ ***Dyna*Text Browser executable(s):** MB

3. **Online book collections.** Each online book collection's auxiliary files require approximately 100K (0.10MB) of disk space. For example, if the SyBooks CD from which you are installing contains three online book collections, and you plan to install all of them, the combined auxiliary files would require 300K of disk space (3 collections x 100K).

✔ **Book collections:** MB

4. Online books. Disk space requirements for each online book on this SyBooks CD are listed in the *SyBooks Contents List* included with this CD. Decide which online books you want to install and add their space requirements to obtain a final value for this step.

✔ **Online books:** MB

5. ***Dyna*****Text/SyBooks documentation collection**. An additional collection containing the online *DynaText Reader Guide and SyBooks Frequently Asked Questions* is automatically installed with every SyBooks installation. Therefore, the disk space requirement for this collection is a constant value for all UNIX platforms.

   ✔ ***Dyna*****Text/SyBooks documentation:** 1.56MB

6. Add the values for steps 1–5 to obtain the disk space requirements for your SyBooks installation.

   ✔ **Total disk space required:** MB

Installing SyBooks

The SyBooks installation program for UNIX is a text-based application. Detailed instructions are provided throughout the installation; you are prompted for information to tailor the SyBooks environment, including:

- The directory in which SyBooks will be installed
- The UNIX platform from which SyBooks will be installed
- The UNIX platforms on which SyBooks will be viewed
- The Sybase books that will be installed

You can terminate the installation at any time during installation prior to the actual writing of data. The location at which SyBooks is to be installed will remain untouched.

It is highly recommended that you execute the SyBooks installation program inside an X-window that has scroll bars.

If you have an existing SyBooks installation, you must execute the SyBooks installation program as a SyBooks user in order to properly install additional books, collections, and executables. That is, the SYBROOT and EBTRC environment variables must be defined in your environment.

To execute the SyBooks installation program for UNIX:

1. Change directories to the *unix* directory on the SyBooks CD. For example, assuming that the CD-ROM drive is mounted as */cdrom*, enter:

   ```
   cd /cdrom/sybooks/unix
   ```

2. Execute the installation program as follows:

   - If you are installing SyBooks from an HP 9000 system running HP-UX, an AT&T system running SVR4, or a Digital UNIX system running OSF/1, version 1.x, execute the installation program from the /cdrom/*sybooks/unix* directory with this command:

     ```
     INSTALL.ME*
     ```

   - If you are installing SyBooks from any other platform, execute the installation program from the */cdrom/sybooks/unix* directory with this command:

     ```
     install.me
     ```

Upon completing successfully, the SyBooks installation program stores a record of the work performed in a log file located in *<SyBooks_root>/config/log.cur*. If the log file from a previous SyBooks installation exists at this location, it is renamed *log.old*. A directory tree of the resulting SyBooks installation is located in the *sybooks/readme.unx* file on the CD.

The *Dyna*Text Configuration File: *.ebtrc*

For each version of the *Dyna*Text Browser installed, the SyBooks installation program for UNIX creates a separate *Dyna*Text configuration file, *.ebtrc*, which tailors the Browser to the system on which it is installed. Each *.ebtrc* file is stored in the *<SyBooks_root>/<platform _name>* directory. For further information about the .ebtrc configuration file, refer to the online document *SyBooks Frequently Asked Questions.*

Collection-Level Indexing

Collection-level indexes are required for cross-collection searches (that is, searches across all installed books within a single collection or multiple collections). The SyBooks installation program for UNIX automatically generates collection-level indexes.

Post-Installation Procedures

Following installation, the System Administrator must perform the following **for each user** who wants to view SyBooks:

1. Create a directory within the user's home directory for private SyBooks annotations. The path and name of this directory must be:

   ```
   ~/sybooks/annot
   ```

2. Set the user's SYBROOT environment variable to point to the directory path where SyBooks is installed. (This is the value of *<SyBooks_root>*.)

   For example, if SyBooks is installed in */usr/local* and has the default directory name of *sybooks*, set the SYBROOT environment variable as follows:

   C shell:

   ```
   setenv SYBROOT /usr/local/sybooks
   ```

   Bourne or Korn shell:

   ```
   SYBROOT=/usr/local/sybooks; export SYBROOT
   ```

3. Set the user's EBTRC environment variable to point to the *.ebtrc* configuration file for the version of *Dyna*Text with which the user will view SyBooks. Set EBTRC as follows:

   C shell:

   ```
   setenv EBTRC $SYBROOT/<platform_name>/.ebtrc
   ```

   Bourne or Korn shell:

   ```
   EBTRC=$SYBROOT/<platform_name>/.ebtrc; export EBTRC
   ```

   Refer to the SyBooks *Release Bulletin* for a list of platform directory names.

   If SYBROOT has not been set, or if the *.ebtrc* file has been moved from its default location, substitute the path associated with *<SyBooks_root>* in place of SYBROOT.

4. Add the SyBooks executable path to the user's path. This points to the version of *Dyna*Text with which the user will view SyBooks. After installation, SyBooks executables are located in *<SyBooks_root>/<platform_name>/bin.*

5. If your SyBooks installation is distributed over a network, particularly if a user is viewing SyBooks on an X terminal remotely logged into the SyBooks host, you must:
   - Set the user's DISPLAY environment variable to point to the user's machine.
   - Add the user's machine to the list of those allowed to make connections to your X server.

   To do this, execute the following commands in the **rlogin** session window on the user's workstation:

   C shell:

   ```
   xhost +local_machine_name
   setenv DISPLAY local_machine_name:0.0
   ```

   Bourne or Korn shell:

   ```
   xhost +local_machine_name
   DISPLAY=local_machine_name:0.0; export DISPLAY
   ```

Starting SyBooks

When all post-installation steps are complete, use the following command to start SyBooks:

```
sybooks
```

Installation Notes and Troubleshooting

*Dyna*Text Browser, Versions 2.0 and 2.3 Compatibility

SyBooks includes version 2.3 of EBT's *Dyna*Text browser.

While version 2.3 of the browser can read online documentation generated for use with earlier versions of the browser, the reverse is not true. Versions of the *Dyna*Text browser earlier than version 2.3 cannot be expected to read online documentation generated for use with version 2.3.

If a version of the *Dyna*Text browser earlier than version 2.3 is currently installed, it is recommended that it be updated to version 2.3. The SyBooks installation program automatically updates earlier versions of the *Dyna*Text Browser that were installed with previous installations of SyBooks.

Updating Annotations from Previous SyBooks Releases

This release of SyBooks does not take advantage of *Dyna*Text's ability to maintain user-created annotations (including bookmarks, internal hypertext links, and margin notes) across successive releases of an online document. However, the SyBooks installation program saves annotations from any previous installation of SyBooks. Old annotations are saved in *<SyBooks_root>/config/annotold*.

Motif Applications and OpenWindows

All versions of *Dyna*Text for UNIX included with SyBooks are Motif applications. Starting Motif applications while running OpenWindows on SunOS 4.x or 5.x operating systems can introduce a variety of problems. The following are problems you can expect when running SyBooks under OpenWindows:

- Double-clicking in any text entry using any mouse button can crash the *Dyna*Text Browser.
- Starting SyBooks can crash the OpenWindows XNEWS server before the *Dyna*Text Browser library window appears.

To resolve these problems, obtain the following patches from Sun and install them on the system on which the SyBooks executable is located:

Table 3-2: Sun patches required to resolve Open Windows problems

Patch Number	Patch Name
100444-58	OpenWindows 3.0: OpenWindows V3.0 Server Patch 3
100512-04	OpenWindows 3.0: libXt CTE Jumbo Patch

Motif 1.2.2: Errors Mapping Pop-Up Menus

A Motif 1.2.2 bug can prevent *Dyna*Text from mapping pop-up menus. If your UNIX environment supplies Motif 1.2 dynamically linked libraries, or if you are using the toolkit to link to Motif 1.2.2, add the following resources to the *Dyna*Text applications defaults file, Dtext, located in *<SyBooks_root>/<data/X_platform_directory>/defaults/C:*

```
dtext.motif122bug:          TRUE
*whichButton:               5
```

Solaris on Sun Sparc and i86-Based Machines

If revelatory windows appear partially or completely black when using the Solaris version of *Dyna*Text on a Sun Sparc or i86-based workstation, add the following resource to the *.Xebt* file located in each user's home directory:

```
motifResizeBug:             TRUE
```

Translation Table Warnings and the *XKeysymDB* File

On UNIX systems on which Motif is not installed, starting SyBooks can generate many "translation table" warning messages, such as:

```
Warning: translation table syntax error:
Unknown keysym . . .
Warning: . . . found while parsing . . .
```

These messages are merely warnings and do not affect the performance of either SyBooks or the *Dyna*Text Browser.

To resolve this problem, there must be an *XKeysymDB* file in the */usr/lib/X11* directory. An *XKeysymDB* file is installed with SyBooks and is located in *SyBooks_root/data/misc.*

Perform the following:

- **If an *XKeysymDB* file is not already located in */usr/lib/X11*,** copy the *XKeysymDB* file installed with SyBooks to /usr/lib/X11.

  If your UNIX environment does not have a */usr/lib/X11* directory, you must create this directory before copying the *XKeysymDB* file to it.
- **If an *XKeysymDB* file is already located in */usr/lib/X11*,** append the contents of the *XKeysymDB* file installed with SyBooks to the present *XKeysymDB* file in */usr/lib/X11*.

If the UNIX workstation from which SyBooks is started has a *usr* directory, an *XKeysymDB* file must be located in the */usr/lib/X11* directory. Repeat the steps outlined above for the XKeysymDB file on the workstation.

SyBooks on AT&T: "Can't find libXt.so.1" Error

If you get this error when you start SyBooks on an AT&T platform:

```
dynamic linker: ncr/bin/sybooks: can't find libXt.so.1
```

you must create a link called "libXt.so.1" in the */usr/lib* directory pointing to the most recent version of this file (for example, */usr/lib/libXt.so.5.0*).

Unable to View Books

If you can start SyBooks but cannot view books, perform the following steps:

1. Ensure that a *map.txt* file exists in the following location for each SyBooks collection installed:

   ```
   <SyBooks_root>/<col_name>/ents/map.txt
   ```
2. If the *map.txt* files are empty or do not exist, create a map.txt file for each collection installed containing the following line:

   ```
   -//SYBOOKS//<col_name> Styles//EN $SYBROOT/<col_name>/styles
   ```

   where *<col_name>* specifies the name of a directory beneath *<SyBooks_root>* containing a collection's ancillary files and book data. For example:

   ```
   -//SYBOOKS//srv10023 Styles//EN $SYBROOT/srv10023/styles
   ```

This problem is known to occur on AT&T workstations and is due to the erroneous reading of files from the CD during installation.

"Could not open DATA_DIR (check your .ebtrc)" Error

If starting SyBooks generates the following error:

```
Could not open DATA_DIR (check your .ebtrc).
```

ensure that the following conditions have been met:

- The SYBROOT environment variable is set to the directory path where SyBooks is installed.
- The EBTRC environment variable is set to the directory path and file name of the *.ebtrc* configuration file.
- The DATA_DIR value set in the *.ebtrc* configuration file is set to the directory in which *Dyna*Text data files are located (for example, *$SYBROOT/data*).

Finally, set or unset the LANG environment variable as follows:

- If the LANG environment variable is set, unset it.
- If the LANG environment variable is not set, set it to the value "en_us" as follows:

  ```
  setenv LANG en_us
  ```

X Terminal Fonts

If SyBooks is started from an X terminal and *Dyna*Text Browser text does not appear in the same font as on other UNIX platforms, it is possible that all fonts were not installed when the X terminal software was installed.

To resolve this problem, install all the fonts included with the X terminal software.

Book Window Size Too Large

If DynaText book windows are too large for your monitor, the window's geometry can be adjusted by changing the values in the parameter **fulltext.geometry* in the file *<SyBooks_root>/data/<X_directory>/defaults/C/Dtext.color.*

UNIX Environment-Specific Installation Options

During installation, you are prompted for information about:

- The environment to which your CD-ROM drive is locally attached (from which you are installing SyBooks)
- The environments for which you want to install *Dyna*Text browsers

Table 3-3 shows the configurations that correspond to the environment from which you are installing SyBooks.

If you install SyBooks for an operating system other than the one on which you are performing the installation, the disk device on which SyBooks is installed must be NFS mounted and accessible directly by the other operating system.

If users are logging in remotely from one operating system to a local operating system on which SyBooks is installed, it is only necessary to install SyBooks for the local operating system. For example, if remote users running Solaris remotely log into a machine running AIX to view SyBooks, it is only necessary to install SyBooks for AIX.

♦ *Warning!*

If you are running DEC OSF 1 1.x, choose option 4, HP 9000 HP-UX, as the UNIX environment from which you are installing SyBooks. DEC OSF 1 1.x does not interpret file names read from a CD-ROM drive verbatim; choosing HP 9000 HP-UX forces the SyBooks installation program to anticipate the problem and correct for it. If you are running DEC OSF 1 2.x or later, choose option 7, DEC Alpha OSF 1.

Table 3-3: Installation Environment Options

Installer Option No.	Machine	Operating System
1	Sun SPARC	SunOS 4.x
2	Sun SPARC	Solaris 2.x
3	IBM RS6000	AIX
4	HP 9000	HP-UX
5	AT&T	AT&T SVR4
6	SGI MIPS	IRIX
7	DEC Alpha	OSF/1
8	Intel x86	Solaris 2.x
9	Intel x86	UnixWare

Table 3-4 shows the configurations that corresponds to the browser environments.

Table 3-4: Browser environment options

Installer Option Number	Machine	Operating System	SyBooks Directory Name
1	Sun SPARC	SunOS 4.1.x Motif	sun4m
2	Sun SPARC	SunOS 4.1.x OpenWindows	sun4mol
3	Sun SPARC	Solaris 2.x Motif	sun5m
4	Sun SPARC	Solaris 2.x OpenWindows	sun5mol
5	IBM RS6000	AIX 3.2	ibm
6	HP 9000	HP-UX 9.0	hp
7	AT&T	AT&T SVR4	att
8	SGI MIPS	IRIX 5.2	sgi5
9	DEC Alpha	DEC OSF/1	decosf
10	Intel x86	Solaris 2.x Motif	i86m
11	Intel x86	Solaris 2.x OpenWindows	i86mol
12	Intel x86	UnixWare 1.1	uw

SunOS 4.1.x: Motif vs. OpenWindows Installation

If you are running SunOS 4.1.x using OpenWindows, you can choose between two SyBooks environments during installation:

- Option 1: SunOS 4.1.x running Motif
- Option 2: SunOS 4.1.x running OpenWindows

Depending on the configuration at your site, one choice may yield better visual results than the other. You can install both and then experiment to determine which looks best on your monitor.

In either case, you must install the Sun patches discussed in "Motif Applications and OpenWindows" on page 28.

Exiting and Restarting the Installation Program

You can exit the SyBooks installation program at any user prompt by entering either "Q" or "q", or at any time by pressing Ctrl-c.

If you exit before all user options have been chosen and confirmed, only a log file located at $HOME/*log.cur* will remain; nothing else in your environment will be affected. If you exit after the final option confirmation, the user-specified SyBooks directory will have been created and populated with directories and files.

If you abort the installation, you must rerun it, and it must complete successfully before SyBooks will be properly installed.

The installation program must complete without errors and generate the following message:

```
End of SyBooks Installation Program
```

before the SyBooks installation can be considered successful. Each user who wants to view SyBooks must then be configured according to the post-installation instructions described in"Post-Installation Procedures" on page 24.

install.me Installation Program Not Found

Occasionally, the UNIX shell cannot find the **install.me** installation program, although the program is visible in the file system. Typical error messages generated when this occurs are as follows:

```
csh: Can't find file install.me
csh: ERROR: install.me: command not found
```

If these errors appear, perform the following:

1. Ensure that your CD-ROM drive is mounted correctly.
2. Do one of the following:
   - Add "." (the current directory) to your path, or
   - Invoke **install.me** using its full path name, as follows:

     ```
     <CD_ROM_mount_point>/unix/install.me
     ```
3. If step 2 fails, ensure that *<CD_ROM_mount_point>/unix* is the current directory, and invoke **install.me** with its own Bourne shell:

   ```
   sh install.me
   ```

"tar: Tape read error" Error

If you receive the following error during installation:

```
tar: Tape read error
```

you must restart the SyBooks installation program for UNIX. This error is generated when either of the following occurs (listed in order of likelihood):

- A read error on the CD-ROM drive
- A physical problem with the SyBooks CD

Moving SyBooks

If you want to move a SyBooks installation to a different location on the same file system, you can use the UNIX mv command. However, if you want to move SyBooks to a different file system, use the installation program to create a new installation. Do not use the cp or cp -r command, as this replaces symbolic links with physical files and thus occupies unnecessary disk space.

4. Installing SyBooks on Windows

Preparing to Install SyBooks

Before installing SyBooks, be aware of the following:

- You can use the installation program to:
    - Install new collections
    - Install new books in existing collections, if the book and the collection have the same release number
    - Delete previously installed collections and books from your installation, or delete entire installations
    - Update the *Dyna*Text browser and environment
- The minimum system requirements are:
    - A CD-ROM drive
    - A hard drive with about 10MB free space available
    - 4MB RAM
- The operating systems supported are:
    - DOS 4.01 or later and Windows 3.1x
    - Windows 95
    - Windows NT 3.x
    - OS/2 2.x or later (WinOS2)
- The directory path where SyBooks will be installed is referred to in this guide as *<SyBooks_root>*. For example, if you choose to install SyBooks at the default location, *<SyBooks_root>* would represent *C:\sybooks*.

Running SyBooks from the CD

You can run SyBooks from the CD, however you will not be able to use annotations or modify the collections on the CD in any other way. If performance is a concern, you should skip this section and install SyBooks to a hard drive.

To run the *Dyna*Text browser from the CD:

1. Insert the SyBooks CD into the CD-ROM drive.
2. Open Windows File Manager and change to the *<cd_drive>:\sybooks\windows\bin* directory.
3. Double-click on the *sybooks.exe* file.

Using Windows 95 with the AutoPlay Feature

If you are using Windows 95 with the AutoPlay feature:

1. Insert the SyBooks CD into the CD-ROM drive.
2. Click the right mouse button on the CD-ROM drive icon and select Run from CD.

Installing SyBooks to a Hard Drive

To run the SyBooks installation program for Windows:

1. Insert the SyBooks CD into the CD-ROM drive.
2. Open the Windows File Manager. Change the current drive to the CD-ROM drive, and change the current directory to *<drive_letter>:\pc\install.*
3. Double-click on the *setup.exe* file.

Windows 95

If you are using Windows 95:

1. Insert the SyBooks CD into the CD-ROM drive.
2. Click the right mouse button on the SyBooks CD-ROM drive icon and select Install/Deinstall.

Starting SyBooks

The SyBooks installation program can create a program group and icon for the *Dyna*Text browser. The browser is located at *<SyBooks_root>\bin\sybooks.exe.* By default, a SyBooks icon is created in a group called SyBooks.

To start SyBooks:

1. Open the SyBooks group.
2. Double-click on the SyBooks icon.

Installation Notes and Troubleshooting

Additional Installation Information in *readme.win*

For up-to-date information, see the *readme.win* file in the *<cd_drive>:\sybooks* directory on the CD. If you are using **Windows 95** with the AutoPlay feature, click the right mouse button on the CD-ROM drive icon and select Read Me.

The *readme.win* file contains a directory tree of a valid SyBooks installation. You can use this information to restore the directory structure if you quit the installation program during the installation or deinstallation.

Compatibility Between *Dyna*Text Browser Versions

SyBooks includes version 2.3 of EBT's *Dyna*Text browser. While version 2.3 of the browser can read online documentation generated for use with earlier versions of the browser, the reverse is not true. Versions of the *Dyna*Text browser earlier than version 2.3 might not be able to read online documents generated for use with version 2.3.

If a version of the *Dyna*Text browser earlier than version 2.3 is installed, it is recommended that it be updated to version 2.3. The SyBooks installation program updates earlier versions of the *Dyna*Text browser that were installed with previous installations of SyBooks.

Memory Requirements for Installing SyBooks

Stack Space

If you are using **Windows 3.1x** or **Windows 95**, make sure you have enough stack space defined by checking the *STACKS* setting in the *\config.sys* file. The statement should say *STACKS=9, 256*.

Conventional Memory

Insufficient conventional memory (under 640K) might prevent the collection indexing program (*mkcolidx.exe*) from running during the installation or deinstallation.

Reduce the number of unnecessary device drivers and TSRs loaded during the installation. About 600K or more of conventional DOS memory should be free.

Systems with 8MB of RAM or Less

Additional operating system swap and page file requirements might be required on systems with 8MB of RAM or less. If you see "Out of Stack Space" error messages during the installation, you should examine the swap and page file settings to see if they need to be increased.

If you are using **Windows NT**, also make sure that the TEMP environment variable points to a valid drive and directory with sufficient disk space. See the operating system documentation for more information about paging and swap files.

Hard Drive Space Requirements for Installing SyBooks

Installation Drive Requirements

In addition to the space requirements shown during the installation program, you should have at least an additional 3MB of free space on the installation drive (2MB for compact installations). It is recommended that you ensure there is enough space on the drive before running the installation program.

Be aware that other processes might access the installation drive during the installation and consume additional drive space, which might result in a disk full error. For example, if you are installing SyBooks to the drive used by the operating system for paging and swapping, an additional 6MB of disk space or more might be consumed during the installation. In general, it is not a good idea to attempt to fit SyBooks on a drive that has barely enough space for the installation.

Temporary Space Requirements

The TEMP environment variable should be set to a drive and directory with at least 1MB of free space available for logging installation and deinstallation events and configuration options.

If you are using **Windows 3.x** or **Windows 95**, you must:

1. Exit Windows or restart your system in DOS mode.
2. At the DOS prompt, set the TEMP variable. Enter:

   SET TEMP=<*temp_directory*>
3. Restart Windows.

Or, you can put the SET statement in the *\autoexec.bat* file so that the setting takes effect when you start your computer.

If you are using **OS/2**, put the *SET* statement in the *\autoexec.bat* file so that the value takes effect when you start a WinOS2 session.

If you are using **Windows NT**, double-click on the System icon in Control Panel to set the TEMP variable.

Installing to an Existing SyBooks Directory

If you are installing to or removing SyBooks from an existing directory, make sure no other processes are accessing the directory when the installation program is running. For example, you must close any instances of the *Dyna*Text browser that are accessing the directory, and change directories if any DOS sessions are using the directory as the current directory.

Failure to take these actions might prevent the SyBooks installer from installing files and removing directories. If you notice that the SyBooks directory is not removed after you attempt a full deinstallation, you can delete it, or install a new SyBooks installation into the same directory.

In addition, make sure you have full read and write access in the installation directory and *\autoexec.bat* file. If you see path or file access errors during the installation or deinstallation:

- Obtain the necessary privileges and retry the operation, or
- Quit and rerun the installation program and install SyBooks to a different drive or directory that you have read and write access to.

If a Full installation is selected, all collections and books available on the CD that are already installed on the hard drive are still displayed as available for installation. These collections and books are installed over the corresponding collections and books on the hard drive during the installation. The installation program intentionally overwrites the SyBooks files and directories on the hard drive that might have been invalidly or unintentionally modified.

Installing SyBooks v2.0 and v2.1 CDs

If you are installing several SyBooks CDs, you should install the SyBooks v2.2 CDs **after** any SyBooks v1.x, v2.0, and v2.1 CDs are installed.

If you have already installed collections from a SyBooks v2.2 CD and need to install collections from earlier SyBooks v2.0 or v2.1 CDs, you can use the SyBooks v2.2 installation program to install these earlier CDs by following these steps:

1. Insert the SyBooks v2.2 CD into the CD-ROM drive.
2. Copy the files in the *<cd_drive>:\sybooks\windows* directory to a diskette or directory on the hard drive.
3. Insert the SyBooks v2.0 or v2.1 CD into the CD-ROM drive.
4. From Windows Program Manager, click on File...Run and enter:

   `<drive>:\<directory>\setup <cd_drive>:`
5. Repeat steps 3 and 4 for each v2.0 or v2.1 CD you want to install.

The SyBooks v2.2 installation program **cannot** install SyBooks v1.x CDs. You must install the v1.x CDs before installing any other SyBooks CDs.

Attempting to install a SyBooks v1.x, v2.0, or v2.1 CD using the older installation programs over an existing SyBooks v2.2 installation will overwrite the pointers to the collections installed using v2.2. You can restore the pointers by editing the *<SyBooks_root>\bin\dynatext.ini* and *colls?.cfg* files and adding the directory paths and collection aliases to those files. Follow the example of the existing collection pointers in those files.

Installing Across Both CD-ROM and Hard Drives

If you want to conserve hard drive space by installing the browser to the hard drive and reading the collections and books from the SyBooks CD (Compact installation), be aware that only full collections can be read from the CD. That is, you cannot read a partial collection from the CD because the *Dyna*Text browser requires all files of a single collection to be contained within the collection directory.

Likewise, if you install a partial collection on the hard drive, you cannot read the remainder of the collection from the CD. If your goal is to conserve hard drive space, you should deinstall the partial collection from the hard drive and perform a Compact installation to read the entire collection from the CD.

If a collection that is available on the CD is partially or fully installed on the hard drive, the collection is not displayed when a Compact installation is selected. Likewise, if a collection is being read from the CD, the collection is not displayed as an available collection when a Full or Custom installation is selected.

Installing over Previous Compact Installations

If there is a previous Compact installation on the system that you want to remove, you must run the SyBooks installation program from a drive other than the CD-ROM drive. If you attempt to run the installation program from the CD, a system error might occur during the step when you must remove the CD during the installation. To copy and run the SyBooks installation program from a different drive:

1. Insert the SyBooks v2.2 CD into the CD-ROM drive.
2. Copy the files in the *<cd_drive>:\sybooks\windows* directory to a diskette or directory on the hard drive.
3. From Windows Program Manager, click on File...Run and enter:

   `<drive>:\<directory>\setup <cd_drive>:`

Installing SyBooks on a Network

If you intend to install SyBooks to or from a network drive, you must map the device to a drive letter before you begin the installation. Universal network connection paths are not supported. The absolute drive letter is used in the *Dyna*Text configuration files and the browser, and the browser will not work properly if the drive is remapped to a different letter after the installation.

If you attempt to install SyBooks to an NFS-mounted UNIX drive, the browser might not run even though the installation was successful. This configuration is not supported.

During the initial scan for existing installations, only local hard drives are searched. If you want the SyBooks installation program to search all available, mapped network drives, specify *setup /net* when you run the SyBooks installation program. Network CD-ROM drives might be searched if they are attached as a network drive.

If you are connected to several local or network hard drives and the initial scan for existing installations takes too long, you can click on the Skip button during the search to bypass the scan. After the scan completes, you can change the installation path to the drive and directory of your choice. Another action you can take before starting the installation to minimize the search time is to set the SYBROOT environment variable to point to the drive and directory of an existing SyBooks installation.

Installing SyBooks on OS/2 (WinOS2)

If you are using OS/2, you should run the SyBooks installation program from a WinOS2 Full-screen session, or from a windowed Program Manager session. In any case, Program Manager must be running in the same WinOS2 session in order for any new icons and program groups to be added to the system.

When removing books from a collection and installing new collections and books, the collection indexing program will start in a DOS session off the OS/2 Desktop. The SyBooks installation program will not wait for the collection indexing to end, and will indicate that the installation has completed. You can safely exit the installation program at this point. However, do not attempt to use the *Dyna*Text browser until the DOS collection indexing session completes successfully.

If you are using OS/2 Warp and notice that the DOS collection indexing session is running slowly, it is possible that the WinOS2 session priority is set at a higher level relative to the DOS session. To speed up the collection indexing, either close the WinOS2 session, or increase the session priority of the DOS session. See the operating system documentation for more information about session priority.

Installation Progress Estimates

The installation progress meter and time estimates give only an approximate indication of the status of the installation or deinstallation based upon the known SyBooks files and directories found.

The installation program does not take into account any non-SyBooks files or unreferenced files that exist in the installation directory structure. Therefore, it is possible for the time estimations to significantly differ from the actual installation or deinstallation time required.

Creating Collection-Level Indexes

Collection-level indexes are provided for the full collections available on the CD. If you perform a Full installation, these collection indexes are installed to the hard drive. If you perform a Custom installation, collection-level indexes are automatically built by the installation program for the partial collections installed.

If you need to build the indexes for the entire set of newly installed partial collections, follow these steps:

1. After the installation program ends, go to a DOS prompt (native DOS or a DOS session).
2. Change to the drive where you installed SyBooks by entering:

   ```
   <drive_letter>:
   ```
3. Change to the SyBooks *config* directory by entering:

   ```
   cd\<SyBooks_directory>\config
   ```
4. To index the newly installed partial collections, enter:

   ```
   indexall
   ```

   If you need to build a single collection index, follow these steps:

1. After the installation program has ended, go to a DOS prompt (native DOS or a DOS session).
2. Change to the drive where you installed SyBooks by entering:

   ```
   <drive_letter>:
   ```
3. Change to the SyBooks directory by entering:

   ```
   cd\<SyBooks_directory>
   ```
4. Look at the collection subdirectories by entering:

   ```
   dir /w.
   ```

   Collection subdirectories begin with three letters and are followed by five digits. For example, for *SyBase Open Client/Server Release 10.0.2*, the collection subdirectory is called *con10021*.
5. Change to the SyBooks binaries directory by entering:

   ```
   cd bin
   ```
6. To index the collection, enter:

   ```
   index <collection_subdirectory>
   ```
7. Repeat steps 3 through 6 for each collection you want to index.

If Indexing Fails

If the *mkcolidx.exe* collection indexing program fails due to insufficient memory:

1. Examine the *\config.sys* and *\autoexec.bat* files on the boot drive.
2. Increase the amount of conventional memory available (below 640K) by temporarily disabling unnecessary device or network drivers and TSRs.

3. Reboot and try the indexing the collection. After you build the indexes for the collections, restore the driver and TSR configuration and reboot again, if necessary.

If you are using **Windows NT 3.1**, the installation program might indicate that collection indexing was performed when, in fact, no collection index was created.

During the installation, the installation program runs *command.com* to start the DOS collection indexing session. Check the system PATH setting to determine whether the DOS *command.com* is being invoked instead of the Windows NT *command.com*. You can either temporarily rename the DOS *command.com* file (for example, to *command.dos*) or change the order of directories in the path so that the Windows NT *command.com* file is found first. After you install SyBooks, restore the path or DOS *command.com* file name to the original setting.

If you are reading books from the CD, collection-level indexes are provided for the full collections on the CD. You cannot build new collection-level indexes for collections read from the CD.

The DynaText Configuration File: dynatext.ini

The SyBooks installation program for Windows creates a *Dyna*Text configuration file, *dynatext.ini*, which tailors the browser to the system on which SyBooks is installed. The *dynatext.ini* file is stored in the *<SyBooks_root>\bin* directory. For further information about the *dynatext.ini* configuration file, refer to the online document, *SyBooks Frequently Asked Questions*.

Setting the SYBROOT and SYBVIDEO Environment Variables

The SYBROOT Environment Variable

SyBooks for Windows provides the ability to tailor the default font size for viewing the online documentation. The font size is determined by the SYBVIDEO environment variable. The value of SYBVIDEO indicates the default point size for the body text in the online documentation. The SYBVIDEO value can range from 10 to 20, depending on the screen resolution. If SYBVIDEO is not set, the online documentation will appear in 18-point type.

The SYBVIDEO Environment Variable

The SYBROOT environment variable points to the drive and directory path where you installed SyBooks. SYBROOT is used by the installation program when searching for previous collections. If SYBROOT is not defined, the installation program searches all available hard drives (including network drives) on the system for a previous installation. The search ends when an existing installation is found, or when no installations are found.

autoexec.bat File and Environment Variables

The SyBooks installation program modifies the *\autoexec.bat* file by adding or updating two lines in the file to set the SYBVIDEO and SYBROOT environment variables. A backup file called *autoexec.bak* is stored in the *<SyBooks_root>\config* directory before any modifications are made. Defining these environment variables is optional but recommended.

These environment variable settings are removed when you completely deinstall SyBooks, and an *\autoexec.bak* backup file is created on the boot drive before any modifications are made.

Setting SYBROOT and SYBVIDEO

The environment variable settings take effect when you restart the system, or whenever those statements are executed.

- If you are using a **DOS/Windows 3.1** system, you can exit Windows, enter those statements at the native DOS prompt, and then restart Windows to have those settings take effect without having to reboot the machine.
- If you are using a **Windows NT** system, the environment settings take effect immediately because the SyBooks installation program notifies Windows *Program Manager* of the environment changes in the registry.
- If you are using OS/2, the settings take effect whenever a WinOS2 session is started.

Windows NT Registry and Environment Variable Changes

If you are installing SyBooks on a Windows NT system, the SYBVIDEO and SYBROOT environment variables are recorded in the registry under the *HKEY_CURRENT_USER/Environment* key. These environment settings are removed when you completely deinstall SyBooks. You should use the SyBooks installation program to install and deinstall collections and books so that the registry entries and environment variables are properly maintained.

If you need to modify the environment variables in Windows NT, click on the System icon in Control Panel.

Windows 95 Registry and Deinstallation

The Windows 95 registry is not updated by the SyBooks installation program. Deinstallation of SyBooks using the Windows 95 Add/Remove Programs function is not supported. Deinstallation functions are provided in the SyBooks installation program.

Installing and Deinstalling Icons and Program Groups

If you deinstall an entire SyBooks installation, the program group is removed only if the group name is *SyBooks*. The installer does not remove non-SyBooks program groups that might contain icons for other applications installed on the system.

Windows NT

If you are using Windows NT and the program group is called SyBooks (Common), the group and icon might not be removed. To remove the group or icon, you (or the system administrator) must log onto the system with the necessary privileges to delete the group or icon.

Windows 95

If you are using Windows 95, only one SyBooks icon can exist in a folder. Therefore, if you choose to install a new icon in an existing group that already has a SyBooks icon, the existing icon will be updated and no new icons are created as a result of the installation.

You might see an error message regarding an icon not found when the installation program attempts to remove the SyBooks icon and group. Ignore the error and continue. If the SyBooks program group is empty, you can remove it by dragging it from Windows Explorer to the Recycle Bin.

Updating Annotations from Previous Installations

This release of SyBooks does not take advantage of *Dyna*Text's ability to maintain user-created annotations (including bookmarks, internal hypertext links, and margin notes) across successive versions of an online book. However, the SyBooks installation program for Windows saves annotations from previous installations. Old annotations are saved in *<SyBooks_root>\config\annotold.*

Moving SyBooks to a Different Location

If you move the entire SyBooks environment to a different location, you must edit the contents of the *Dyna*Text configuration file, *dynatext.ini*, located in *<SyBooks_root>\bin*. All paths pointing to the **previous** *<SyBooks_root>* directory must be replaced with paths pointing to the **new** *<SyBooks_root>* directory.

The *Dyna*Text-specific environment variables, which you must edit, include:

COLLECTION
SYSCONFIG
DATA_DIR
PRIVATE_DIR
PUBLIC_DIR

Change PRIVATE_DIR and PUBLIC_DIR only if their values include <SyBooks_root>

You must also edit these files in *<SyBooks_root>\bin:*

colls1.cfg
colls2.cfg
.
.
collsn.cfg

For further explanation of these DynaText configuration file variables, refer to the online document *SyBooks Frequently Asked Questions*.

Using the Log for Troubleshooting Installation Errors

If you encounter any problems or errors during the installation, you can consult the *log.cur* file in the directory pointed to by the TEMP environment variable (before the actual installation has started), or in the *<SyBooks_root>\config* directory, if the installation has started. If you encounter deinstallation problems, consult the *log.cur* file in the directory pointed to by the TEMP environment variable.

Information in the *log.cur* file and other files in this directory can be used for diagnosis and recovery purposes. Try to save these files, especially if you plan to contact Sybase Technical Support for further assistance.

5. The DynaText Browser

➤ *Note*

The screen diagrams in this chapter demonstrate DynaText for Microsoft Windows 3.1. DynaText for UNIX and Apple Macintosh offers identical functionality and a similar graphical user interface.

Using the *Dyna*Text Browser

When you start SyBooks, the DynaText library window appears.

The library window is divided into two views: on the left is a **collection** view (listing the available collections, or groups of related books). On the right is a **book** view (listing the titles of books in the selected collection). Selecting a different collection displays the titles of the books in that collection.

To open a book, select its title in the book view. When you open a book, a *Dyna*Text book window appears, containing the contents of the selected book.

Like the library window, the book window is divided into two views: on the left is a **table of contents** view, displaying a structural hierarchy of the book. On the right is a **text** view, displaying the contents of the book. When you select a section heading in the table of contents view, the corresponding section appears in the text view.

*Dyna*Text Browser Online Help

SyBooks does not include printed documentation for the *Dyna*Text Browser. However, you can access the DynaText Browser's online Help through the Help menu. The topics included in the Help menu vary, depending upon where you are when you access Help:

- **Accessed from a library window**, the Help menu displays collection-level help topics.
- **Accessed from a book window**, the Help menu displays book-level help topics.

The complete *DynaText Reader Guide* is available through both library and book window Help menus using the Windows *Dyna*Text Browser. To open the *DynaText Reader Guide*, choose Reader Guide from the Help menu.

➤ *Note*

On UNIX platforms, the DynaText Reader Guide cannot be opened from a book window's Help menu; it must be opened from a library window's Help menu.

For further instruction on using the *Dyna*Text Browser, refer to the online *DynaText Reader Guide.*

For More Information

For more information about topics such as printing sections of the online documentation, locating *Dyna*Text configuration files, and searching in online documents, see the online document *SyBooks Frequently Asked Questions.*

6. Printing the PostScript Files

PostScript versions of all the Sybase documents included on this CD are located in the */sybooks/ps* directory. These files are organized in directories according to the *Dyna*Text collection in which they are located online. These files can be printed on PostScript printers, enabling you to print high-quality paper documentation at no additional cost.

Sybase customers have limited rights to reproduce the Sybase documentation. For details, see the license agreement included with this CD.

Contact the vendor of your PostScript driver for information about how to print these files on your system.

Printing the Files

- PostScript files can be printed only on PostScript printers.
- For Macintosh users, printing PostScript files may be slow. If possible, print the files from a UNIX system.
- The files should be printed at 300 dpi only.
- All of the PostScript files are formatted to print on 8-1/2-by-11-inch or A4-size paper.

71999-01-0220-01
February 9, 1996

Release Bulletin
SyBooks™ Release 2.2

1. Product Summary

1.1. Supported Platforms

Enclosed is SyBooks, the CD-ROM online documentation for Sybase® products. Included with SyBooks are multiple versions of Electronic Book Technologies, Inc.'s (EBT) full-runtime *Dyna*Text browser for viewing the online documentation. Platforms and operating systems for which *Dyna*Text Browsers are included are as shown in Table 1.

Table 1: EBT DynaText Browsers Included with SyBooks

Browser Platform	Operating System	Browser RAM Requirements	Notes
DEC	OSF/1	12MB	X requirements: X11R4-R5 and Motif 1.1.x
HP	HP-UX 9.0	12MB	X requirements: X11R4-R5 and Motif 1.2.x
IBM	AIX 3.2	12MB	X requirements: X11R4-R5 and Motif 1.2.x
Intel x86	Solaris 2.x	12MB	X requirements: X11R5 and either OpenWindows 3.x or Motif 1.2.x
AT&T	SVR4	12MB	X requirements: X11R4 and Motif 1.2.2
SGI	IRIX 5.2	12MB	X requirements: X11R4-R5 and Motif 1.2.x
Sun SPARC	SunOS 4.1.x	12MB	X requirements: X11R4-R5 and either OpenWindows 3.x or Motif 1.1.x
Sun SPARC	Solaris 2.x	12MB	X requirements: X11R4-R5 and either OpenWindows 3.x or Motif 1.1.x
Intel x86	UnixWare 1.1	12MB	X requirements: X11R4 and Motif 1.2.2
Apple Macintosh	System 7.x	6MB	
Intel x86	Microsoft Windows	4MB	Includes the following operating systems: • MS DOS 4.01 or later, and Microsoft Windows 3.1x • Microsoft Windows 95 • Microsoft Windows NT 3.1 or later • IBM OS/2 2.1 or later

1.2. SyBooks Information on the World Wide Web

Information regarding SyBooks can be found on the World Wide Web by navigating from the following location:

http://www.sybase.com

Follow the hypertext links from this page to view:

- Product Information. A high-level description of SyBooks features including a list of platforms on which SyBooks can be viewed.
- Online Publications from SyBooks. A list of the Sybase online document titles currently distributed via SyBooks CD-ROM and the World Wide Web.
- SyBooks Problem Descriptions and Patches. A list of problems associated with SyBooks and, when possible, hypertext links to download available patches.

2. What's New in SyBooks Release 2.2?

2.1. SyBooks for Macintosh and Windows

SyBooks release 2.2 includes the following features for Apple Macintosh and Microsoft Windows platforms:

- **A new installation program.** The new installation program has a graphical user interface that provides disk space requirements for the installation options selected. New collections are automatically indexed during installation. The installation program can also remove existing SyBooks installations.
- **Ability to run SyBooks from the CD.** Users can insert the CD-ROM and run SyBooks without having to install any files to the hard drive.

3. Upgrading Previous SyBooks Installations

The SyBooks installation programs on this CD are capable of upgrading previous installations of SyBooks and, by default, will install an updated version of the *Dyna*Text browser, *Dyna*Text v2.3.

Earlier versions of the SyBooks installation programs did not have the capability to upgrade. Using an earlier version of the installation program might delete—not upgrade—any previous installation of SyBooks that exists in your environment.

Table 2 lists the product identification numbers of previously released SyBooks CDs (printed on the face of the CD) that cannot upgrade a previous installation of SyBooks.

Table 2: Upgrade Limitations of Previous SyBooks Installation Programs

SyBooks CD Product ID Number	Cannot Upgrade These Versions of SyBooks
94515-55-1002-01 94515-55-1002-02	2.0, 2.1, 2.2
94515-55-1002-03	2.2
94517-55-1010-01	
38800-55-1002-01 91516-55-1002-01	

IMPORTANT—READ CAREFULLY BEFORE OPENING

SYBASE, INC. LICENSE AGREEMENT (THIS IS A LICENSE AND NOT A SALE)

SYBASE'S ACCEPTANCE OF YOUR ORDER AND DELIVERY OF THIS SOFTWARE ARE EXPRESSLY CONDITIONED ON YOUR AGREEING TO THE FOLLOWING LICENSE AGREEMENT.

BY OPENING THIS PACKAGE, YOU INDICATE YOUR AGREEMENT WITH THE FOLLOWING.

1. **LICENSE.** You may use those enclosed software programs (and accompanying documentation) which were ordered by you ("Programs") solely for your internal business purposes. No more than the number of User's for which the license was ordered are authorized to access such Program at any one time. A User is a person (or identifiable unique accessor of information used in place of human interaction) who is authorized by you to access the Program or use a foreground or background process to access a Program.

2. **COPYRIGHT AND OWNERSHIP.** The Programs are owned by Sybase and are protected by United States and Canadian copyright laws and international treaty provisions. You acquire only the right to use the Programs and do not acquire any rights of ownership in the Programs or the media on which they are provided.

3. **COPY RESTRICTIONS AND OTHER RESTRICTIONS.** You may copy the Programs except to make up to one (1) copy for each User and one copy (1) for backup or archival purposes. You may not copy the written materials and manuals accompanying the Programs assigned, or otherwise conveyed (whether by operation of law or otherwise) to another party without Sybase's prior written consent. You may not use the Programs for timesharing, rental or service bureau purposes. You shall not remove any product identification, copyright notices or other notices or proprietary restrictions from the Programs. Upon reasonable notice to you, Sybase may audit the number of Users using the Programs and the number of copies of the Programs in use by you.

4. **U.S. GOVERNMENT RESTRICTED RIGHTS.** If this license is acquired under a U.S. Government contract, use, duplication or disclosure by the U.S. Government is subject to restrictions as set forth in DFARS 252.227–7013(c)(ii) for Department of Defense contracts and as set forth in FAR 52.227–19(a)–(d) for civilian agency contracts. Sybase reserves all unpublished rights under the United States copyright laws.

5. **TERMINATION.** Either party may terminate this Agreement if the other party breaches any of its obligations hereunder and such breach is not cured within sixty (60) days after written notice. Sybase may terminate this Agreement if you fail to make any payment when due to Sybase and such failure is not cured within fifteen (15) days after written notice. Upon termination, you shall cease using the Programs and shall return to Sybase all copies of the Programs and Documentation in any form.

6. **LIMITED WARRANTY AND LIABILITY.** Sybase warrants that the Programs when properly used, will operate in all material respects in conformity with Sybase published specifications for the applicable version, and the Program media shall be free of defects, for one (1) year from the date of shipment of such version to you. In the event of a failure to meet the foregoing limited warranty, your sole remedy in the event of nonconformity of a Program, at Sybase's option, shall be replacement of the defective materials or a refund of the license fees paid for the affected Program. This limited warranty gives you specific legal rights. **SYBASE DISCLAIMS ALL OTHER WARRANTIES AND CONDITIONS, EXPRESS OR IMPLIED, INCLUDING WITHOUT LIMITATION THE IMPLIED WARRANTIES OR CONDITIONS OF MERCHANTABLE QUALITY AND FITNESS FOR A PARTICULAR PURPOSE, AND WHETHER ARISING BY STATUTE OR IN LAW OR AS A RESULT OF A COURSE OF DEALING OR USAGE OF TRADE, WITH RESPECT TO THE PROGRAMS OR THE DOCUMENTATION. NO WARRANTY IS MADE REGARDING THE RESULTS OF ANY PROGRAM OR INFORMATION CONTAINED THEREIN, THAT ALL ERRORS IN THE PROGRAMS WILL BE CORRECTED, OR THAT THE PROGRAMS' FUNCTIONALITY WILL MEET YOUR REQUIREMENTS. IN NO EVENT WILL SYBASE OR ITS SUPPLIERS BE LIABLE FOR ANY LOSS OR INACCURACY OF DATA, LOSS OF PROFITS OR INDIRECT, SPECIAL, INCIDENTAL OR CONSEQUENTIAL DAMAGES, EVEN IF SYBASE HAS BEEN ADVISED OF THE POSSIBILITY OF SUCH DAMAGES. SYBASE'S TOTAL LIABILITY, IF ANY, ARISING OUT OF OR RELATING TO THIS AGREEMENT SHALL NOT EXCEED THE LICENSE FEES PAID BY YOU FOR THE PROGRAMS. THE FOREGOING RESTRICTIONS, DISCLAIMERS AND LIMITATIONS SHALL APPLY AND REMAIN IN FORCE EVEN IN THE EVENT OF A BREACH BY SYBASE HEREUNDER OF A CONDITION OR FUNDAMENTAL TERM HEREUNDER, OR IN THE EVENT OF A BREACH WHICH CONSTITUTES A FUNDAMENTAL BREACH.**

7. **GOVERNING LAW; COMPLETE AGREEMENT.** THIS AGREEMENT IS GOVERNED BY THE LAWS OF THE STATE OF CALIFORNIA IF THE USER IS LOCATED IN THE UNITED STATES, AND BY THE LAWS OF THE PROVINCE OF ONTARIO IF THE USER IS LOCATED IN CANADA, AND CONSTITUTES THE COMPLETE AGREEMENT BETWEEN THE PARTIES WITH RESPECT TO THE PROGRAMS. The terms of this Agreement supersede the terms of any purchase order, order letter or other document issued or signed by you to authorize its license of the Programs. If any provision of this Agreement is held to be unenforceable, such provision shall be limited, modified or severed as necessary to eliminate its unenforceability, and all other provisions shall remain unaffected.

8. **WAIVERS.** The failure or delay of either party to exercise any of its rights shall not be deemed a waiver thereof and no waiver by either party of any breach of this Agreement shall constitute a waiver of any other subsequent breach.

9. **TRANSLATION.** The parties have requested that this Agreement and all documents contemplated hereby be drawn up in English. Les parties aux presentes ont exigé que cerre entente et tous nutree documents envisagés par les présentes soíent rédigés en anglais.